VOLUME 2

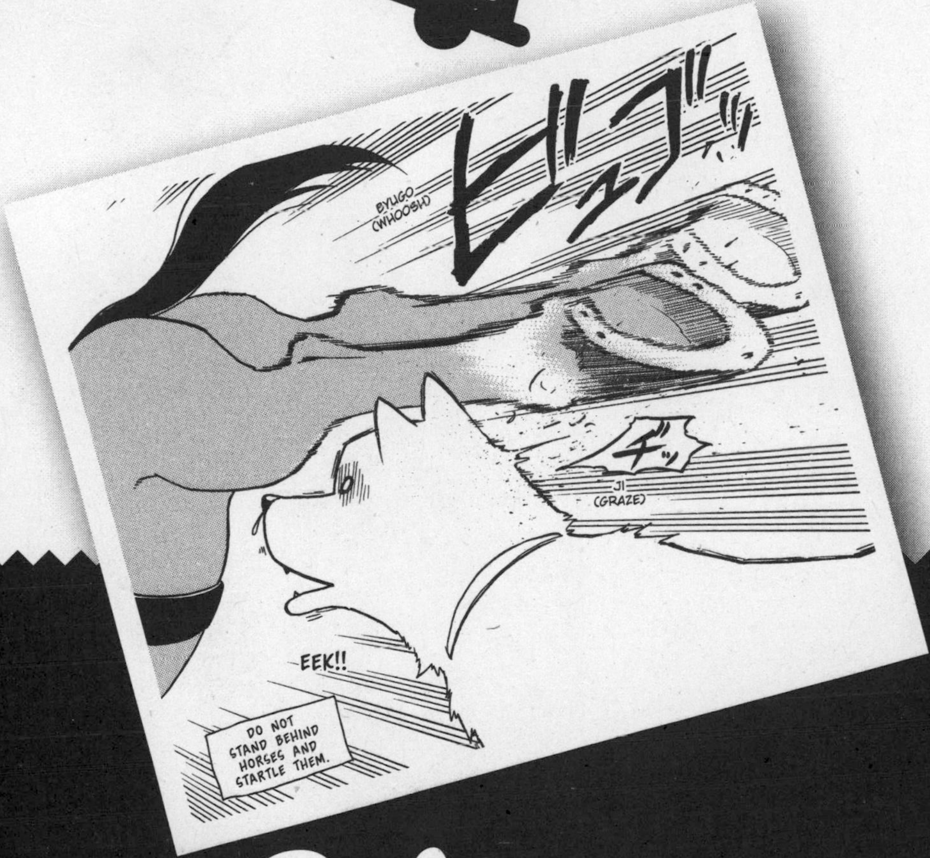
ビュゴッ
BYUGO (WHOOSH)
ヂッ
JI (GRAZE)
EEK!!
DO NOT STAND BEHIND HORSES AND STARTLE THEM.

Silver Spoon

HIROMU ARAKAWA

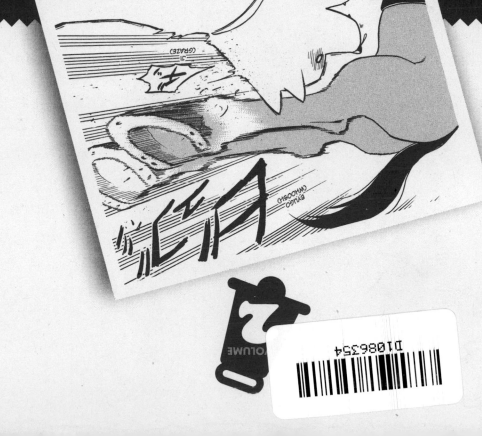

STORY & CHARACTERS

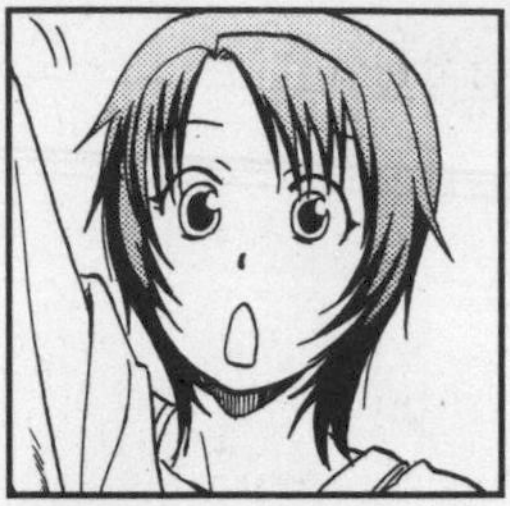

AKI MIKAGE

A first-year student at Ooezo Agricultural High School, enrolled in the Dairy Science Program. Her family keeps cows and horses. Applied to Ezo Ag because she's thinking about carrying on the family business.

YUUGO HACHIKEN

A first-year student at Ooezo Agricultural High School, enrolled in the Dairy Science Program. A city kid from Sapporo who got in through the general entrance exam. His reason for applying? Because there's a dorm...

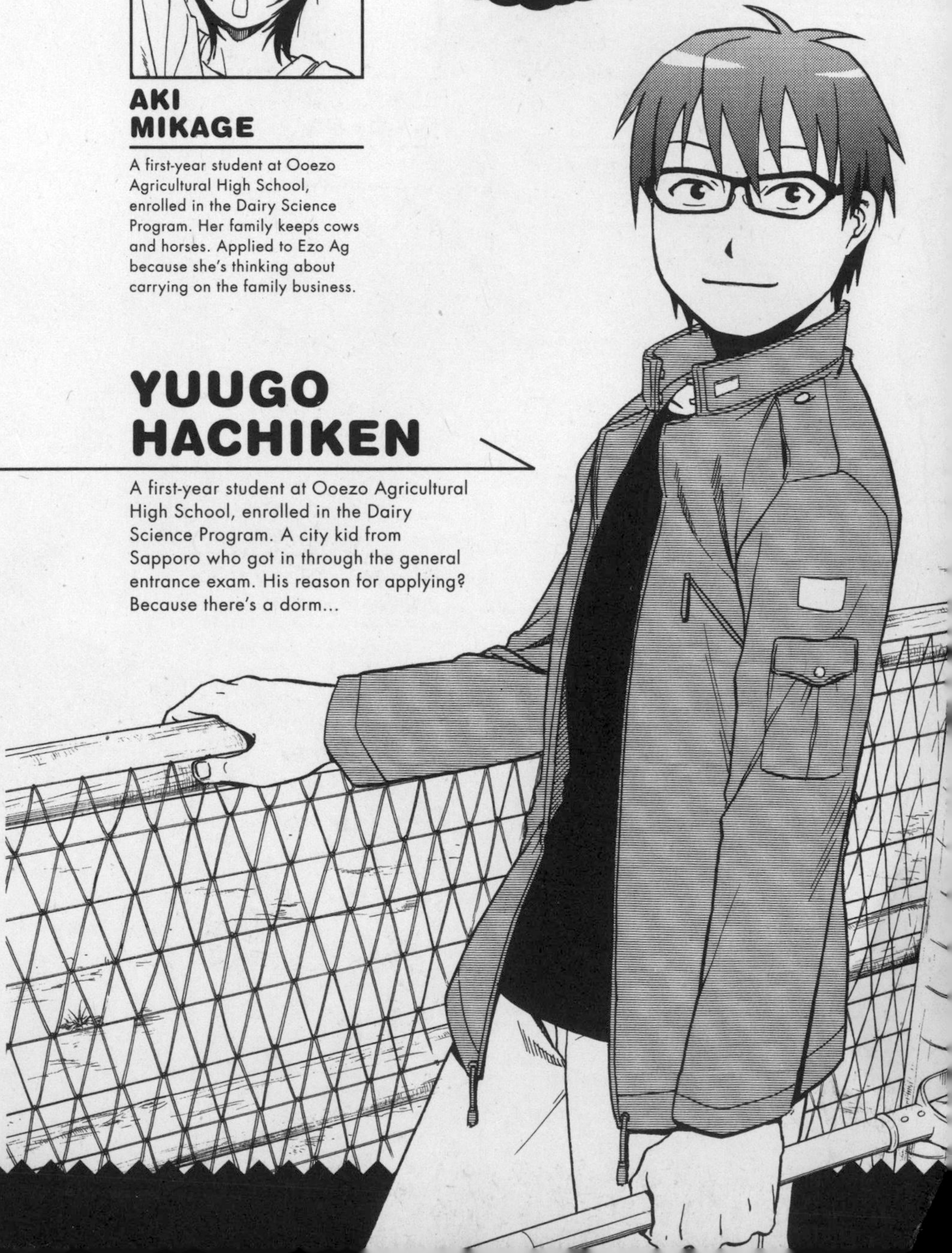

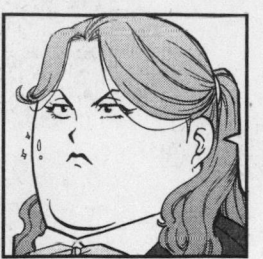

TAMAKO INADA

A first-year student at Ooezo Agricultural High School, enrolled in the Dairy Science Program. A complete enigma.

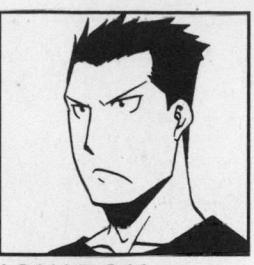

ICHIROU KOMABA

A first-year student at Ooezo Agricultural High School, enrolled in the Dairy Science Program. Plans on taking over the family farm after graduation. Member of the baseball team.

The Story Thus Far:

Goalless, dreamless city kid, Yuugo Hachiken, is accepted at Ooezo Agricultural High School... but farm school isn't the walk in the park he expected. Not only does he feel increasingly inferior next to his classmates who already have concrete plans for their futures, but between hands-on lessons and mandatory club activities, the schoolwork is a grueling physical struggle! Then comes Ezo Ag's big spring cleanup of the sprawling campus, when Hachiken finds a strange object buried in the piles of garbage...

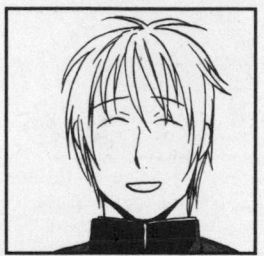

SHINNOSUKE AIKAWA

A first-year student at Ooezo Agricultural High School, enrolled in the Dairy Science Program. His dream is to become a veterinarian.

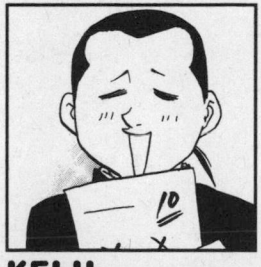

KEIJI TOKIWA

A first-year student at Ooezo Agricultural High School, enrolled in the Dairy Science Program. Son of chicken farmers. Awful at academics.

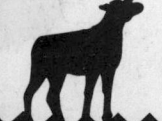

CONTENTS

Silver Spoon

Chapter 9:
Tale of Spring ⑨

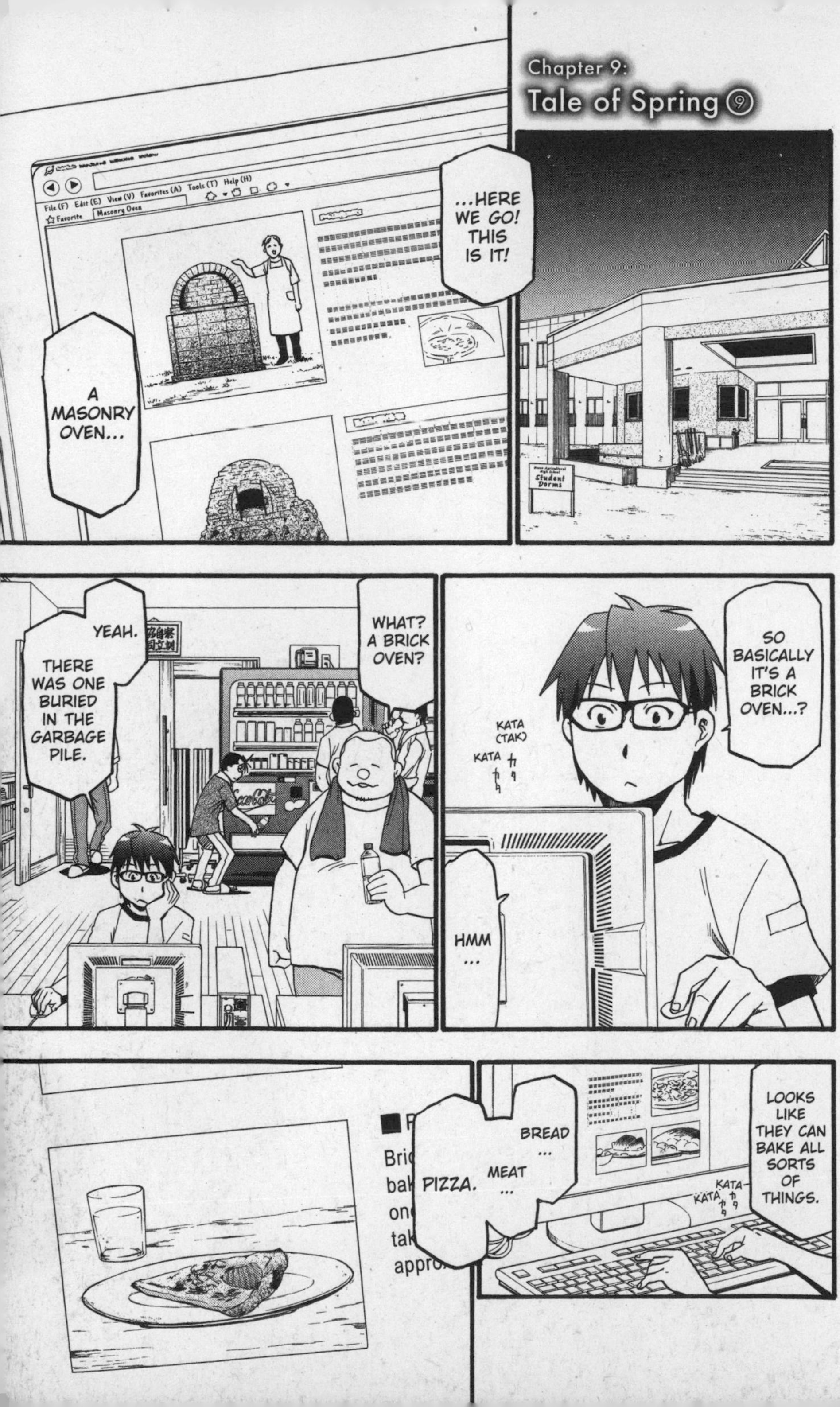
Student Dorms
...HERE WE GO! THIS IS IT!
File (F) Edit (E) View (V) Favorites (A) Tools (T) Help (H)
Favorite Masonry Oven
A MASONRY OVEN...
SO BASICALLY IT'S A BRICK OVEN...?
KATA (TAK) KATA
HMM ...
WHAT? A BRICK OVEN?
YEAH.
THERE WAS ONE BURIED IN THE GARBAGE PILE.
LOOKS LIKE THEY CAN BAKE ALL SORTS OF THINGS.
KATA- KATA
BREAD ...
MEAT ...
PIZZA.

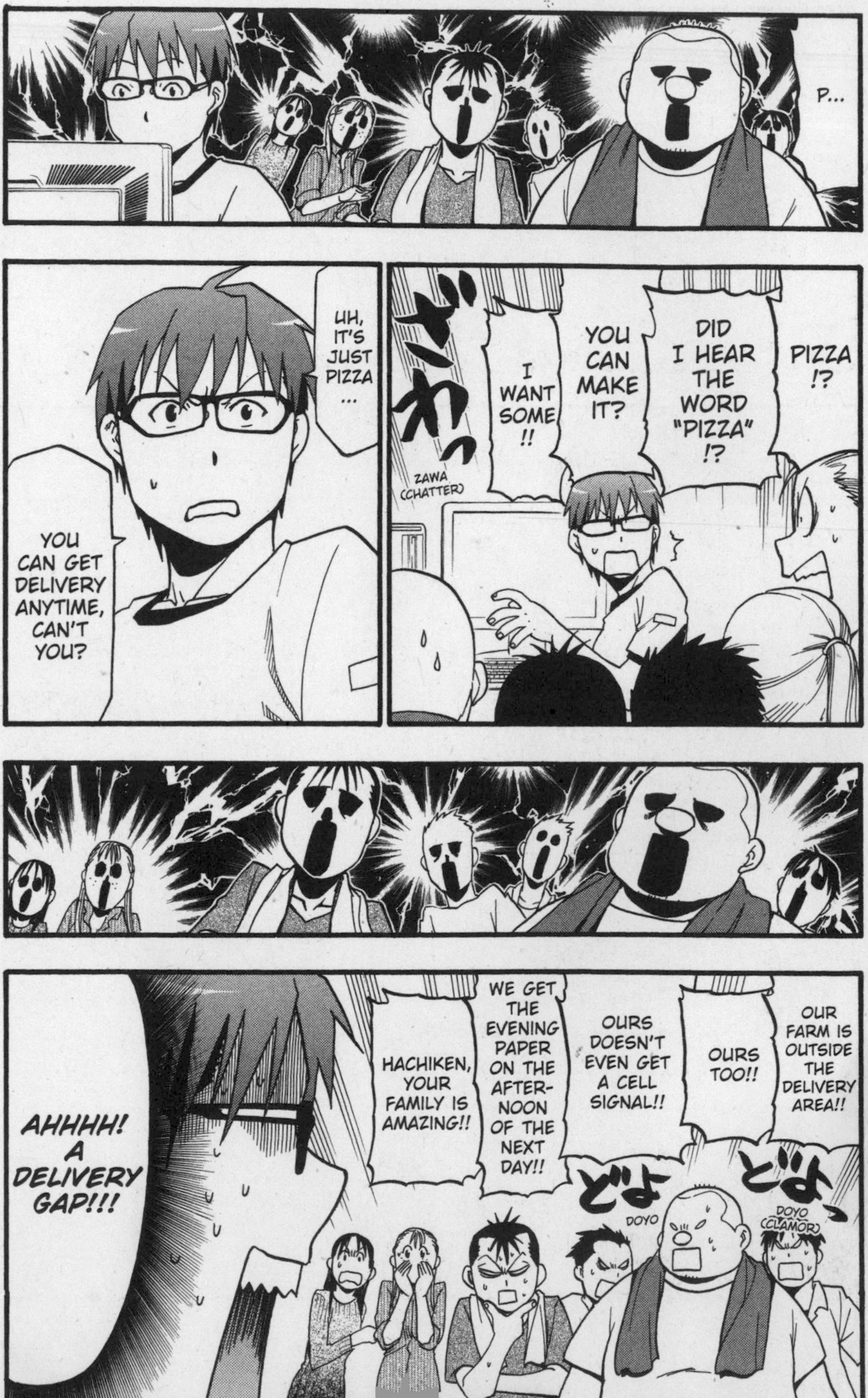
P...
PIZZA !?
DID I HEAR THE WORD "PIZZA" !?
YOU CAN MAKE IT?
I WANT SOME !!
ざわっ
ZAWA (CHATTER)
UH, IT'S JUST PIZZA ...
YOU CAN GET DELIVERY ANYTIME, CAN'T YOU?
OUR FARM IS OUTSIDE THE DELIVERY AREA!!
OURS TOO!!
OURS DOESN'T EVEN GET A CELL SIGNAL!!
WE GET THE EVENING PAPER ON THE AFTER-NOON OF THE NEXT DAY!!
HACHIKEN, YOUR FAMILY IS AMAZING!!
どよっ
DOYO (CLAMOR)
どよ
DOYO
AHHHH! A DELIVERY GAP!!!

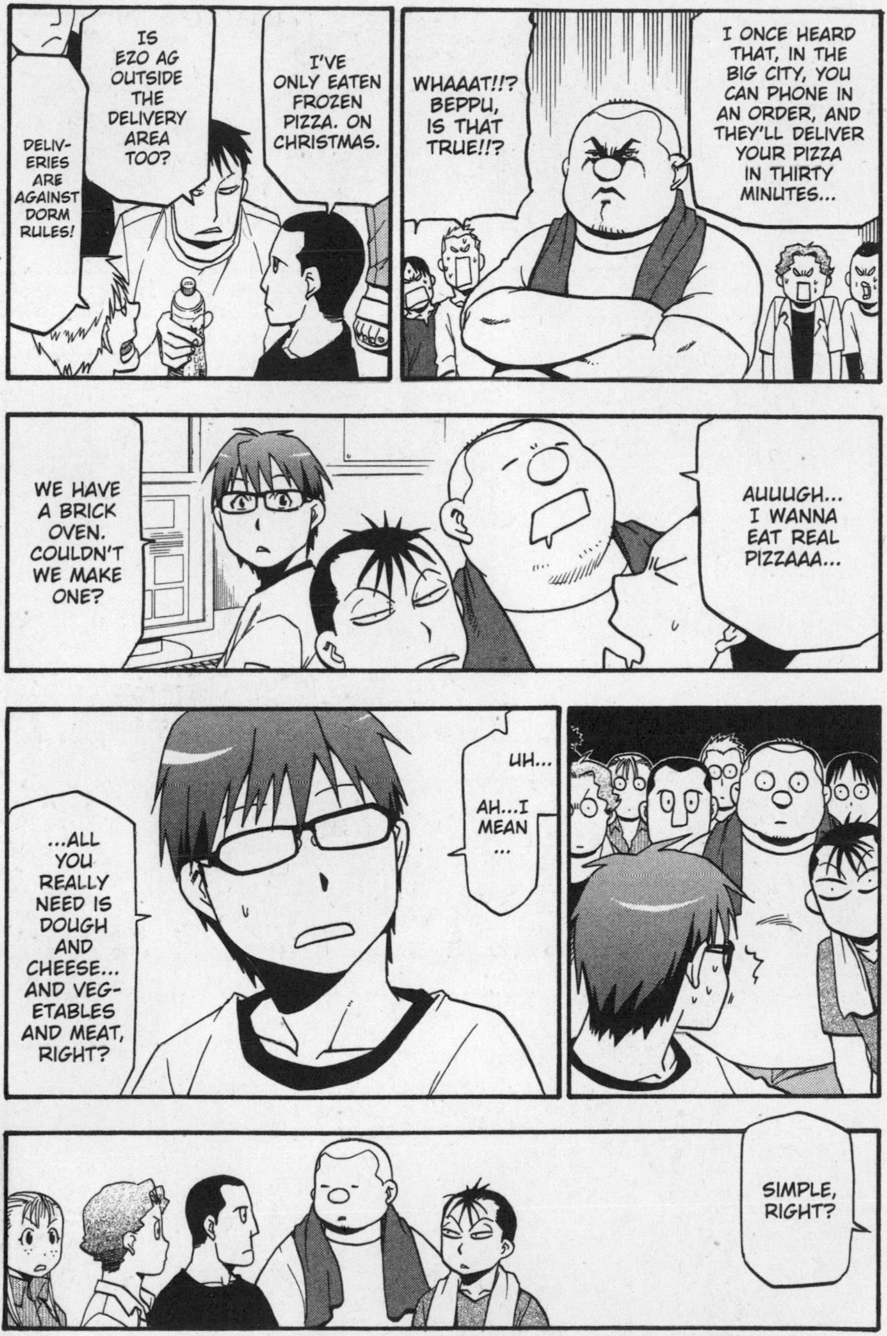
I ONCE HEARD THAT, IN THE BIG CITY, YOU CAN PHONE IN AN ORDER, AND THEY'LL DELIVER YOUR PIZZA IN THIRTY MINUTES...
WHAAAT!!? BEPPU, IS THAT TRUE!!?
I'VE ONLY EATEN FROZEN PIZZA. ON CHRISTMAS.
IS EZO AG OUTSIDE THE DELIVERY AREA TOO?
DELIV-ERIES ARE AGAINST DORM RULES!
AUUUGH... I WANNA EAT REAL PIZZAAA...
WE HAVE A BRICK OVEN. COULDN'T WE MAKE ONE?
UH...
AH...I MEAN ...
...ALL YOU REALLY NEED IS DOUGH AND CHEESE... AND VEG-ETABLES AND MEAT, RIGHT?
SIMPLE, RIGHT?

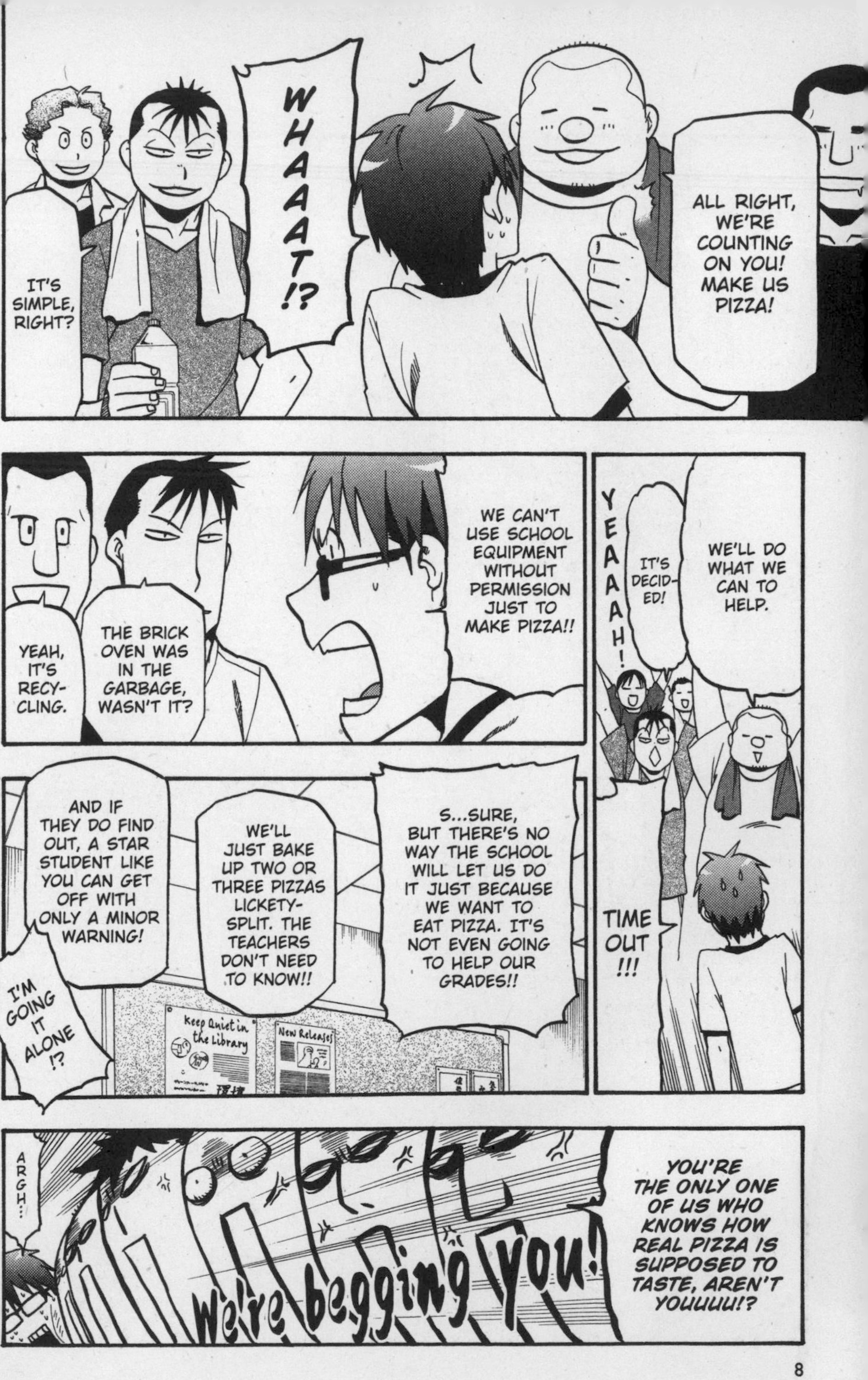
ALL RIGHT, WE'RE COUNTING ON YOU! MAKE US PIZZA!
WHAAAT!?
IT'S SIMPLE, RIGHT?
WE'LL DO WHAT WE CAN TO HELP.
IT'S DECIDED!
YEAAAH!
TIME OUT!!!
WE CAN'T USE SCHOOL EQUIPMENT WITHOUT PERMISSION JUST TO MAKE PIZZA!!
THE BRICK OVEN WAS IN THE GARBAGE, WASN'T IT?
YEAH, IT'S RECYCLING.
S...SURE, BUT THERE'S NO WAY THE SCHOOL WILL LET US DO IT JUST BECAUSE WE WANT TO EAT PIZZA. IT'S NOT EVEN GOING TO HELP OUR GRADES!!
WE'LL JUST BAKE UP TWO OR THREE PIZZAS LICKETY-SPLIT. THE TEACHERS DON'T NEED TO KNOW!!
AND IF THEY DO FIND OUT, A STAR STUDENT LIKE YOU CAN GET OFF WITH ONLY A MINOR WARNING!
I'M GOING IT ALONE!?
Keep Quiet in the Library
New Releases
YOU'RE THE ONLY ONE OF US WHO KNOWS HOW REAL PIZZA IS SUPPOSED TO TASTE, AREN'T YOUUUU!?
We're begging you!
ARGH...

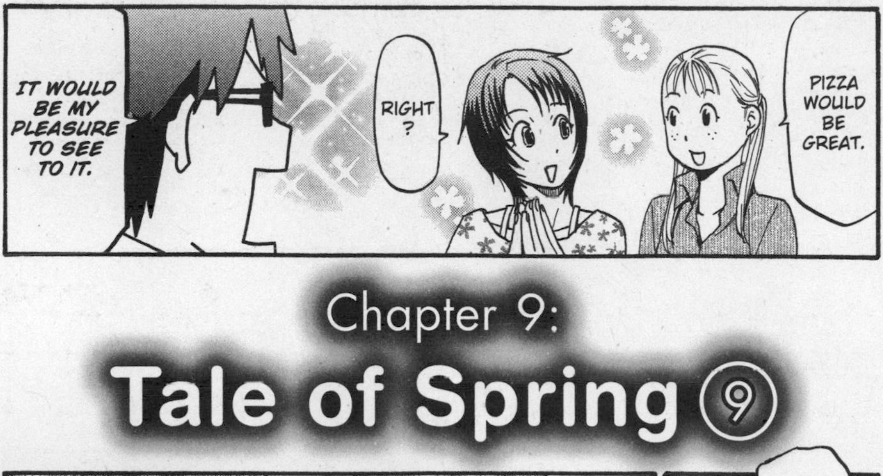
PIZZA WOULD BE GREAT.
RIGHT?
IT WOULD BE MY PLEASURE TO SEE TO IT.

Chapter 9:
Tale of Spring ⑨

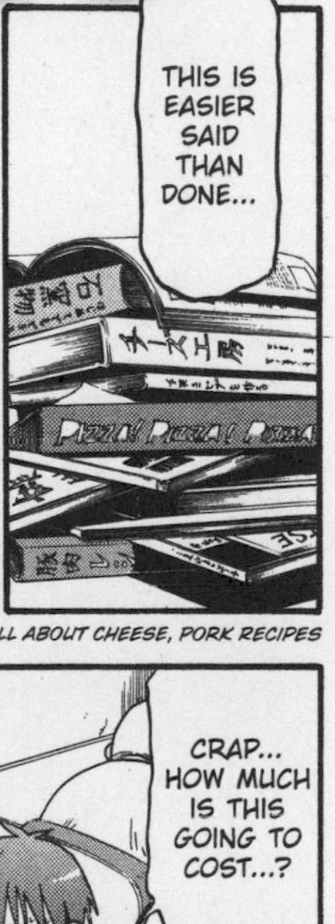
THIS IS EASIER SAID THAN DONE...

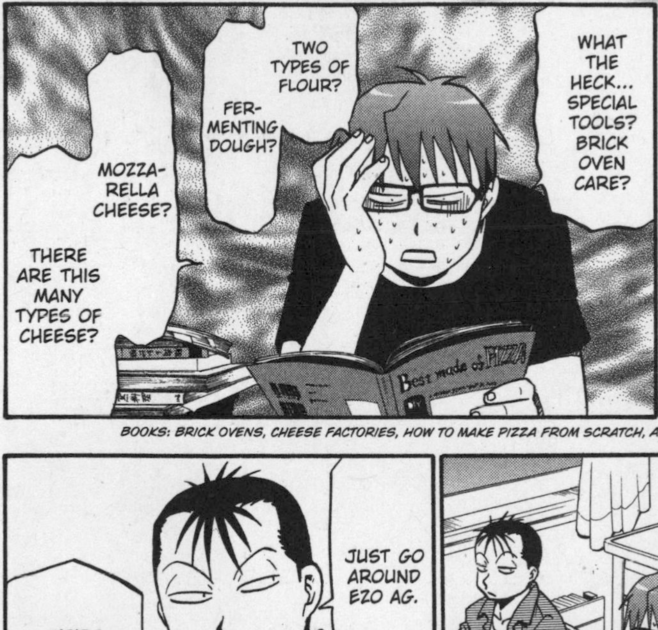
WHAT THE HECK... SPECIAL TOOLS? BRICK OVEN CARE?
TWO TYPES OF FLOUR?
FER-MENTING DOUGH?
MOZZA-RELLA CHEESE?
THERE ARE THIS MANY TYPES OF CHEESE?
Best made of PIZZA

BOOKS: BRICK OVENS, CHEESE FACTORIES, HOW TO MAKE PIZZA FROM SCRATCH, ALL ABOUT CHEESE, PORK RECIPES

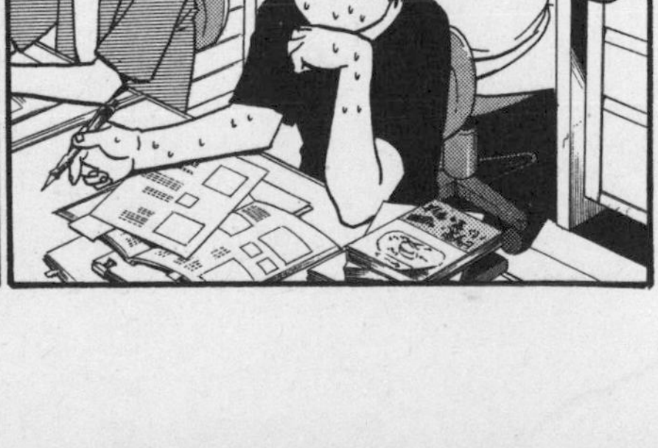
CRAP... HOW MUCH IS THIS GOING TO COST...?

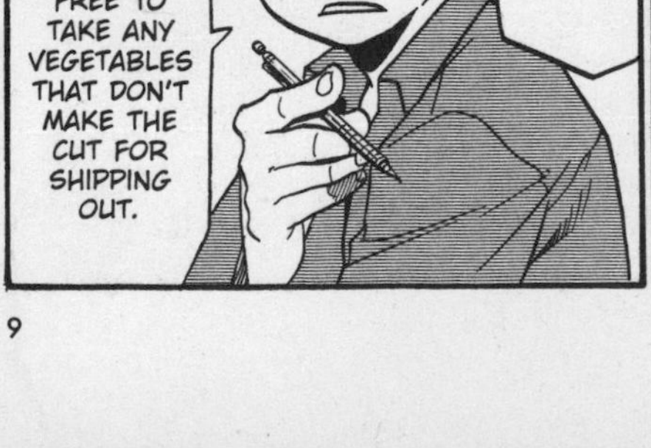
JUST GO AROUND EZO AG.
WE'RE FREE TO TAKE ANY VEGETABLES THAT DON'T MAKE THE CUT FOR SHIPPING OUT.

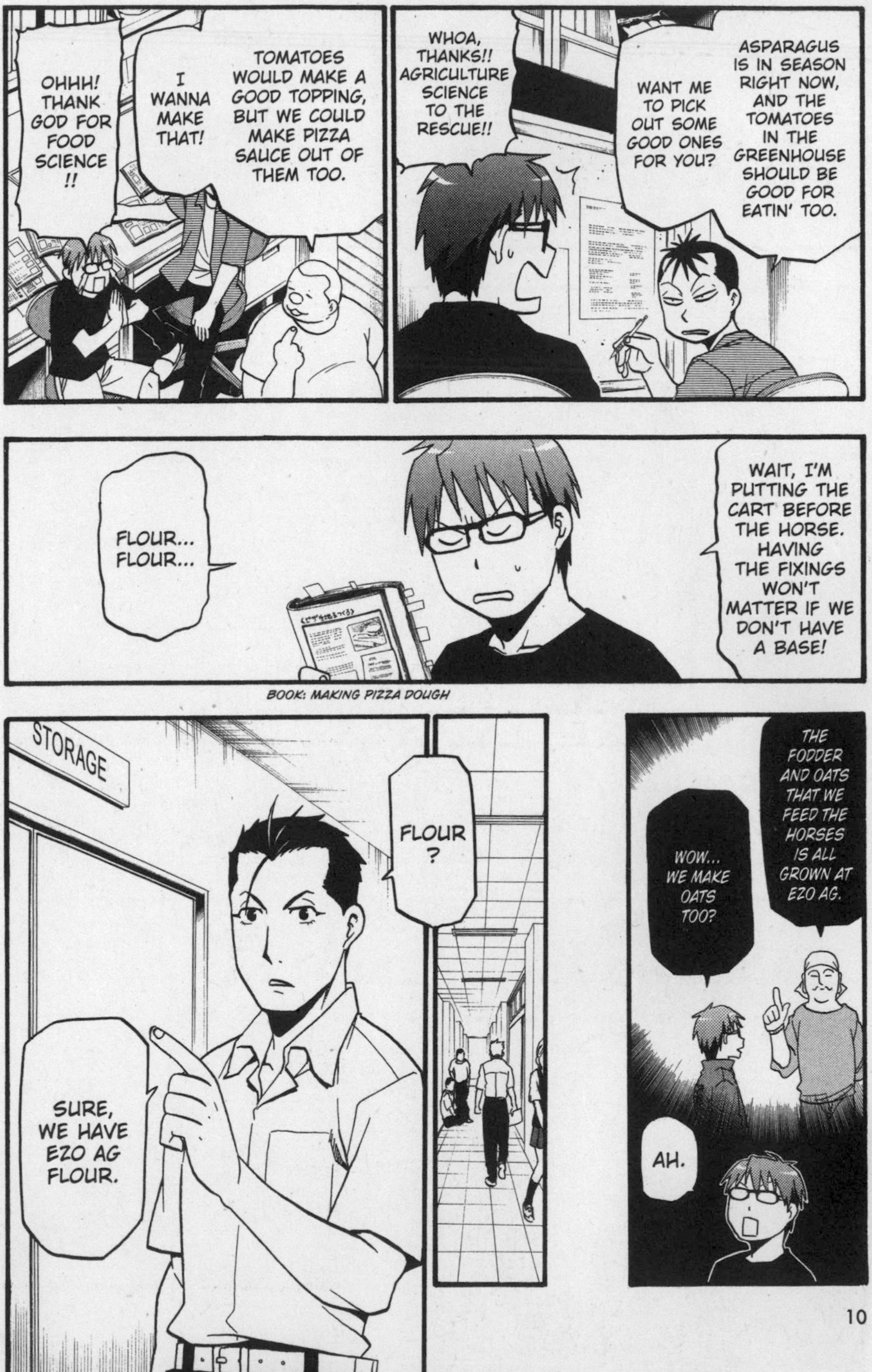
ASPARAGUS IS IN SEASON RIGHT NOW, AND THE TOMATOES IN THE GREENHOUSE SHOULD BE GOOD FOR EATIN' TOO.
WANT ME TO PICK OUT SOME GOOD ONES FOR YOU?
WHOA, THANKS!! AGRICULTURE SCIENCE TO THE RESCUE!!
TOMATOES WOULD MAKE A GOOD TOPPING, BUT WE COULD MAKE PIZZA SAUCE OUT OF THEM TOO.
I WANNA MAKE THAT!
OHHH! THANK GOD FOR FOOD SCIENCE !!
WAIT, I'M PUTTING THE CART BEFORE THE HORSE. HAVING THE FIXINGS WON'T MATTER IF WE DON'T HAVE A BASE!
FLOUR... FLOUR...
BOOK: MAKING PIZZA DOUGH
THE FODDER AND OATS THAT WE FEED THE HORSES IS ALL GROWN AT EZO AG.
WOW... WE MAKE OATS TOO?
AH.
STORAGE
FLOUR ?
SURE, WE HAVE EZO AG FLOUR.

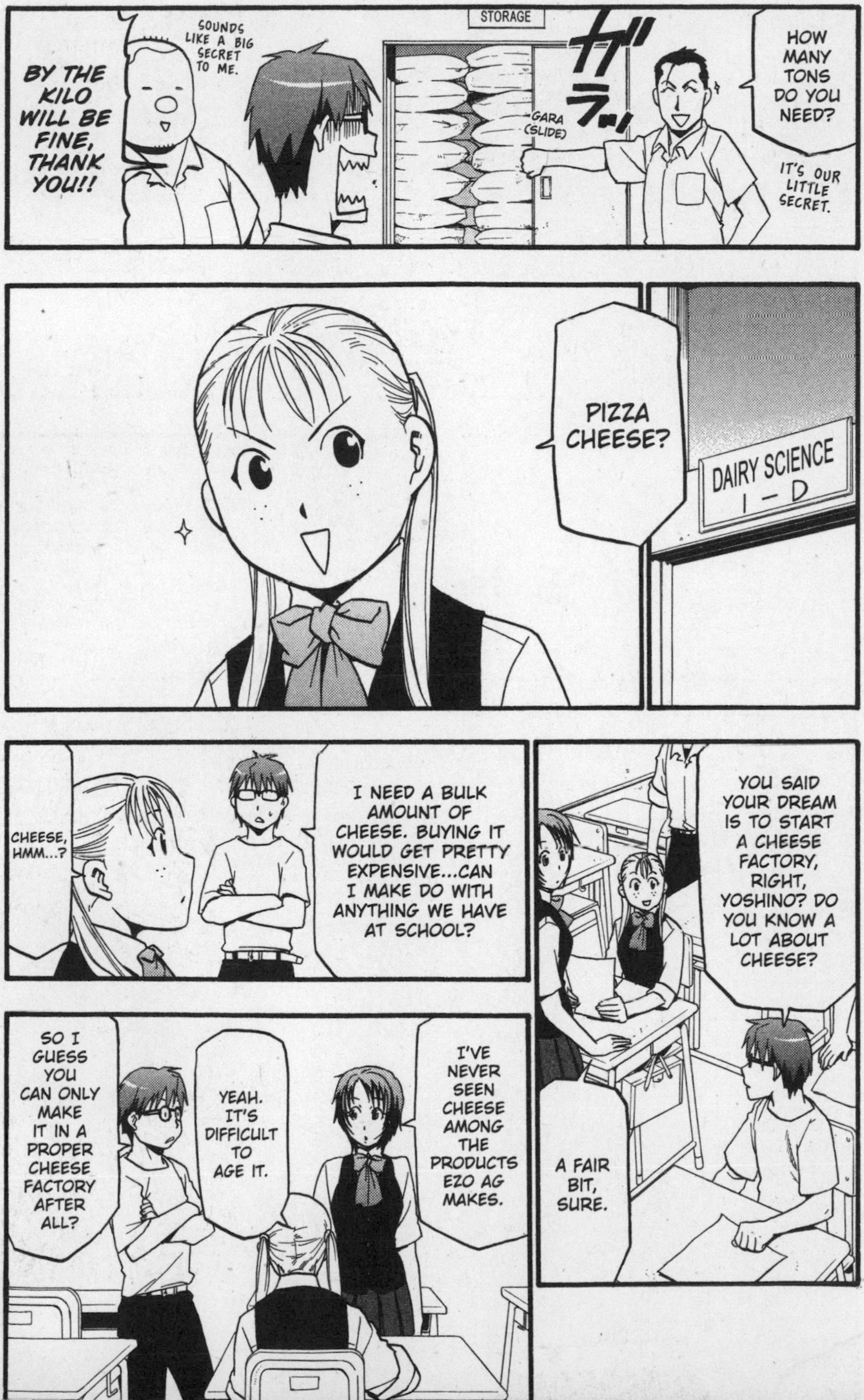
HOW MANY TONS DO YOU NEED?
IT'S OUR LITTLE SECRET.
GARA (SLIDE)
STORAGE
SOUNDS LIKE A BIG SECRET TO ME.
BY THE KILO WILL BE FINE, THANK YOU!!
DAIRY SCIENCE 1-D
PIZZA CHEESE?
YOU SAID YOUR DREAM IS TO START A CHEESE FACTORY, RIGHT, YOSHINO? DO YOU KNOW A LOT ABOUT CHEESE?
A FAIR BIT, SURE.
I NEED A BULK AMOUNT OF CHEESE. BUYING IT WOULD GET PRETTY EXPENSIVE...CAN I MAKE DO WITH ANYTHING WE HAVE AT SCHOOL?
CHEESE, HMM...?
I'VE NEVER SEEN CHEESE AMONG THE PRODUCTS EZO AG MAKES.
YEAH. IT'S DIFFICULT TO AGE IT.
SO I GUESS YOU CAN ONLY MAKE IT IN A PROPER CHEESE FACTORY AFTER ALL?

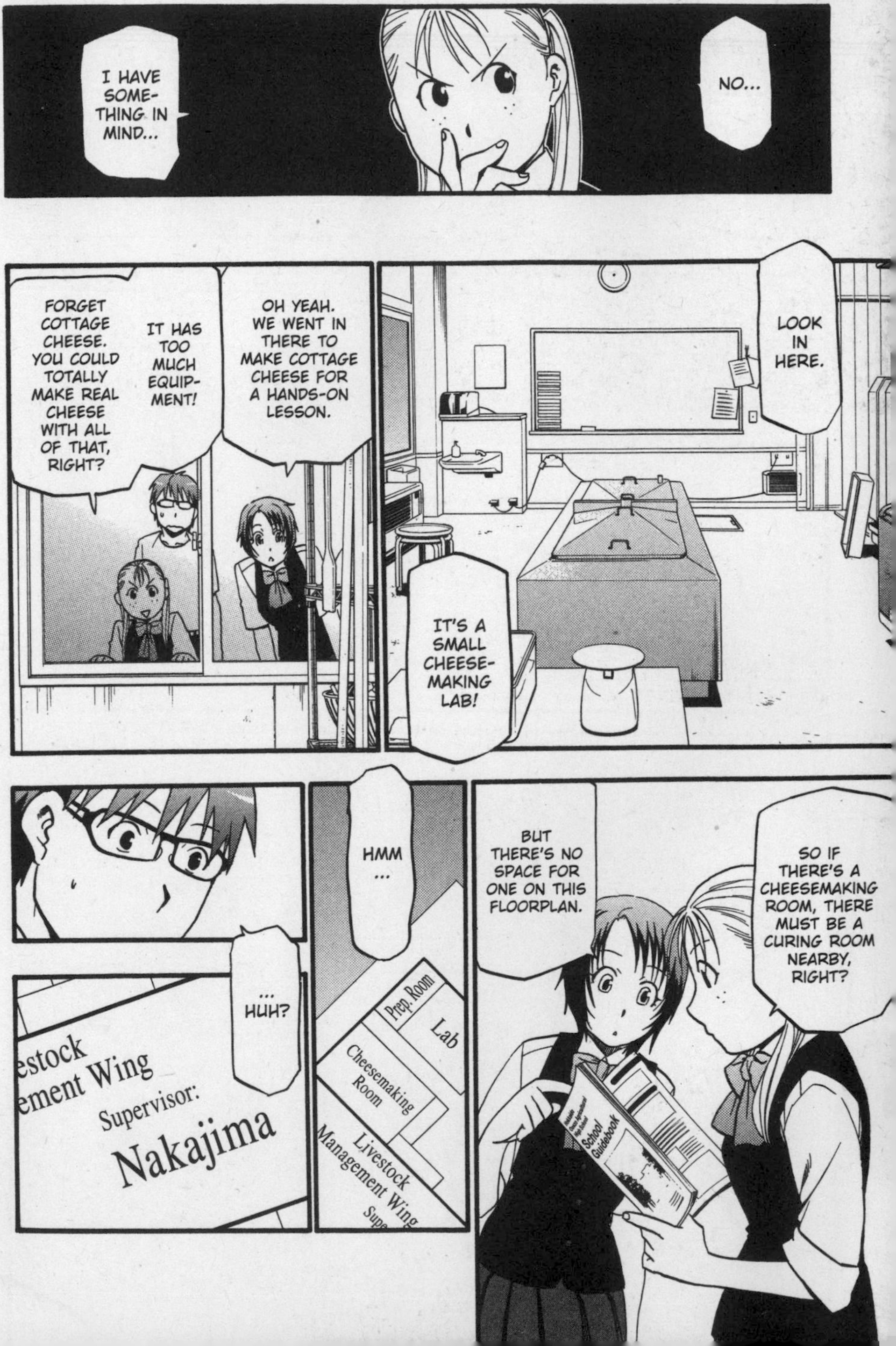
NO...
I HAVE SOMETHING IN MIND...
LOOK IN HERE.
IT'S A SMALL CHEESE-MAKING LAB!
OH YEAH. WE WENT IN THERE TO MAKE COTTAGE CHEESE FOR A HANDS-ON LESSON.
IT HAS TOO MUCH EQUIPMENT!
FORGET COTTAGE CHEESE. YOU COULD TOTALLY MAKE REAL CHEESE WITH ALL OF THAT, RIGHT?
SO IF THERE'S A CHEESEMAKING ROOM, THERE MUST BE A CURING ROOM NEARBY, RIGHT?
School Guidebook
BUT THERE'S NO SPACE FOR ONE ON THIS FLOORPLAN.
HMM...
Prep. Room
Lab
Cheesemaking Room
Livestock Management Wing
...HUH?
estock
ement Wing
Supervisor:
Nakajima

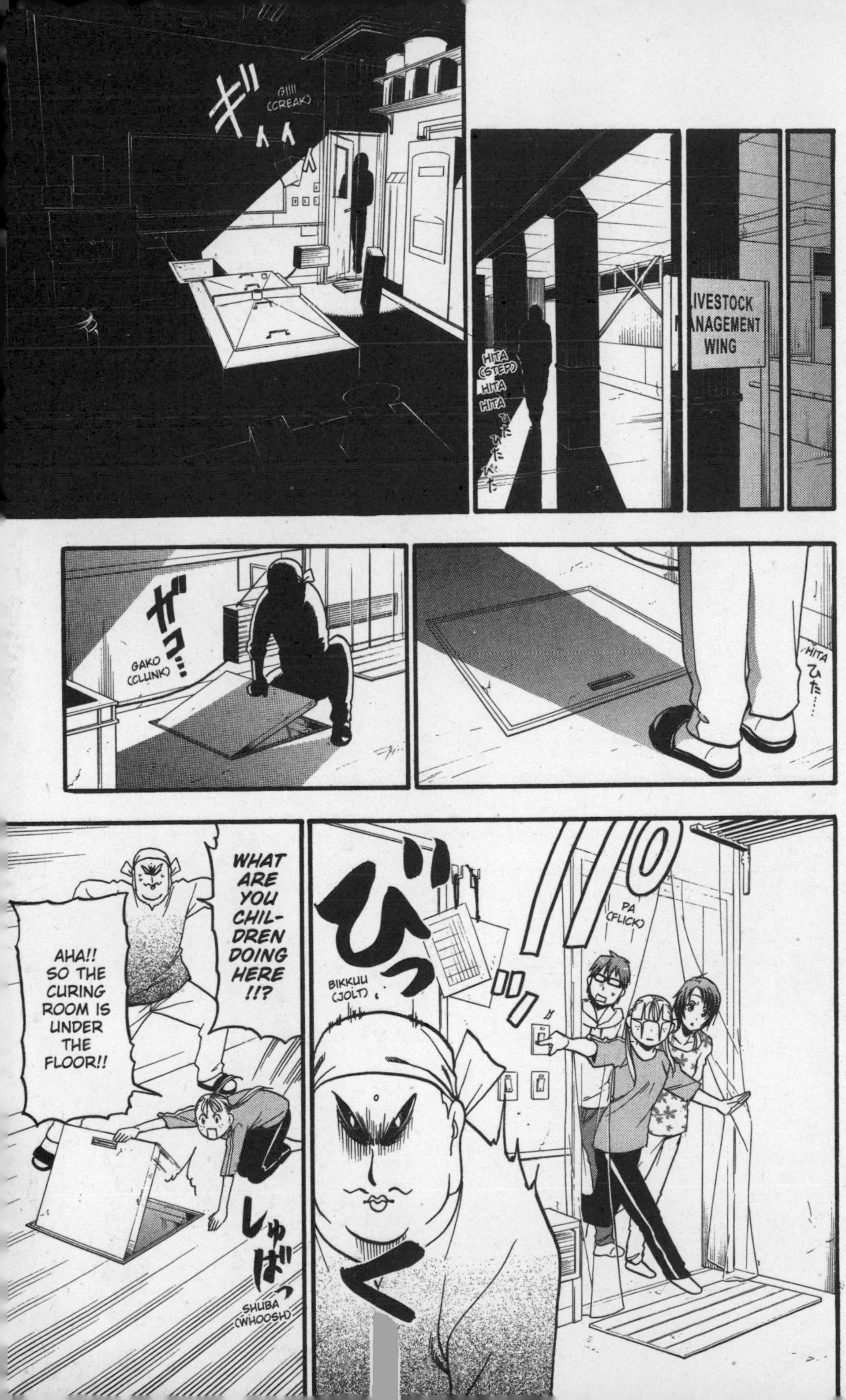

LIVESTOCK MANAGEMENT WING
HITA (STEP) HITA HITA
ひたひたひた
GIIII (CREAK)
ギィィ
HITA
ひた……
GAKO (CLUNK)
ガコ…
PA (FLICK)
BIKKUU (JOLT)
ひっ
WHAT ARE YOU CHIL-DREN DOING HERE !!?
AHA!! SO THE CURING ROOM IS UNDER THE FLOOR!!
SHUBA (WHOOSH)
しゅばっ

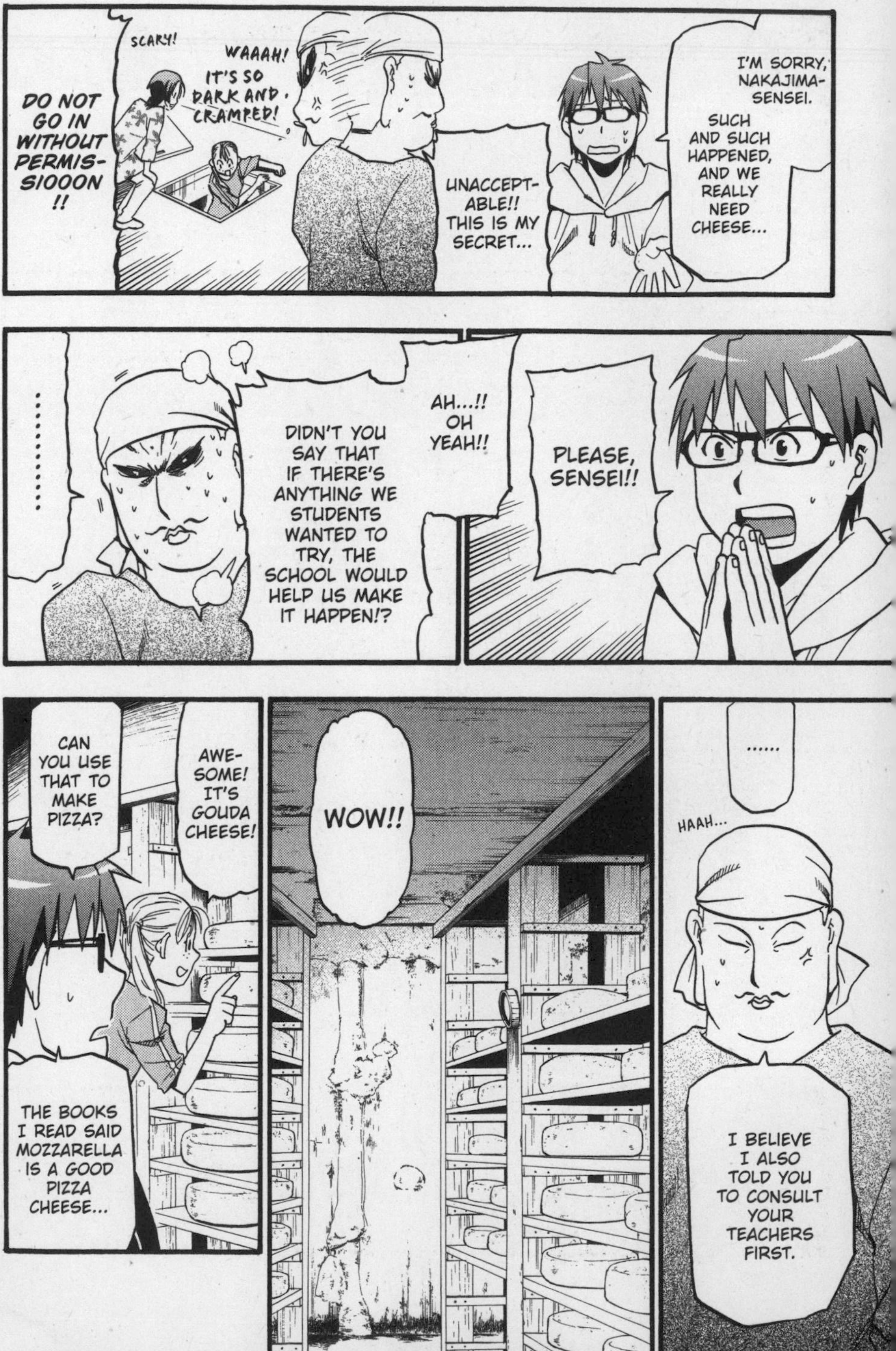
I'M SORRY, NAKAJIMA-SENSEI.
SUCH AND SUCH HAPPENED, AND WE REALLY NEED CHEESE...
UNACCEPTABLE!! THIS IS MY SECRET...
WAAAH!
IT'S SO DARK AND CRAMPED!
SCARY!
DO NOT GO IN WITHOUT PERMISSIOOON!!
PLEASE, SENSEI!!
AH...!! OH YEAH!!
DIDN'T YOU SAY THAT IF THERE'S ANYTHING WE STUDENTS WANTED TO TRY, THE SCHOOL WOULD HELP US MAKE IT HAPPEN!?
....
......
HAAH...
I BELIEVE I ALSO TOLD YOU TO CONSULT YOUR TEACHERS FIRST.
WOW!!
AWESOME! IT'S GOUDA CHEESE!
CAN YOU USE THAT TO MAKE PIZZA?
THE BOOKS I READ SAID MOZZARELLA IS A GOOD PIZZA CHEESE...

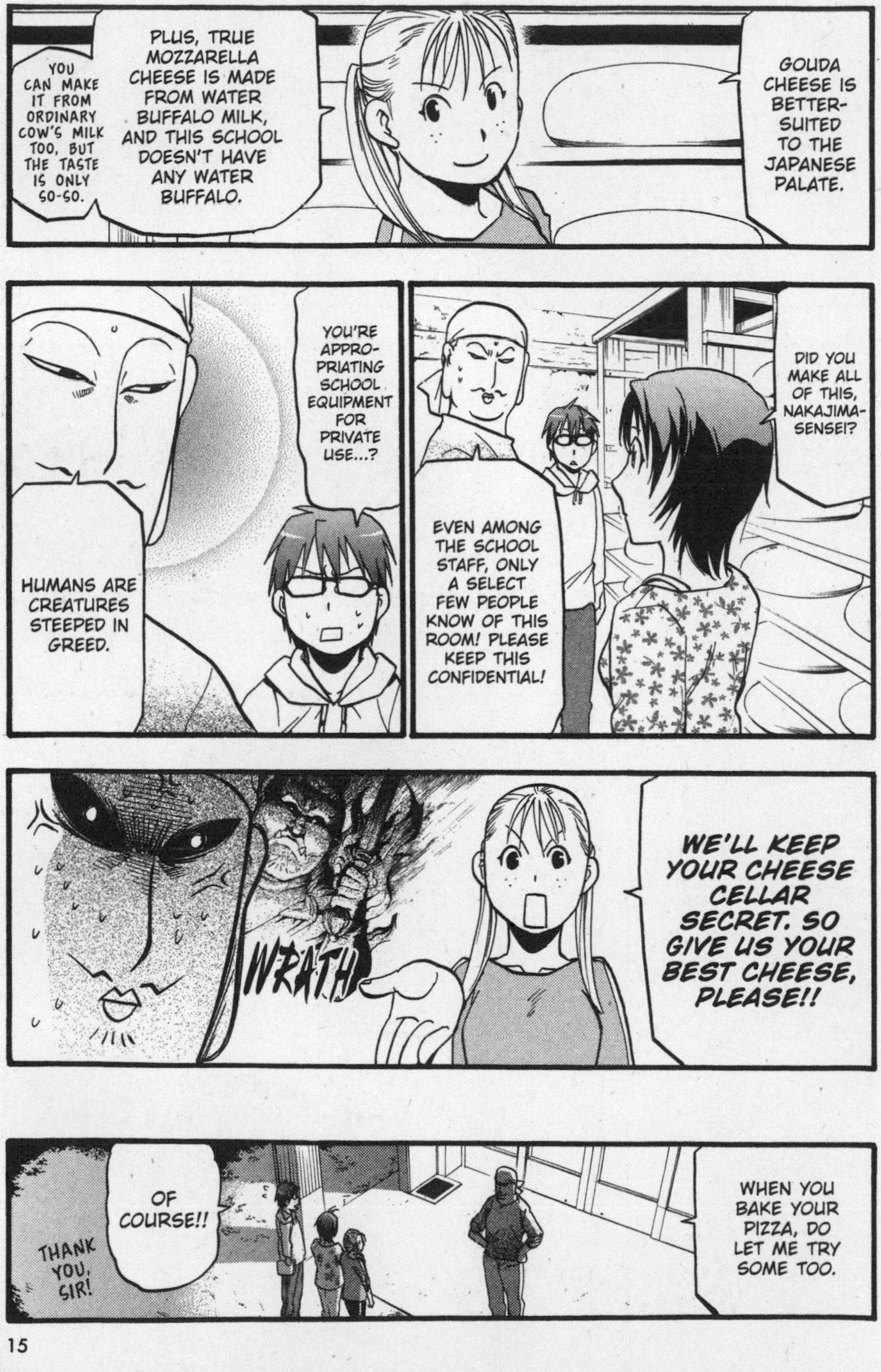
GOUDA CHEESE IS BETTER-SUITED TO THE JAPANESE PALATE.
PLUS, TRUE MOZZARELLA CHEESE IS MADE FROM WATER BUFFALO MILK, AND THIS SCHOOL DOESN'T HAVE ANY WATER BUFFALO.
YOU CAN MAKE IT FROM ORDINARY COW'S MILK TOO, BUT THE TASTE IS ONLY SO-SO.
DID YOU MAKE ALL OF THIS, NAKAJIMA-SENSEI?
EVEN AMONG THE SCHOOL STAFF, ONLY A SELECT FEW PEOPLE KNOW OF THIS ROOM! PLEASE KEEP THIS CONFIDENTIAL!
YOU'RE APPRO-PRIATING SCHOOL EQUIPMENT FOR PRIVATE USE...?
HUMANS ARE CREATURES STEEPED IN GREED.
WE'LL KEEP YOUR CHEESE CELLAR SECRET. SO GIVE US YOUR BEST CHEESE, PLEASE!!
WRATH
WHEN YOU BAKE YOUR PIZZA, DO LET ME TRY SOME TOO.
OF COURSE!!
THANK YOU, SIR!

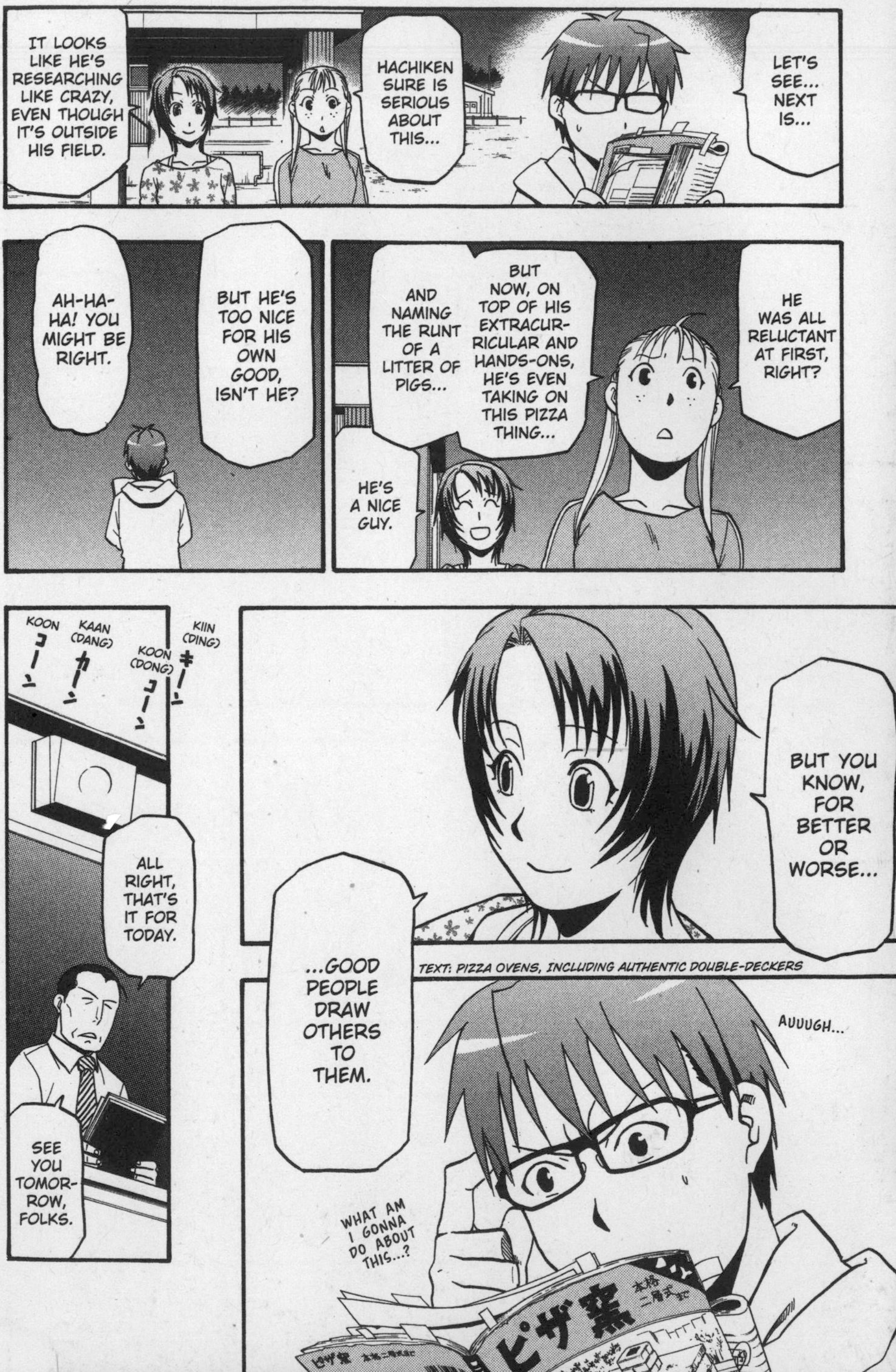
LET'S SEE... NEXT IS...
HACHIKEN SURE IS SERIOUS ABOUT THIS...
IT LOOKS LIKE HE'S RESEARCHING LIKE CRAZY, EVEN THOUGH IT'S OUTSIDE HIS FIELD.
HE WAS ALL RELUCTANT AT FIRST, RIGHT?
BUT NOW, ON TOP OF HIS EXTRACURRICULAR AND HANDS-ONS, HE'S EVEN TAKING ON THIS PIZZA THING...
AND NAMING THE RUNT OF A LITTER OF PIGS...
HE'S A NICE GUY.
BUT HE'S TOO NICE FOR HIS OWN GOOD, ISN'T HE?
AH-HA-HA! YOU MIGHT BE RIGHT.
BUT YOU KNOW, FOR BETTER OR WORSE...
...GOOD PEOPLE DRAW OTHERS TO THEM.
TEXT: PIZZA OVENS, INCLUDING AUTHENTIC DOUBLE-DECKERS
AUUUGH...
WHAT AM I GONNA DO ABOUT THIS...?
KOON
KAAN (DANG)
KOON (DONG)
KIIN (DING)
ALL RIGHT, THAT'S IT FOR TODAY.
SEE YOU TOMORROW, FOLKS.

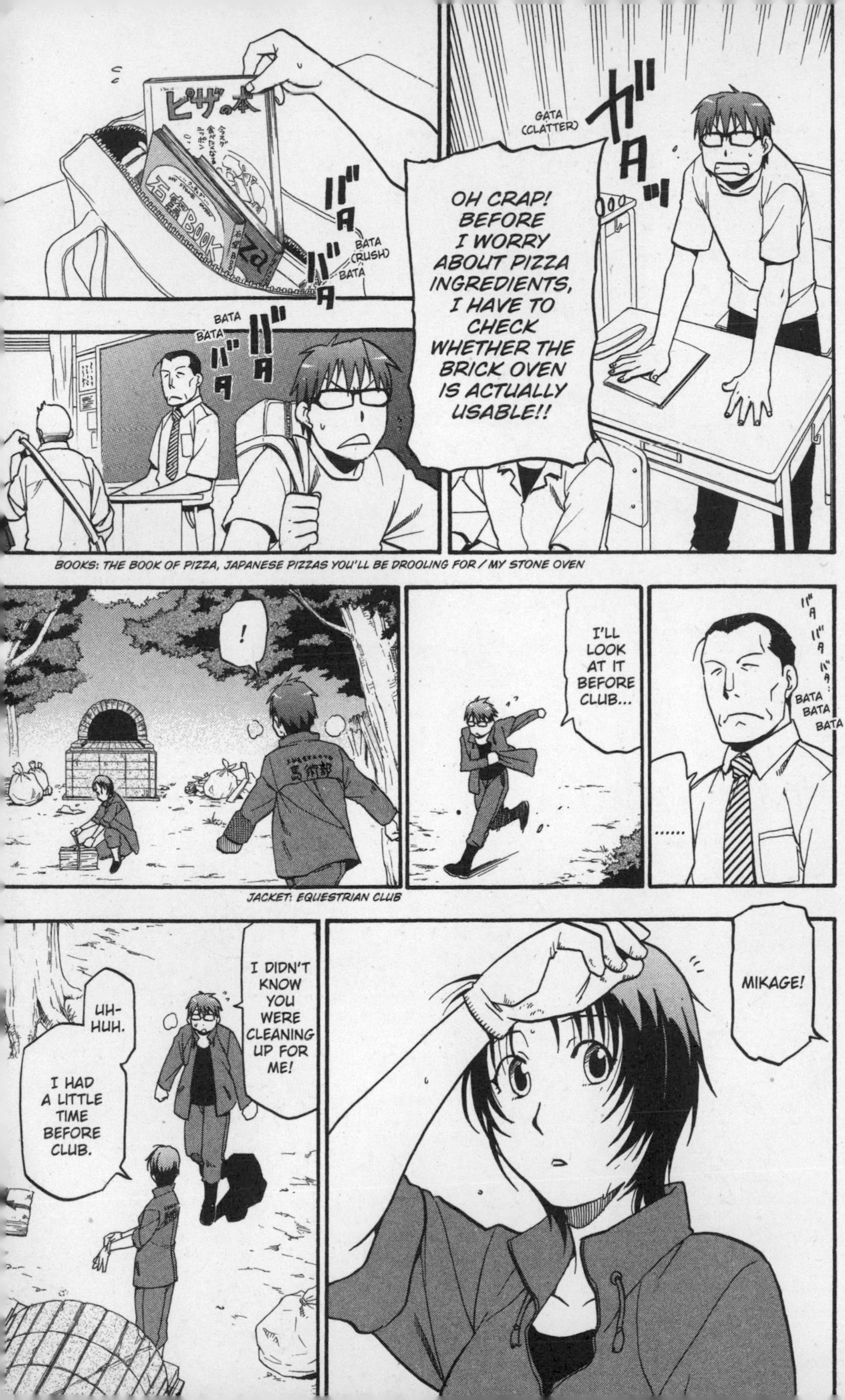
GATA (CLATTER)
OH CRAP! BEFORE I WORRY ABOUT PIZZA INGREDIENTS, I HAVE TO CHECK WHETHER THE BRICK OVEN IS ACTUALLY USABLE!!
BATA (RUSH) BATA
BATA BATA
BOOKS: THE BOOK OF PIZZA, JAPANESE PIZZAS YOU'LL BE DROOLING FOR / MY STONE OVEN
BATA BATA BATA
......
I'LL LOOK AT IT BEFORE CLUB...
!
JACKET: EQUESTRIAN CLUB
MIKAGE!
I DIDN'T KNOW YOU WERE CLEANING UP FOR ME!
UH-HUH.
I HAD A LITTLE TIME BEFORE CLUB.

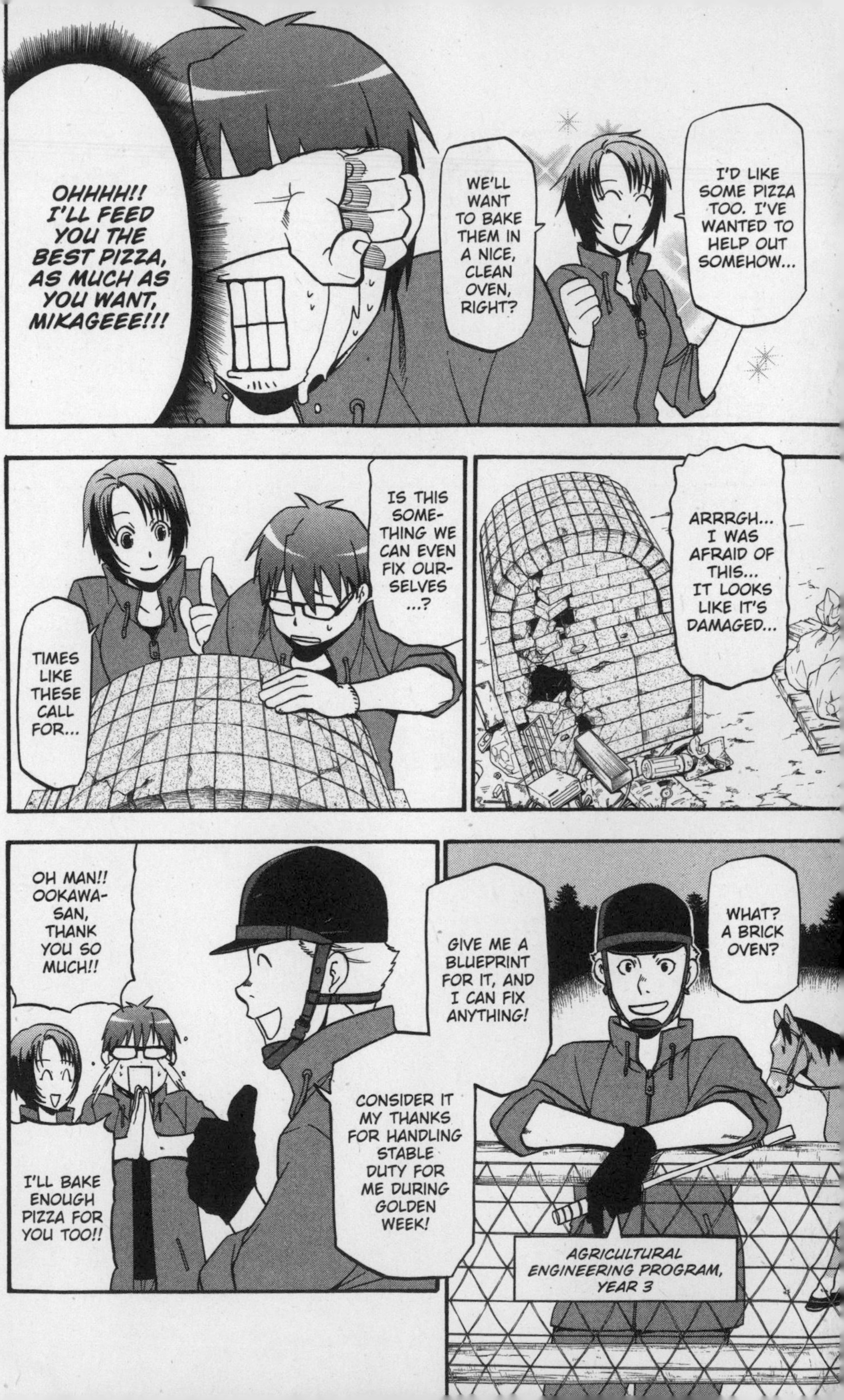
I'D LIKE SOME PIZZA TOO. I'VE WANTED TO HELP OUT SOMEHOW...
WE'LL WANT TO BAKE THEM IN A NICE, CLEAN OVEN, RIGHT?
OHHHH!! I'LL FEED YOU THE BEST PIZZA, AS MUCH AS YOU WANT, MIKAGEEE!!!
ARRRGH... I WAS AFRAID OF THIS... IT LOOKS LIKE IT'S DAMAGED...
IS THIS SOMETHING WE CAN EVEN FIX OURSELVES ...?
TIMES LIKE THESE CALL FOR...
WHAT? A BRICK OVEN?
GIVE ME A BLUEPRINT FOR IT, AND I CAN FIX ANYTHING!
AGRICULTURAL ENGINEERING PROGRAM, YEAR 3
CONSIDER IT MY THANKS FOR HANDLING STABLE DUTY FOR ME DURING GOLDEN WEEK!
OH MAN!! OOKAWA-SAN, THANK YOU SO MUCH!!
I'LL BAKE ENOUGH PIZZA FOR YOU TOO!!

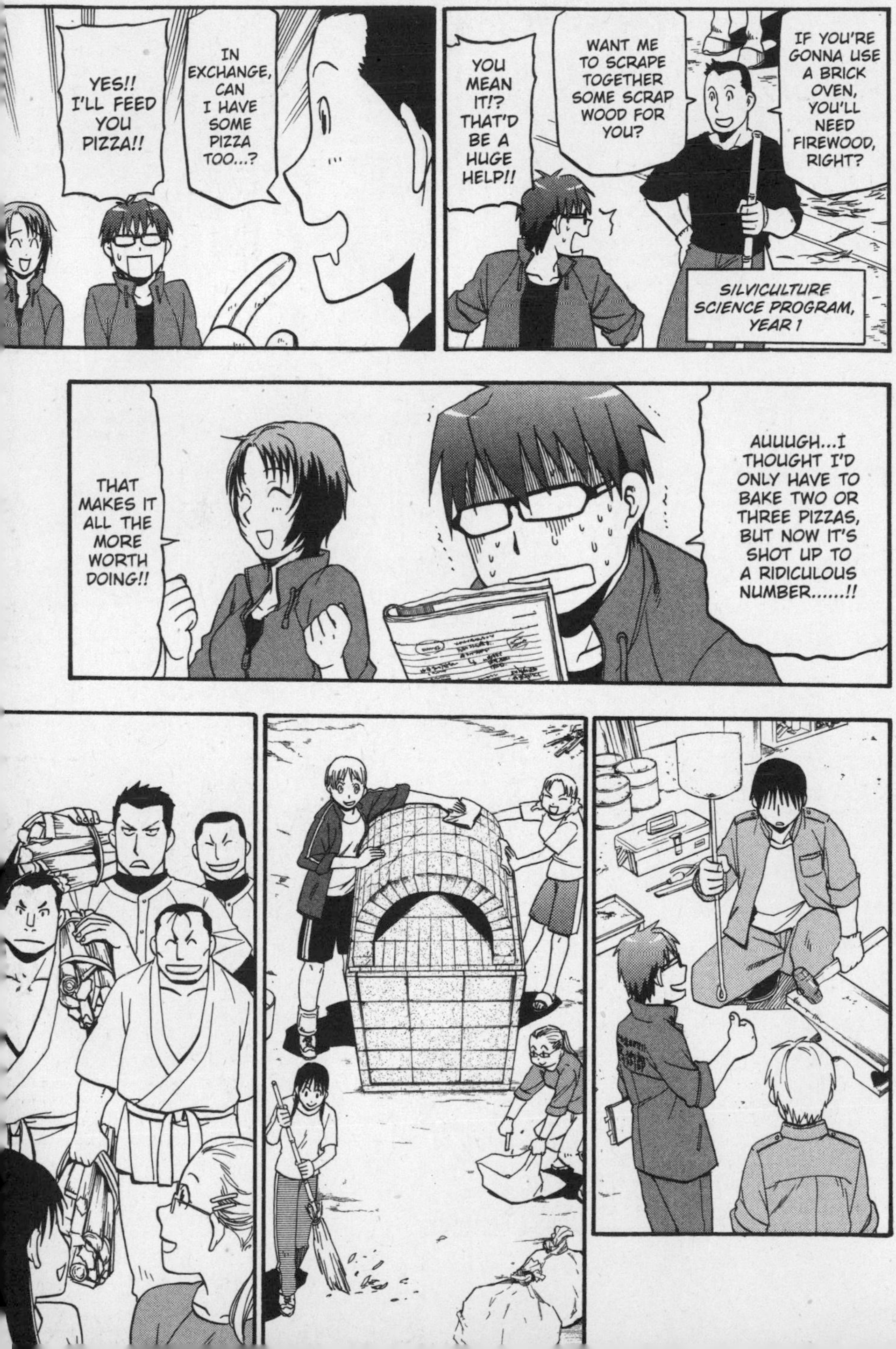
IF YOU'RE GONNA USE A BRICK OVEN, YOU'LL NEED FIREWOOD, RIGHT?
SILVICULTURE SCIENCE PROGRAM, YEAR 1
WANT ME TO SCRAPE TOGETHER SOME SCRAP WOOD FOR YOU?
YOU MEAN IT!? THAT'D BE A HUGE HELP!!
IN EXCHANGE, CAN I HAVE SOME PIZZA TOO...?
YES!! I'LL FEED YOU PIZZA!!
AUUUGH...I THOUGHT I'D ONLY HAVE TO BAKE TWO OR THREE PIZZAS, BUT NOW IT'S SHOT UP TO A RIDICULOUS NUMBER......!!
THAT MAKES IT ALL THE MORE WORTH DOING!!

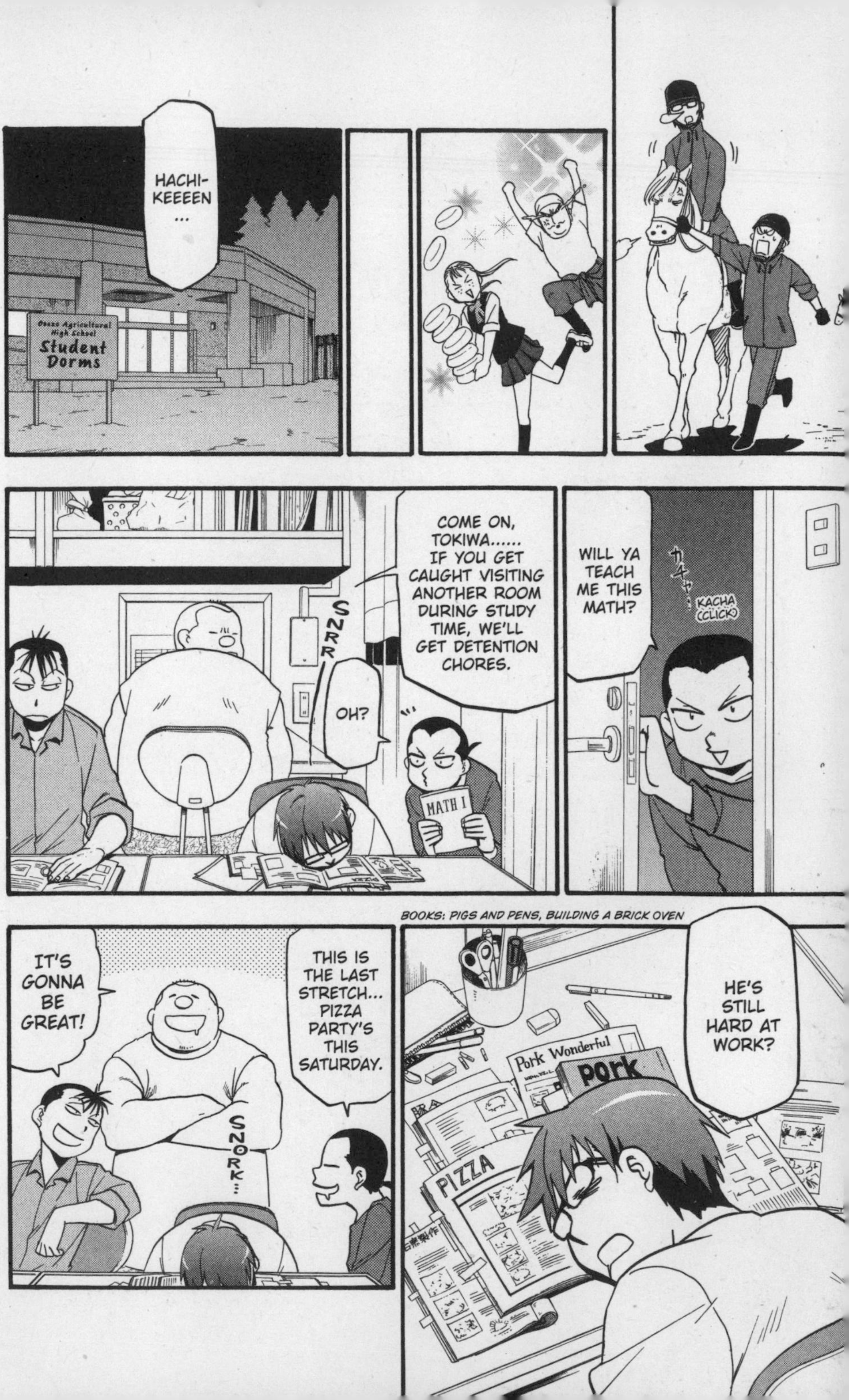
Ooezo Agricultural High School Student Dorms
HACHI-KEEEEN...
カチャ
KACHA (CLICK)
WILL YA TEACH ME THIS MATH?
COME ON, TOKIWA...... IF YOU GET CAUGHT VISITING ANOTHER ROOM DURING STUDY TIME, WE'LL GET DETENTION CHORES.
OH?
SNRR
MATH I
BOOKS: PIGS AND PENS, BUILDING A BRICK OVEN
HE'S STILL HARD AT WORK?
Pork Wonderful
PORK
PIZZA
THIS IS THE LAST STRETCH... PIZZA PARTY'S THIS SATURDAY.
IT'S GONNA BE GREAT!
SNORK...

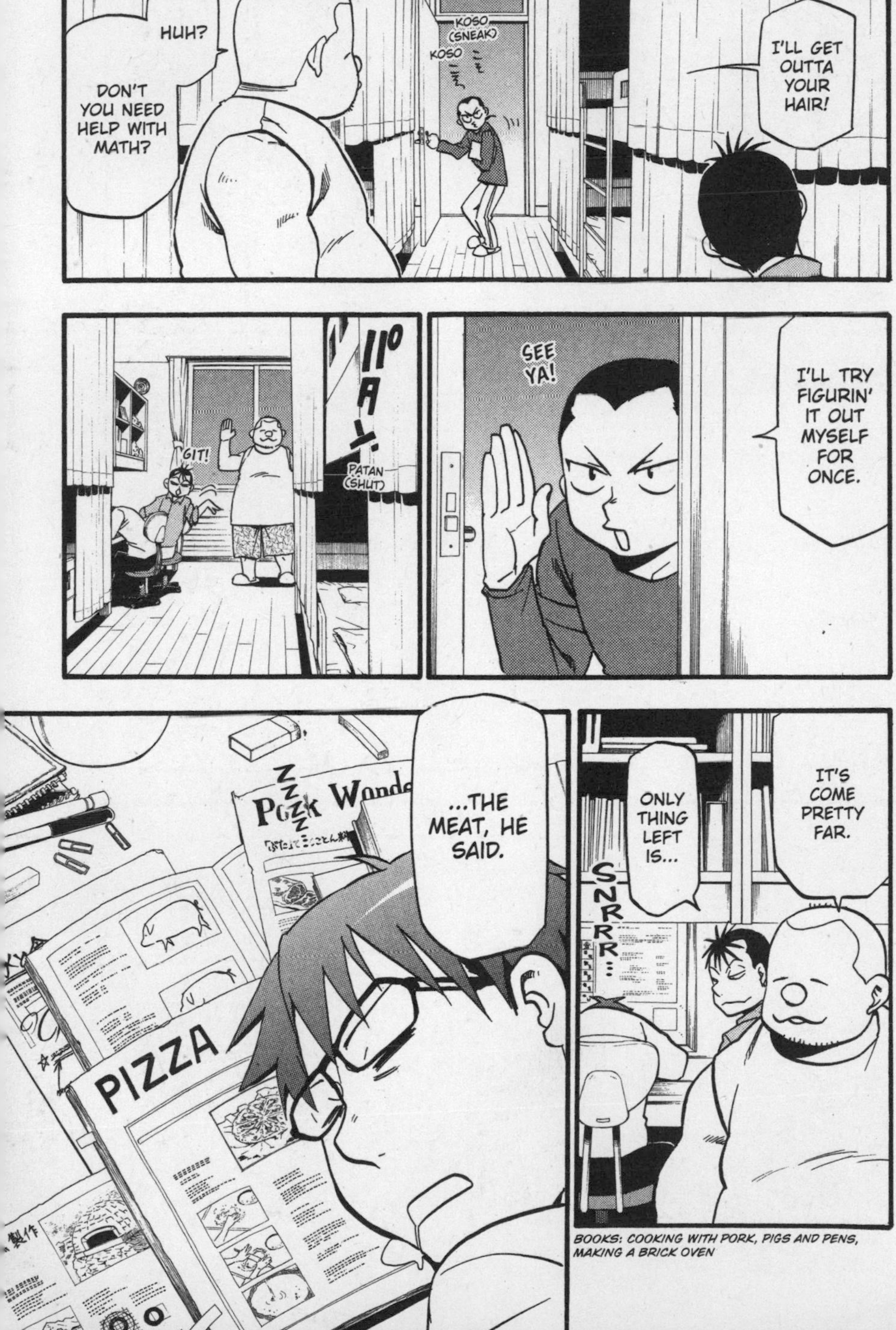
I'LL GET OUTTA YOUR HAIR!
KOSO (SNEAK)
KOSO
HUH?
DON'T YOU NEED HELP WITH MATH?
I'LL TRY FIGURIN' IT OUT MYSELF FOR ONCE.
SEE YA!
PATAN (SHUT)
GIT!
IT'S COME PRETTY FAR.
ONLY THING LEFT IS...
SNRRR...
...THE MEAT, HE SAID.
ZZZZ
PIZZA
BOOKS: COOKING WITH PORK, PIGS AND PENS, MAKING A BRICK OVEN

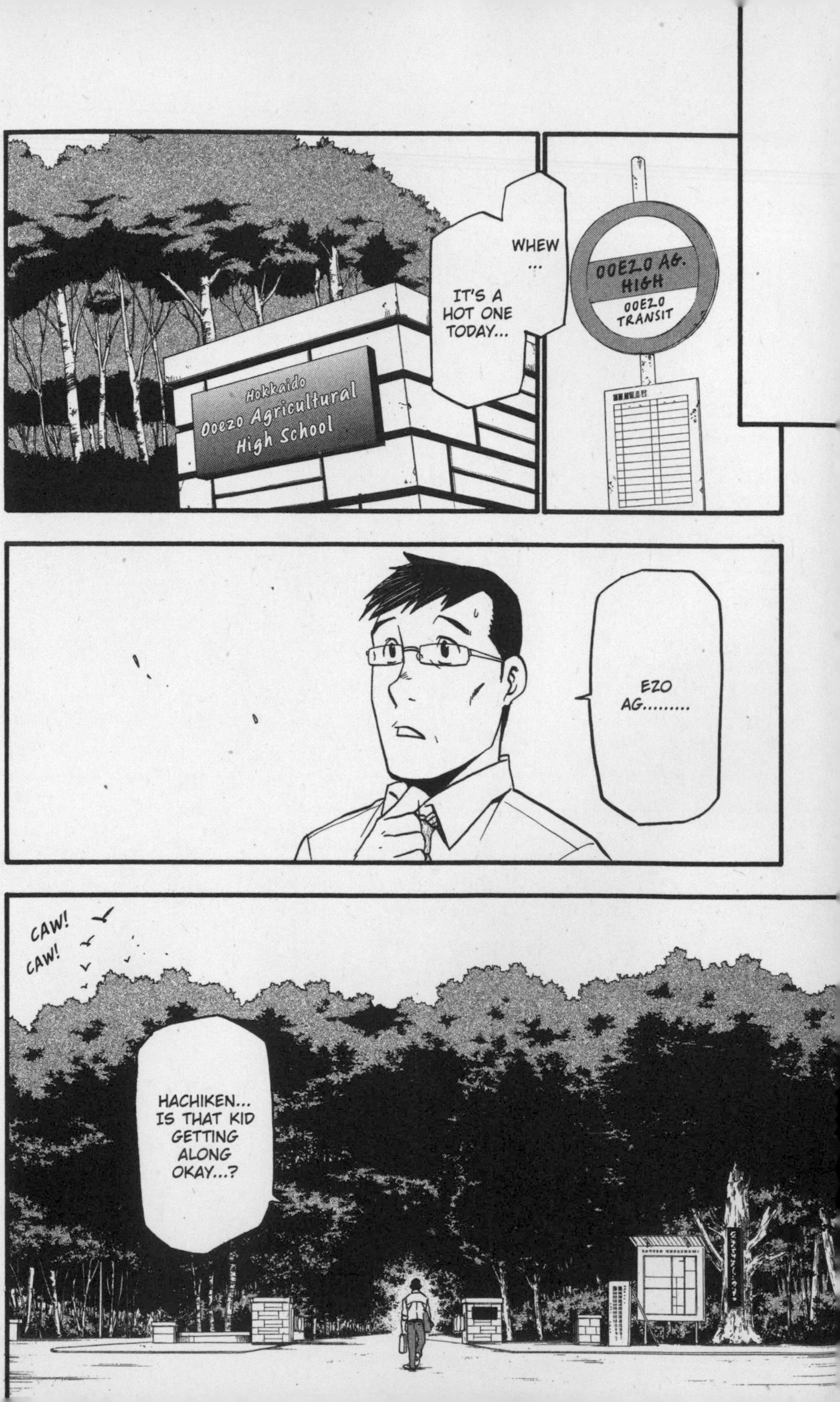
OOEZO AG. HIGH
OOEZO TRANSIT
WHEW ... IT'S A HOT ONE TODAY...
Hokkaido Ooezo Agricultural High School
EZO AG.........
CAW! CAW!
HACHIKEN... IS THAT KID GETTING ALONG OKAY...?

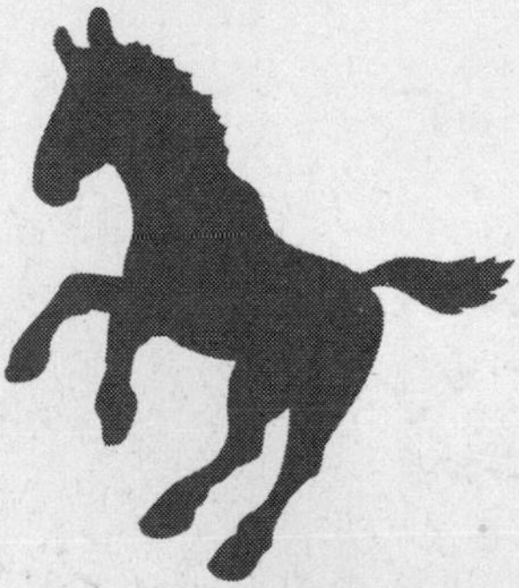

Silver Spoon

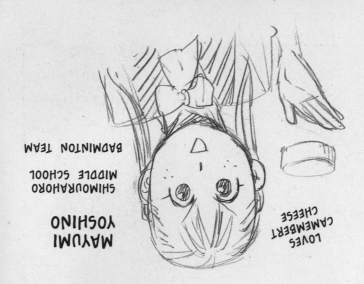

MAYUMI
YOSHINO

SHIMOURAHORO
MIDDLE SCHOOL

BADMINTON TEAM

LOVES
CAMEMBERT
CHEESE

Chapter 10:
Tale of Spring ⑩

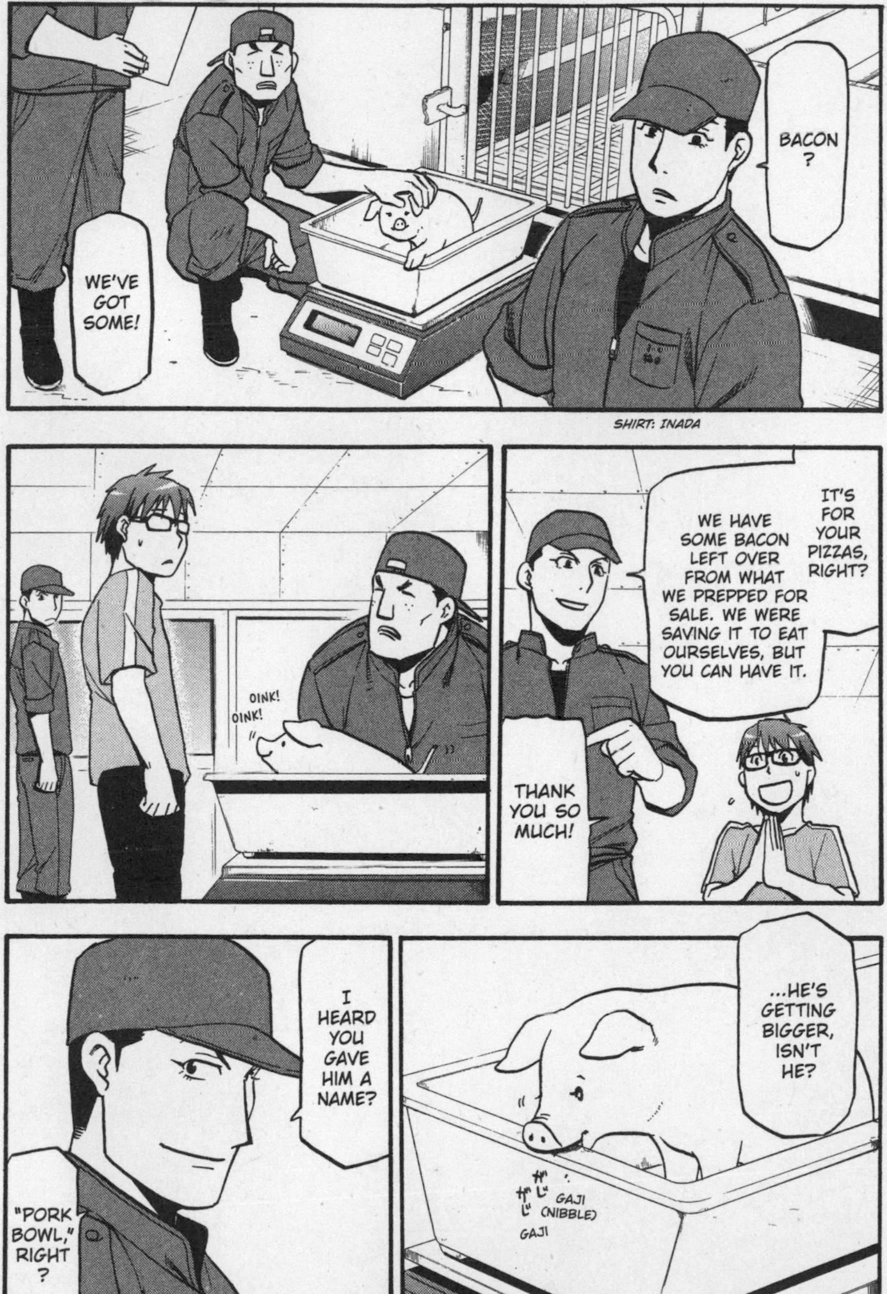
BACON ?
WE'VE GOT SOME!
SHIRT: INADA
IT'S FOR YOUR PIZZAS, RIGHT?
WE HAVE SOME BACON LEFT OVER FROM WHAT WE PREPPED FOR SALE. WE WERE SAVING IT TO EAT OURSELVES, BUT YOU CAN HAVE IT.
THANK YOU SO MUCH!
OINK! OINK!
...HE'S GETTING BIGGER, ISN'T HE?
GAJI GAJI (NIBBLE)
I HEARD YOU GAVE HIM A NAME?
"PORK BOWL," RIGHT ?

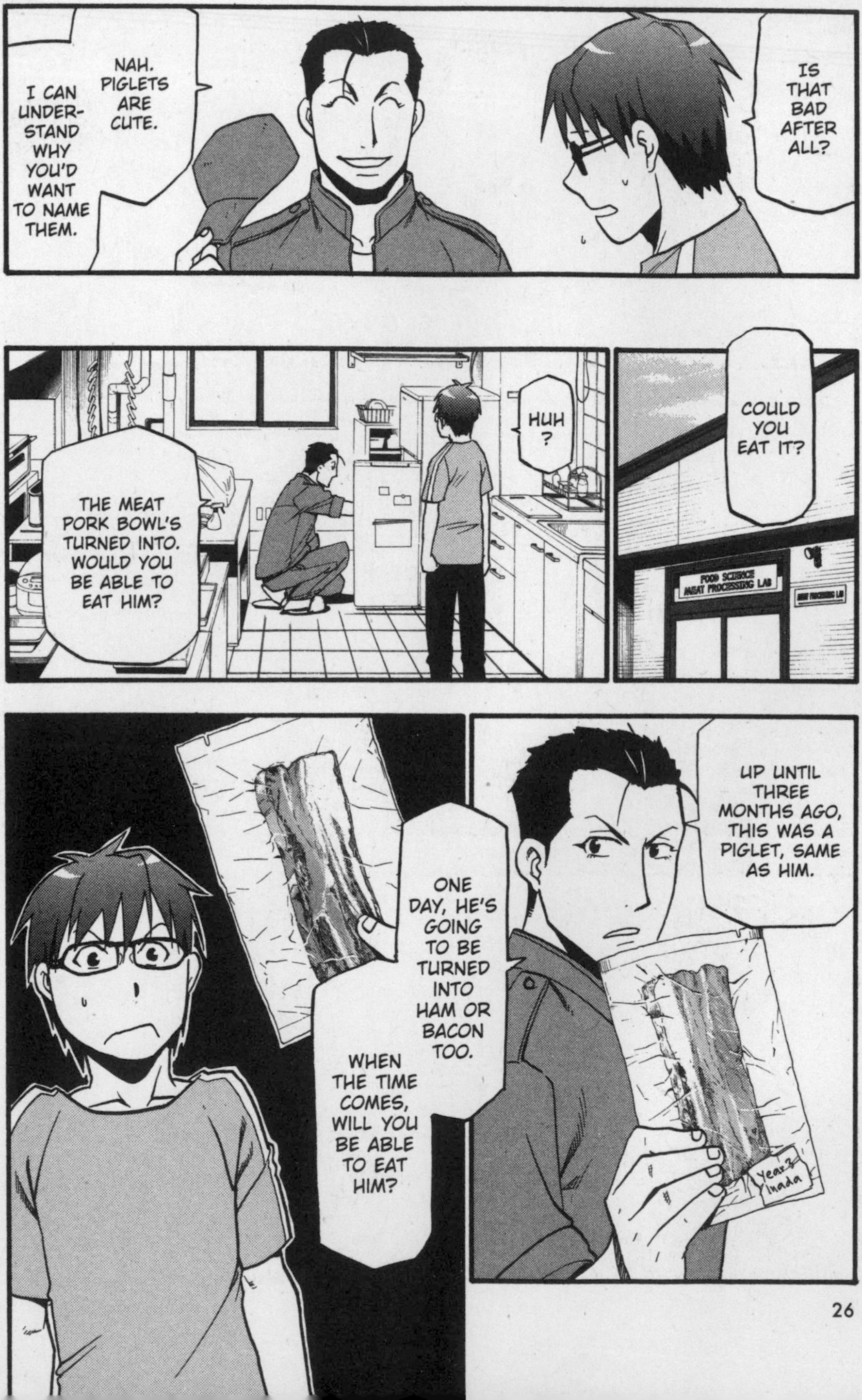
IS THAT BAD AFTER ALL?
NAH. PIGLETS ARE CUTE.
I CAN UNDER-STAND WHY YOU'D WANT TO NAME THEM.
COULD YOU EAT IT?
FOOD SCIENCE MEAT PROCESSING LAB
HUH?
THE MEAT PORK BOWL'S TURNED INTO. WOULD YOU BE ABLE TO EAT HIM?
UP UNTIL THREE MONTHS AGO, THIS WAS A PIGLET, SAME AS HIM.
Year 3 Inada
ONE DAY, HE'S GOING TO BE TURNED INTO HAM OR BACON TOO.
WHEN THE TIME COMES, WILL YOU BE ABLE TO EAT HIM?

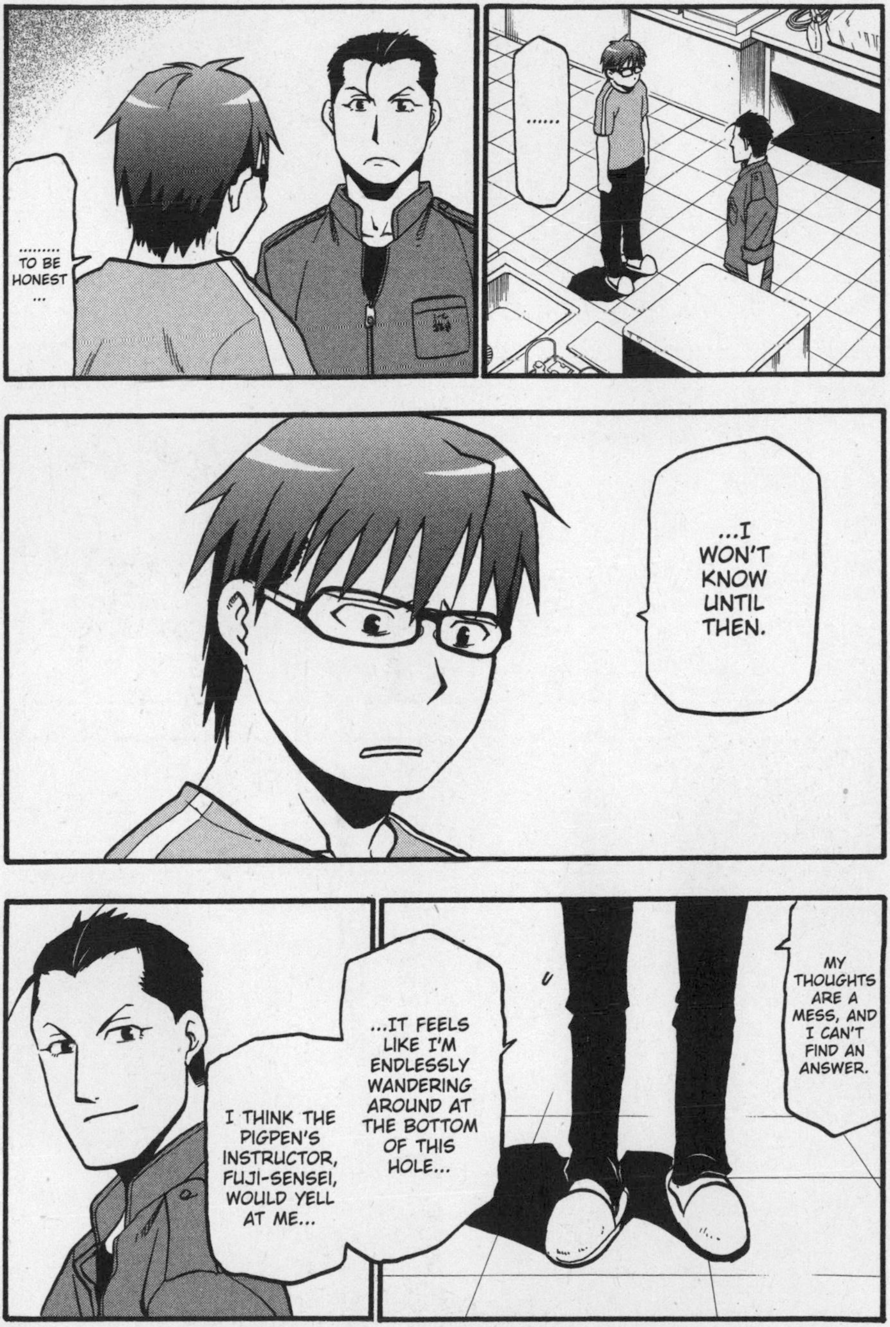
......
.........TO BE HONEST...
...I WON'T KNOW UNTIL THEN.
MY THOUGHTS ARE A MESS, AND I CAN'T FIND AN ANSWER.
...IT FEELS LIKE I'M ENDLESSLY WANDERING AROUND AT THE BOTTOM OF THIS HOLE...
I THINK THE PIGPEN'S INSTRUCTOR, FUJI-SENSEI, WOULD YELL AT ME...

IF YOU'RE WANDERING AROUND CONFLICTED, THAT MEANS YOU'RE STILL SEARCHING FOR THE EXIT.
ZAKUN (THNK)
YOU HAVEN'T STOPPED THINKING.
YOU HAVE TO EXPERIENCE IT PERSONALLY AND FIND THE EXIT YOURSELF, OR IT WON'T BECOME A REAL PART OF YOU.
HERE. TASTE IT.
......THANK YOU.
PAKU (CHOMP)
......
MOGU (CHEW) MOGU
ARGH... I'M SO CON-FLICTED ...
WHYYYY ...?

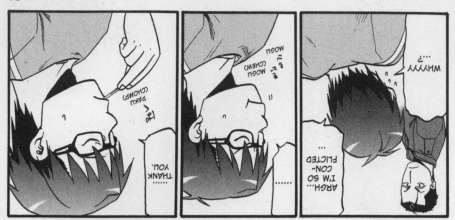

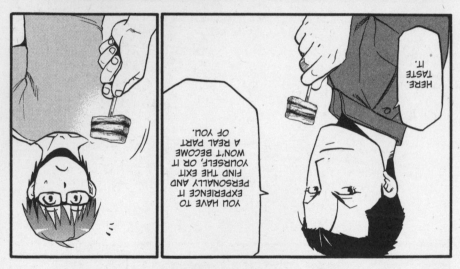

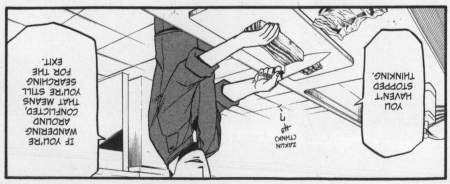

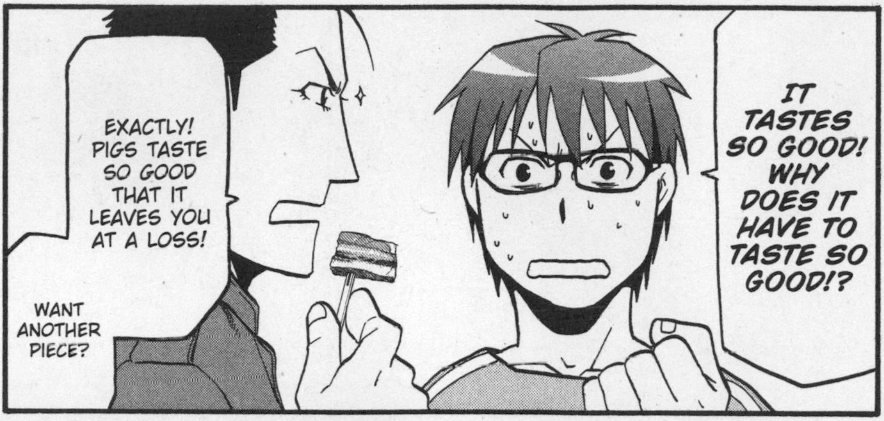
IT TASTES SO GOOD! WHY DOES IT HAVE TO TASTE SO GOOD!?
EXACTLY! PIGS TASTE SO GOOD THAT IT LEAVES YOU AT A LOSS!
WANT ANOTHER PIECE?

Chapter 10: Tale of Spring ⑩

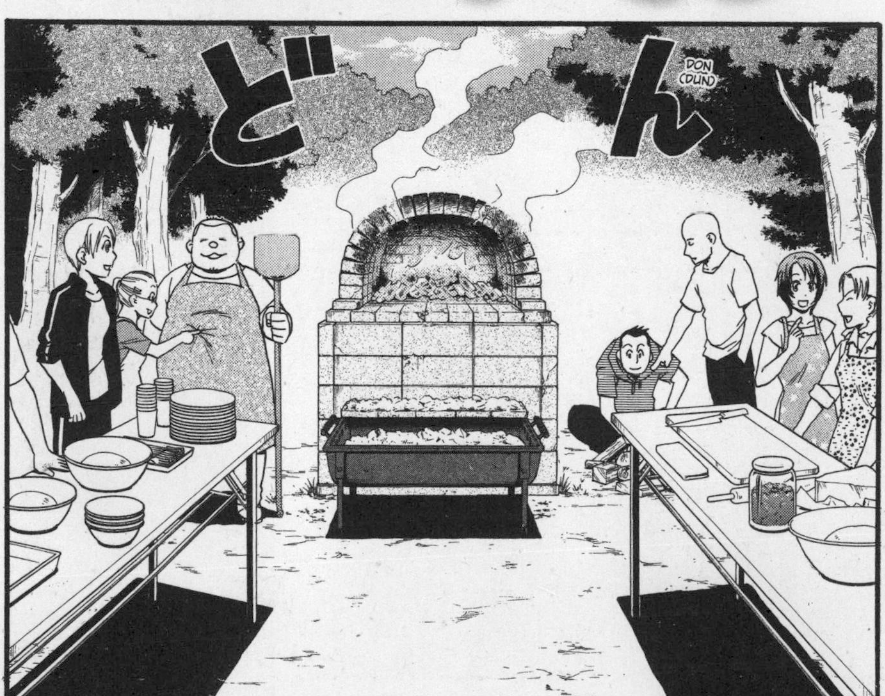
どん
DON (DUN)

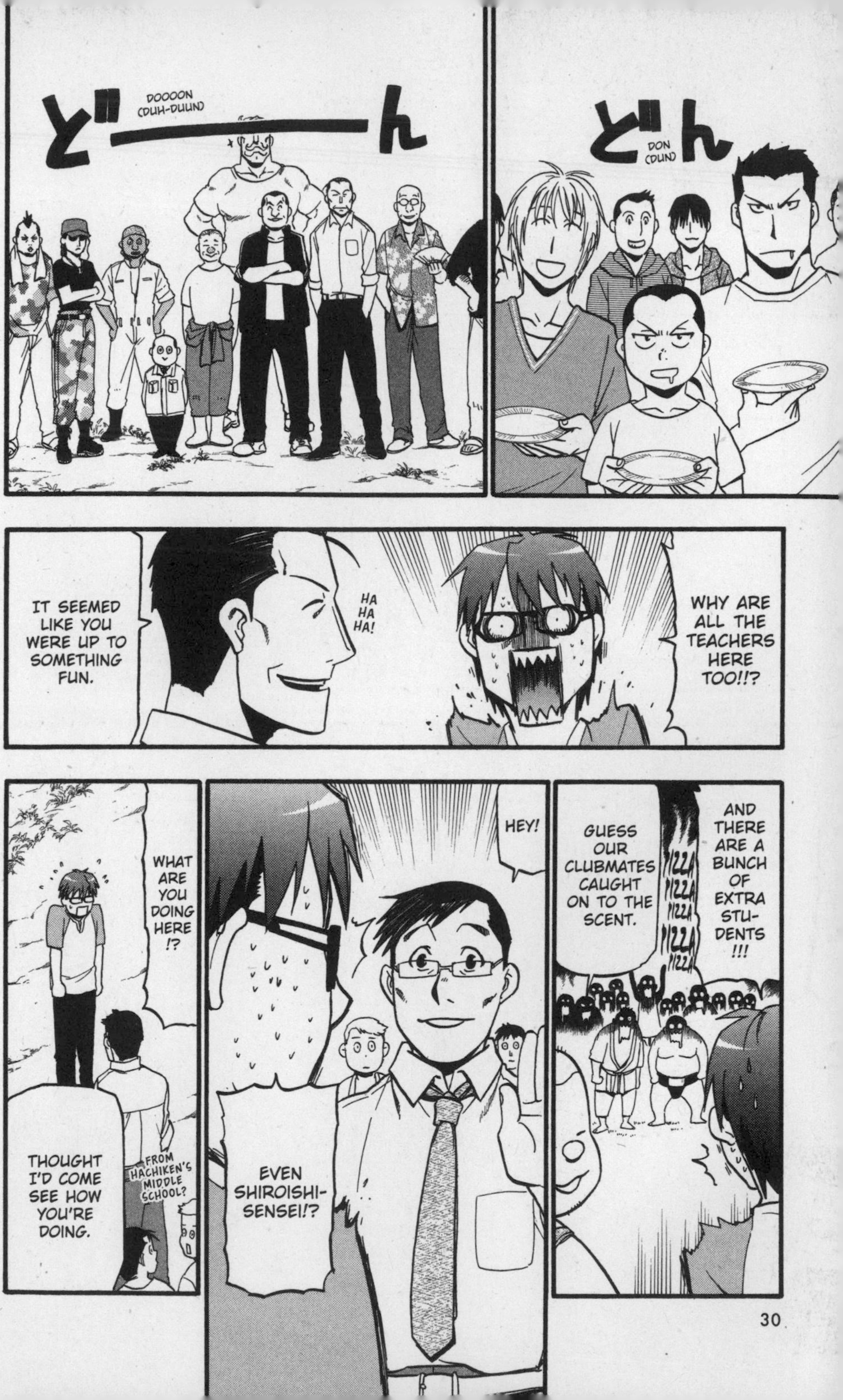
どん
DON (DUN)
どーーーん
DOOOON (DUH-DUUN)
WHY ARE ALL THE TEACHERS HERE TOO!!?
HA HA HA!
IT SEEMED LIKE YOU WERE UP TO SOMETHING FUN.
AND THERE ARE A BUNCH OF EXTRA STU-DENTS!!!
PIZZA PIZZA PIZZA PIZZA PIZZA
GUESS OUR CLUBMATES CAUGHT ON TO THE SCENT.
HEY!
EVEN SHIROISHI-SENSEI!?
WHAT ARE YOU DOING HERE!?
FROM HACHIKEN'S MIDDLE SCHOOL?
THOUGHT I'D COME SEE HOW YOU'RE DOING.

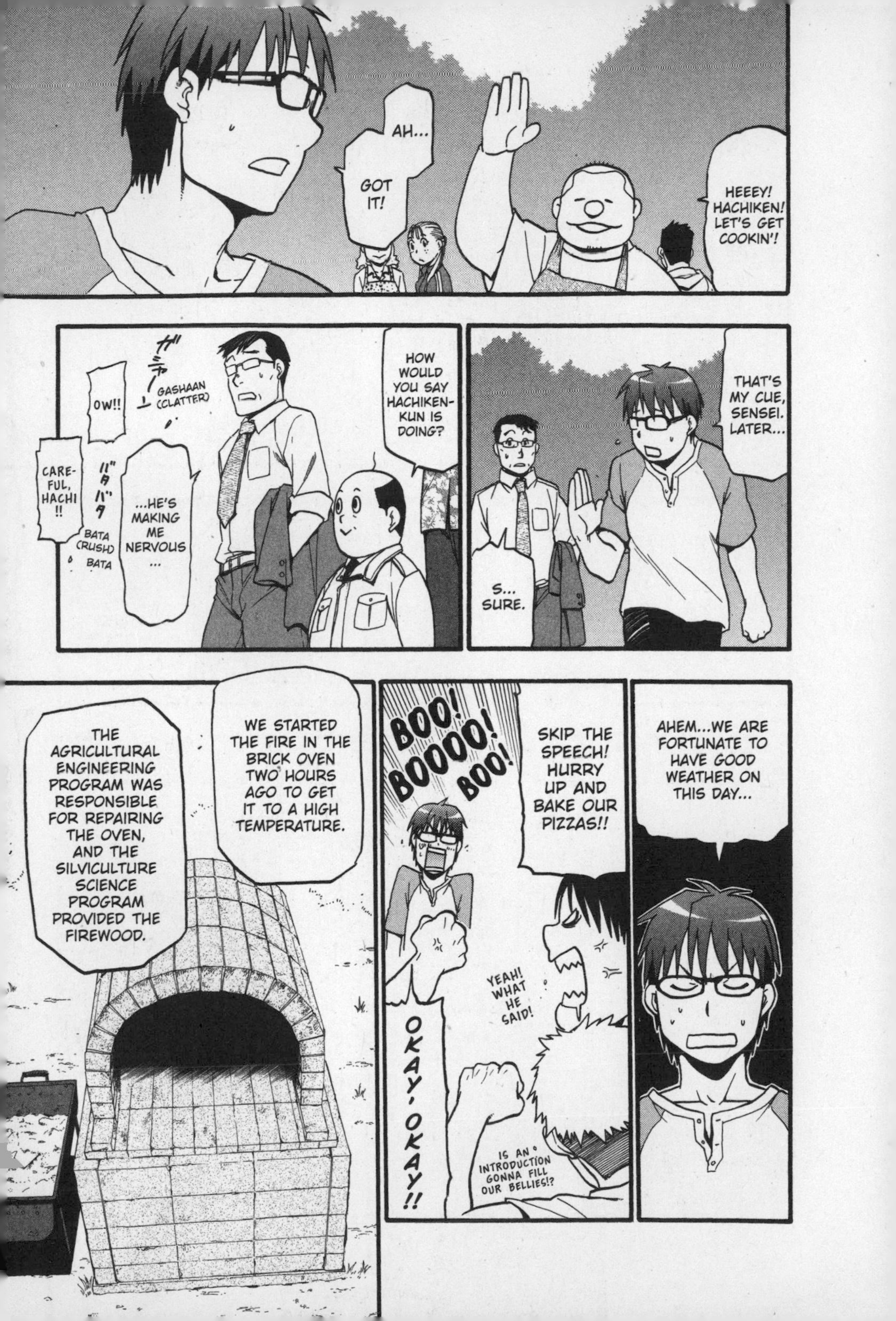
HEEEY! HACHIKEN! LET'S GET COOKIN'!
AH...
GOT IT!
THAT'S MY CUE, SENSEI. LATER...
S... SURE.
HOW WOULD YOU SAY HACHIKEN-KUN IS DOING?
GASHAAN (CLATTER)
OW!!
...HE'S MAKING ME NERVOUS...
BATA (RUSH) BATA
CARE-FUL, HACHI!!
AHEM...WE ARE FORTUNATE TO HAVE GOOD WEATHER ON THIS DAY...
SKIP THE SPEECH! HURRY UP AND BAKE OUR PIZZAS!!
BOO! BOOOOO! BOO!
YEAH! WHAT HE SAID!
OKAY, OKAY!!
IS AN INTRODUCTION GONNA FILL OUR BELLIES!?
WE STARTED THE FIRE IN THE BRICK OVEN TWO HOURS AGO TO GET IT TO A HIGH TEMPERATURE.
THE AGRICULTURAL ENGINEERING PROGRAM WAS RESPONSIBLE FOR REPAIRING THE OVEN, AND THE SILVICULTURE SCIENCE PROGRAM PROVIDED THE FIREWOOD.

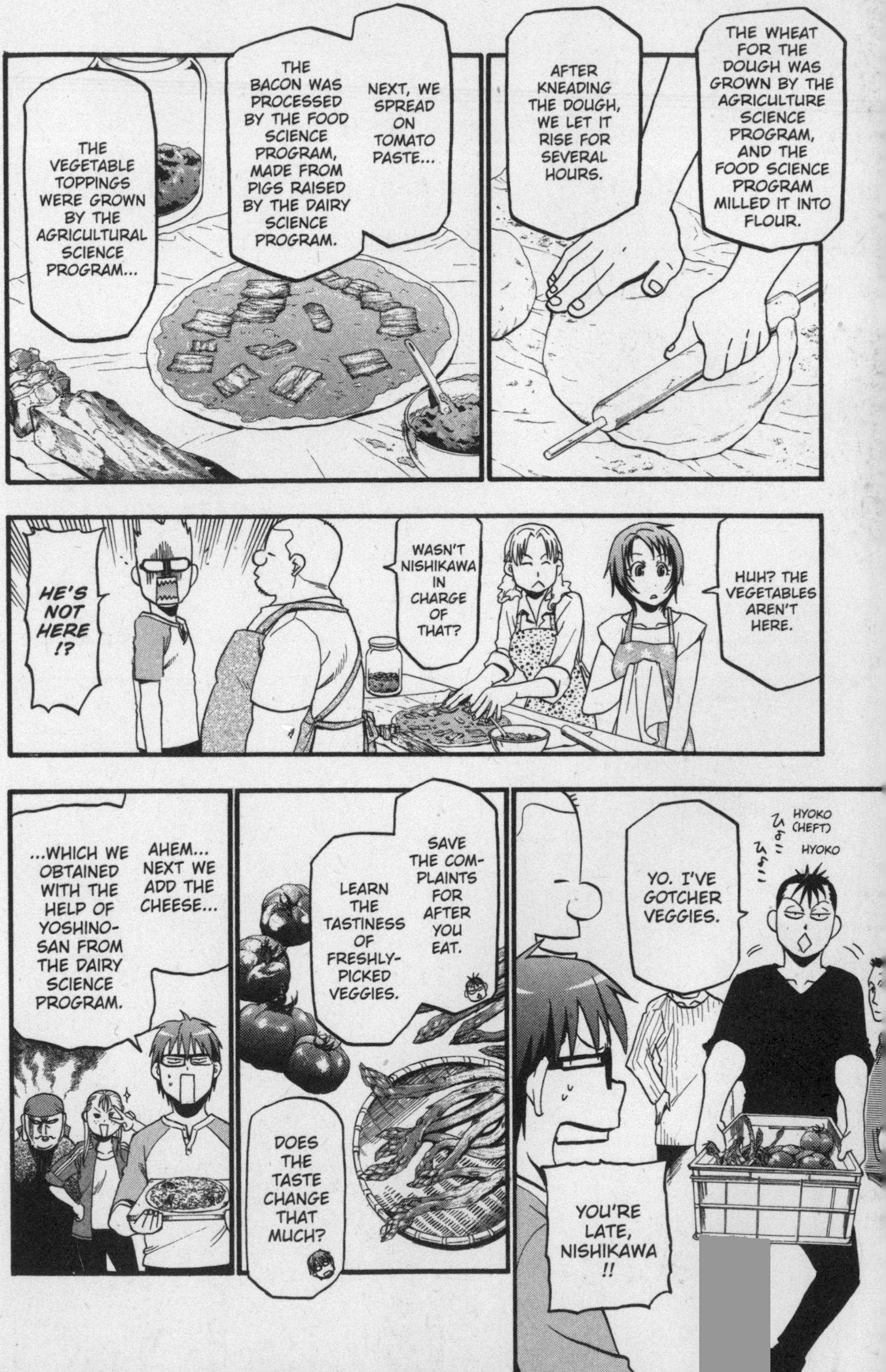
THE WHEAT FOR THE DOUGH WAS GROWN BY THE AGRICULTURE SCIENCE PROGRAM, AND THE FOOD SCIENCE PROGRAM MILLED IT INTO FLOUR.
AFTER KNEADING THE DOUGH, WE LET IT RISE FOR SEVERAL HOURS.
NEXT, WE SPREAD ON TOMATO PASTE...
THE BACON WAS PROCESSED BY THE FOOD SCIENCE PROGRAM, MADE FROM PIGS RAISED BY THE DAIRY SCIENCE PROGRAM.
THE VEGETABLE TOPPINGS WERE GROWN BY THE AGRICULTURAL SCIENCE PROGRAM...
HUH? THE VEGETABLES AREN'T HERE.
WASN'T NISHIKAWA IN CHARGE OF THAT?
HE'S NOT HERE !?
HYOKO (HEFT)
HYOKO
YO. I'VE GOTCHER VEGGIES.
YOU'RE LATE, NISHIKAWA !!
SAVE THE COM- PLAINTS FOR AFTER YOU EAT.
LEARN THE TASTINESS OF FRESHLY- PICKED VEGGIES.
DOES THE TASTE CHANGE THAT MUCH?
AHEM... NEXT WE ADD THE CHEESE...
...WHICH WE OBTAINED WITH THE HELP OF YOSHINO- SAN FROM THE DAIRY SCIENCE PROGRAM.

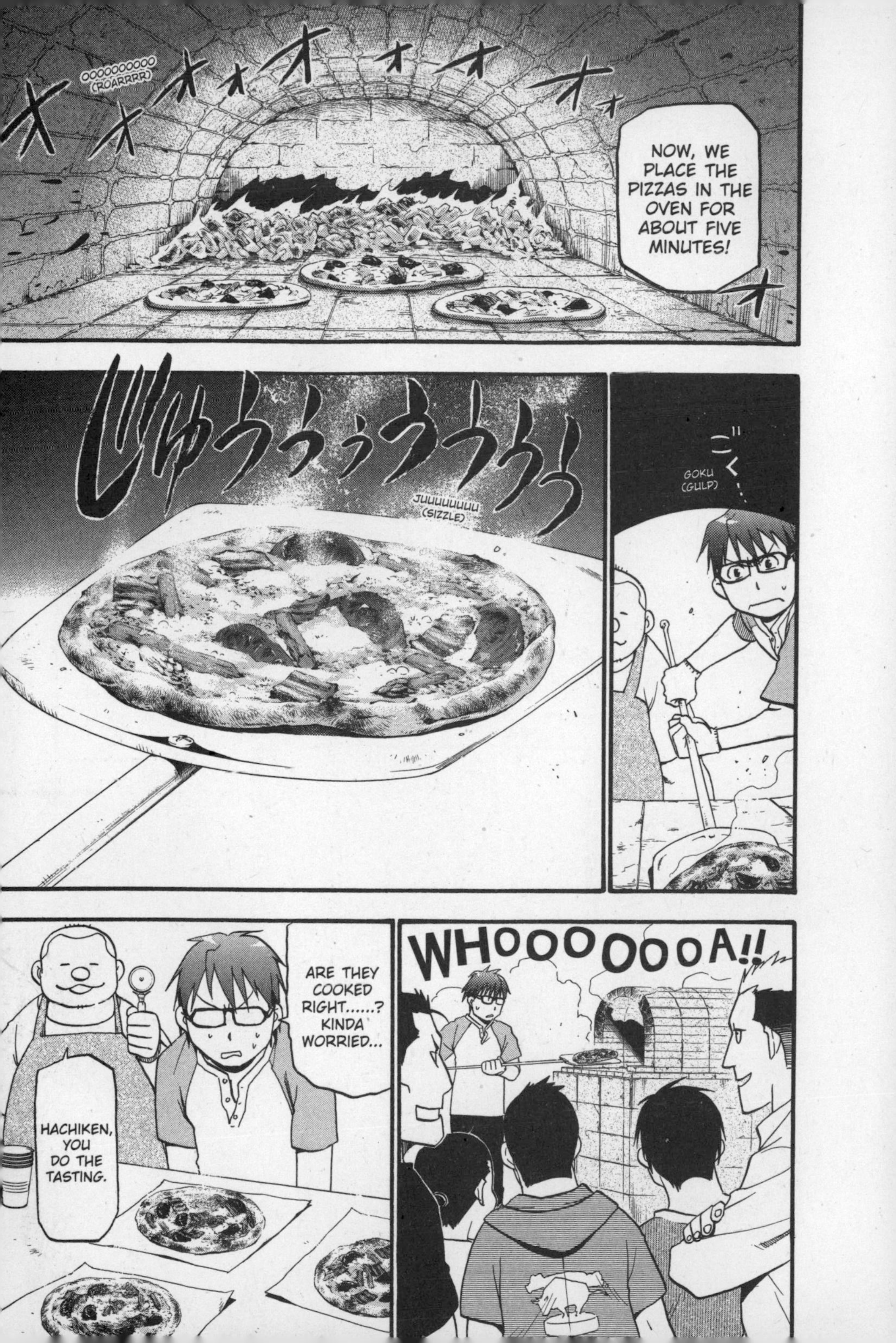
OOOOOOOOOO (ROARRRR)
NOW, WE PLACE THE PIZZAS IN THE OVEN FOR ABOUT FIVE MINUTES!
GOKU (GULP)
JUUUUUUUUU (SIZZLE)
WHOOOOOOA!!
ARE THEY COOKED RIGHT......? KINDA WORRIED...
HACHIKEN, YOU DO THE TASTING.

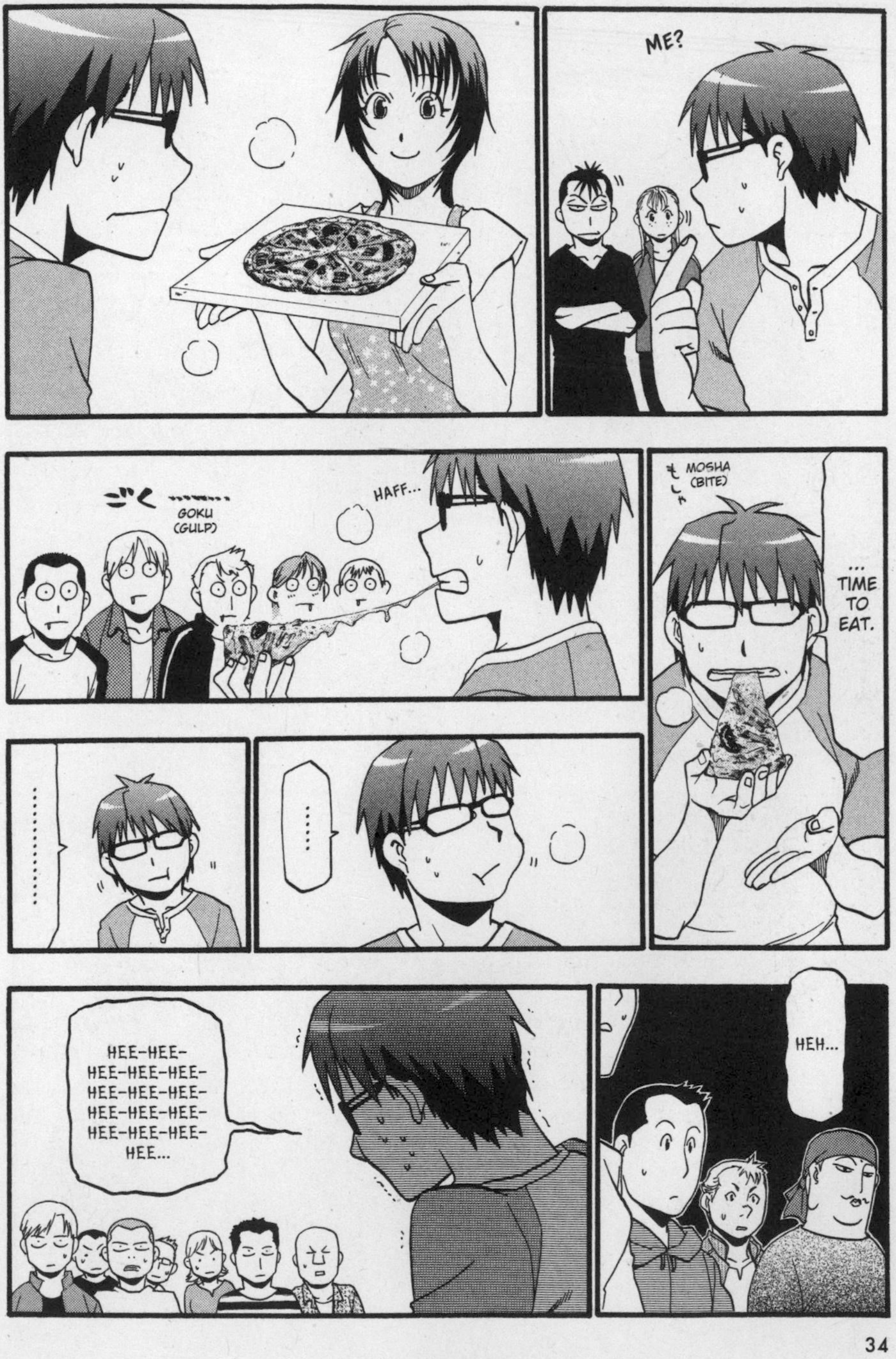
ME?
もしゃ MOSHA (BITE)
...TIME TO EAT.
HAFF...
ごく GOKU (GULP)
......
......
HEH...
HEE-HEE-HEE-HEE-HEE-HEE-HEE-HEE-HEE-HEE-HEE-HEE-HEE-HEE-HEE...

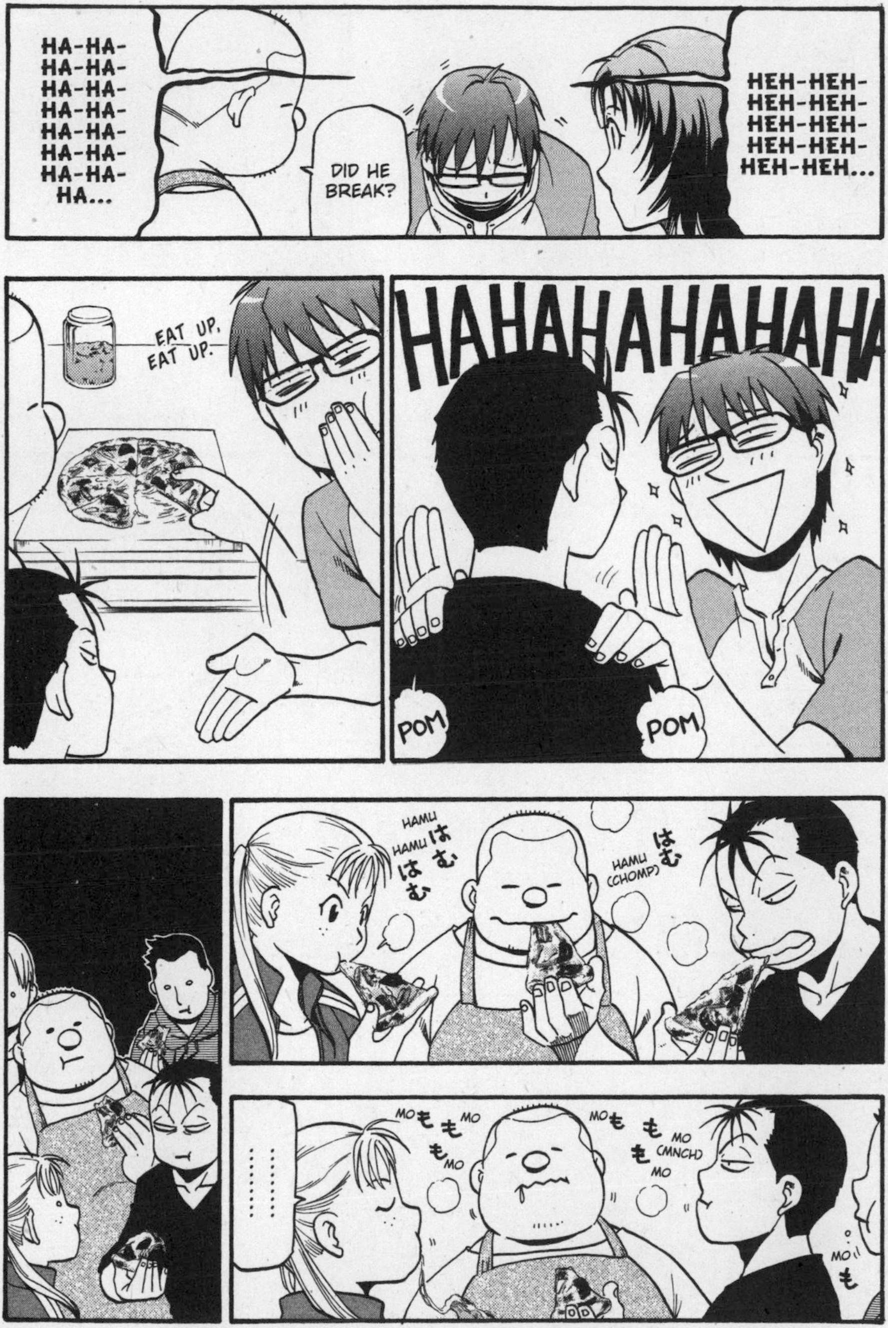
HEH-HEH-HEH-HEH-HEH-HEH-HEH-HEH-HEH-HEH...
DID HE BREAK?
HA-HA-HA-HA-HA-HA-HA-HA-HA-HA-HA-HA-HA-HA-HA...
HAHAHAHAHAHAHA
POM
POM
EAT UP, EAT UP.
はむ
HAMU (CHOMP)
HAMU はむ
HAMU はむ
MO も
MO もMO も MO (MNCH)
MO も MO もMO も MO
......

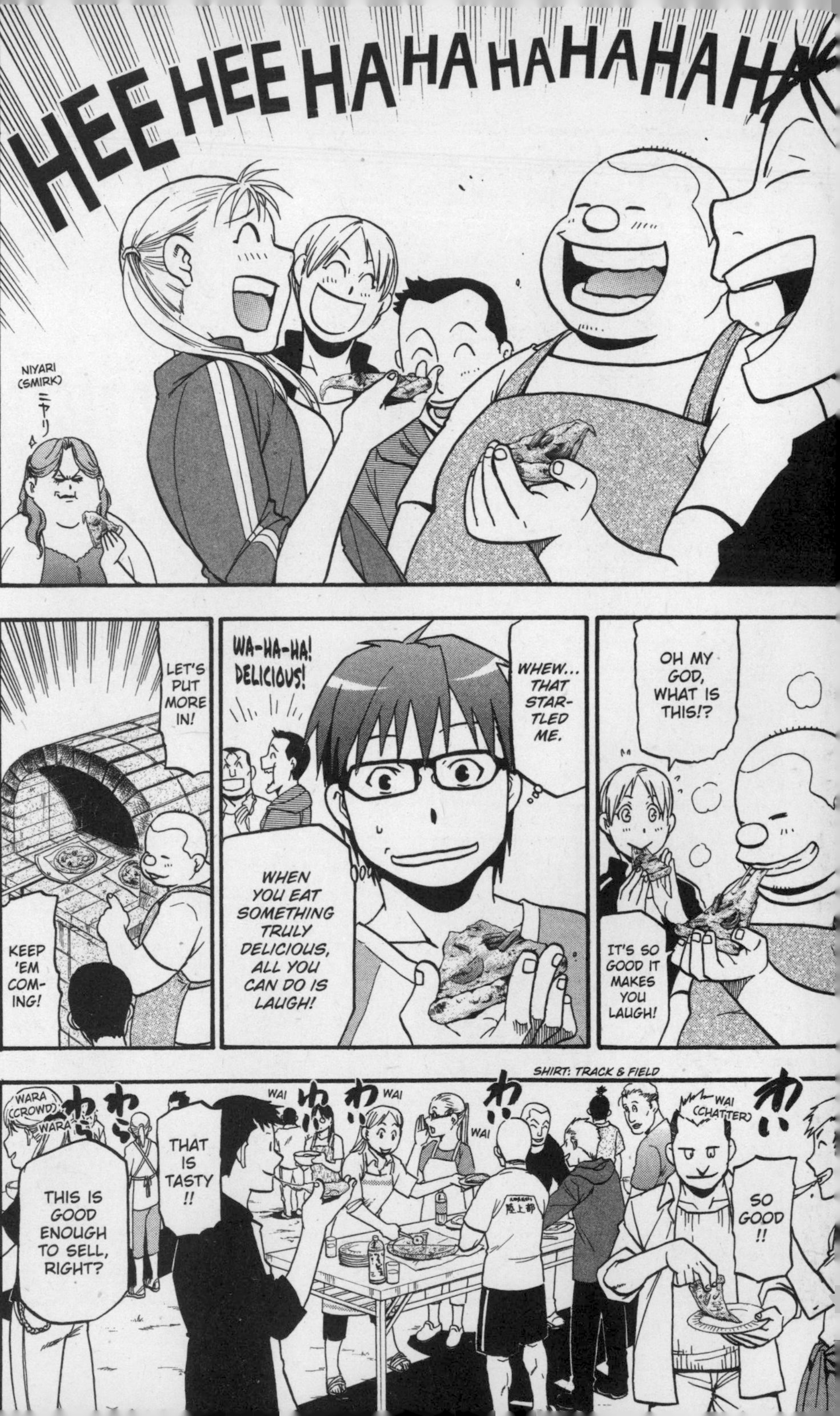
HEE HEE HA HA HA HA HA HA
NIYARI (SMIRK)
ニヤリ
OH MY GOD, WHAT IS THIS!?
IT'S SO GOOD IT MAKES YOU LAUGH!
WHEW... THAT STARTLED ME.
WA-HA-HA! DELICIOUS!
WHEN YOU EAT SOMETHING TRULY DELICIOUS, ALL YOU CAN DO IS LAUGH!
LET'S PUT MORE IN!
KEEP 'EM COMING!
SHIRT: TRACK & FIELD
WAI (CHATTER)
SO GOOD !!
WAI
WAI
WAI
THAT IS TASTY !!
WARA (CROWD) WARA
THIS IS GOOD ENOUGH TO SELL, RIGHT?

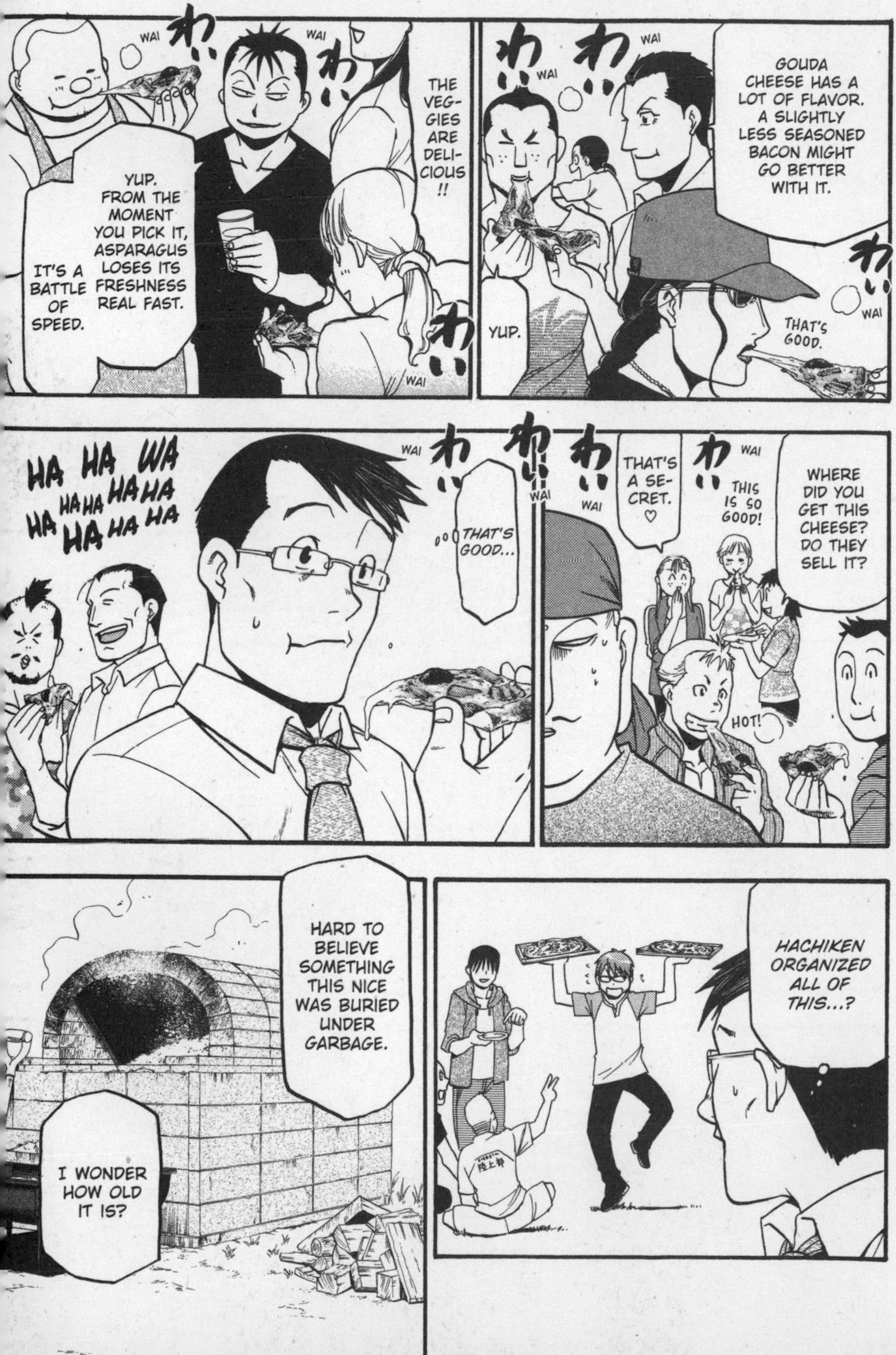
GOUDA CHEESE HAS A LOT OF FLAVOR. A SLIGHTLY LESS SEASONED BACON MIGHT GO BETTER WITH IT.
WAI
WAI
WAI
YUP.
THAT'S GOOD.
WAI
THE VEG-GIES ARE DELI-CIOUS!!
WAI
WAI
YUP. FROM THE MOMENT YOU PICK IT, ASPARAGUS LOSES ITS FRESHNESS REAL FAST.
IT'S A BATTLE OF SPEED.
WAI
WAI
WHERE DID YOU GET THIS CHEESE? DO THEY SELL IT?
WAI
THIS IS SO GOOD!
THAT'S A SE-CRET. ♡
WAI
WAI
HOT!
WAI
THAT'S GOOD...
HA HA WA HA HA HA HA HA HA HA HA HA HA
HACHIKEN ORGANIZED ALL OF THIS...?
HARD TO BELIEVE SOMETHING THIS NICE WAS BURIED UNDER GARBAGE.
I WONDER HOW OLD IT IS?

IT'S A HOBBY OVEN, RIGHT?
WHO COULD HAVE MADE IT?
GRK!
THIS WOULD GO GREAT WITH BEER!
SHOULD WE START MAKING EZO AG BEER?
A HIGH SCHOOL MAKING BEER, THOUGH?
WELL, THERE ARE HIGH SCHOOLS THAT MAKE SAKE. WE COULD INTEGRATE IT INTO THE CURRICULUM AS FERMENTATION AND BREWING SCIENCE, OR...
TSUI (POKE)
ついつい
TSUI
Ooezo Agricultural High School
Pizza Festival
Project Proposal
1-D
Tamako Inada
WHY NOT EXPAND THIS PIZZA PARTY INTO AN EVENT THAT WOULD INCLUDE MEMBERS OF THE GENERAL PUBLIC?
I SEE, I SEE...
HMM, HMM...
I SEE YOUR POINT...
WE COULD CHARGE AN ENTRANCE FEE, AND FOR THE BUDGET...
YUM!

SFX: PACHI (CLICK) PACHI PACHI

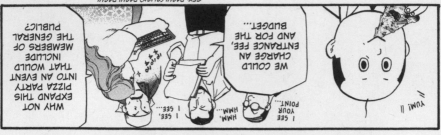

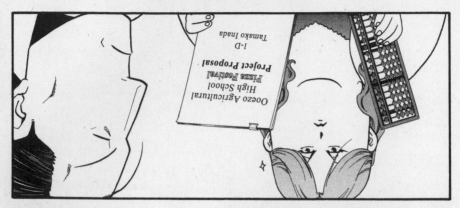

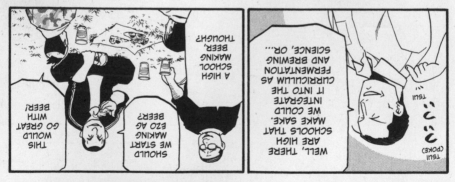

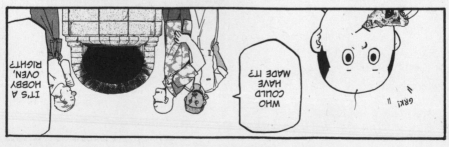

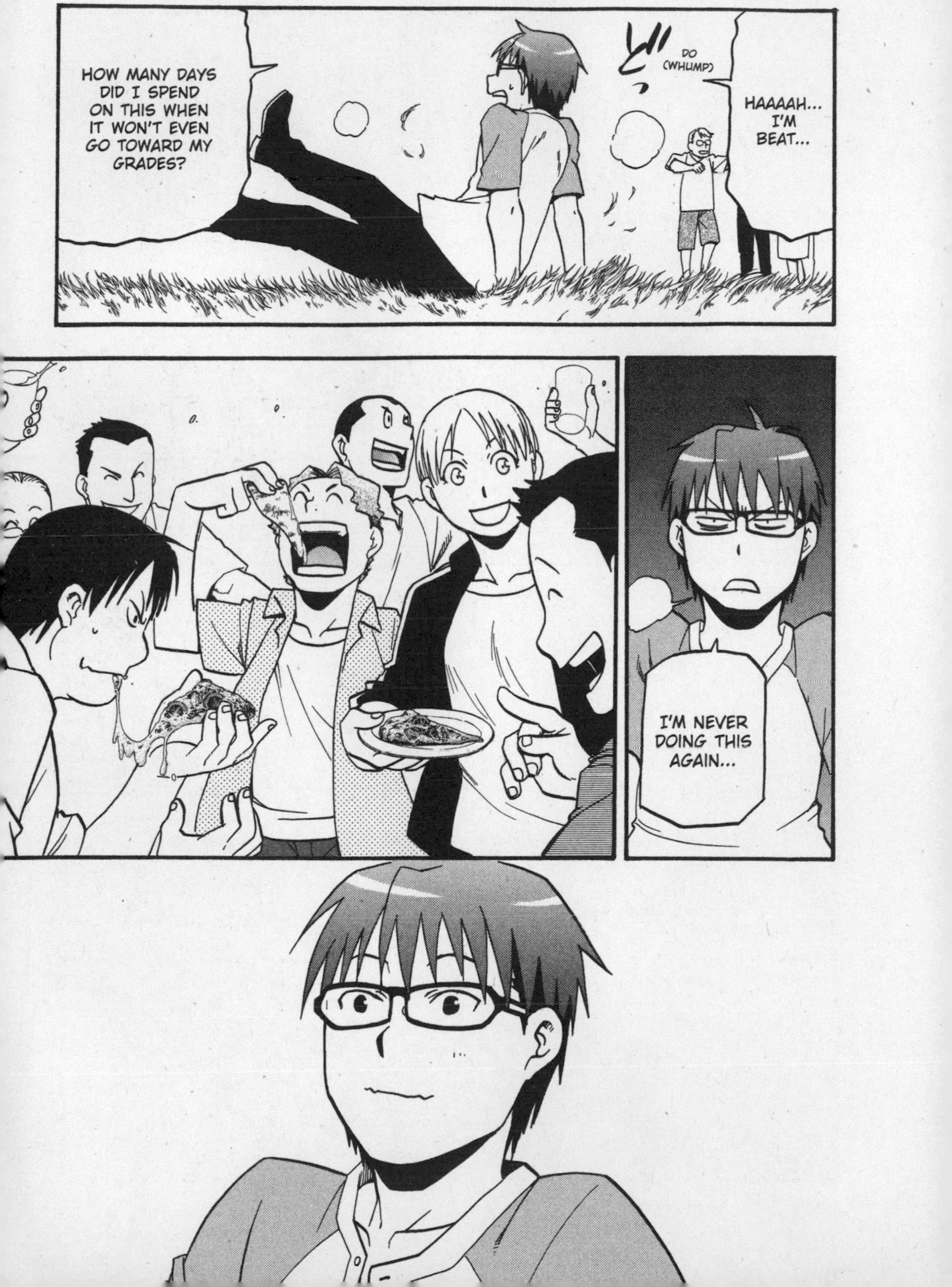
HAAAAH... I'M BEAT...
DO (WHUMP)
HOW MANY DAYS DID I SPEND ON THIS WHEN IT WON'T EVEN GO TOWARD MY GRADES?
I'M NEVER DOING THIS AGAIN...
...

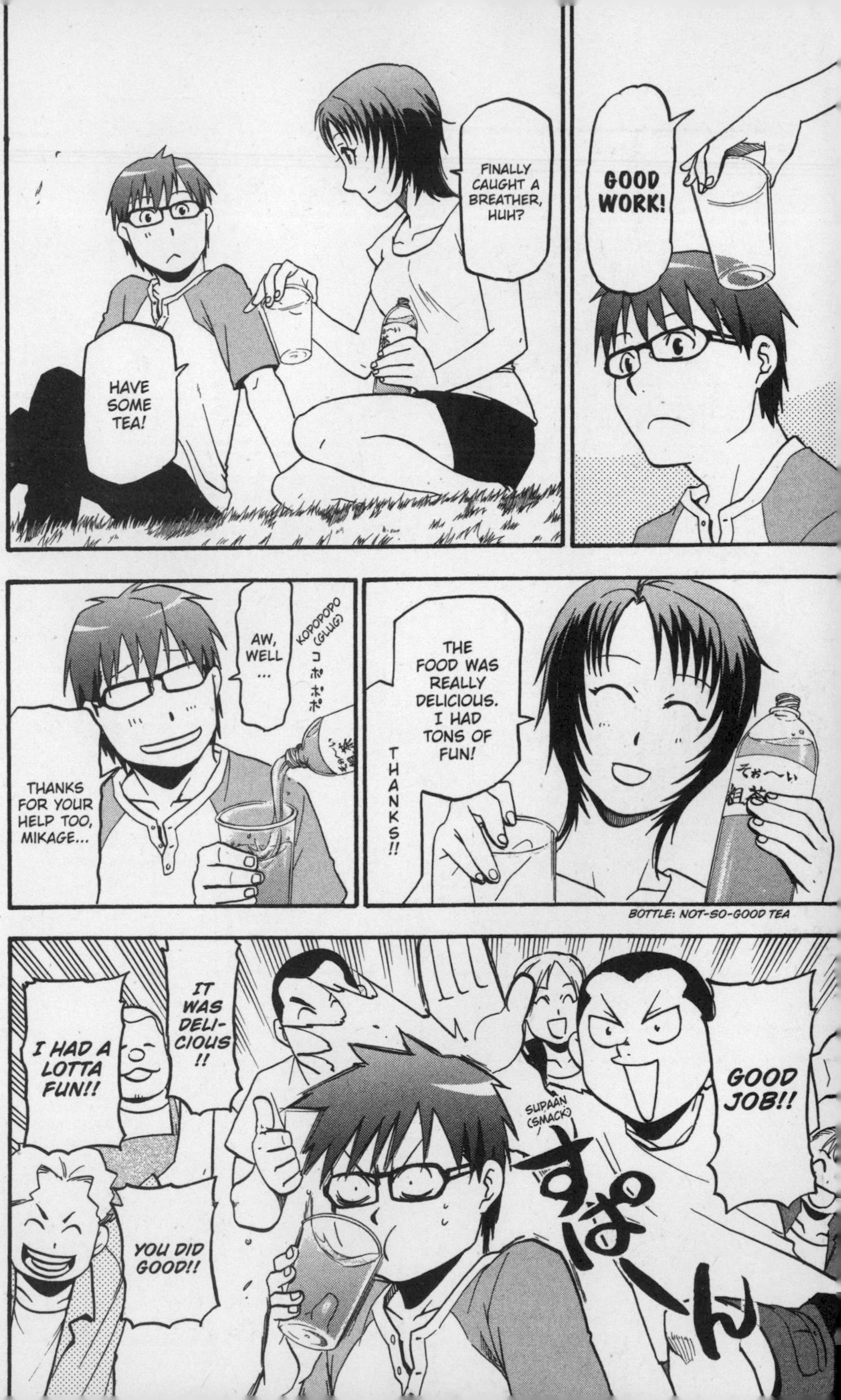
GOOD WORK!
FINALLY CAUGHT A BREATHER, HUH?
HAVE SOME TEA!
THE FOOD WAS REALLY DELICIOUS. I HAD TONS OF FUN!
THANKS!!
KOPOPOPO (GLUG)
コポポポ
AW, WELL ...
THANKS FOR YOUR HELP TOO, MIKAGE...
GOOD JOB!!
SUPAAN (SMACK)
すぱ〜ん
IT WAS DELI-CIOUS!!
I HAD A LOTTA FUN!!
YOU DID GOOD!!
BOTTLE: NOT-SO-GOOD TEA

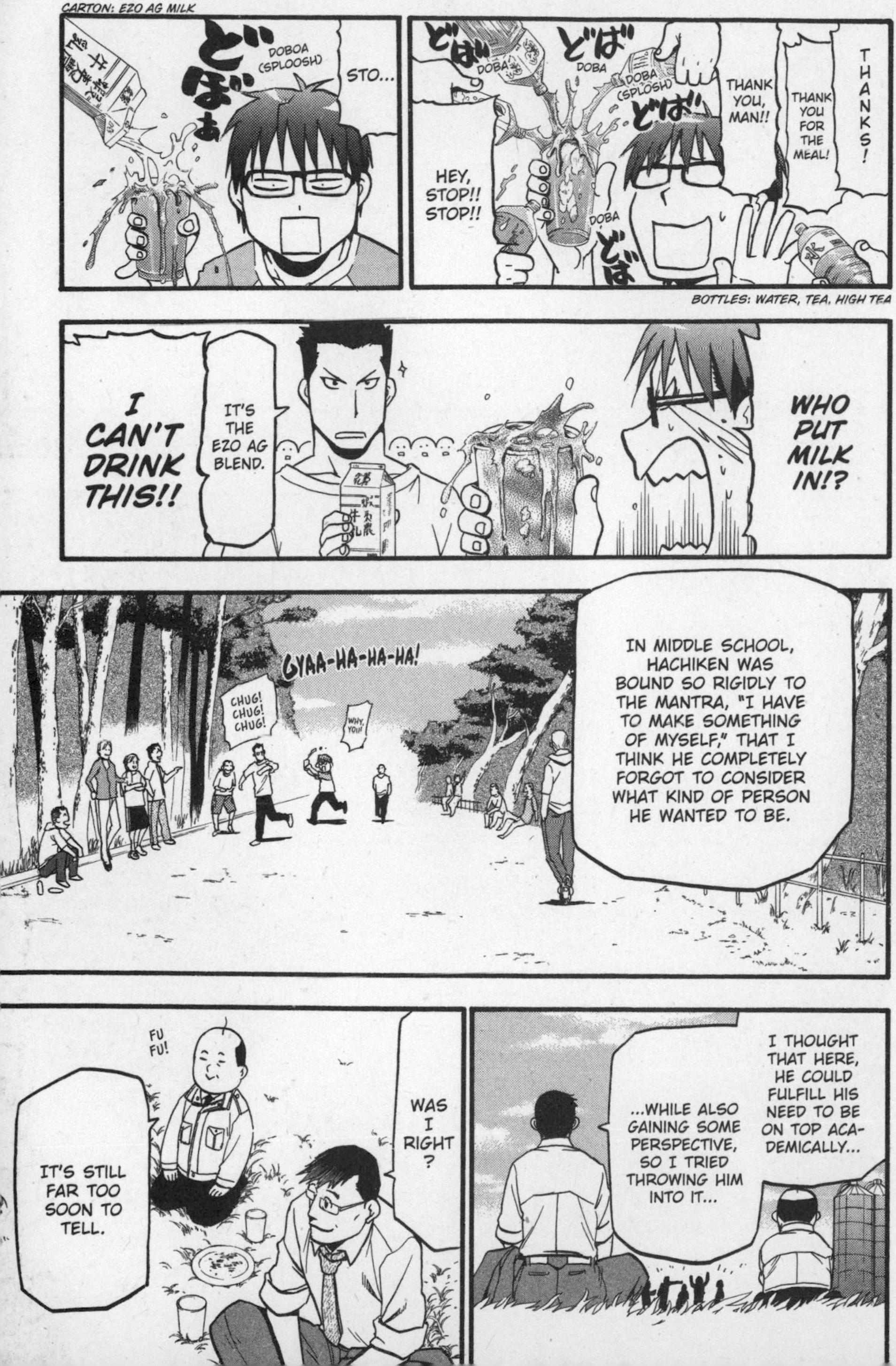

THANKS!
THANK YOU FOR THE MEAL!
THANK YOU, MAN!!
DOBA (SPLOSH)
どば
DOBA
どば
DOBA
どば
HEY, STOP!! STOP!!
DOBA
どば
STO...
DOBOA (SPLOSH)
どぼぉ
WHO PUT MILK IN!?
IT'S THE EZO AG BLEND.
I CAN'T DRINK THIS!!
IN MIDDLE SCHOOL, HACHIKEN WAS BOUND SO RIGIDLY TO THE MANTRA, "I HAVE TO MAKE SOMETHING OF MYSELF," THAT I THINK HE COMPLETELY FORGOT TO CONSIDER WHAT KIND OF PERSON HE WANTED TO BE.
GYAA-HA-HA-HA!
WHY, YOU!
CHUG! CHUG! CHUG!
I THOUGHT THAT HERE, HE COULD FULFILL HIS NEED TO BE ON TOP ACA-DEMICALLY...
...WHILE ALSO GAINING SOME PERSPECTIVE, SO I TRIED THROWING HIM INTO IT...
WAS I RIGHT?
FU FU!
IT'S STILL FAR TOO SOON TO TELL.

CARTON: EZO AG MILK
BOTTLES: WATER, TEA, HIGH TEA

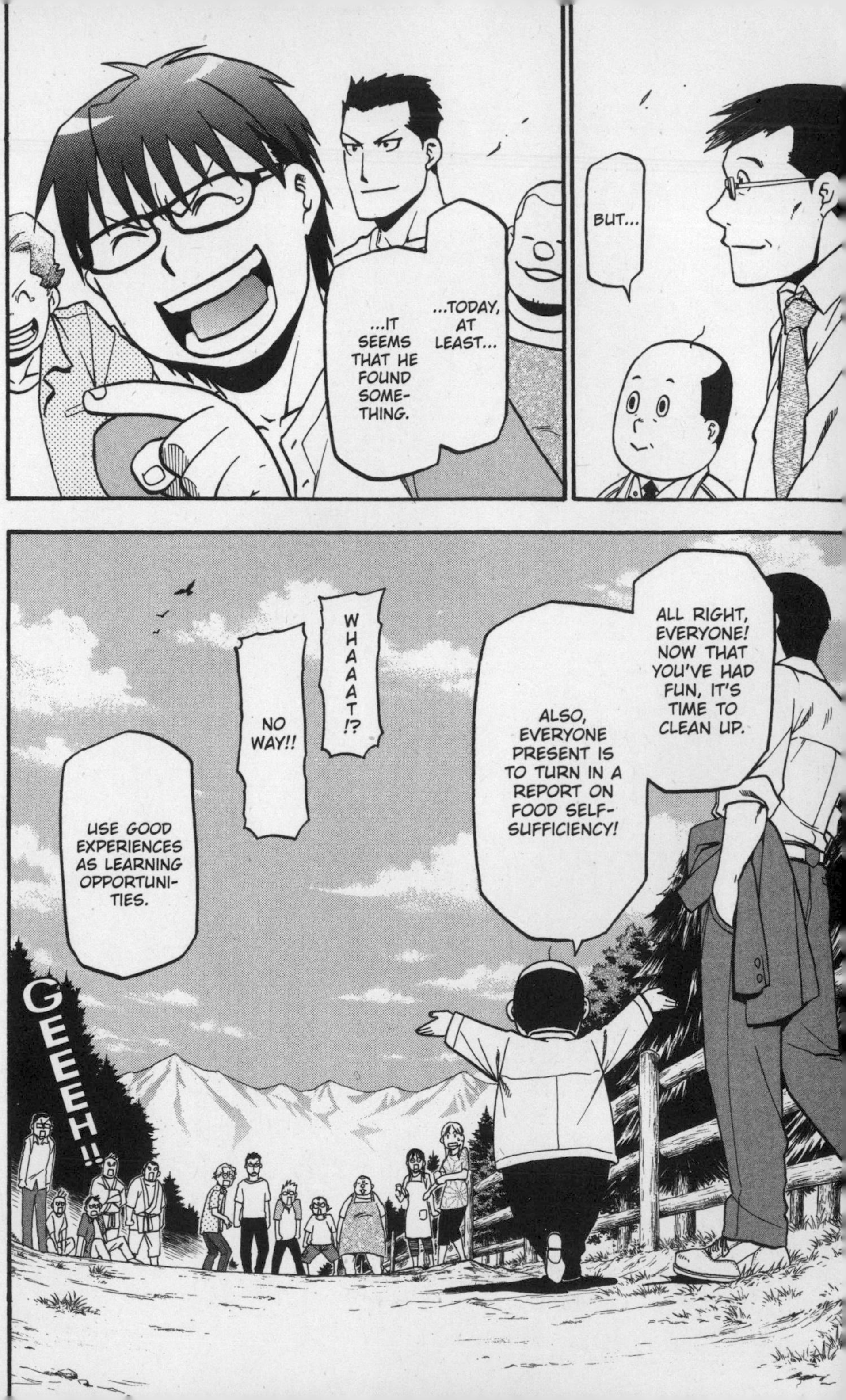
BUT...
...TODAY, AT LEAST...
...IT SEEMS THAT HE FOUND SOME-THING.
ALL RIGHT, EVERYONE! NOW THAT YOU'VE HAD FUN, IT'S TIME TO CLEAN UP.
ALSO, EVERYONE PRESENT IS TO TURN IN A REPORT ON FOOD SELF-SUFFICIENCY!
WHAAAAT!?
NO WAY!!
USE GOOD EXPERIENCES AS LEARNING OPPORTUNI-TIES.
GEEEEH!!

Silver Spoon

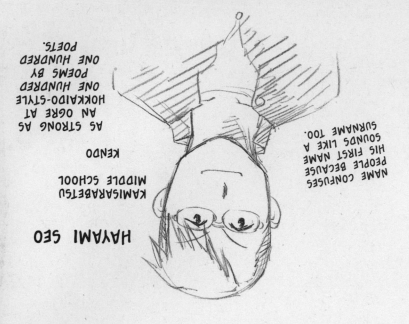

HAYAMI SEO

KAMISARABETSU
MIDDLE SCHOOL

KENDO

AS STRONG AS
AN OGRE AT
HOKKAIDO-STYLE
ONE HUNDRED
POEMS BY
ONE HUNDRED
POETS.

NAME CONFUSES
PEOPLE BECAUSE
HIS FIRST NAME
SOUNDS LIKE A
SURNAME TOO.

Chapter 11: Tale of Summer ①

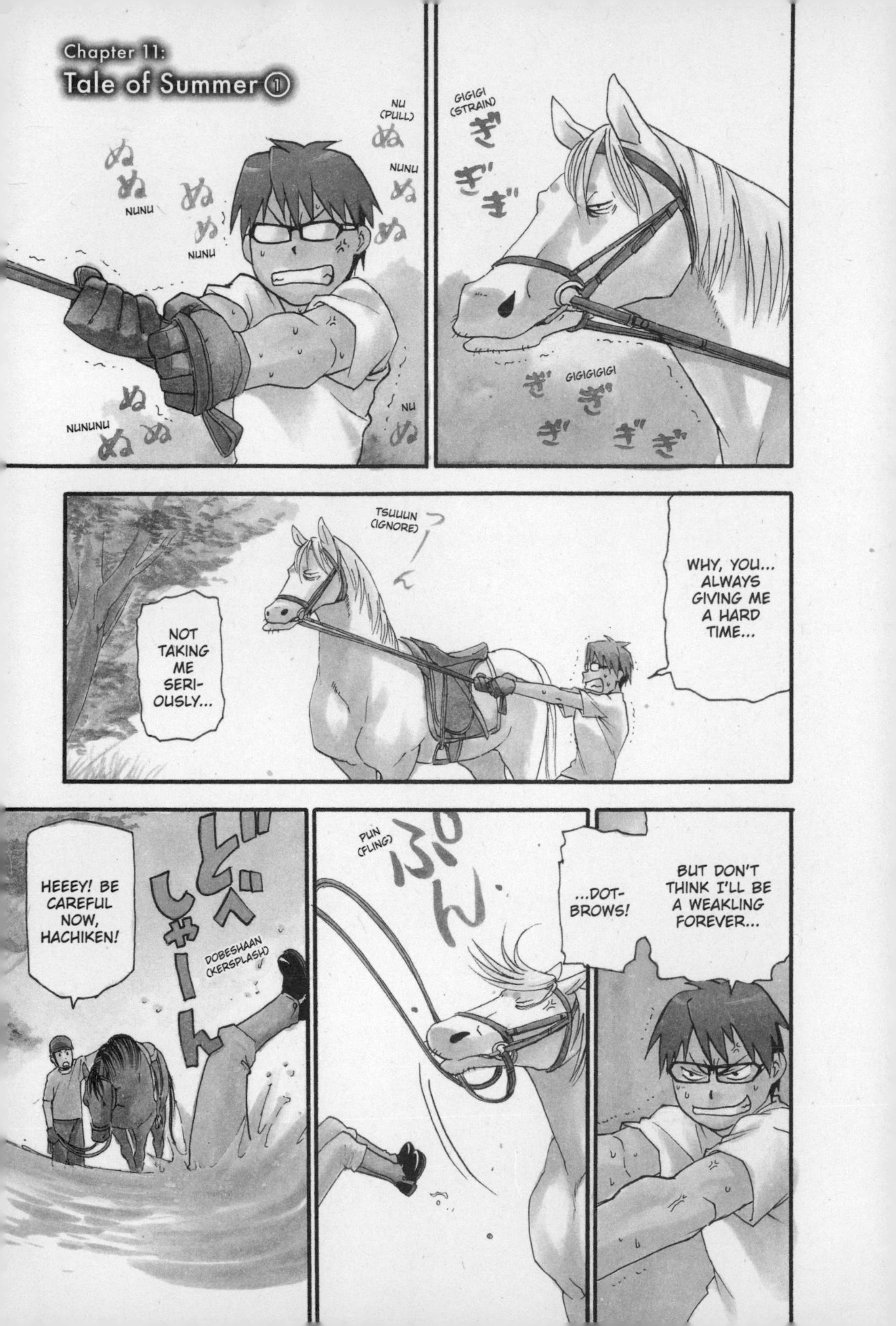
GIGIGI (STRAIN)
ぎぎぎ
GIGIGIGIGI
ぎぎぎぎぎ
NU (PULL)
ぬ
NUNU
ぬぬ
NUNU
ぬぬ
NUNU
ぬぬ
NU
ぬ
NUNUNU
ぬぬぬ
WHY, YOU... ALWAYS GIVING ME A HARD TIME...
TSUUUN (IGNORE)
NOT TAKING ME SERIOUSLY...
BUT DON'T THINK I'LL BE A WEAKLING FOREVER...
...DOT-BROWS!
PUN (FLING)
ぷん
DOBESHAAN (KERSPLASH)
どべしゃーん
HEEEY! BE CAREFUL NOW, HACHIKEN!

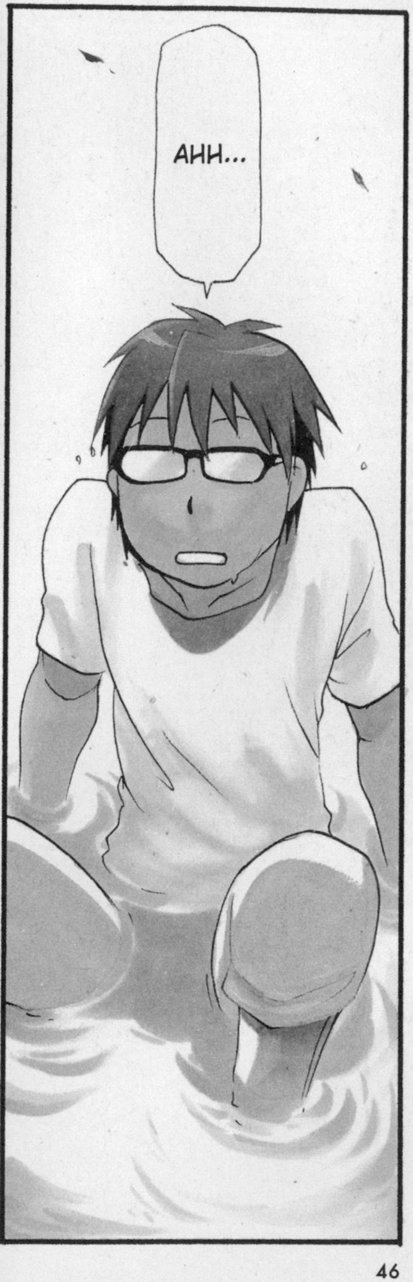
AHH...
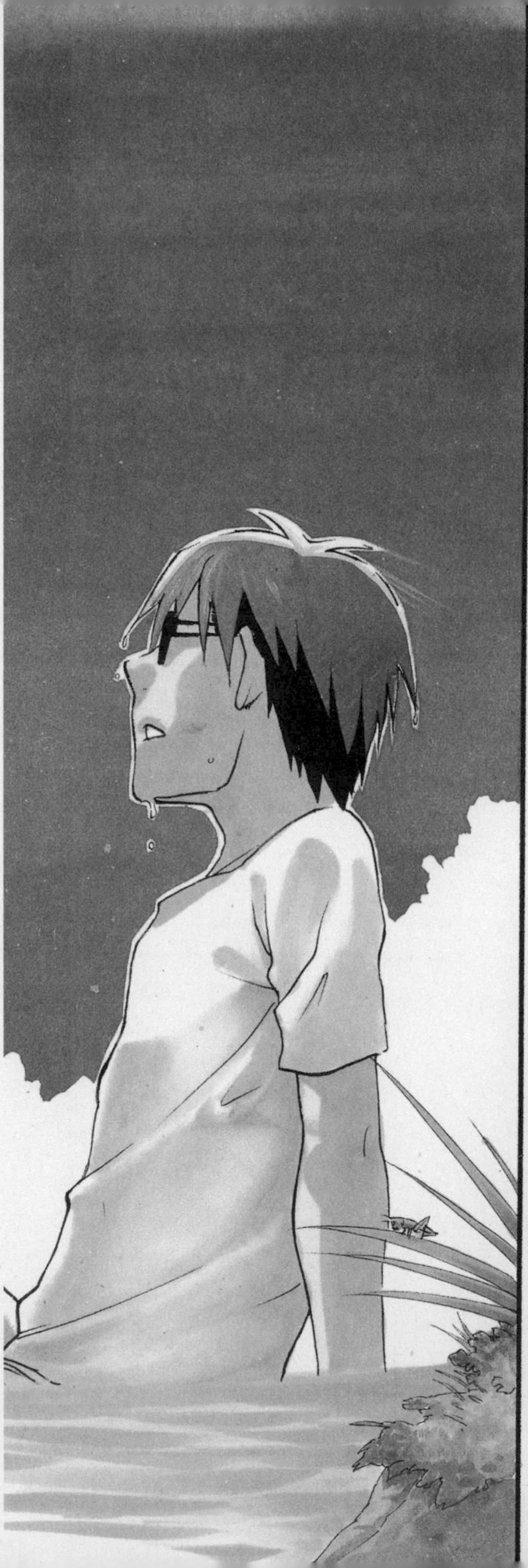

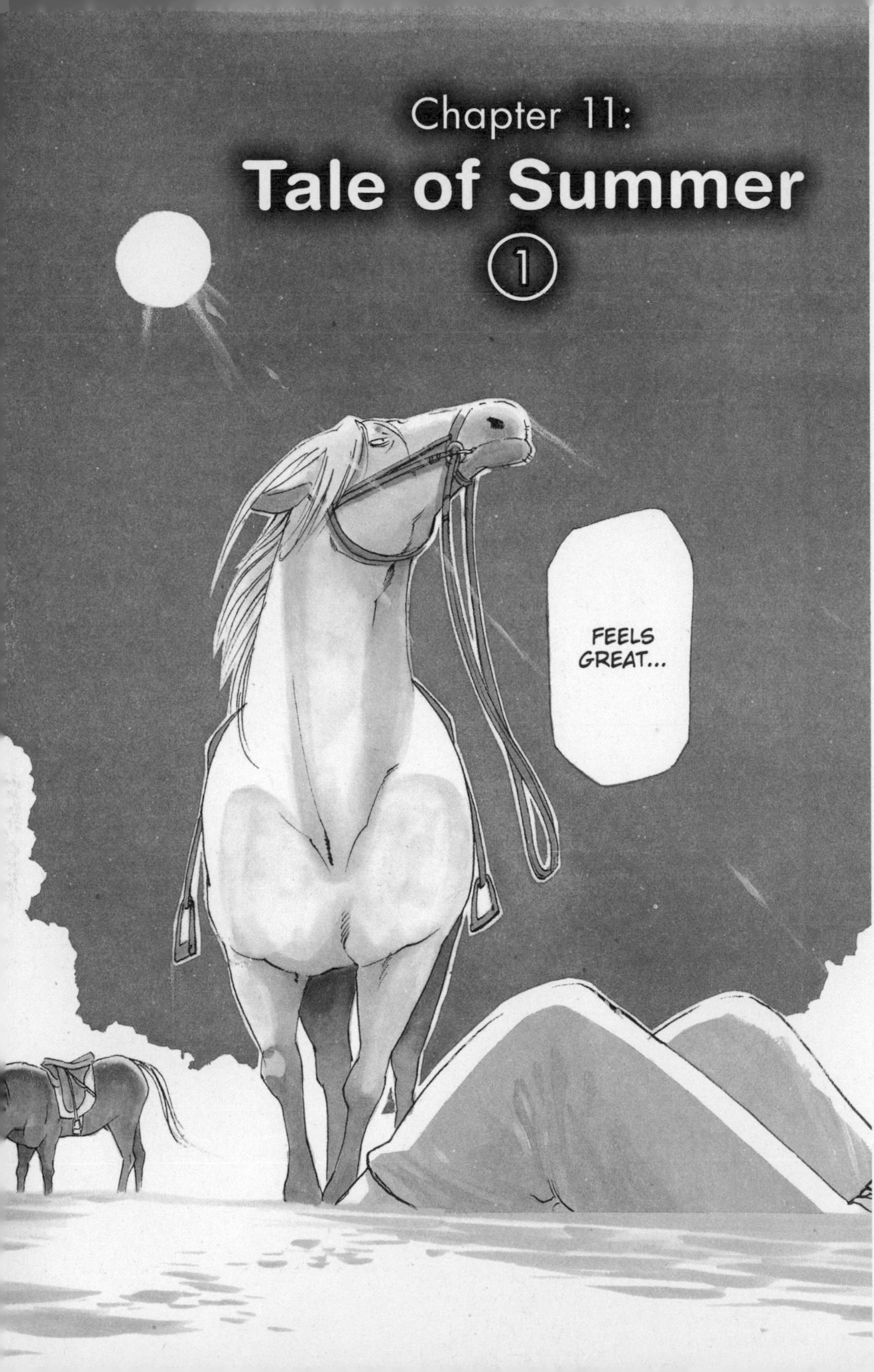
Chapter 11:
Tale of Summer
1
FEELS GREAT...

**SHIGERU
IZUMIKAWA**

BETSUKAI NAKAFUREN
MIDDLE SCHOOL

HE WAS PUT OFF
WHEN HE WENT TO CHECK
OUT THE HOLSTEIN CLUB,
SO HE SWITCHED TO
KARATE CLUB.

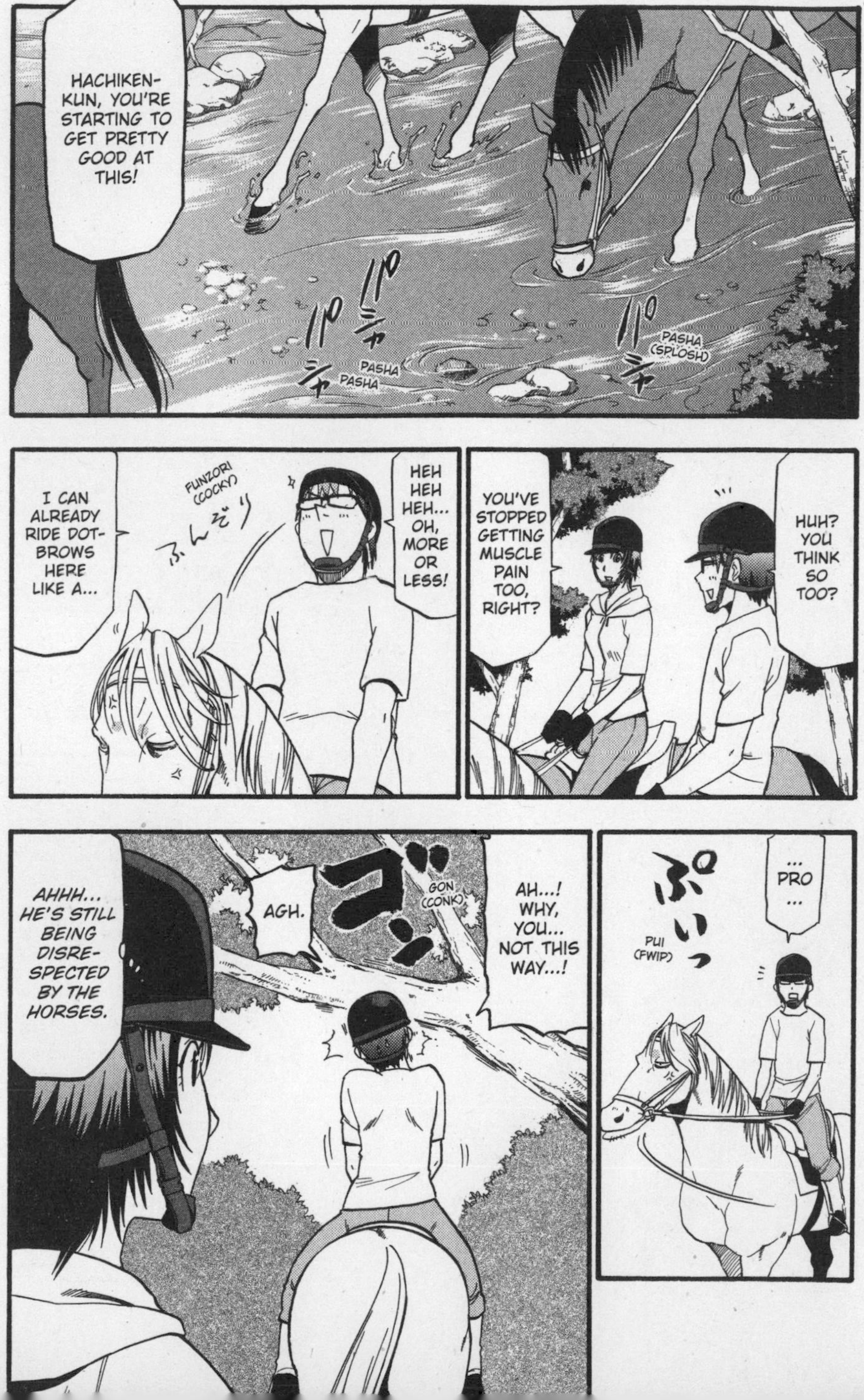
HACHIKEN-KUN, YOU'RE STARTING TO GET PRETTY GOOD AT THIS!
PASHA (SPLOSH)
PASHA PASHA
HUH? YOU THINK SO TOO?
YOU'VE STOPPED GETTING MUSCLE PAIN TOO, RIGHT?
HEH HEH HEH... OH, MORE OR LESS!
FUNZORI (COCKY)
I CAN ALREADY RIDE DOT-BROWS HERE LIKE A...
... PRO ...
PUI (FWIP)
AH...! WHY, YOU... NOT THIS WAY...!
GON (CONK)
AGH.
AHHH... HE'S STILL BEING DISRE-SPECTED BY THE HORSES.

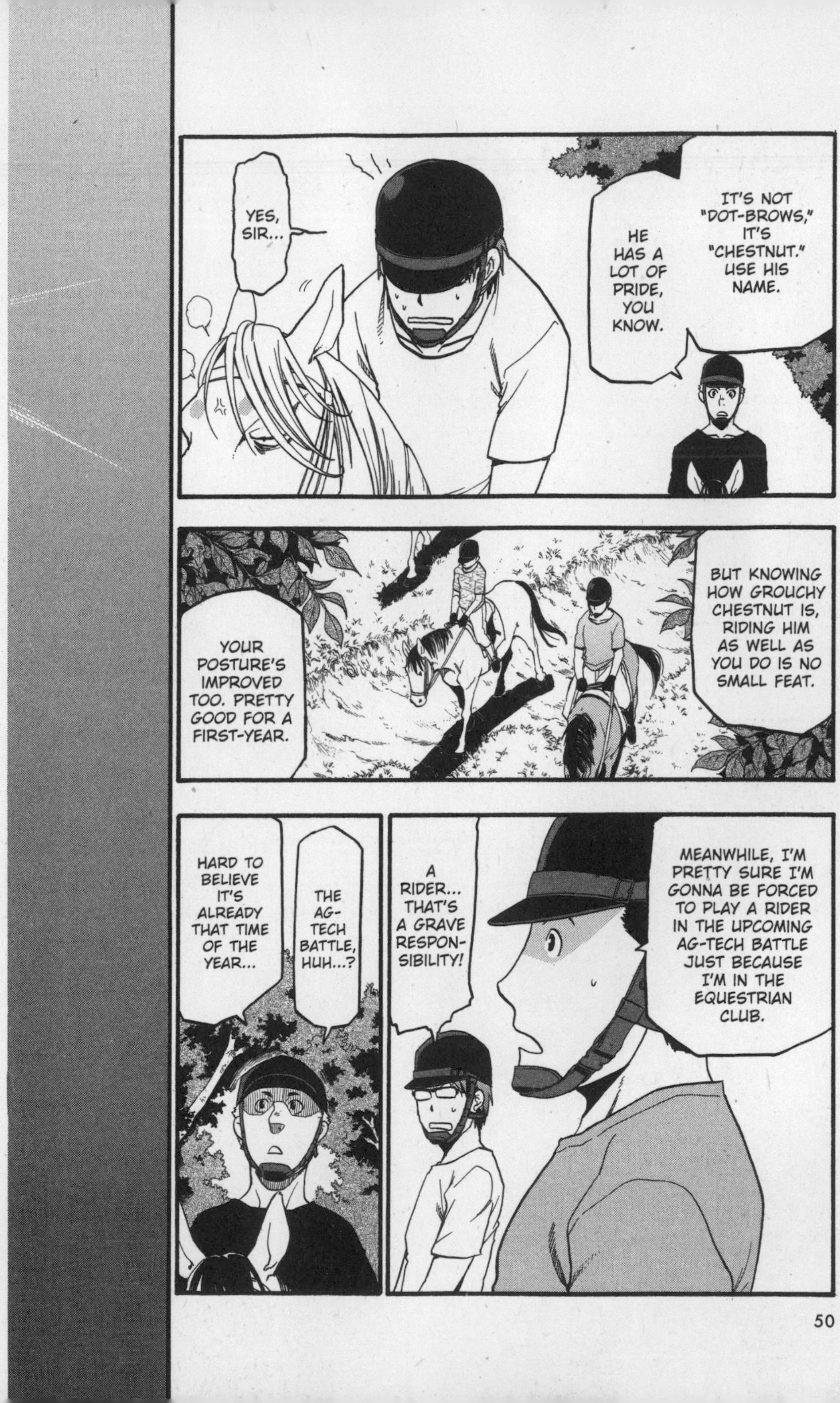
IT'S NOT "DOT-BROWS," IT'S "CHESTNUT." USE HIS NAME.
HE HAS A LOT OF PRIDE, YOU KNOW.
YES, SIR...
BUT KNOWING HOW GROUCHY CHESTNUT IS, RIDING HIM AS WELL AS YOU DO IS NO SMALL FEAT.
YOUR POSTURE'S IMPROVED TOO. PRETTY GOOD FOR A FIRST-YEAR.
MEANWHILE, I'M PRETTY SURE I'M GONNA BE FORCED TO PLAY A RIDER IN THE UPCOMING AG-TECH BATTLE JUST BECAUSE I'M IN THE EQUESTRIAN CLUB.
A RIDER... THAT'S A GRAVE RESPON-SIBILITY!
THE AG-TECH BATTLE, HUH...?
HARD TO BELIEVE IT'S ALREADY THAT TIME OF THE YEAR...

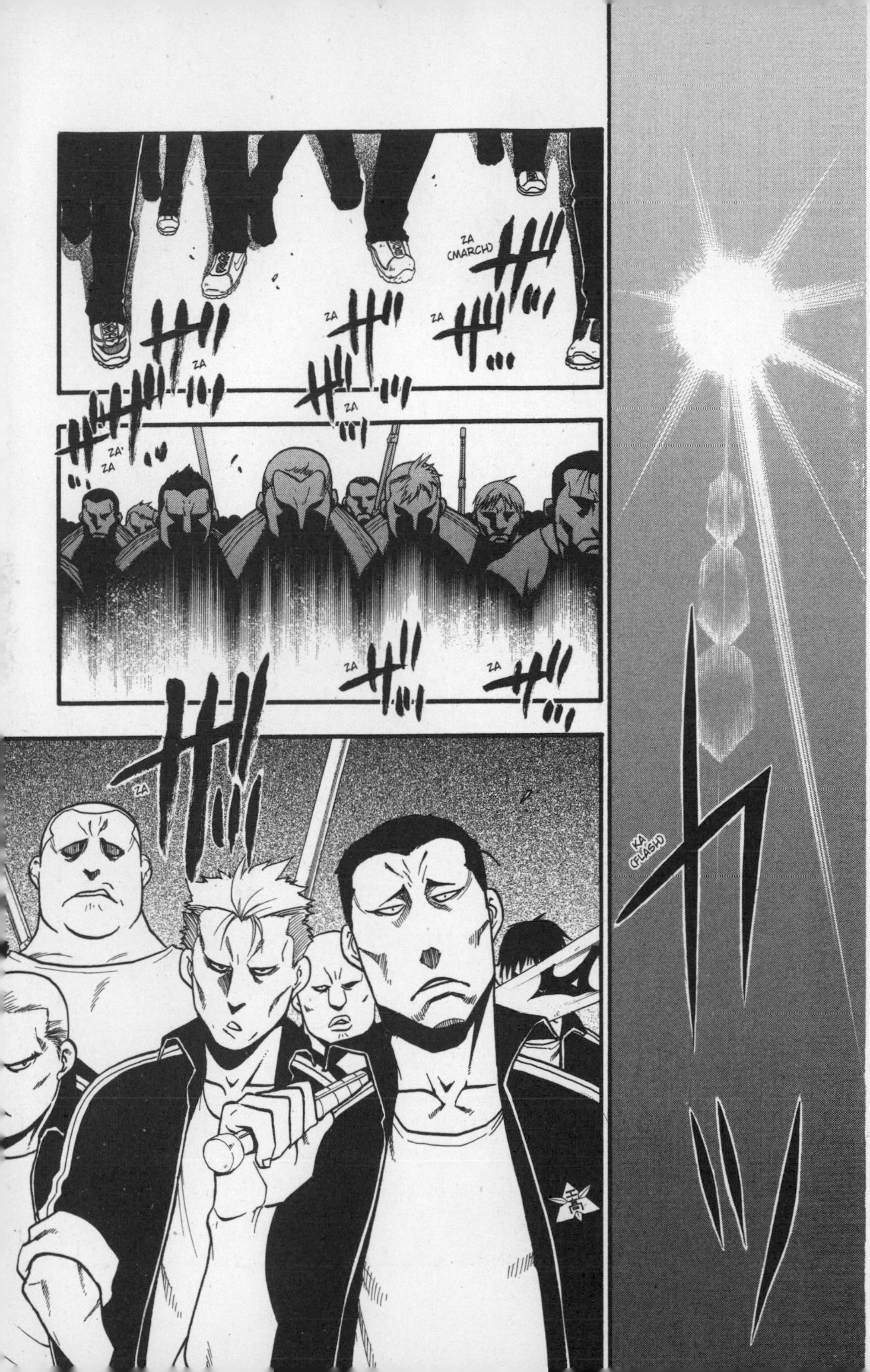
KA (FLASH)
ZA (MARCH)
ZA
ZA
ZA
ZA
ZA
ZA
ZA
ZA
ZA
ZA

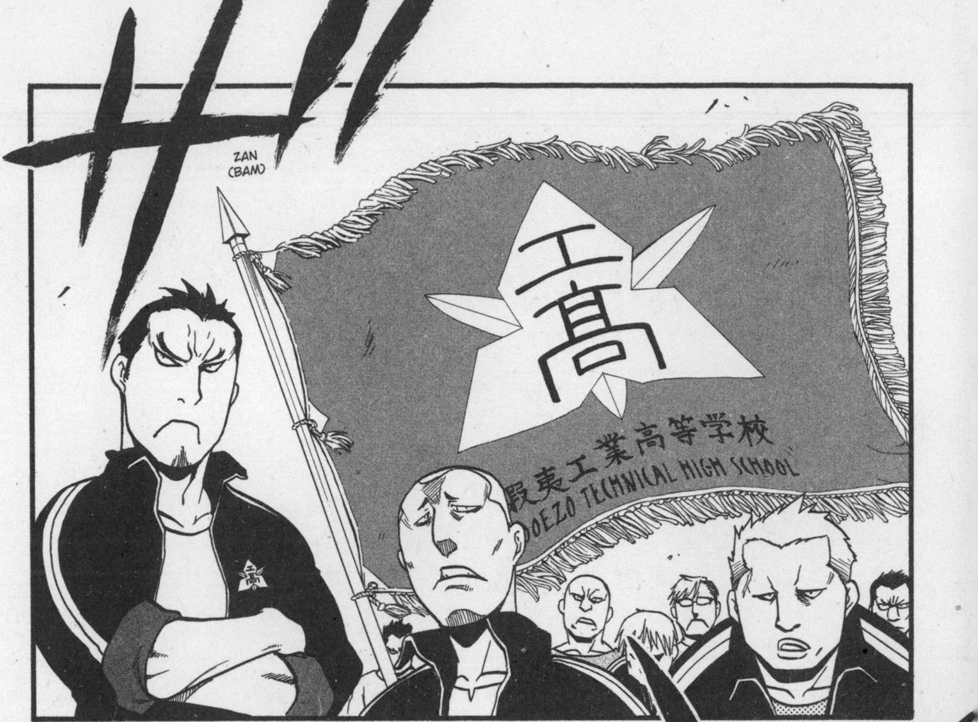
ZAN
(BAM)
工高
TECHNICAL HIGH SCHOOL

FLAGS: (TOP) EZO TECH, (BOTTOM) EZO AG

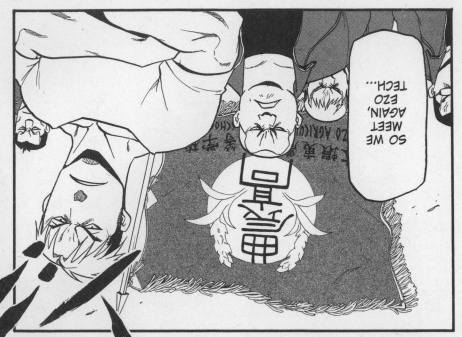

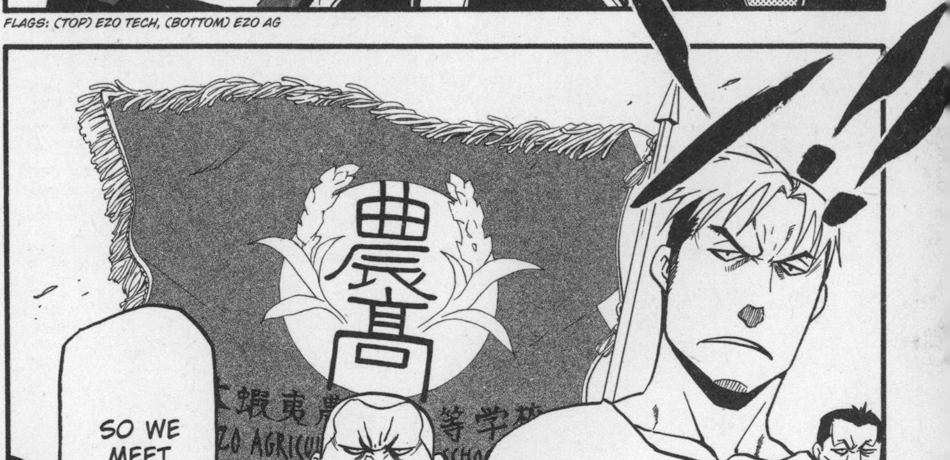
SO WE MEET AGAIN, EZO TECH...

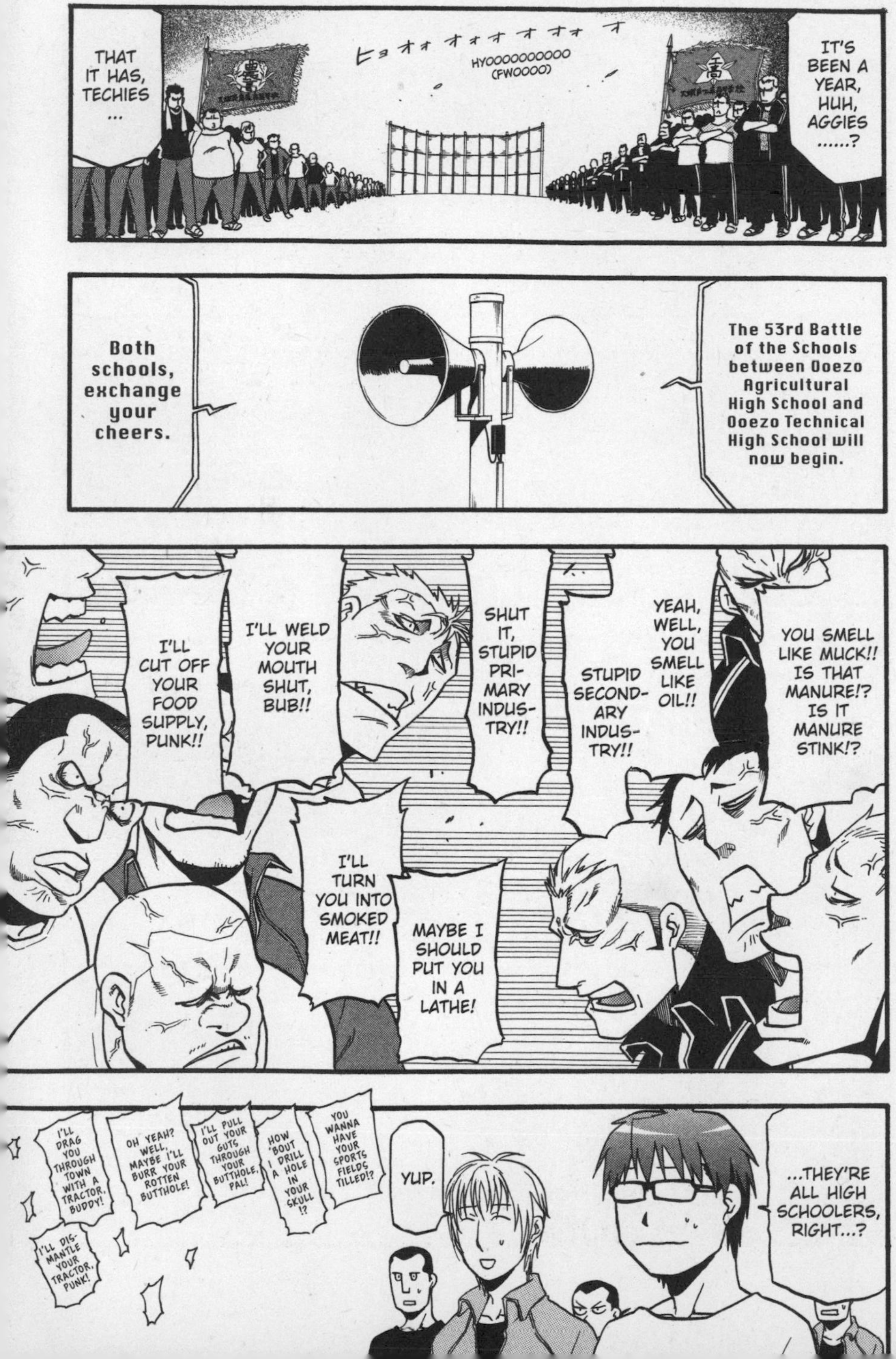
IT'S BEEN A YEAR, HUH, AGGIES ......?
ヒョオォオォオオオォオ
HYOOOOOOOOOO (FWOOOO)
THAT IT HAS, TECHIES ...
The 53rd Battle of the Schools between Ooezo Agricultural High School and Ooezo Technical High School will now begin.
Both schools, exchange your cheers.
YOU SMELL LIKE MUCK!! IS THAT MANURE!? IS IT MANURE STINK!?
YEAH, WELL, YOU SMELL LIKE OIL!!
STUPID SECOND-ARY INDUS-TRY!!
SHUT IT, STUPID PRI-MARY INDUS-TRY!!
I'LL WELD YOUR MOUTH SHUT, BUB!!
I'LL CUT OFF YOUR FOOD SUPPLY, PUNK!!
MAYBE I SHOULD PUT YOU IN A LATHE!
I'LL TURN YOU INTO SMOKED MEAT!!
...THEY'RE ALL HIGH SCHOOLERS, RIGHT...?
YUP.
YOU WANNA HAVE YOUR SPORTS FIELDS TILLED!?
HOW 'BOUT I DRILL A HOLE IN YOUR SKULL !?
I'LL PULL OUT YOUR GUTS THROUGH YOUR BUTTHOLE, PAL!
OH YEAH? WELL, MAYBE I'LL BURR YOUR ROTTEN BUTTHOLE!
I'LL DRAG YOU THROUGH TOWN WITH A TRACTOR, BUDDY!
I'LL DIS-MANTLE YOUR TRACTOR, PUNK!

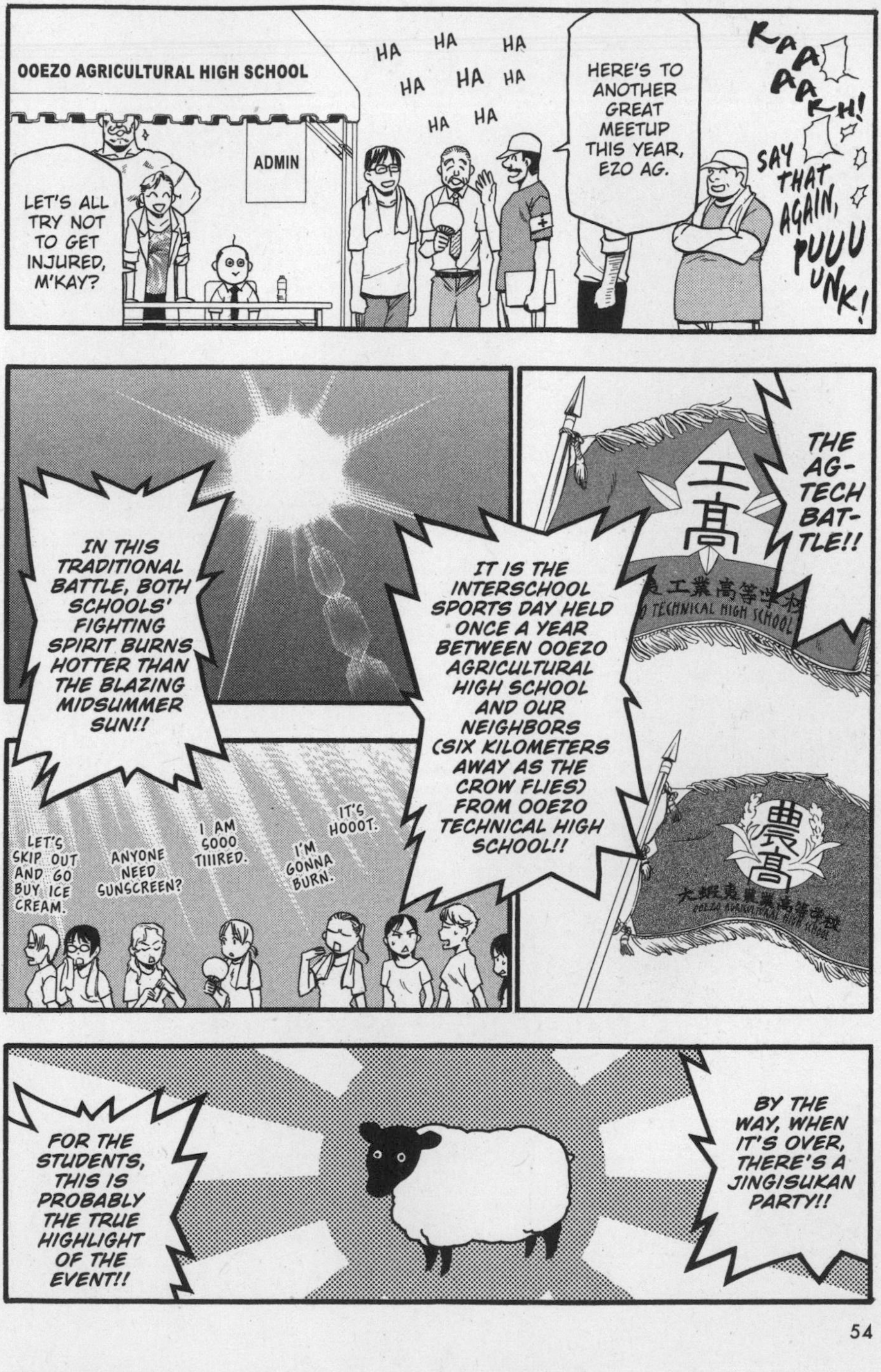
KAAAAKH!
SAY THAT AGAIN, PUUUUNK!
HERE'S TO ANOTHER GREAT MEETUP THIS YEAR, EZO AG.
HA HA HA HA HA HA HA HA
OOEZO AGRICULTURAL HIGH SCHOOL
ADMIN
LET'S ALL TRY NOT TO GET INJURED, M'KAY?
THE AG-TECH BAT-TLE!!
IN THIS TRADITIONAL BATTLE, BOTH SCHOOLS' FIGHTING SPIRIT BURNS HOTTER THAN THE BLAZING MIDSUMMER SUN!!
IT IS THE INTERSCHOOL SPORTS DAY HELD ONCE A YEAR BETWEEN OOEZO AGRICULTURAL HIGH SCHOOL AND OUR NEIGHBORS (SIX KILOMETERS AWAY AS THE CROW FLIES) FROM OOEZO TECHNICAL HIGH SCHOOL!!
IT'S HOOOT.
I'M GONNA BURN.
I AM SOOO TIIIRED.
ANYONE NEED SUNSCREEN?
LET'S SKIP OUT AND GO BUY ICE CREAM.
BY THE WAY, WHEN IT'S OVER, THERE'S A JINGISUKAN PARTY!!
FOR THE STUDENTS, THIS IS PROBABLY THE TRUE HIGHLIGHT OF THE EVENT!!

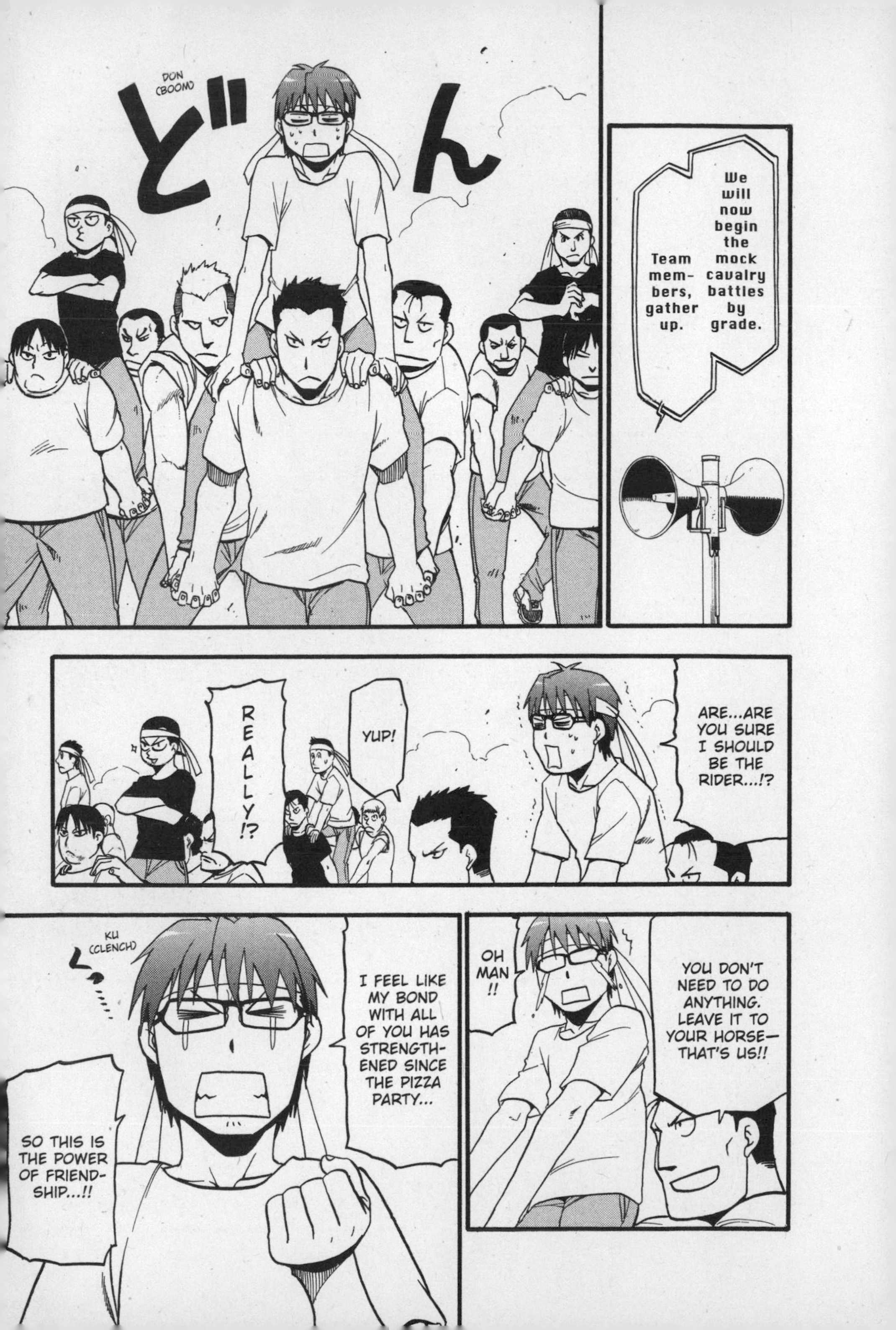
We will now begin the mock cavalry battles by grade. Team members, gather up.
DON (BOOM)
どん
ARE...ARE YOU SURE I SHOULD BE THE RIDER...!?
YUP!
REALLY!?
YOU DON'T NEED TO DO ANYTHING. LEAVE IT TO YOUR HORSE—THAT'S US!!
OH MAN!!
I FEEL LIKE MY BOND WITH ALL OF YOU HAS STRENGTH-ENED SINCE THE PIZZA PARTY...
KU (CLENCH)
SO THIS IS THE POWER OF FRIEND-SHIP...!!

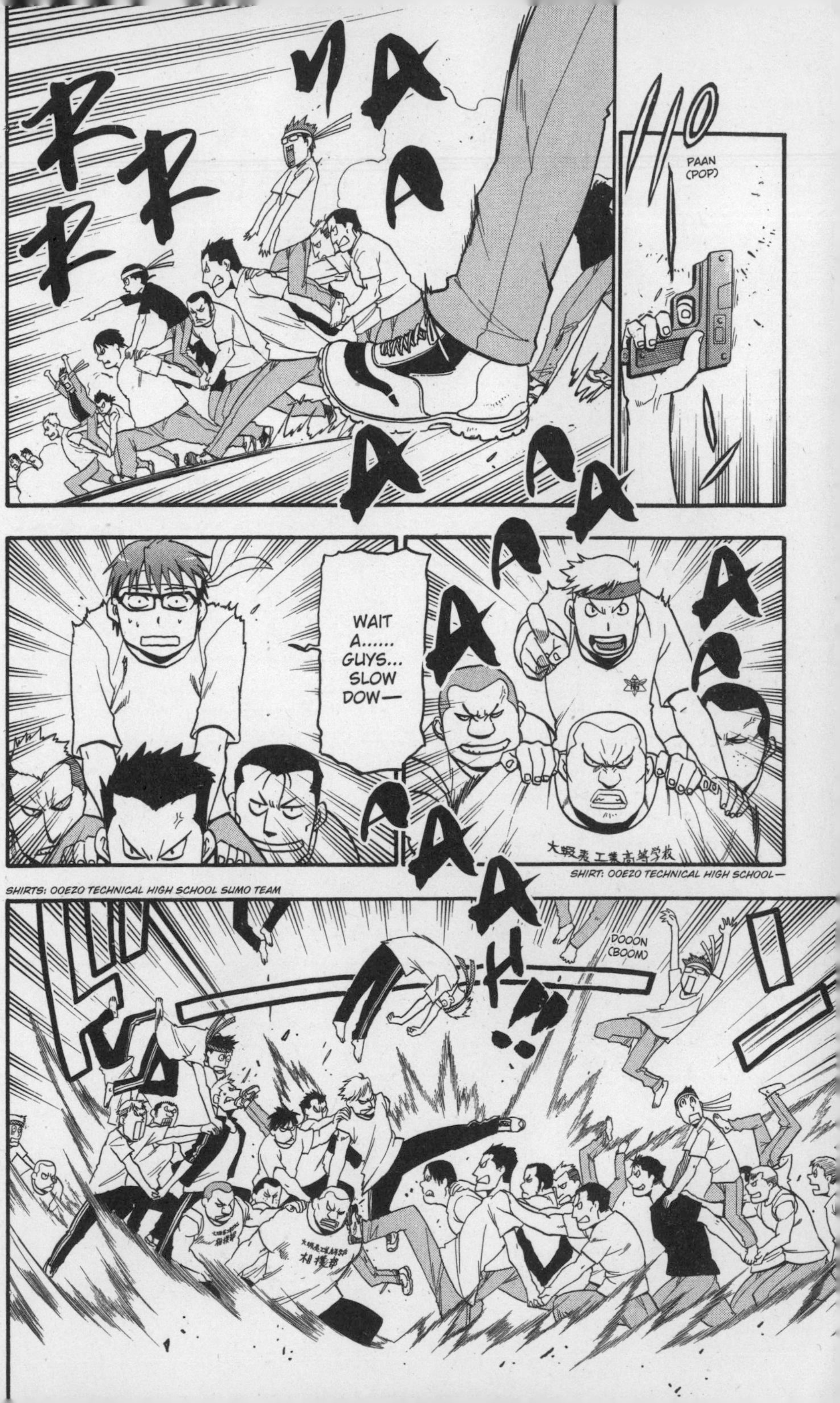
PAAN (POP)
ワワワワ
AAAA
WAIT A...... GUYS... SLOW DOW—
AAAAAAAA
大蝦夷工業高等学校
SHIRT: OOEZO TECHNICAL HIGH SCHOOL—
SHIRTS: OOEZO TECHNICAL HIGH SCHOOL SUMO TEAM
AH!!
DOOON (BOOM)

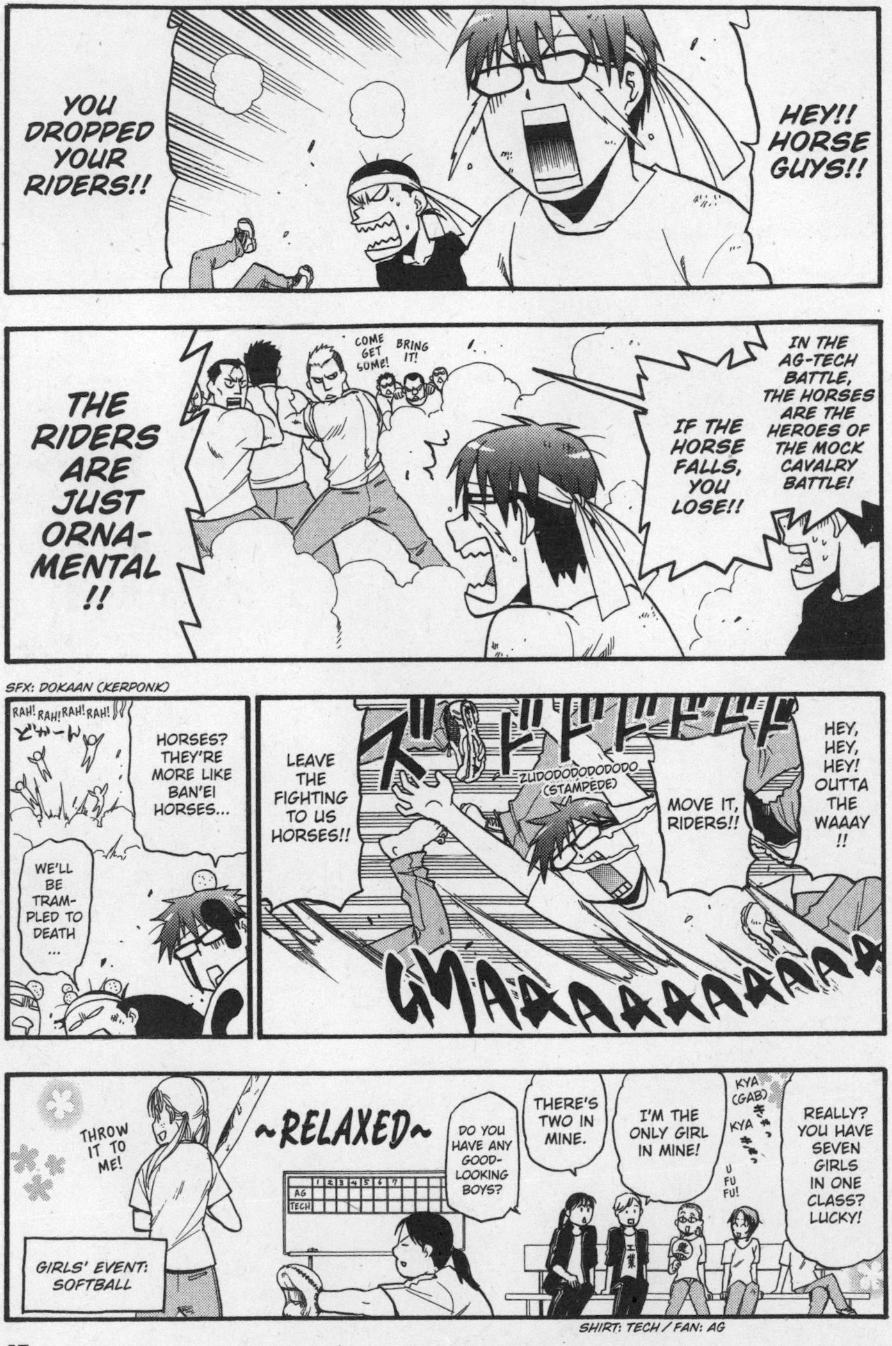
HEY!! HORSE GUYS!!
YOU DROPPED YOUR RIDERS!!
IN THE AG-TECH BATTLE, THE HORSES ARE THE HEROES OF THE MOCK CAVALRY BATTLE!
IF THE HORSE FALLS, YOU LOSE!!
COME GET SOME!
BRING IT!
THE RIDERS ARE JUST ORNA-MENTAL !!
HEY, HEY, HEY! OUTTA THE WAAAY !!
MOVE IT, RIDERS!!
ZUDODODODODODO (STAMPEDE)
LEAVE THE FIGHTING TO US HORSES!!
GWAAAAAAAAAAA
HORSES? THEY'RE MORE LIKE BAN'EI HORSES...
RAH! RAH! RAH! RAH!
WE'LL BE TRAM-PLED TO DEATH ...
REALLY? YOU HAVE SEVEN GIRLS IN ONE CLASS? LUCKY!
KYA (GAB) KYA
U FU FU!
I'M THE ONLY GIRL IN MINE!
THERE'S TWO IN MINE.
DO YOU HAVE ANY GOOD-LOOKING BOYS?
~RELAXED~
AG
TECH
THROW IT TO ME!
GIRLS' EVENT: SOFTBALL

SFX: DOKAAN (KERPONK)

SHIRT: TECH / FAN: AG

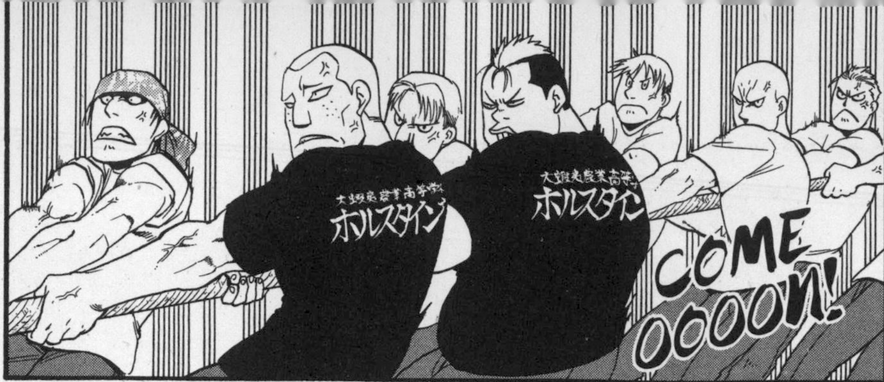
COME OOOOON!

SHIRTS: OOEZO AGRICULTURAL HIGH SCHOOL HOLSTEIN CLUB

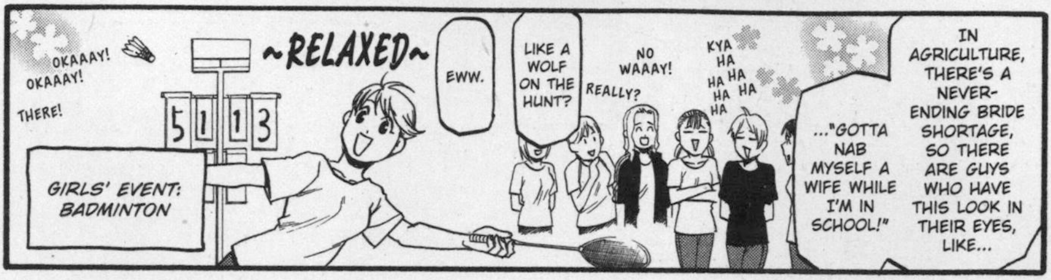
IN AGRICULTURE, THERE'S A NEVER-ENDING BRIDE SHORTAGE, SO THERE ARE GUYS WHO HAVE THIS LOOK IN THEIR EYES, LIKE...
..."GOTTA NAB MYSELF A WIFE WHILE I'M IN SCHOOL!"
KYA HA HA HA HA HA HA
NO WAAAY!
REALLY?
LIKE A WOLF ON THE HUNT?
EWW.
~RELAXED~
OKAAAY!
OKAAAY!
THERE!
GIRLS' EVENT: BADMINTON

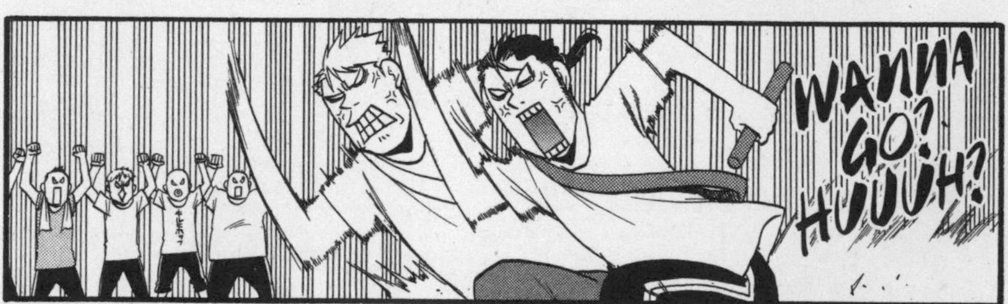
WANNA GO? HUUUH?

SHIRT: KIRCHHOFF

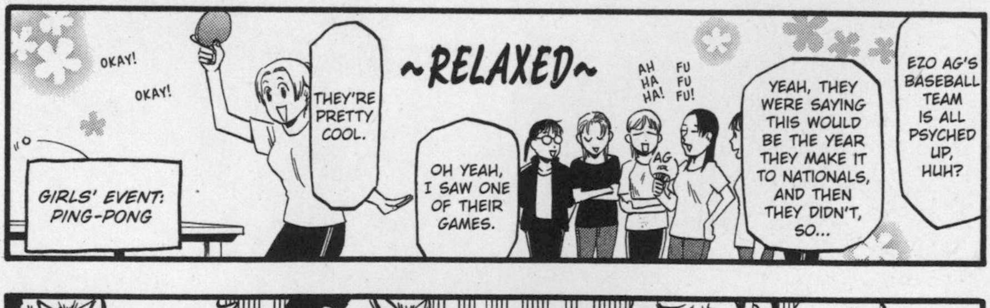
EZO AG'S BASEBALL TEAM IS ALL PSYCHED UP, HUH?
YEAH, THEY WERE SAYING THIS WOULD BE THE YEAR THEY MAKE IT TO NATIONALS, AND THEN THEY DIDN'T, SO...
FU FU FU!
AH HA HA!
AG
OH YEAH, I SAW ONE OF THEIR GAMES.
~RELAXED~
THEY'RE PRETTY COOL.
OKAY!
OKAY!
GIRLS' EVENT: PING-PONG

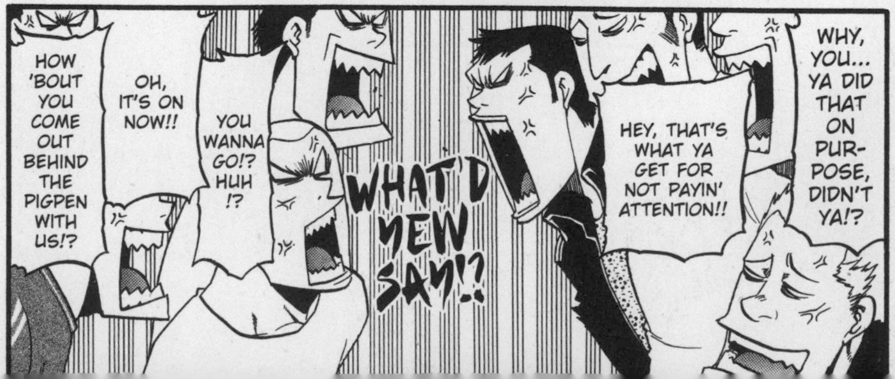
WHY, YOU... YA DID THAT ON PURPOSE, DIDN'T YA!?
HEY, THAT'S WHAT YA GET FOR NOT PAYIN' ATTENTION!!
WHAT'D NEW SAY!?
YOU WANNA GO!? HUH!?
OH, IT'S ON NOW!!
HOW 'BOUT YOU COME OUT BEHIND THE PIGPEN WITH US!?

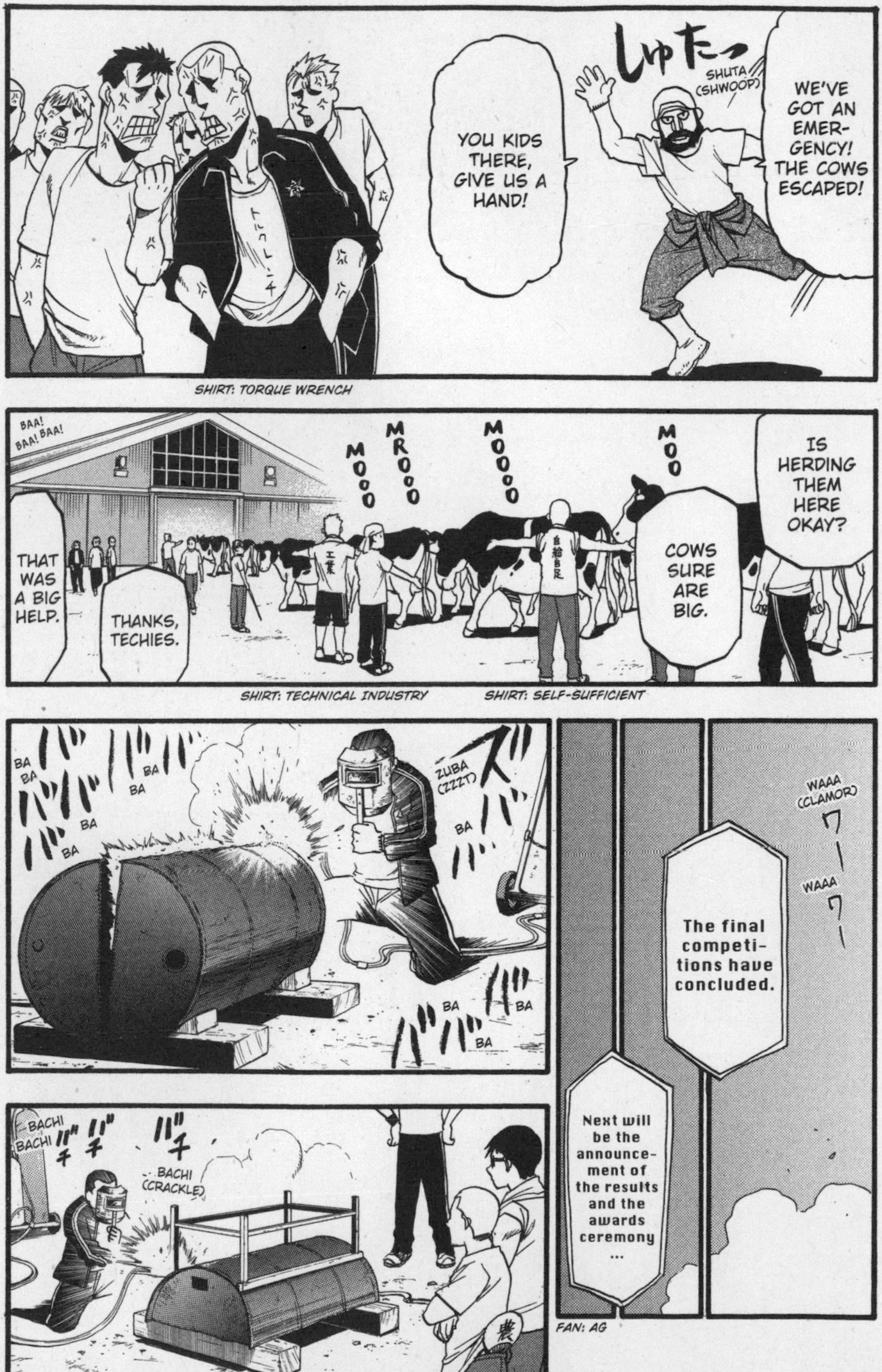
WE'VE GOT AN EMERGENCY! THE COWS ESCAPED!
SHUTA (SHWOOP)
YOU KIDS THERE, GIVE US A HAND!
SHIRT: TORQUE WRENCH
IS HERDING THEM HERE OKAY?
MOO
COWS SURE ARE BIG.
MOOOO
MROOO
MOOO
BAA! BAA! BAA!
THANKS, TECHIES.
THAT WAS A BIG HELP.
SHIRT: TECHNICAL INDUSTRY
SHIRT: SELF-SUFFICIENT
WAAA (CLAMOR)
WAAA
The final competitions have concluded.
Next will be the announcement of the results and the awards ceremony ...
FAN: AG
ZUBA (ZZZT)
BA
BA BA
BA BA
BA BA
BA BA BA
BACHI (CRACKLE)
BACHI BACHI

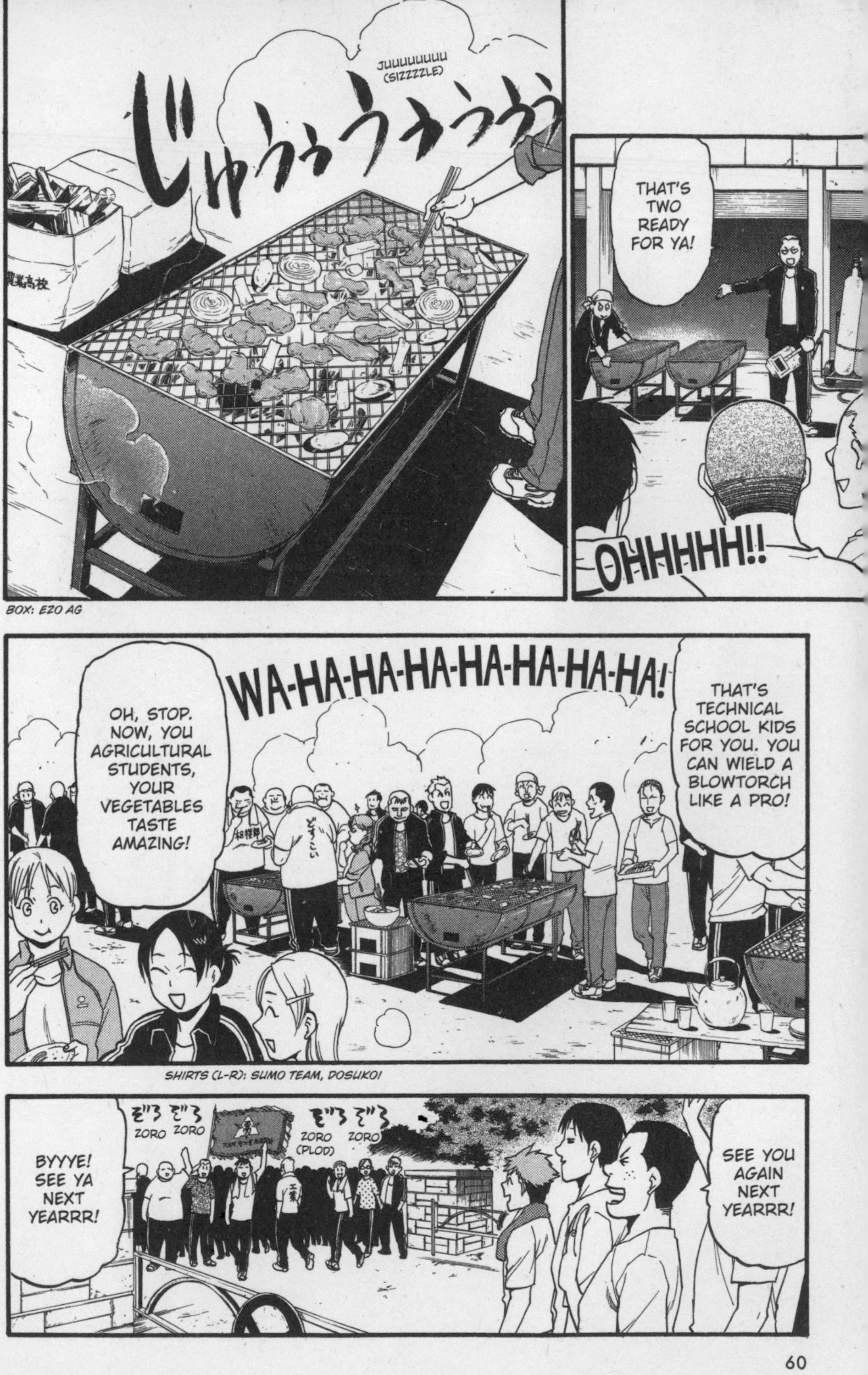
THAT'S TWO READY FOR YA!
OHHHHH!!
じゅううううぅぅう
JUUUUUUUUU (SIZZZZLE)
THAT'S TECHNICAL SCHOOL KIDS FOR YOU. YOU CAN WIELD A BLOWTORCH LIKE A PRO!
WA-HA-HA-HA-HA-HA-HA-HA!
OH, STOP. NOW, YOU AGRICULTURAL STUDENTS, YOUR VEGETABLES TASTE AMAZING!
SEE YOU AGAIN NEXT YEARRR!
ぞろ ぞろ
ZORO (PLOD) ZORO
ぞろ ぞろ
ZORO ZORO
BYYYE! SEE YA NEXT YEARRR!

BOX: EZO AG

SHIRTS (L-R): SUMO TEAM, DOSUKOI

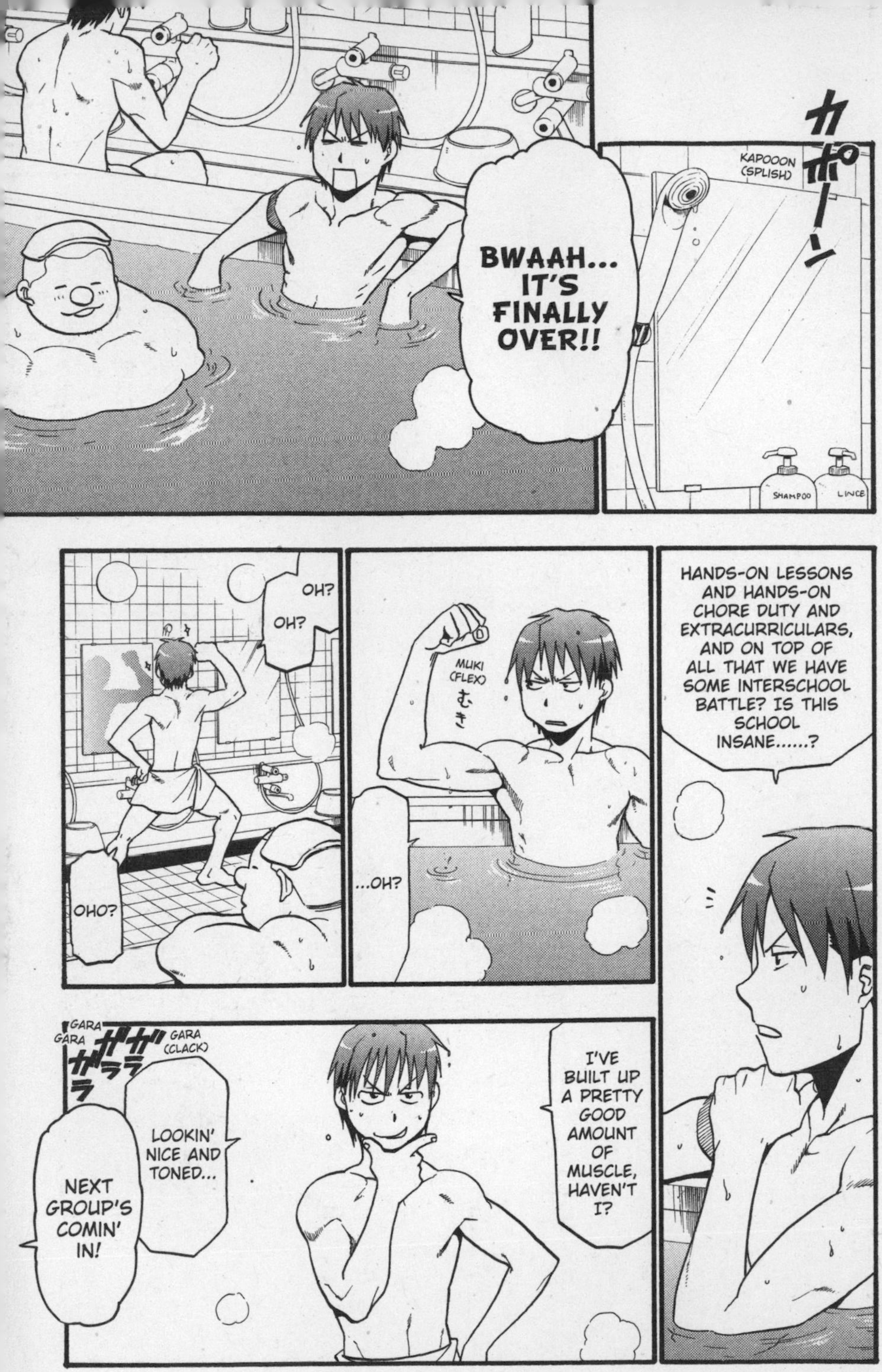
カポーン
KAPOOON (SPLISH)
SHAMPOO
LINCE
BWAAH... IT'S FINALLY OVER!!
HANDS-ON LESSONS AND HANDS-ON CHORE DUTY AND EXTRACURRICULARS, AND ON TOP OF ALL THAT WE HAVE SOME INTERSCHOOL BATTLE? IS THIS SCHOOL INSANE......?
MUKI (FLEX) むき
...OH?
OH?
OH?
OHO?
I'VE BUILT UP A PRETTY GOOD AMOUNT OF MUSCLE, HAVEN'T I?
LOOKIN' NICE AND TONED...
GARA GARA GARA (CLACK) ガラガラ
NEXT GROUP'S COMIN' IN!

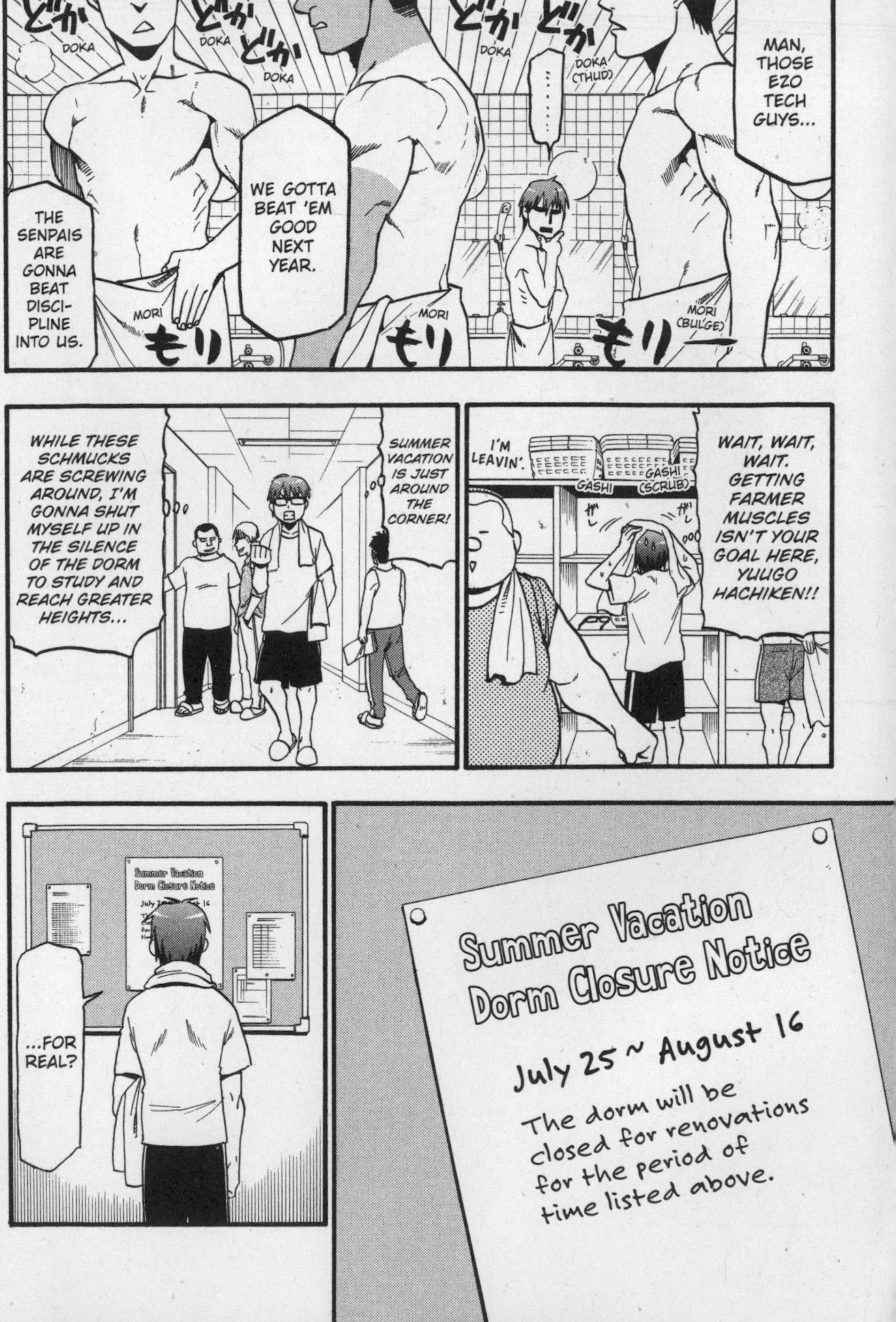

MAN, THOSE EZO TECH GUYS...
どかどか
DOKA DOKA (THUD)
......
もりー
MORI (BULGE)
もり
MORI
WE GOTTA BEAT 'EM GOOD NEXT YEAR.
どかどか
DOKA DOKA
どか
DOKA
THE SENPAIS ARE GONNA BEAT DISCI-PLINE INTO US.
もり
MORI
WAIT, WAIT, WAIT. GETTING FARMER MUSCLES ISN'T YOUR GOAL HERE, YUUGO HACHIKEN!!
GASHI GASHI (SCRUB)
I'M LEAVIN'.
SUMMER VACATION IS JUST AROUND THE CORNER!
WHILE THESE SCHMUCKS ARE SCREWING AROUND, I'M GONNA SHUT MYSELF UP IN THE SILENCE OF THE DORM TO STUDY AND REACH GREATER HEIGHTS...
Summer Vacation Dorm Closure Notice
July 25 ~ August 16
The dorm will be closed for renovations for the period of time listed above.
...FOR REAL?

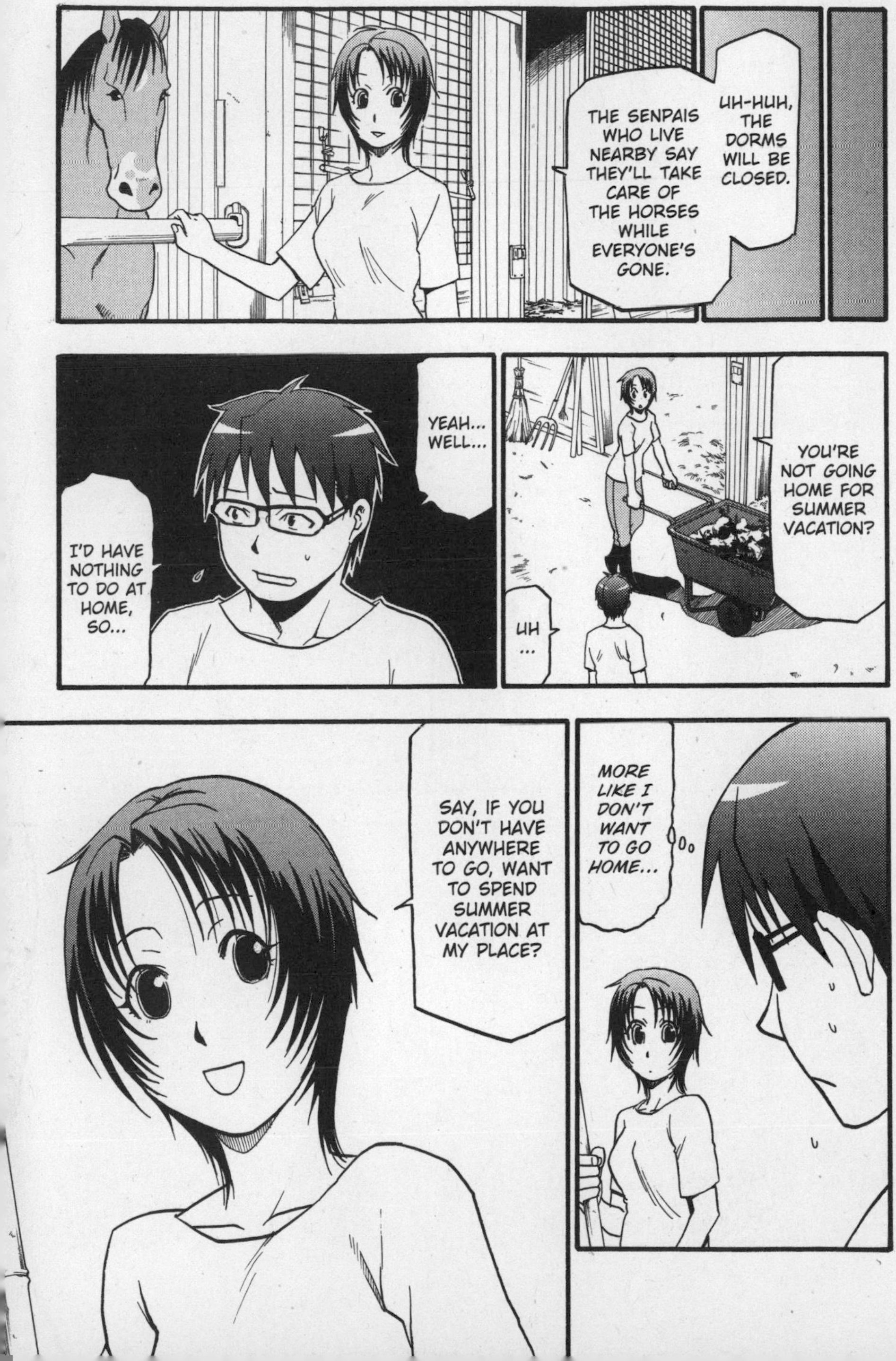
UH-HUH, THE DORMS WILL BE CLOSED.
THE SENPAIS WHO LIVE NEARBY SAY THEY'LL TAKE CARE OF THE HORSES WHILE EVERYONE'S GONE.
YOU'RE NOT GOING HOME FOR SUMMER VACATION?
UH ...
YEAH... WELL...
I'D HAVE NOTHING TO DO AT HOME, SO...
MORE LIKE I DON'T WANT TO GO HOME...
SAY, IF YOU DON'T HAVE ANYWHERE TO GO, WANT TO SPEND SUMMER VACATION AT MY PLACE?

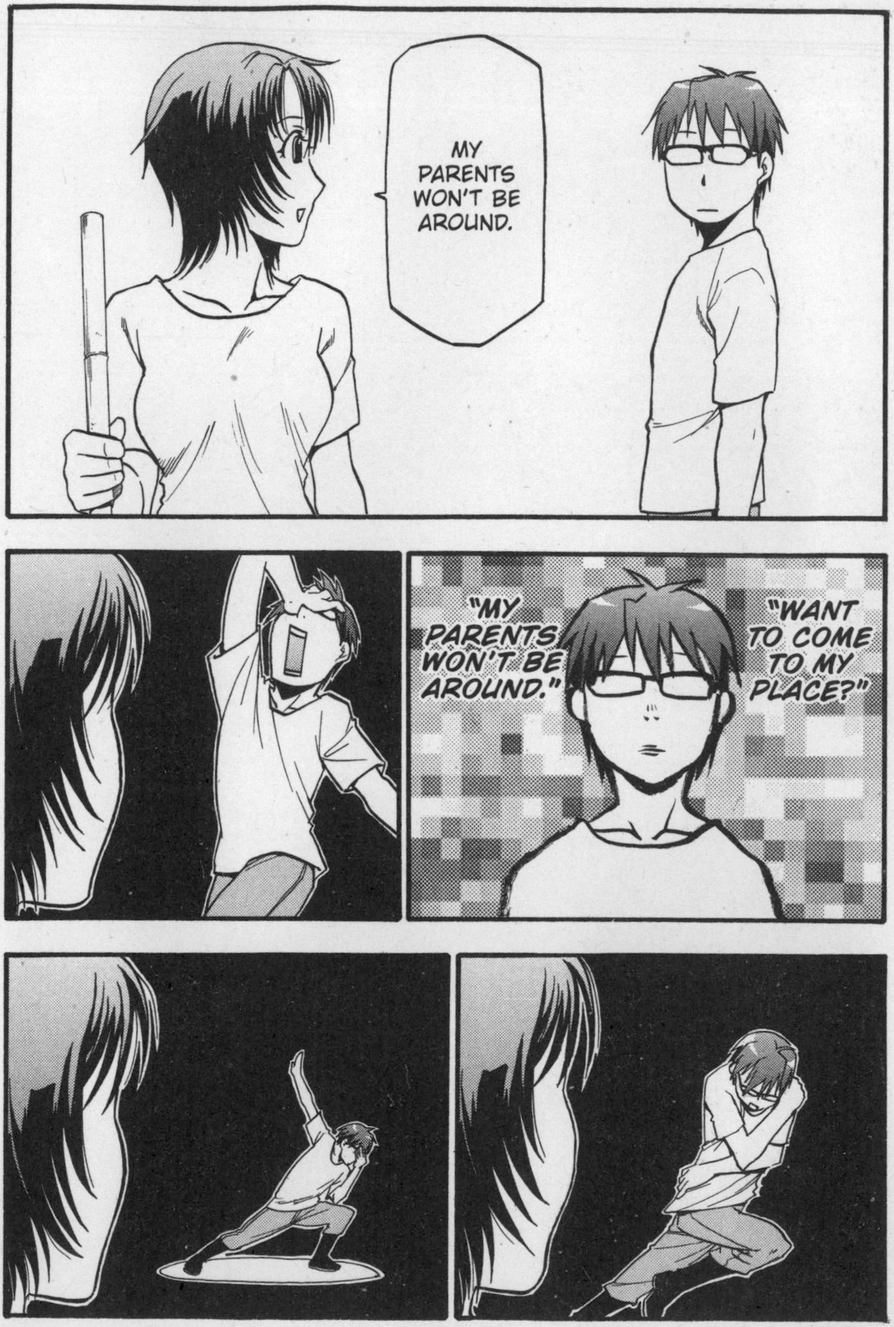
MY PARENTS WON'T BE AROUND.
"WANT TO COME TO MY PLACE?"
"MY PARENTS WON'T BE AROUND."

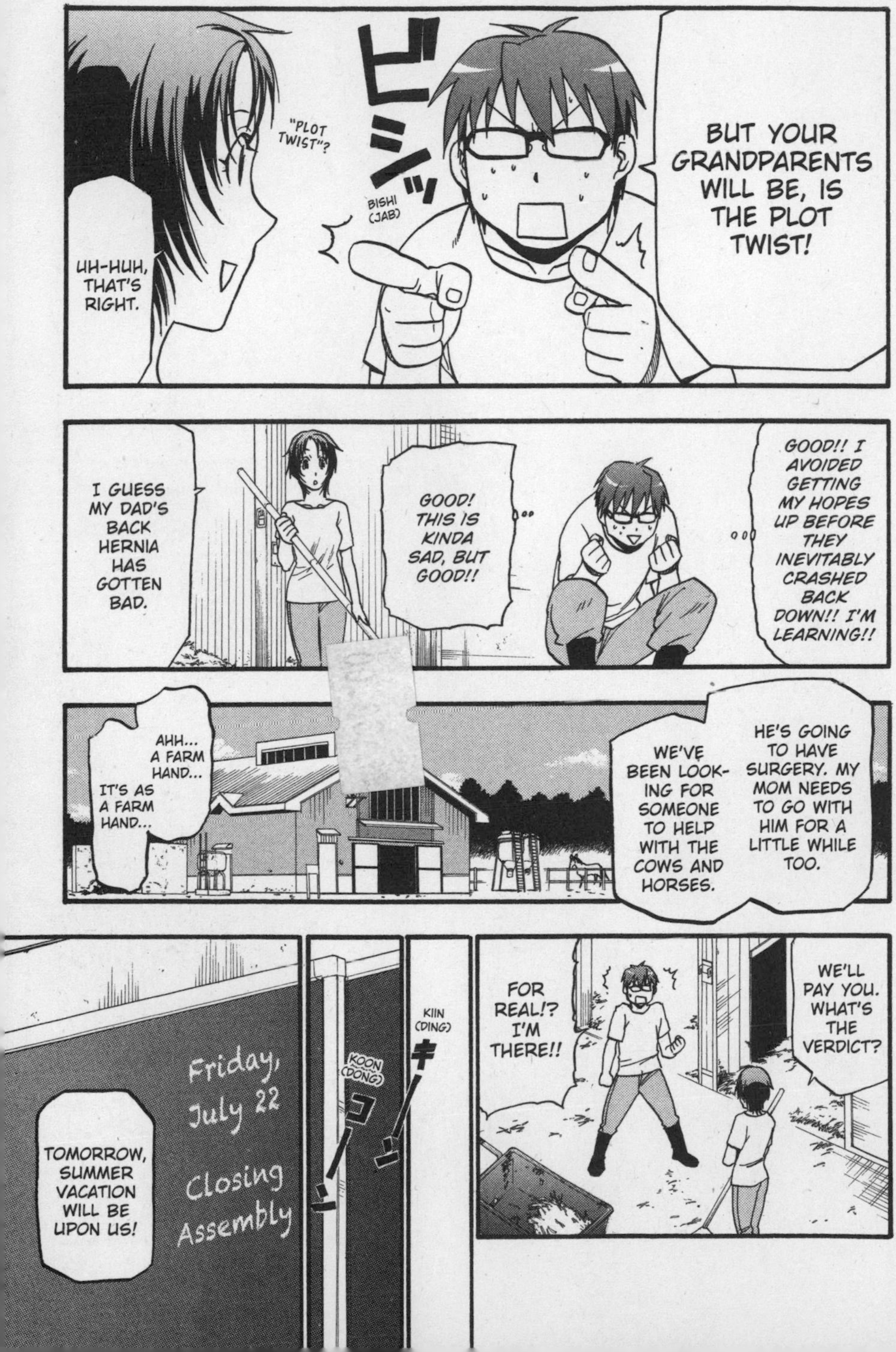
BUT YOUR GRANDPARENTS WILL BE, IS THE PLOT TWIST!
ビシッ
BISHI (JAB)
"PLOT TWIST"?
UH-HUH, THAT'S RIGHT.
GOOD!! I AVOIDED GETTING MY HOPES UP BEFORE THEY INEVITABLY CRASHED BACK DOWN!! I'M LEARNING!!
GOOD! THIS IS KINDA SAD, BUT GOOD!!
I GUESS MY DAD'S BACK HERNIA HAS GOTTEN BAD.
HE'S GOING TO HAVE SURGERY. MY MOM NEEDS TO GO WITH HIM FOR A LITTLE WHILE TOO.
WE'VE BEEN LOOK-ING FOR SOMEONE TO HELP WITH THE COWS AND HORSES.
AHH... A FARM HAND...
IT'S AS A FARM HAND...
WE'LL PAY YOU. WHAT'S THE VERDICT?
FOR REAL!? I'M THERE!!
KIIN (DING)
KOON (DONG)
Friday, July 22
Closing Assembly
TOMORROW, SUMMER VACATION WILL BE UPON US!

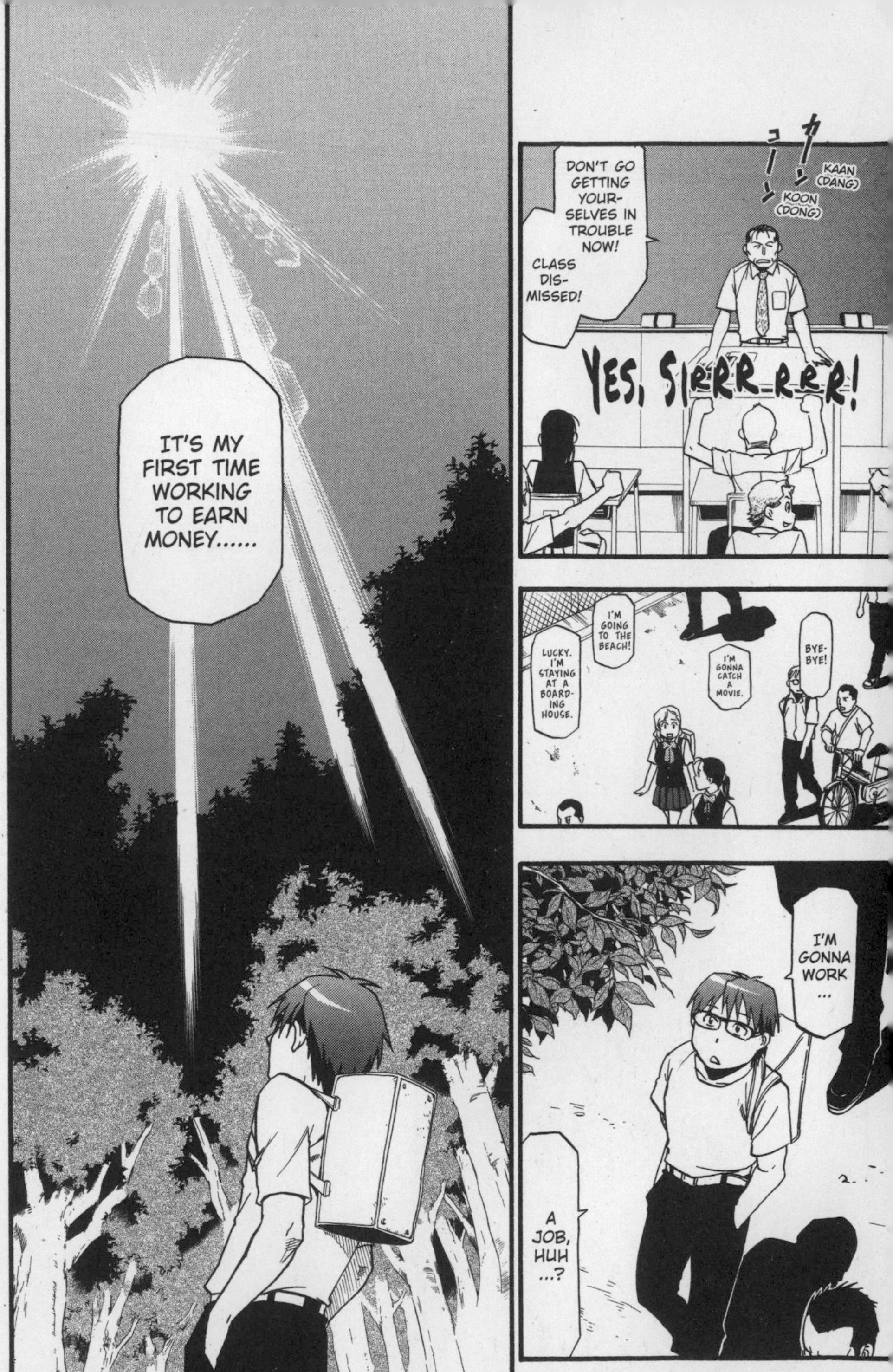

KAAN (DANG)
KOON (DONG)
DON'T GO GETTING YOUR-SELVES IN TROUBLE NOW!
CLASS DIS-MISSED!
YES, SIRRR RRR!
BYE-BYE!
I'M GONNA CATCH A MOVIE.
I'M GOING TO THE BEACH!
LUCKY. I'M STAYING AT A BOARD-ING HOUSE.
I'M GONNA WORK ...
A JOB, HUH ...?
IT'S MY FIRST TIME WORKING TO EARN MONEY......

Silver Spoon

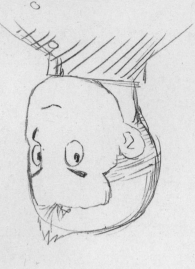

JUN ODA

TAIKI BANSEI
MIDDLE SCHOOL
PING-PONG TEAM

Chapter 12:
Tale of Summer ②

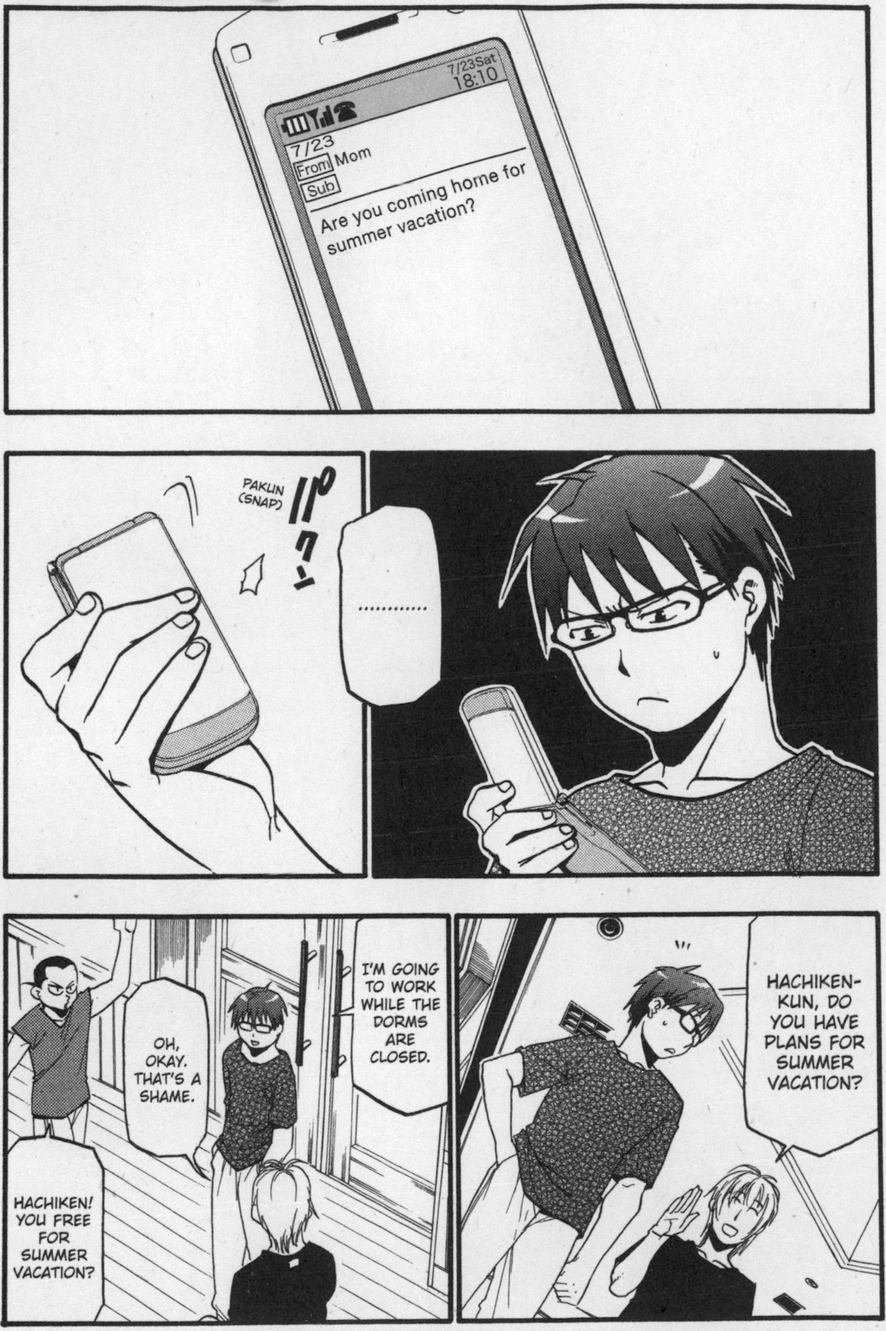
7/23Sat
18:10
7/23
From Mom
Sub
Are you coming home for summer vacation?
......
PAKUN (SNAP)
HACHIKEN-KUN, DO YOU HAVE PLANS FOR SUMMER VACATION?
I'M GOING TO WORK WHILE THE DORMS ARE CLOSED.
OH, OKAY. THAT'S A SHAME.
HACHIKEN! YOU FREE FOR SUMMER VACATION?

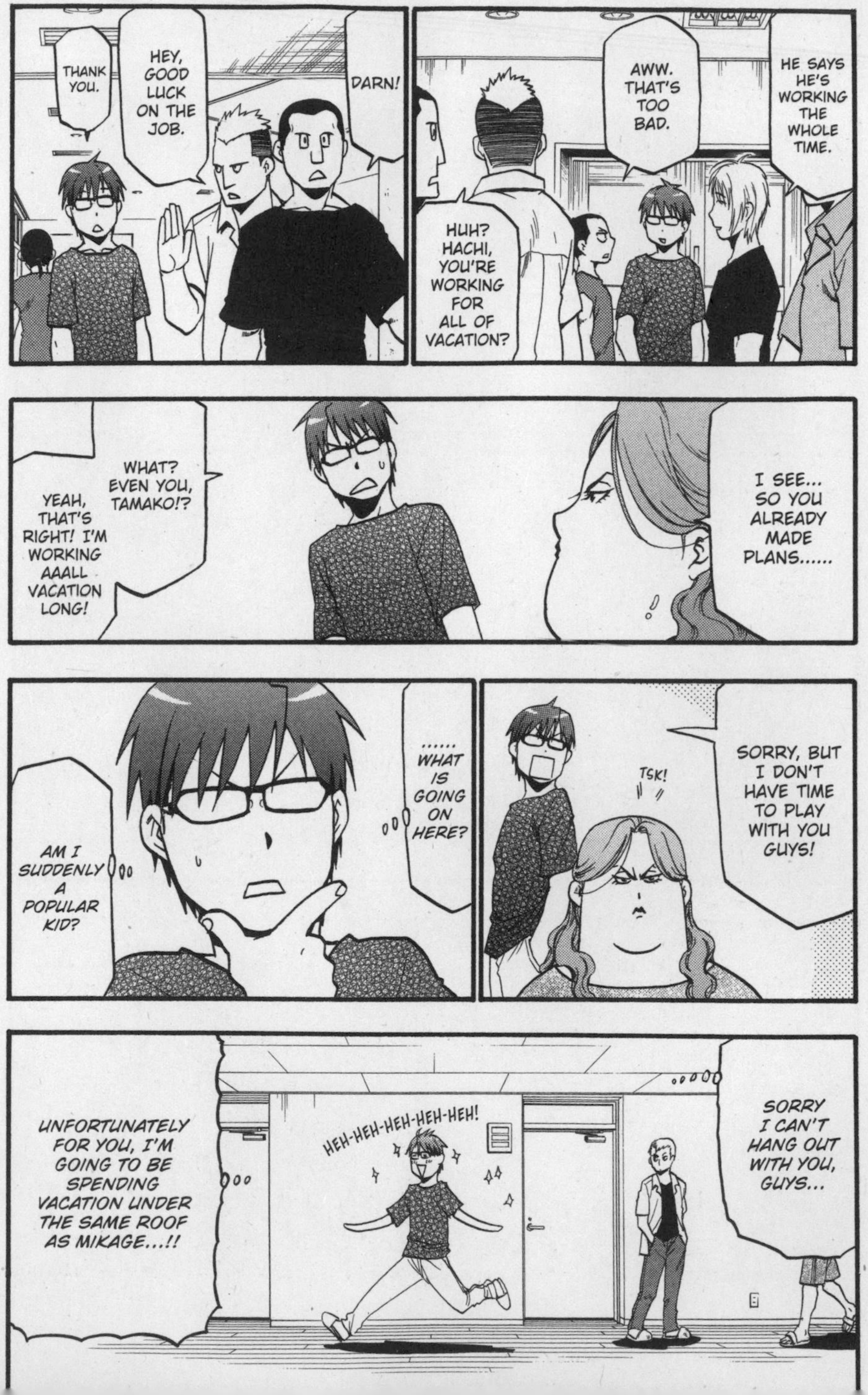
HE SAYS HE'S WORKING THE WHOLE TIME.
AWW. THAT'S TOO BAD.
HUH? HACHI, YOU'RE WORKING FOR ALL OF VACATION?
DARN!
HEY, GOOD LUCK ON THE JOB.
THANK YOU.
I SEE... SO YOU ALREADY MADE PLANS......
!
WHAT? EVEN YOU, TAMAKO!?
YEAH, THAT'S RIGHT! I'M WORKING AAALL VACATION LONG!
SORRY, BUT I DON'T HAVE TIME TO PLAY WITH YOU GUYS!
TSK!
...... WHAT IS GOING ON HERE?
AM I SUDDENLY A POPULAR KID?
SORRY I CAN'T HANG OUT WITH YOU, GUYS...
HEH-HEH-HEH-HEH-HEH!
UNFORTUNATELY FOR YOU, I'M GOING TO BE SPENDING VACATION UNDER THE SAME ROOF AS MIKAGE...!!

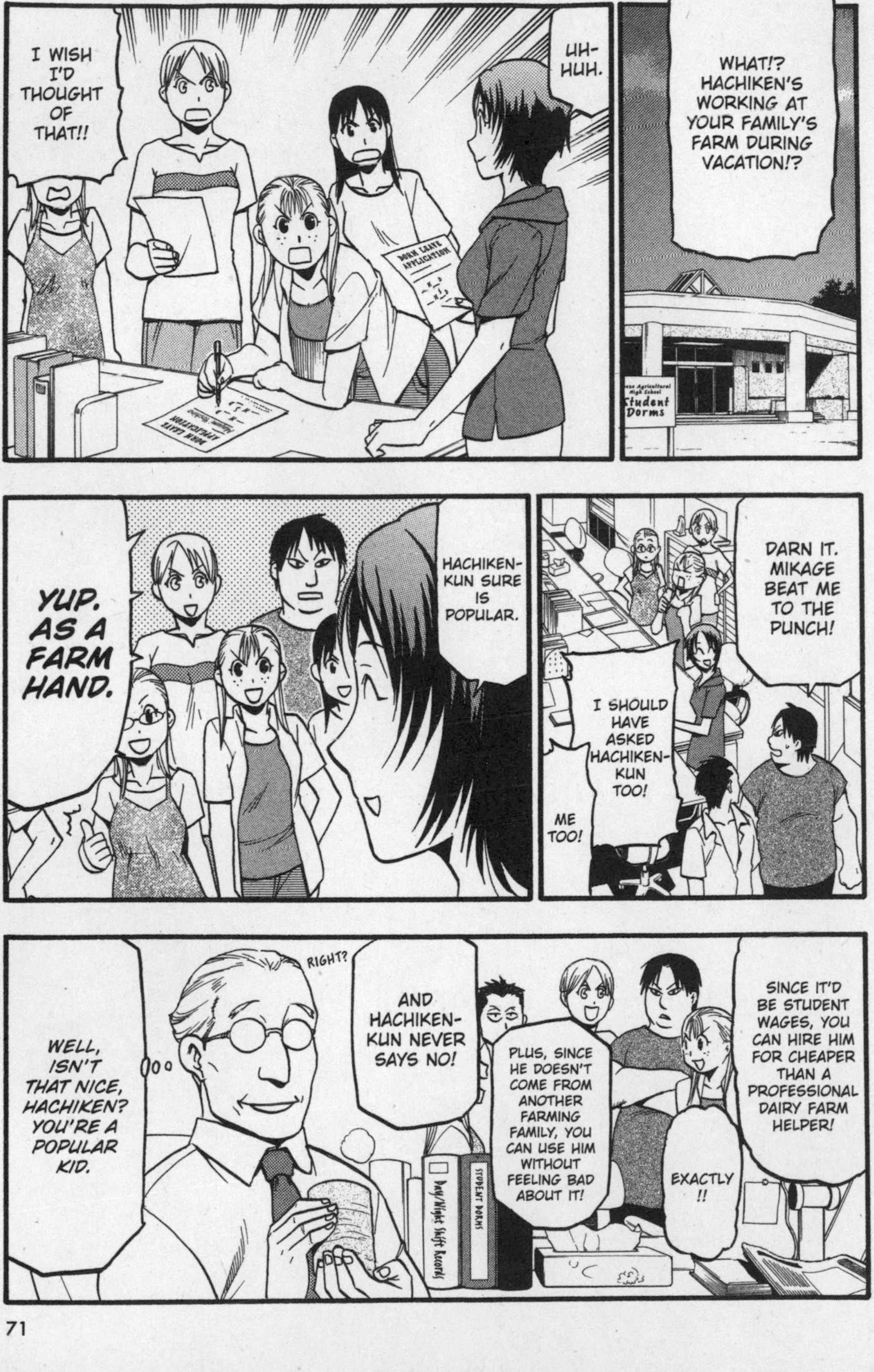
WHAT!? HACHIKEN'S WORKING AT YOUR FAMILY'S FARM DURING VACATION!?
Student Dorms
UH-HUH.
I WISH I'D THOUGHT OF THAT!!
DORM LEAVE APPLICATION
DARN IT. MIKAGE BEAT ME TO THE PUNCH!
I SHOULD HAVE ASKED HACHIKEN-KUN TOO!
ME TOO!
HACHIKEN-KUN SURE IS POPULAR.
YUP. AS A FARM HAND.
SINCE IT'D BE STUDENT WAGES, YOU CAN HIRE HIM FOR CHEAPER THAN A PROFESSIONAL DAIRY FARM HELPER!
EXACTLY !!
PLUS, SINCE HE DOESN'T COME FROM ANOTHER FARMING FAMILY, YOU CAN USE HIM WITHOUT FEELING BAD ABOUT IT!
STUDENT DORMS
Day/Night Shift Records
AND HACHIKEN-KUN NEVER SAYS NO!
RIGHT?
WELL, ISN'T THAT NICE, HACHIKEN? YOU'RE A POPULAR KID.

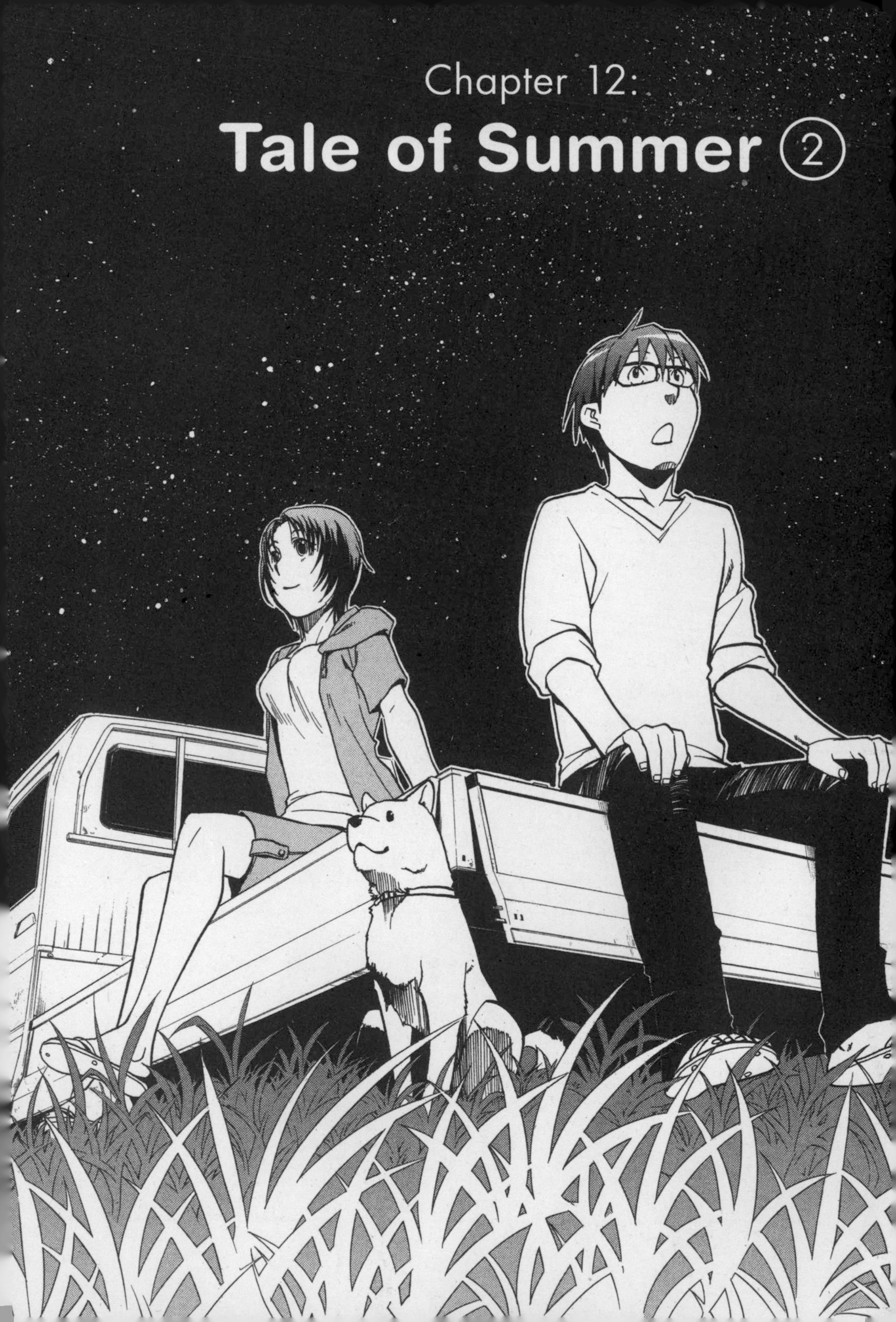
Chapter 12:
Tale of Summer ②

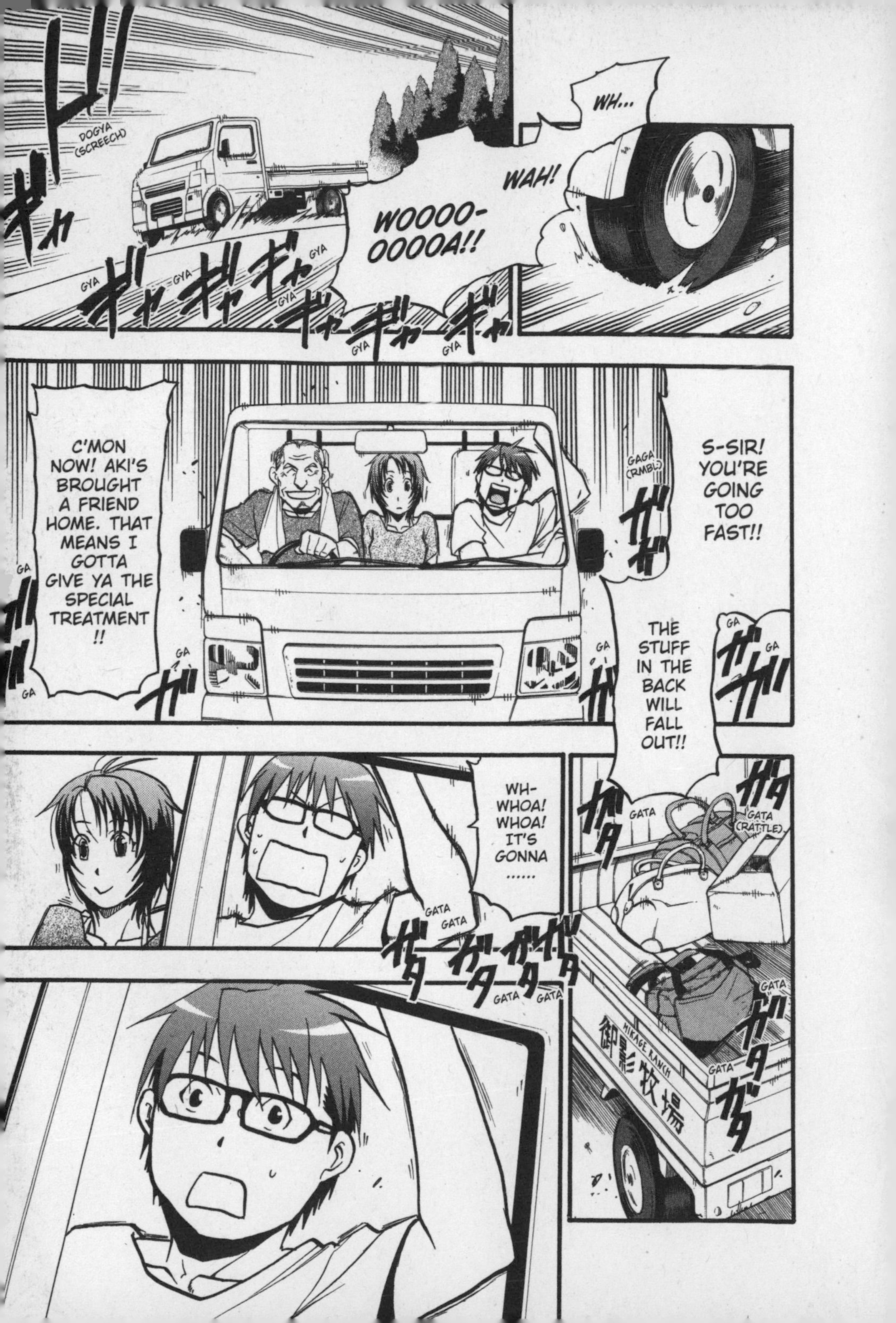
WH...
WAH!
WOOOO-OOOOA!!
DOGYA (SCREECH)
GYA GYA GYA GYA GYA GYA
S-SIR! YOU'RE GOING TOO FAST!!
GAGA (RMBL)
THE STUFF IN THE BACK WILL FALL OUT!!
GA GA
GA
C'MON NOW! AKI'S BROUGHT A FRIEND HOME. THAT MEANS I GOTTA GIVE YA THE SPECIAL TREATMENT!!
GA GA
GA
GATA (RATTLE)
GATA
GATA
GATA
御影牧場
MIKAGE RANCH
WH-WHOA! WHOA! IT'S GONNA ......
GATA GATA
GATA GATA

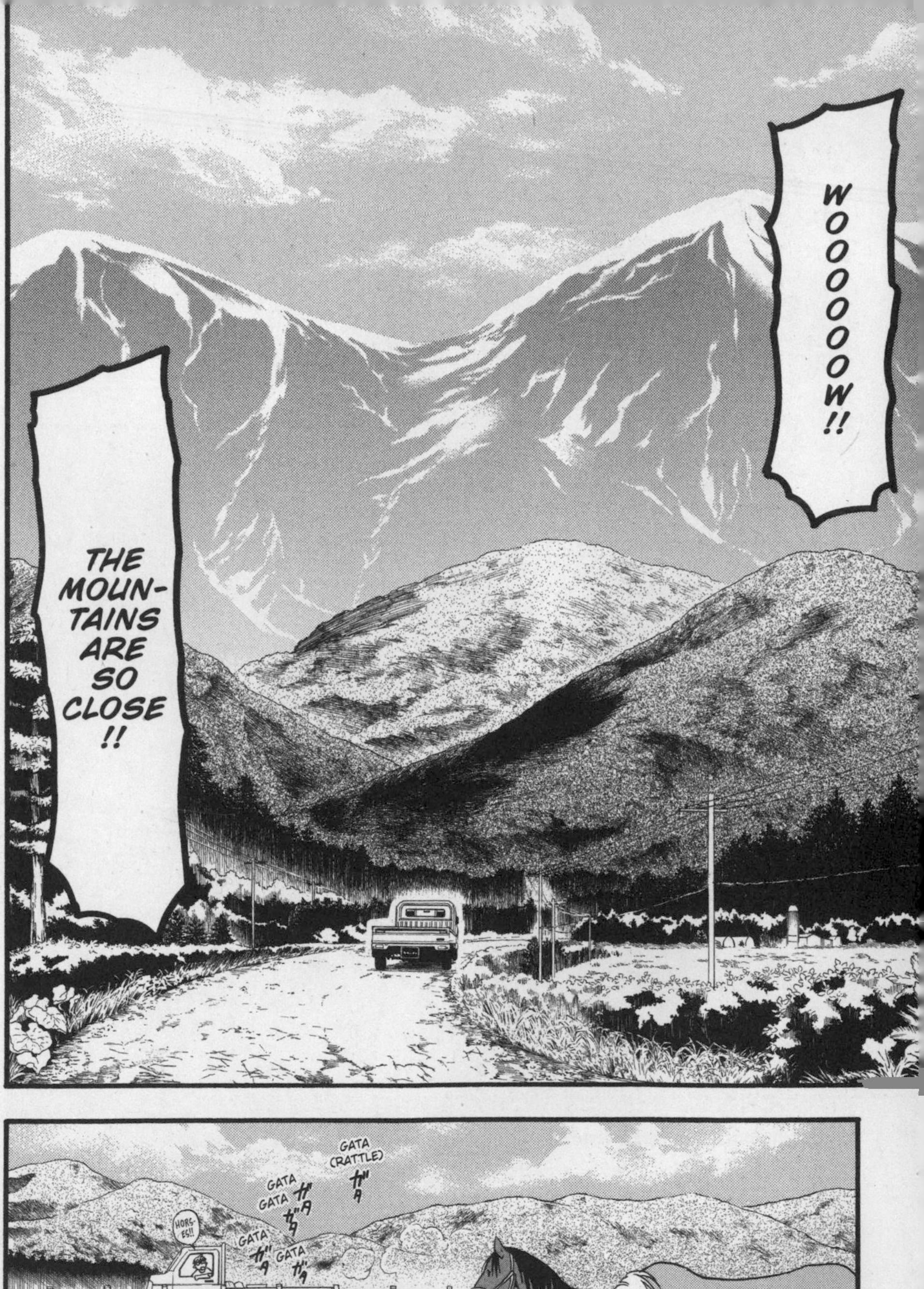
WOOOOOOOW!!
THE MOUNTAINS ARE SO CLOSE!!

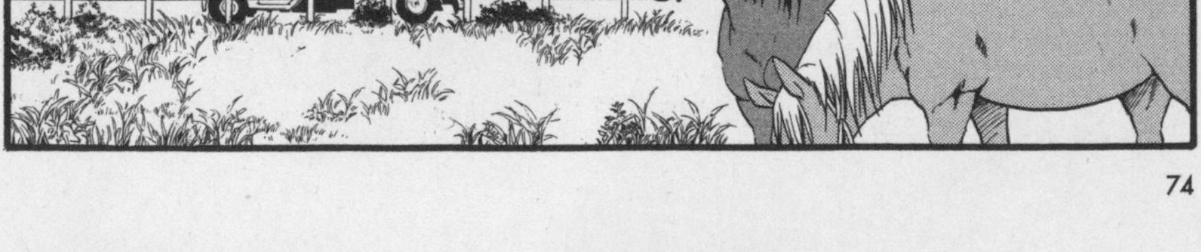
GATA (RATTLE)
GATA GATA
GATA GATA
HORSES!!

BARK! BARK!
BARK!
BARK!
BARK!
KI (SQUEAK)
ARF! ARF! ARF!
YOU MUST BE HACHI-KEN-KUN.
THANKS FOR COMING. I'M AKI'S MOTHER.
ARF!
THANK YOU FOR HAVING ME, MA'AM!
OH PLEASE. YOU'RE THE ONE DOING US A FAVOR!
GARA
GARA (SLIDE)
GARA
AKI'S FATHER IS GOING TO THE HOSPITAL TOMORROW, AND WE WERE HAVING A HARD TIME FINDING ANY HELP.
PA! PA!

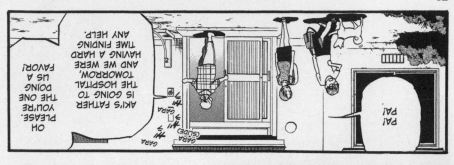

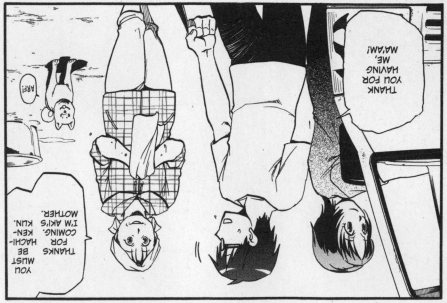

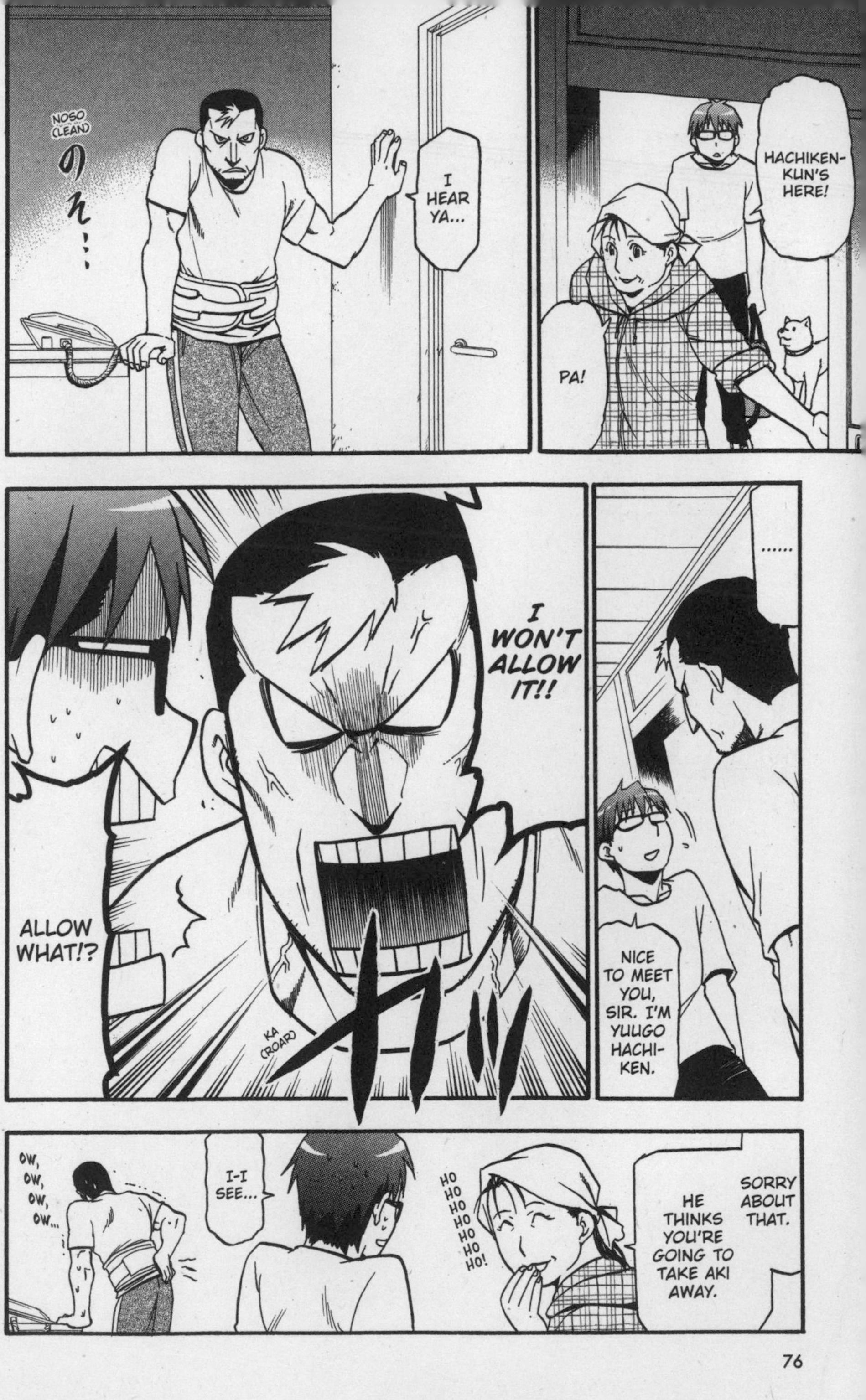
HACHIKEN-KUN'S HERE!
PA!
I HEAR YA...
NOSO (LEAN)
.....
NICE TO MEET YOU, SIR. I'M YUUGO HACHI-KEN.
I WON'T ALLOW IT!!
KA (ROAR)
ALLOW WHAT!?
SORRY ABOUT THAT.
HE THINKS YOU'RE GOING TO TAKE AKI AWAY.
HO HO HO HO HO HO HO HO!
I-I SEE...
OW, OW, OW, OW...

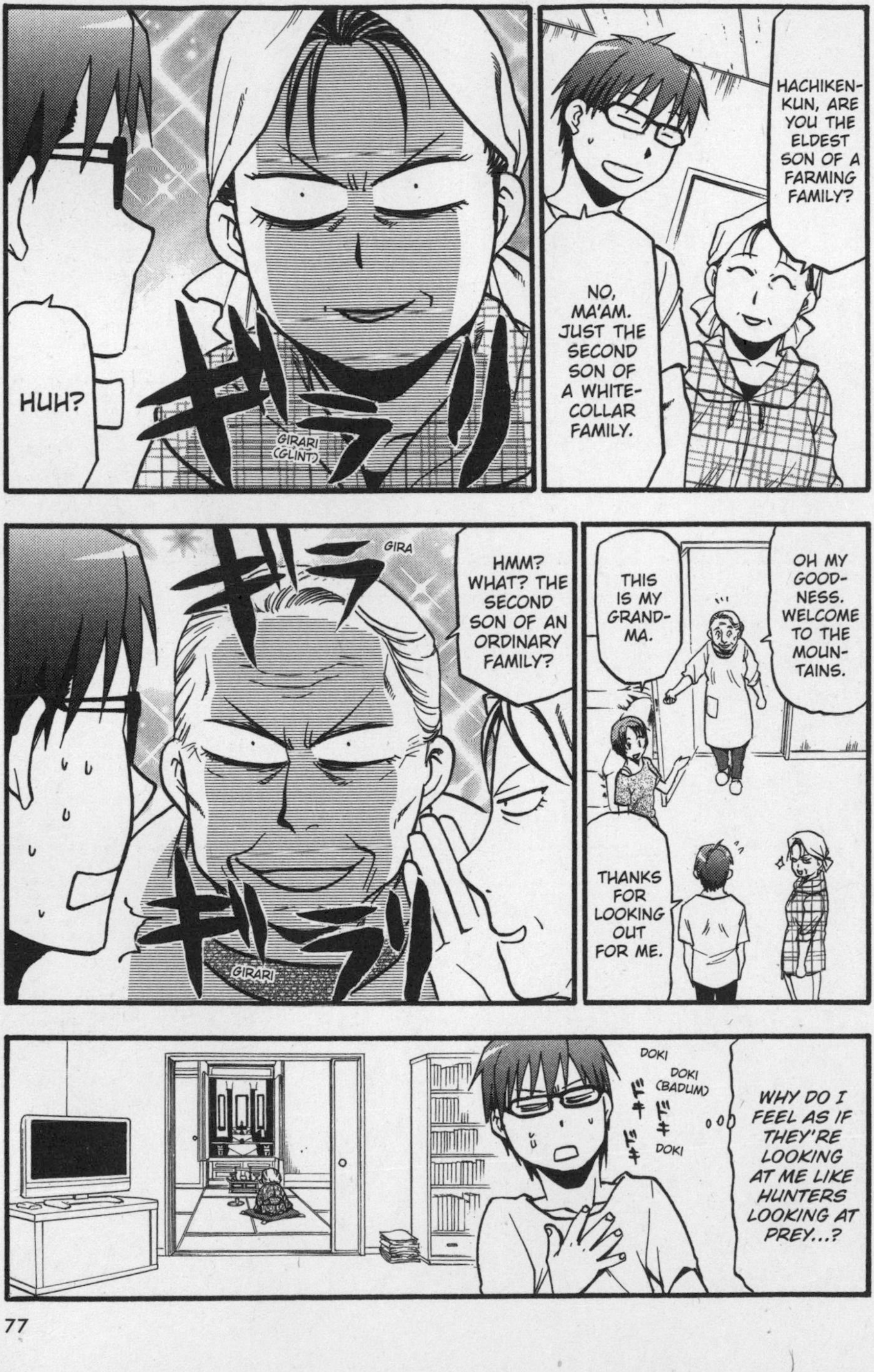
HACHIKEN-KUN, ARE YOU THE ELDEST SON OF A FARMING FAMILY?
NO, MA'AM. JUST THE SECOND SON OF A WHITE-COLLAR FAMILY.
HUH?
GIRARI (GLINT)
OH MY GOODNESS. WELCOME TO THE MOUNTAINS.
THIS IS MY GRANDMA.
THANKS FOR LOOKING OUT FOR ME.
HMM? WHAT? THE SECOND SON OF AN ORDINARY FAMILY?
GIRA
GIRARI
WHY DO I FEEL AS IF THEY'RE LOOKING AT ME LIKE HUNTERS LOOKING AT PREY...?
DOKI
DOKI (BADUM)
DOKI

GREAT-GRANDMA, I'M HOME!
THIS IS MY CLASSMATE, HACHIKEN-KUN. HE'S HERE TO HELP ON THE FARM.
HELLO, MA'AM.
ペこ
PEKO (NOD)
MOGO (CHEW) MOGO
SHE'S 107.
ONE HUN—
UHHH... SO SHE WAS BORN IN THE MEIJI PERIOD?

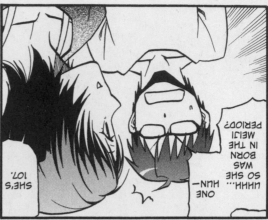

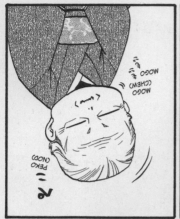

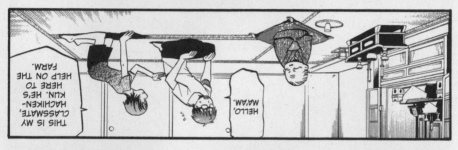

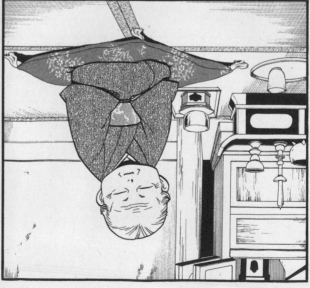

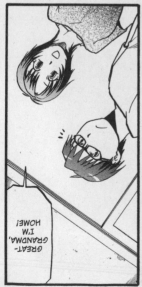

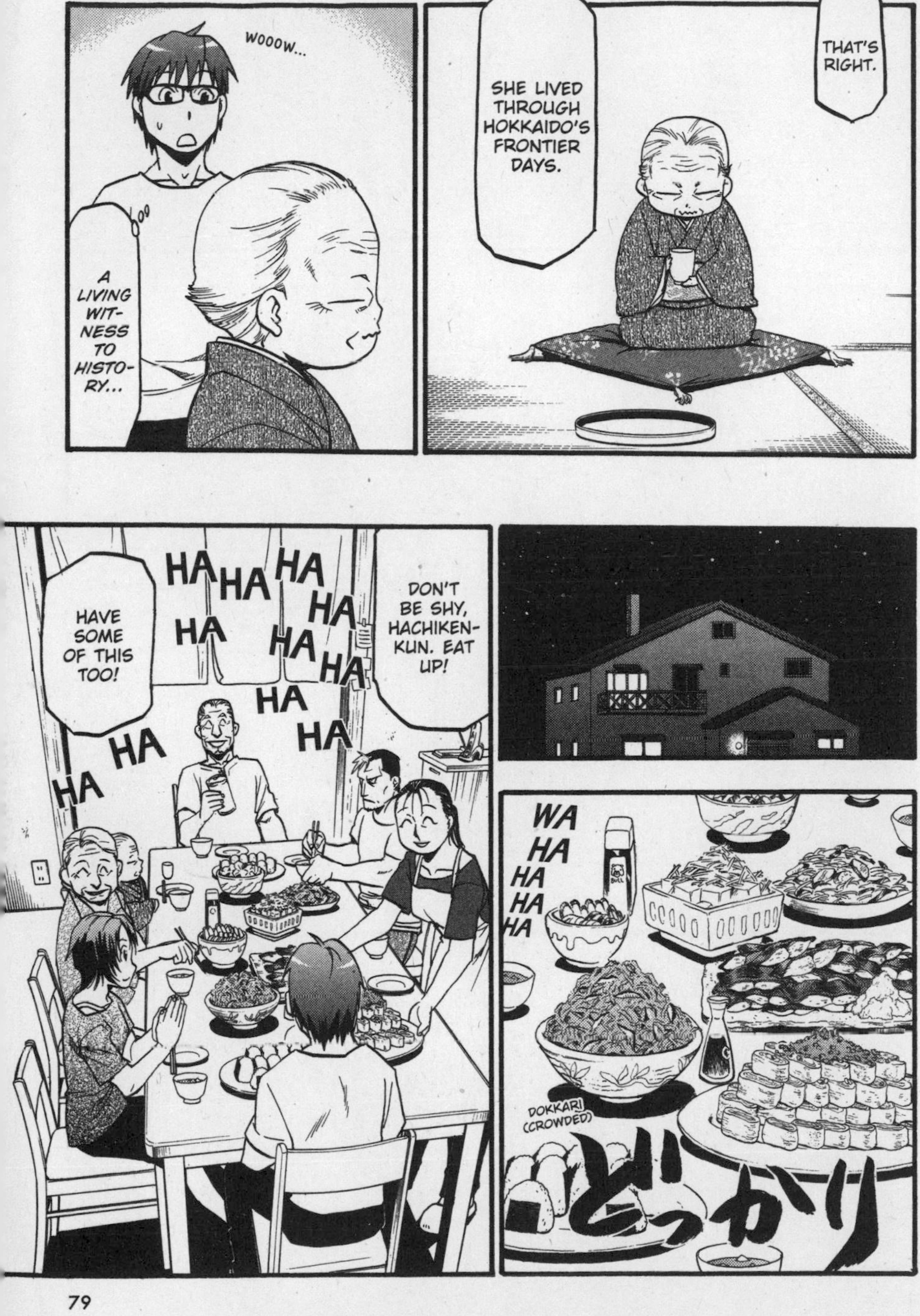
THAT'S RIGHT.
SHE LIVED THROUGH HOKKAIDO'S FRONTIER DAYS.
WOOOW...
A LIVING WIT-NESS TO HISTO-RY...
DON'T BE SHY, HACHIKEN-KUN. EAT UP!
HAVE SOME OF THIS TOO!
HA HA HA HA HA HA HA HA HA HA HA HA
WA HA HA HA HA
DOKKARI (CROWDED)
どっかり

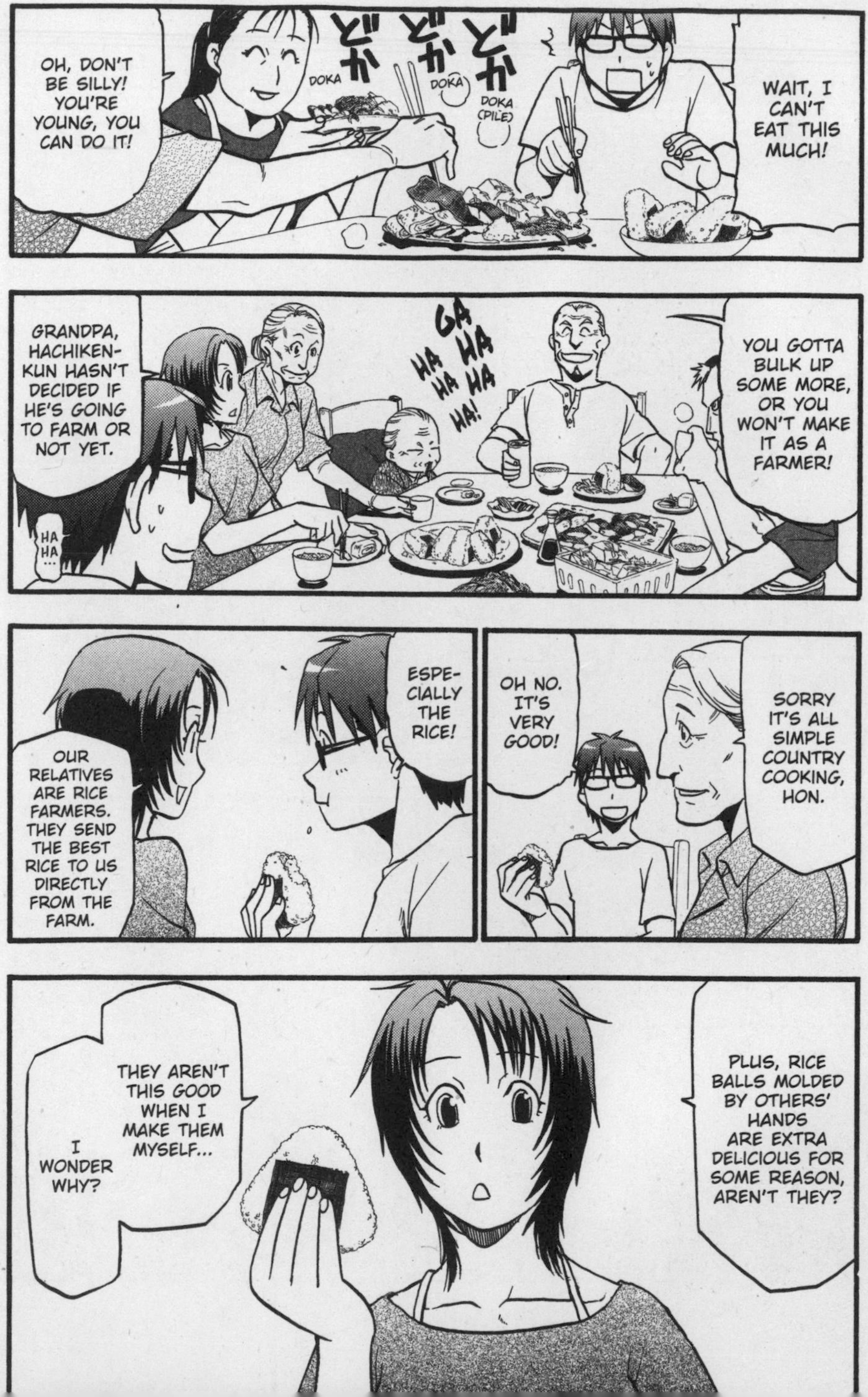
WAIT, I CAN'T EAT THIS MUCH!
どか
どか
どか
DOKA (PILE)
DOKA
DOKA
OH, DON'T BE SILLY! YOU'RE YOUNG, YOU CAN DO IT!
YOU GOTTA BULK UP SOME MORE, OR YOU WON'T MAKE IT AS A FARMER!
GA HA HA HA HA HA HA HA!
GRANDPA, HACHIKEN-KUN HASN'T DECIDED IF HE'S GOING TO FARM OR NOT YET.
HA HA...
SORRY IT'S ALL SIMPLE COUNTRY COOKING, HON.
OH NO. IT'S VERY GOOD!
ESPE-CIALLY THE RICE!
OUR RELATIVES ARE RICE FARMERS. THEY SEND THE BEST RICE TO US DIRECTLY FROM THE FARM.
PLUS, RICE BALLS MOLDED BY OTHERS' HANDS ARE EXTRA DELICIOUS FOR SOME REASON, AREN'T THEY?
THEY AREN'T THIS GOOD WHEN I MAKE THEM MYSELF...
I WONDER WHY?

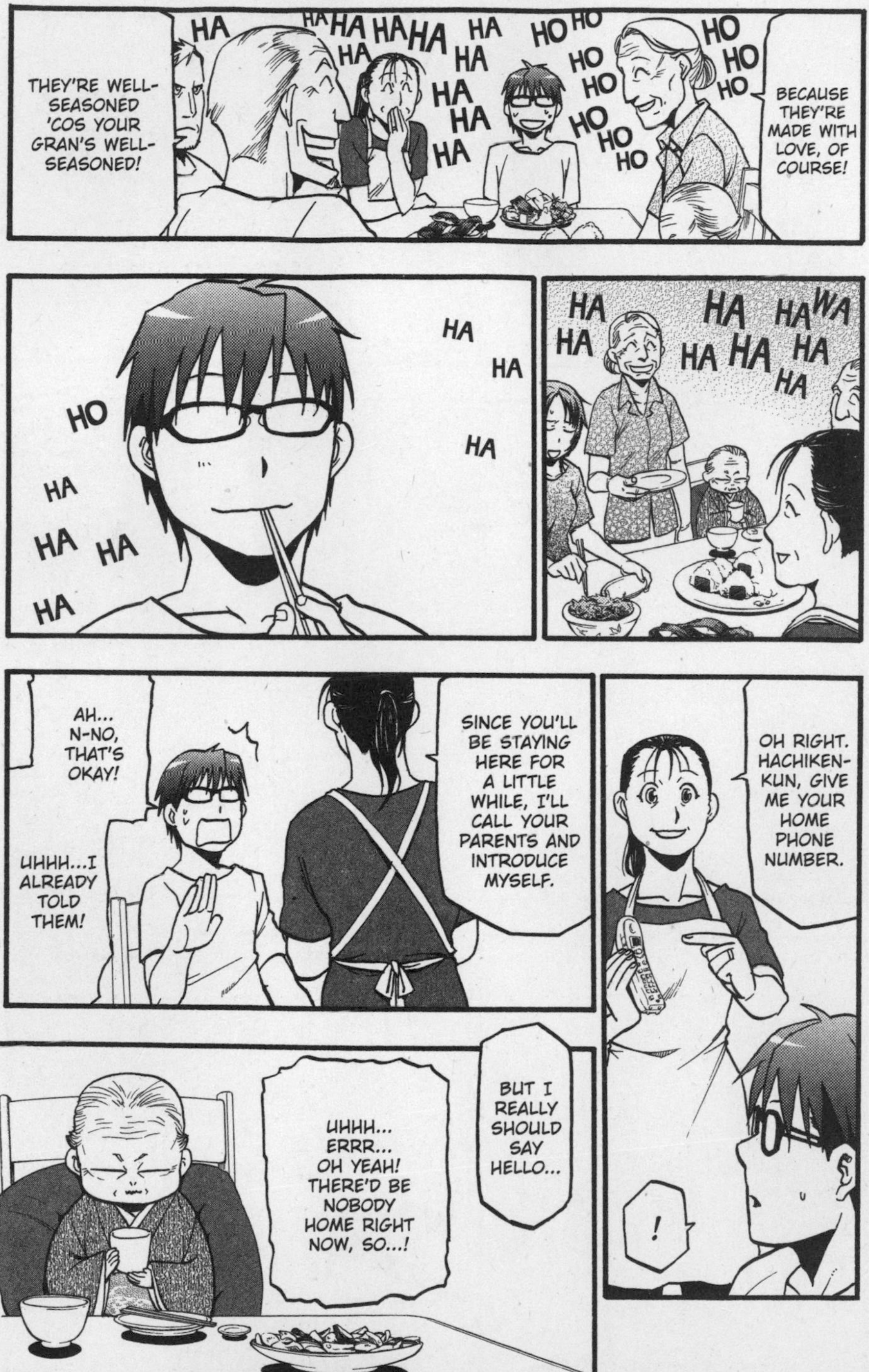
BECAUSE THEY'RE MADE WITH LOVE, OF COURSE!
HO HO HO HO HO HO HO HO HO
HA HA HA HA HA HA HA HA HA HA HA
THEY'RE WELL-SEASONED 'COS YOUR GRAN'S WELL-SEASONED!
HA HA HAWA HA HA HA HA HA
HA HA HO HA HA HA HA
OH RIGHT. HACHIKEN-KUN, GIVE ME YOUR HOME PHONE NUMBER.
SINCE YOU'LL BE STAYING HERE FOR A LITTLE WHILE, I'LL CALL YOUR PARENTS AND INTRODUCE MYSELF.
AH... N-NO, THAT'S OKAY!
UHHH...I ALREADY TOLD THEM!
!
BUT I REALLY SHOULD SAY HELLO...
UHHH... ERRR... OH YEAH! THERE'D BE NOBODY HOME RIGHT NOW, SO...!

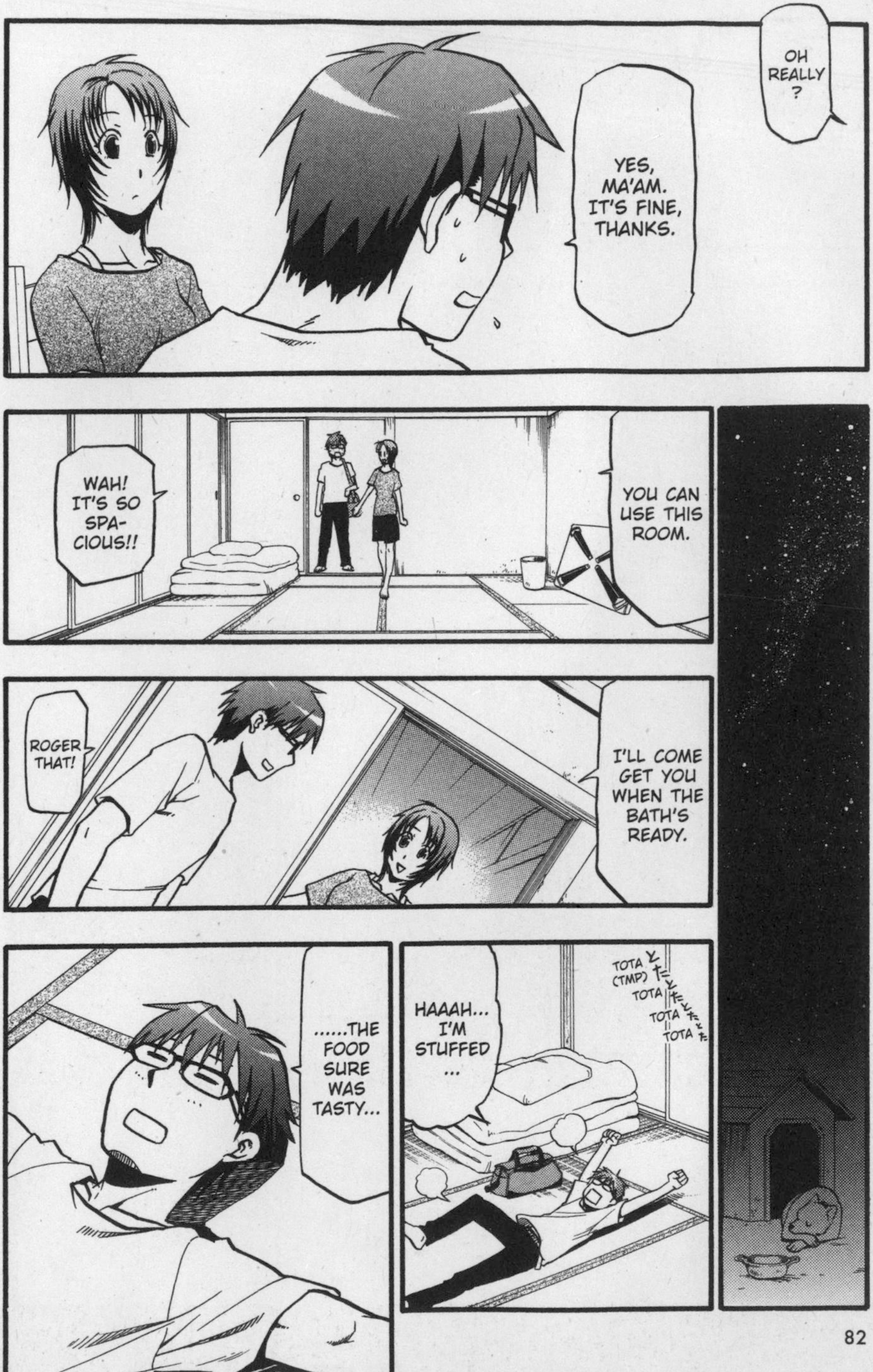
OH REALLY ?
YES, MA'AM. IT'S FINE, THANKS.
YOU CAN USE THIS ROOM.
WAH! IT'S SO SPA-CIOUS!!
I'LL COME GET YOU WHEN THE BATH'S READY.
ROGER THAT!
TOTA (TMP) TOTA TOTA TOTA
HAAAH... I'M STUFFED ...
......THE FOOD SURE WAS TASTY...

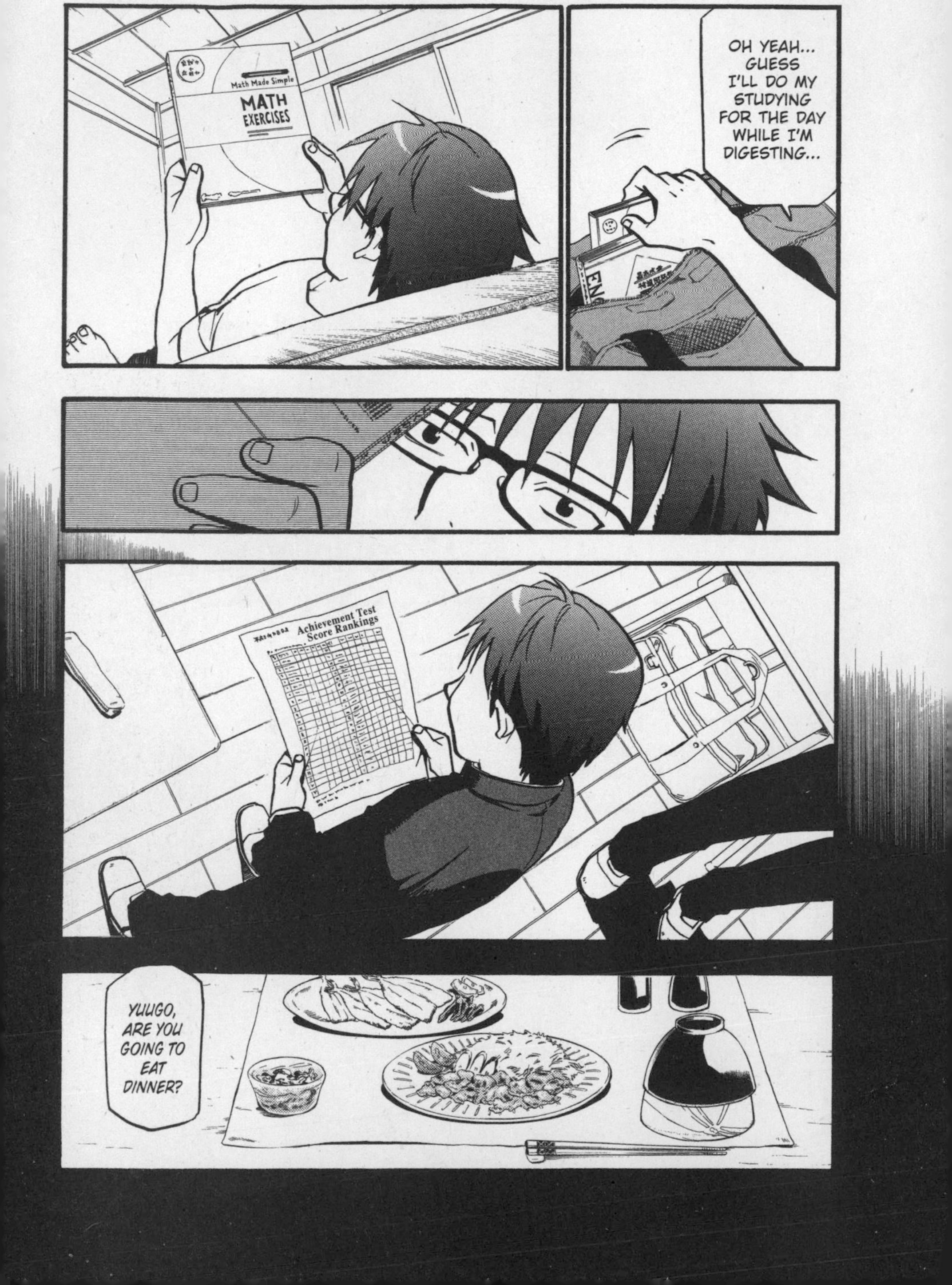
OH YEAH... GUESS I'LL DO MY STUDYING FOR THE DAY WHILE I'M DIGESTING...
Math Made Simple
MATH EXERCISES
Achievement Test Score Rankings
YUUGO, ARE YOU GOING TO EAT DINNER?

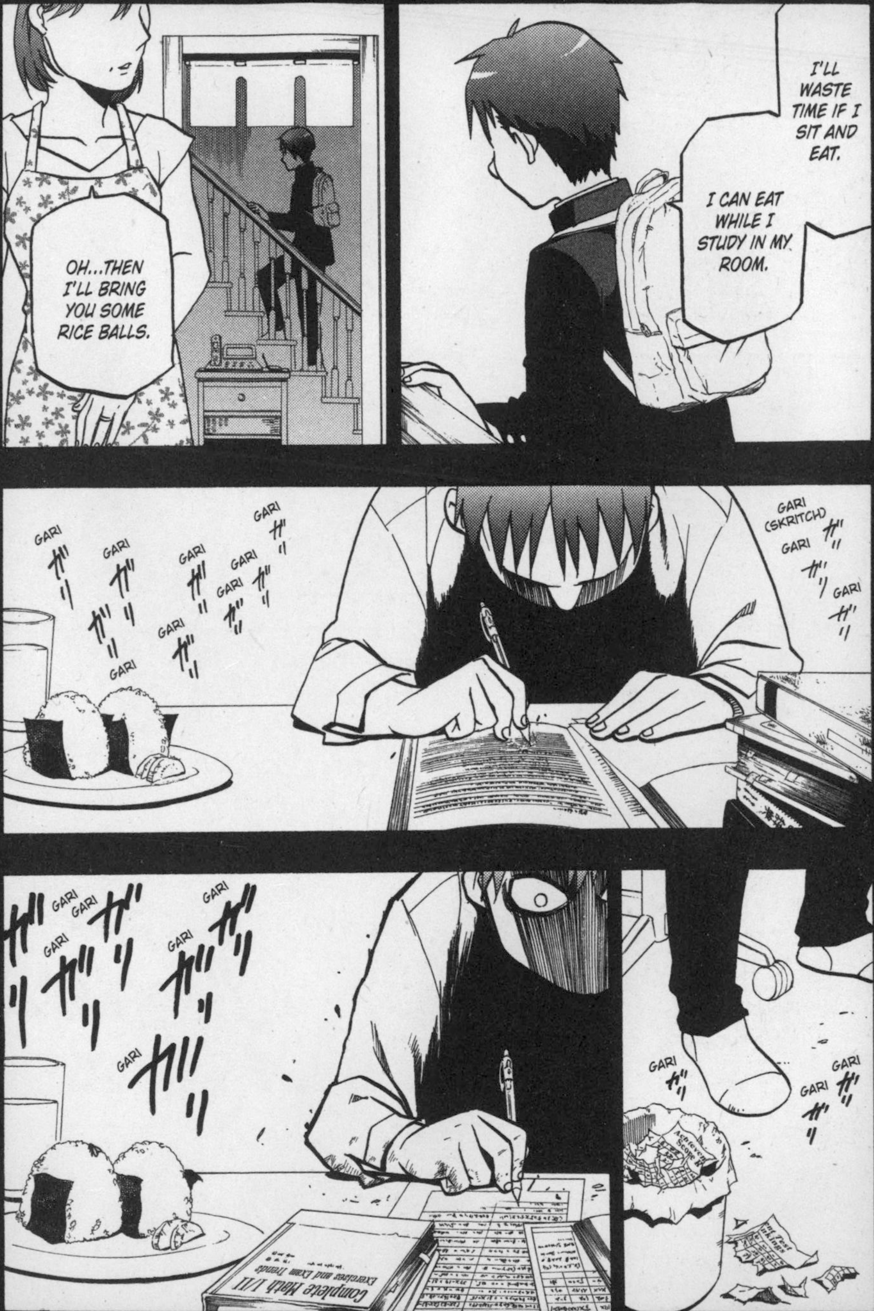
I'LL WASTE TIME IF I SIT AND EAT.
I CAN EAT WHILE I STUDY IN MY ROOM.
OH...THEN I'LL BRING YOU SOME RICE BALLS.
GARI (SKRITCH)
GARI
GARI
GARI
GARI
GARI
GARI
GARI
GARI
GARI
GARI
GARI
GARI
GARI
GARI
GARI
GARI
GARI
GARI
Complete Math I/II
Exercises and Exam Trends

むく……
MUKU (SIT)
カチ.
KACHI (CLICK)
Reply to Sender
OK
To
Sub
Working at a farmer friend's place during vacation.
Can't come home.
カチ
KACHI
カチ
KACHI
カチ…
KACHI
KANJI
AUTOPREDICT
OK
……………

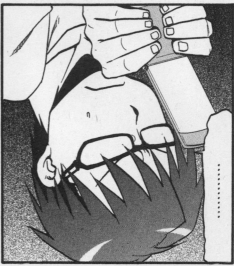

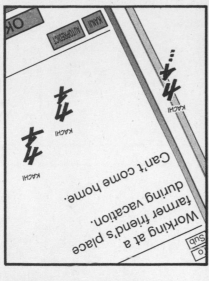

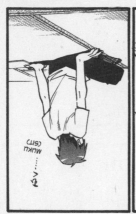

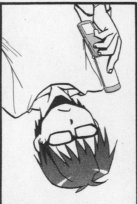

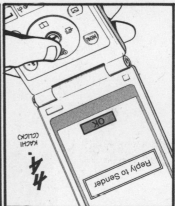

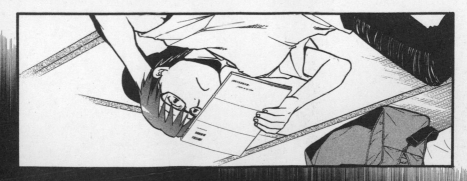

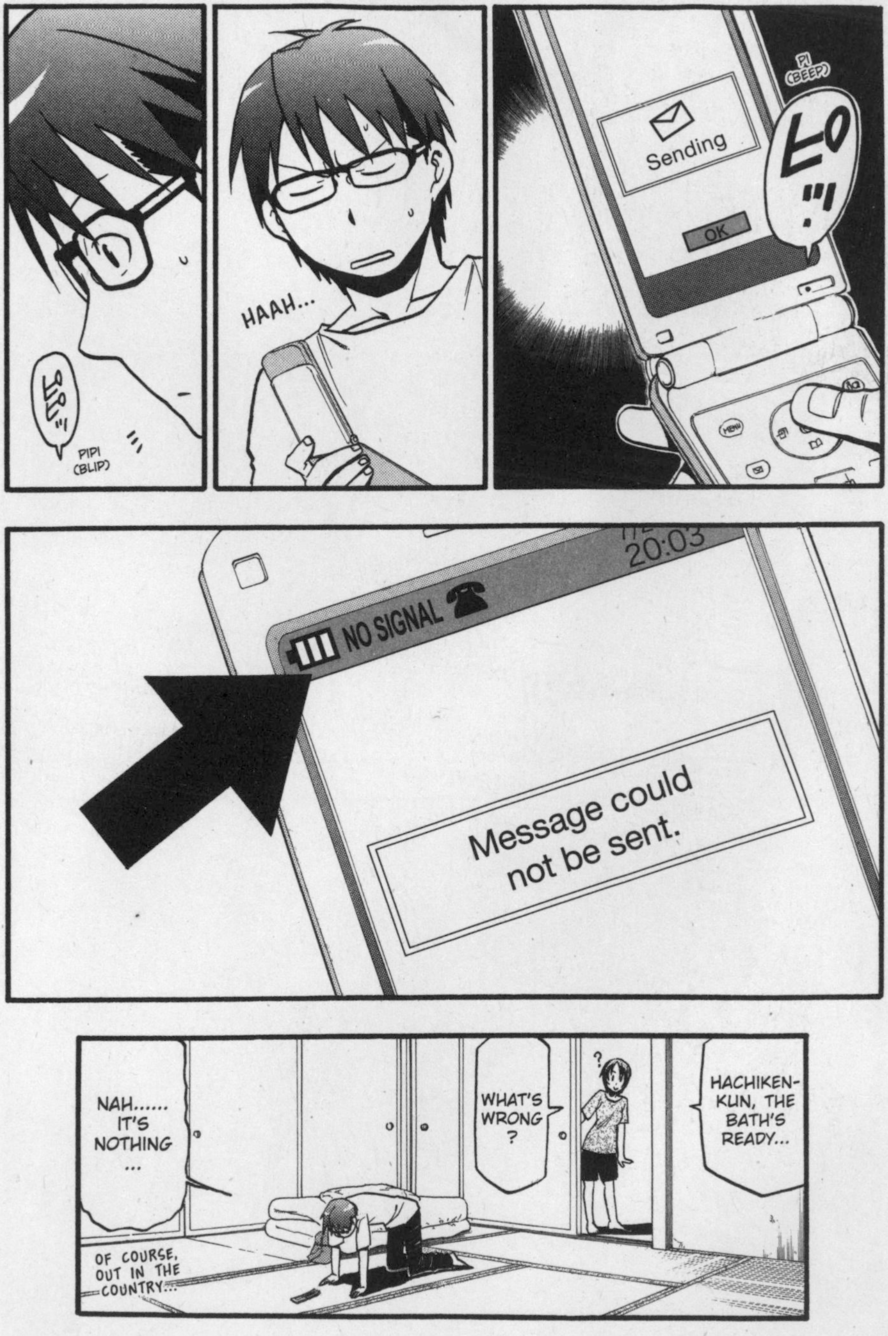
Sending
OK
PI
(BEEP)
HAAH...
PIPI
(BLIP)
20:03
NO SIGNAL
Message could
not be sent.
HACHIKEN-
KUN, THE
BATH'S
READY...
?
WHAT'S
WRONG
?
NAH......
IT'S
NOTHING
...
OF COURSE,
OUT IN THE
COUNTRY...

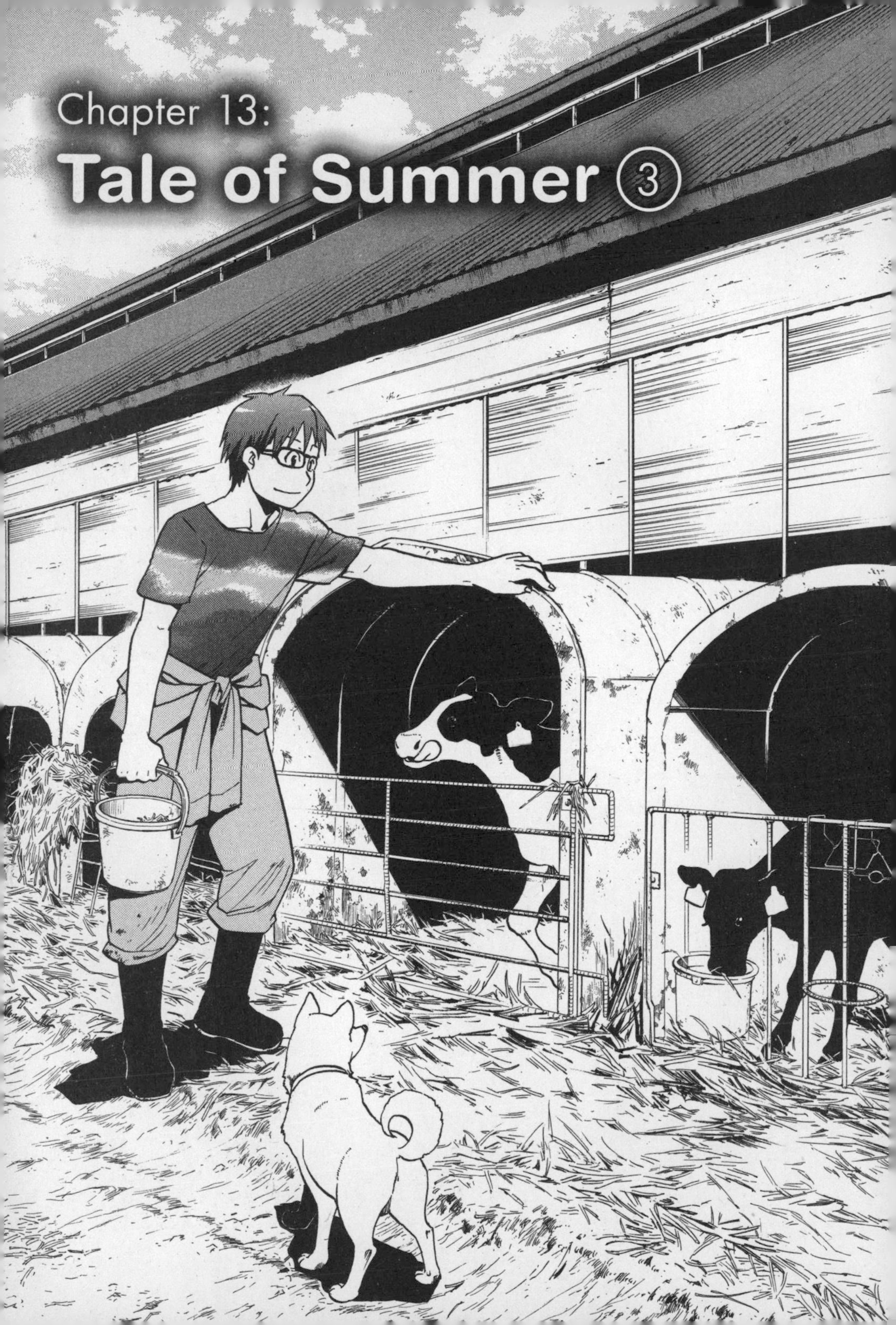
Chapter 13:
Tale of Summer ③

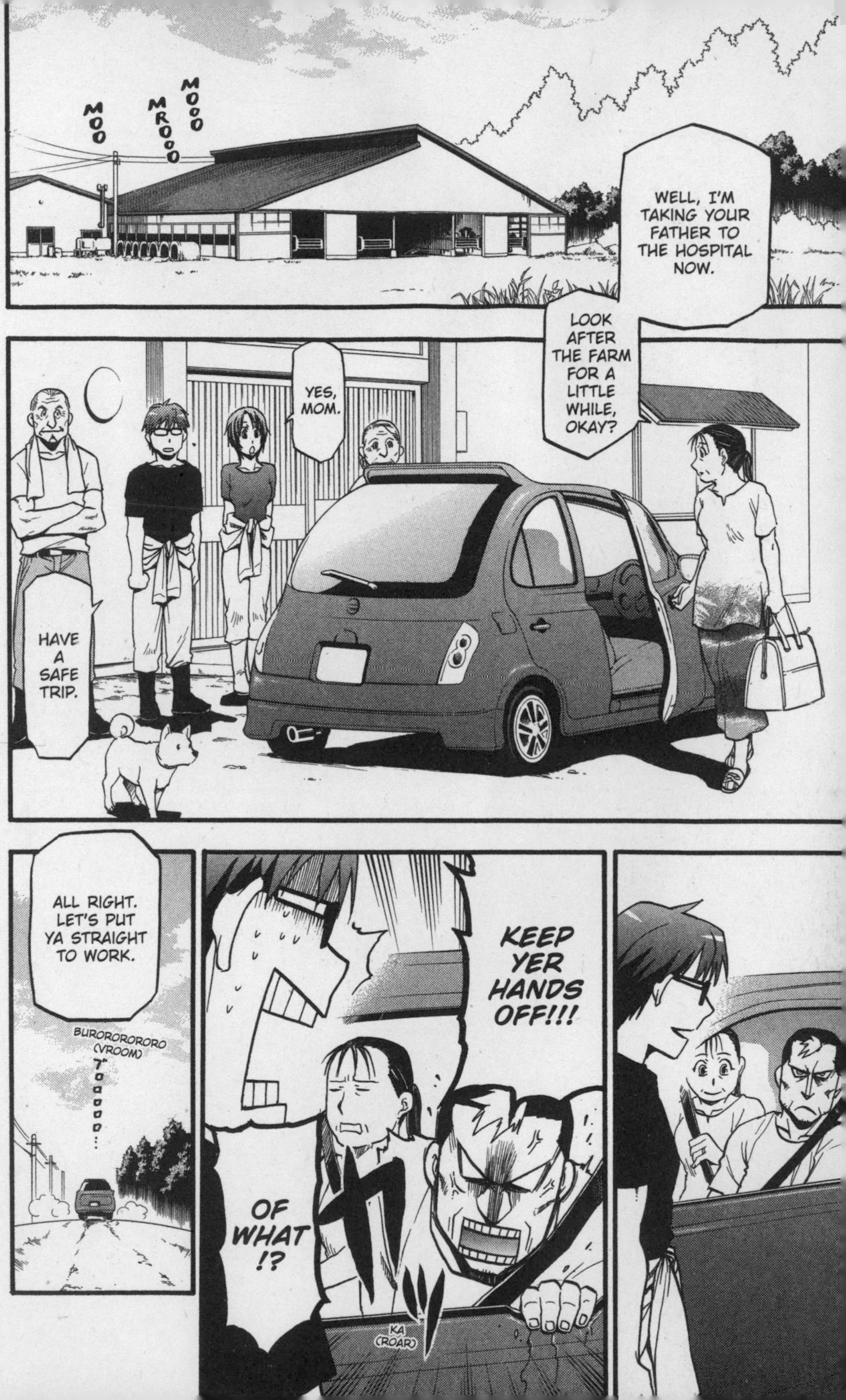
MOO
MROOO
MOOO
WELL, I'M TAKING YOUR FATHER TO THE HOSPITAL NOW.
LOOK AFTER THE FARM FOR A LITTLE WHILE, OKAY?
YES, MOM.
HAVE A SAFE TRIP.
KEEP YER HANDS OFF!!!
OF WHAT !?
KA (ROAR)
ALL RIGHT. LET'S PUT YA STRAIGHT TO WORK.
BURORORORORO (VROOM)
TOOOOOO...

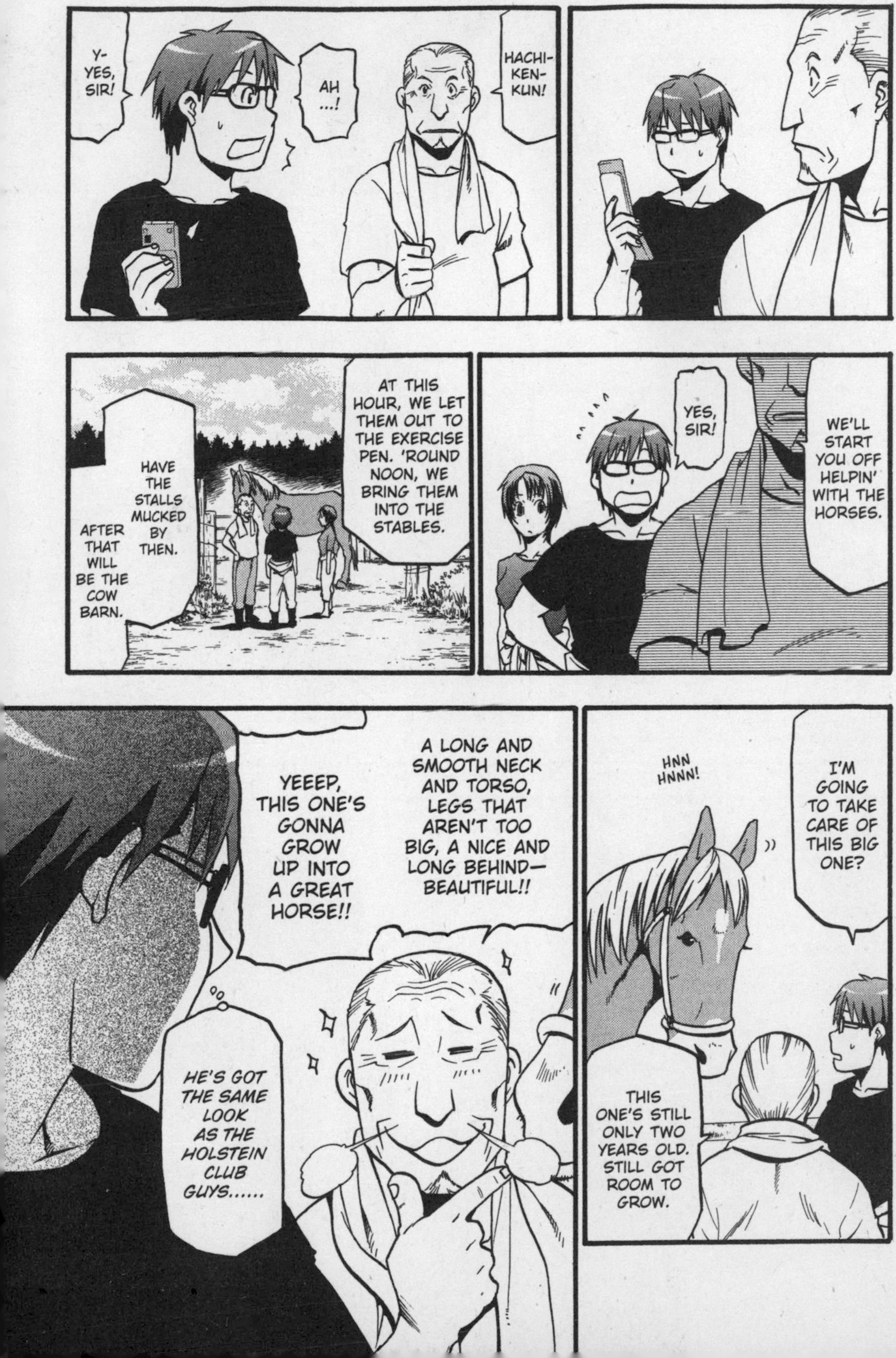
HACHI-KEN-KUN!
AH ...!
Y-YES, SIR!
WE'LL START YOU OFF HELPIN' WITH THE HORSES.
YES, SIR!
AT THIS HOUR, WE LET THEM OUT TO THE EXERCISE PEN. 'ROUND NOON, WE BRING THEM INTO THE STABLES.
HAVE THE STALLS MUCKED BY THEN.
AFTER THAT WILL BE THE COW BARN.
I'M GOING TO TAKE CARE OF THIS BIG ONE?
HNN HNNN!
THIS ONE'S STILL ONLY TWO YEARS OLD. STILL GOT ROOM TO GROW.
A LONG AND SMOOTH NECK AND TORSO, LEGS THAT AREN'T TOO BIG, A NICE AND LONG BEHIND—BEAUTIFUL!!
YEEEP, THIS ONE'S GONNA GROW UP INTO A GREAT HORSE!!
HE'S GOT THE SAME LOOK AS THE HOLSTEIN CLUB GUYS......

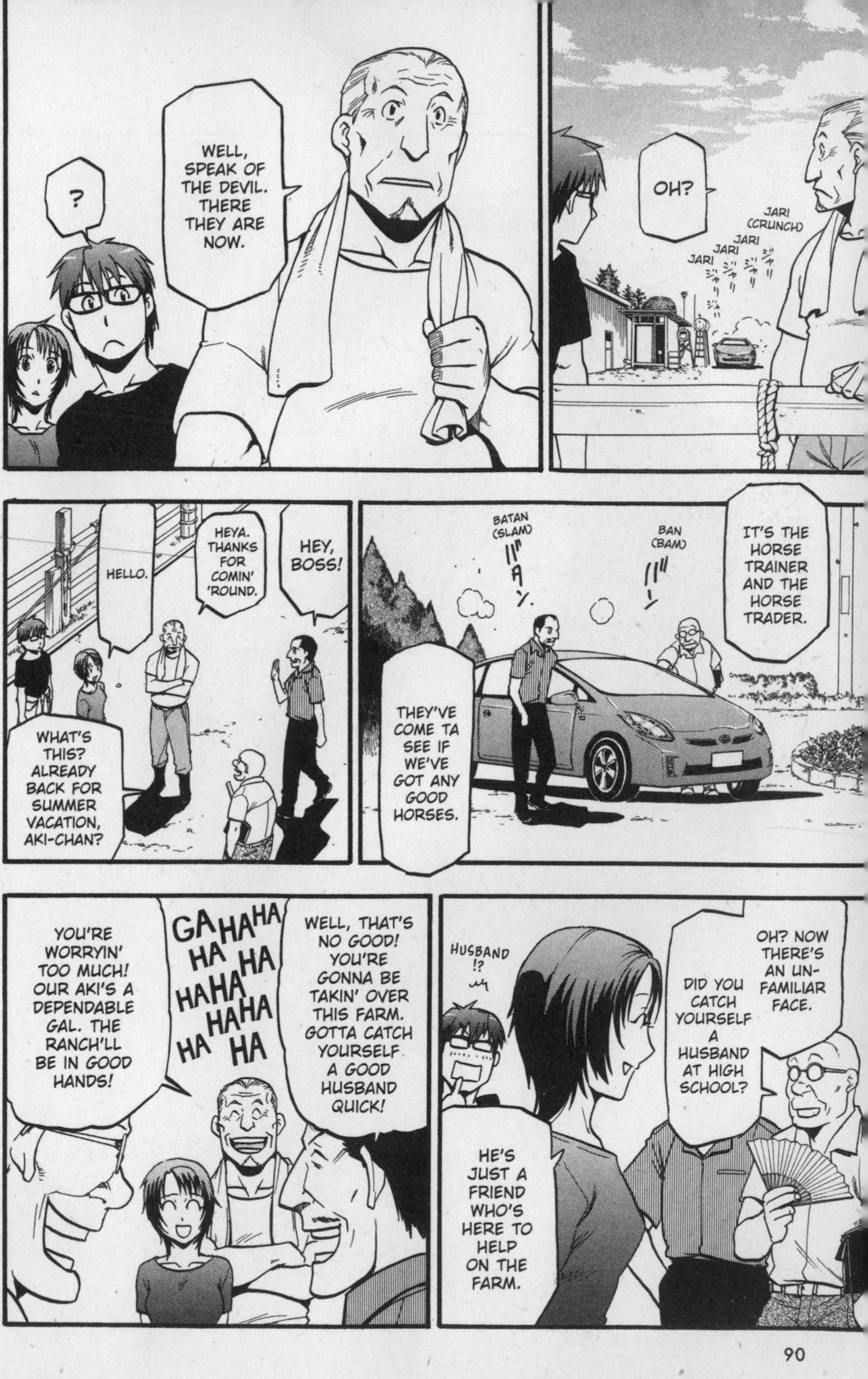
OH?
JARI (CRUNCH)
JARI
JARI
JARI
WELL, SPEAK OF THE DEVIL. THERE THEY ARE NOW.
?
IT'S THE HORSE TRAINER AND THE HORSE TRADER.
BAN (BAM)
BATAN (SLAM)
THEY'VE COME TA SEE IF WE'VE GOT ANY GOOD HORSES.
HEY, BOSS!
HEYA. THANKS FOR COMIN' 'ROUND.
HELLO.
WHAT'S THIS? ALREADY BACK FOR SUMMER VACATION, AKI-CHAN?
OH? NOW THERE'S AN UN-FAMILIAR FACE.
DID YOU CATCH YOURSELF A HUSBAND AT HIGH SCHOOL?
HUSBAND!?
HE'S JUST A FRIEND WHO'S HERE TO HELP ON THE FARM.
WELL, THAT'S NO GOOD! YOU'RE GONNA BE TAKIN' OVER THIS FARM. GOTTA CATCH YOURSELF A GOOD HUSBAND QUICK!
GAHAHA HA HA HAHAHA HA HAHAHA HA
YOU'RE WORRYIN' TOO MUCH! OUR AKI'S A DEPENDABLE GAL. THE RANCH'LL BE IN GOOD HANDS!

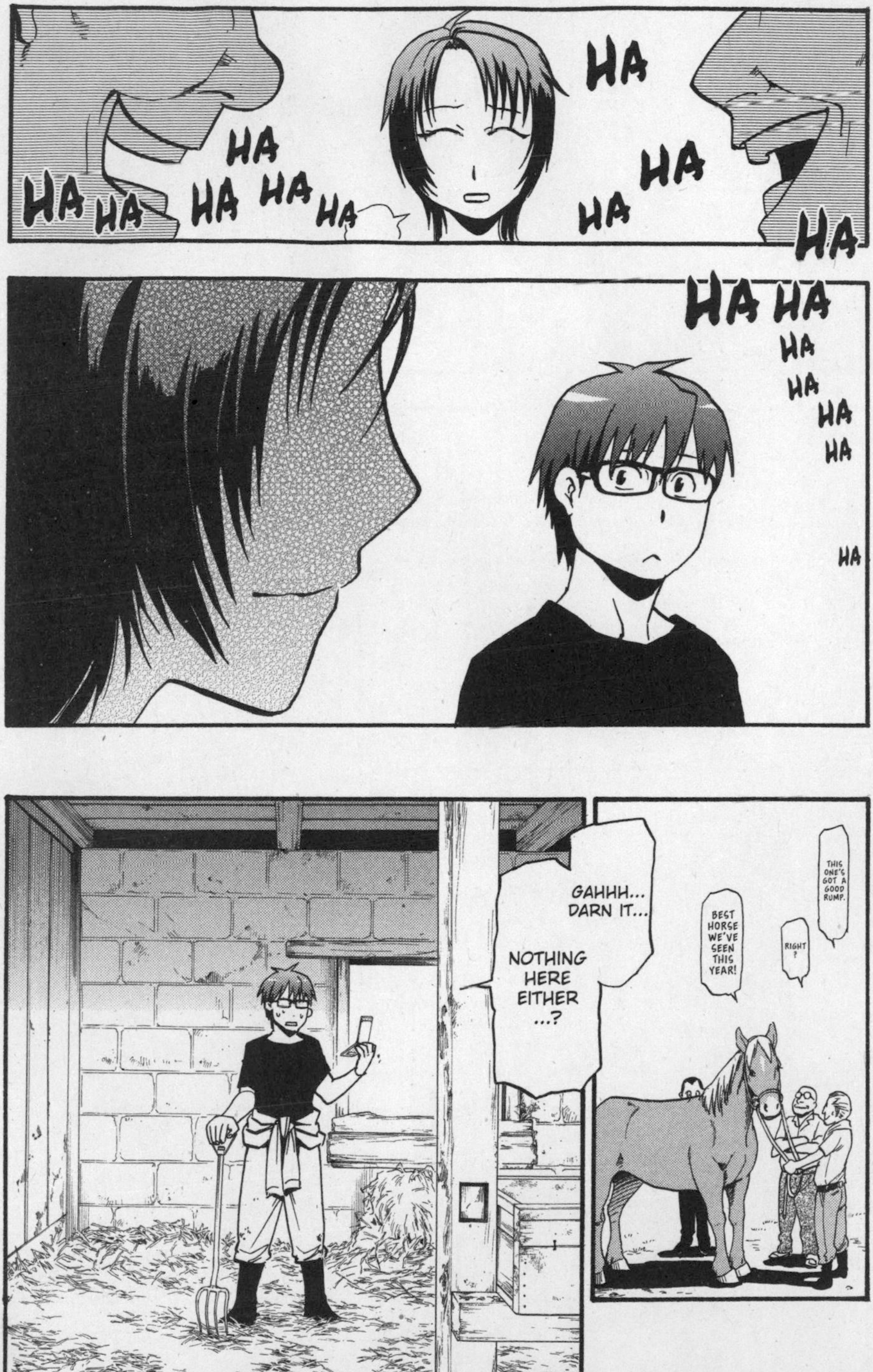
HA
HA HA
HA HA HA HA HA HA
HA
HA HA HA HA HA HA
HA
THIS ONE'S GOT A GOOD RUMP.
RIGHT?
BEST HORSE WE'VE SEEN THIS YEAR!
GAHHH... DARN IT...
NOTHING HERE EITHER ...?

HOW ...
...CAN I...
...GET A...
... SIG-NAL ...!?
STUPID PHONE ...!
AH.
OH MY. HACHIKEN-KUN'S FALLEN HEADFIRST INTO THE MANURE PILE.
UWAH!
HACHI-KEN-KUN, ARE YOU OKAY!?
I...
I'M FOKAY ...
WHAT'S THIS NOW? HE HASN'T GOTTEN ANY OF THE CLEANING DONE.

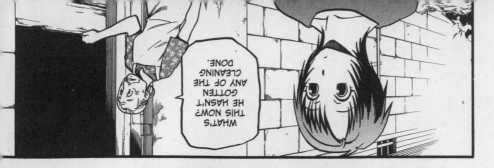

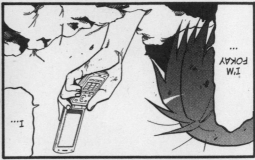

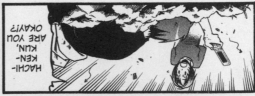

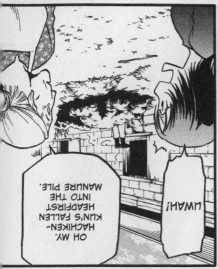

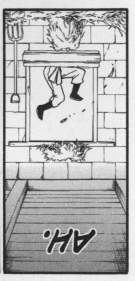

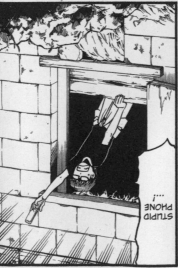

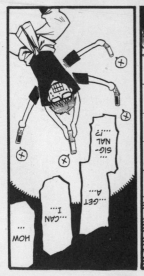

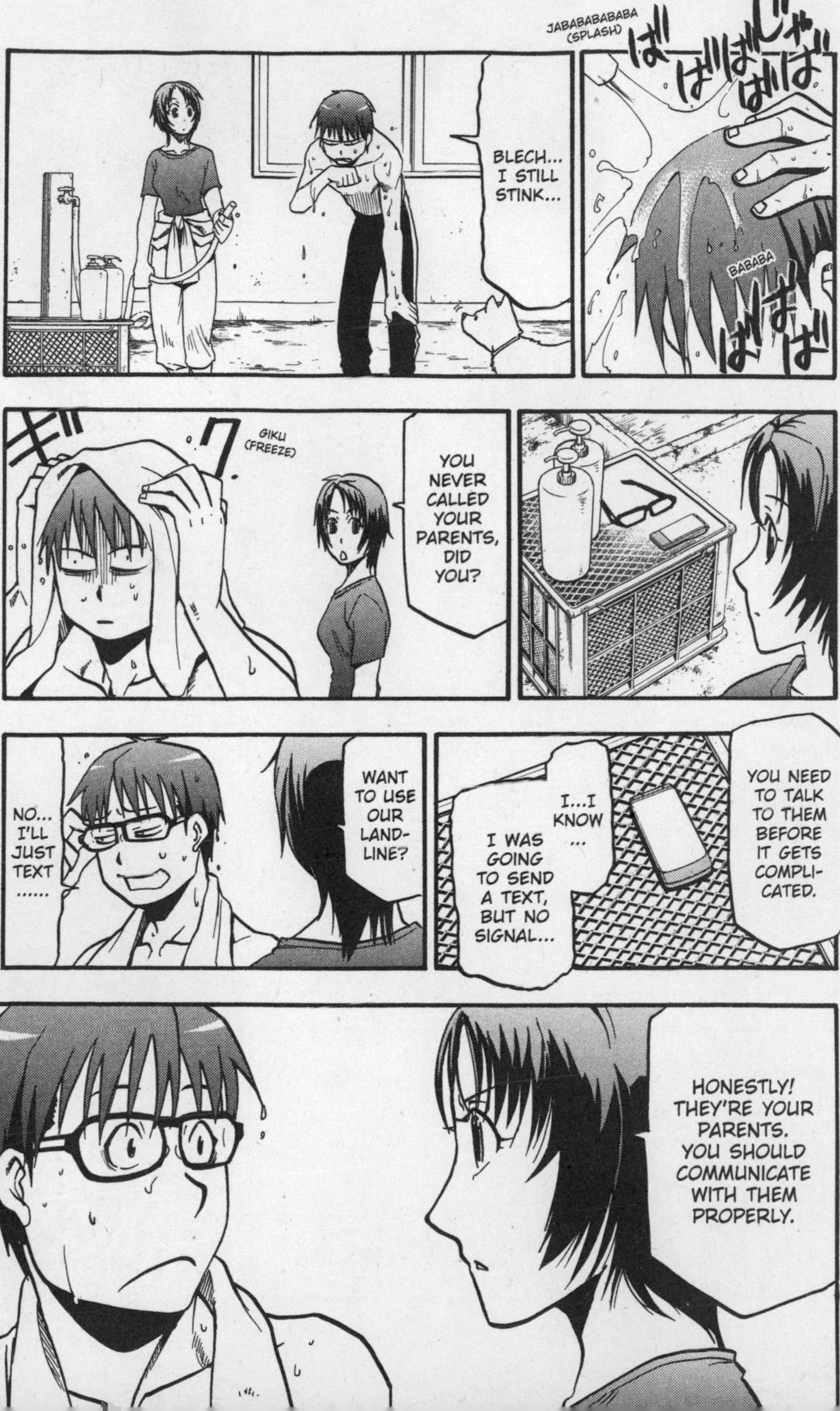
JABABABABABA (SPLASH)
BABABA
BLECH... I STILL STINK...
GIKU (FREEZE)
YOU NEVER CALLED YOUR PARENTS, DID YOU?
YOU NEED TO TALK TO THEM BEFORE IT GETS COMPLI-CATED.
I...I KNOW ...
I WAS GOING TO SEND A TEXT, BUT NO SIGNAL...
WANT TO USE OUR LAND-LINE?
NO... I'LL JUST TEXT ......
HONESTLY! THEY'RE YOUR PARENTS. YOU SHOULD COMMUNICATE WITH THEM PROPERLY.

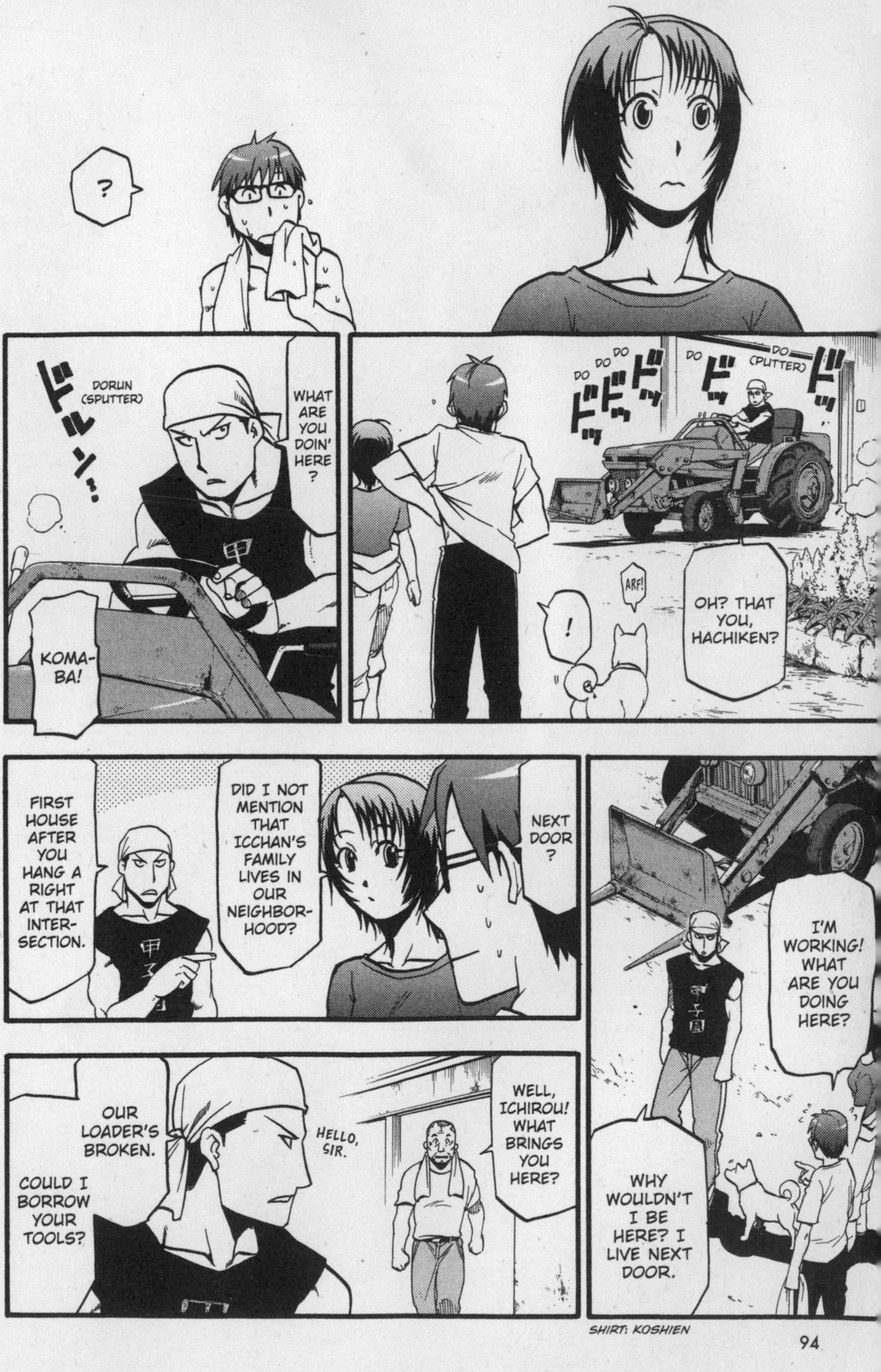
?
DO DO DO DO
(PUTTER)
OH? THAT YOU, HACHIKEN?
ARF!
!
WHAT ARE YOU DOIN' HERE?
DORUN (SPUTTER)
KOMA-BA!
I'M WORKING! WHAT ARE YOU DOING HERE?
WHY WOULDN'T I BE HERE? I LIVE NEXT DOOR.
NEXT DOOR?
DID I NOT MENTION THAT ICCHAN'S FAMILY LIVES IN OUR NEIGHBOR-HOOD?
FIRST HOUSE AFTER YOU HANG A RIGHT AT THAT INTER-SECTION.
WELL, ICHIROU! WHAT BRINGS YOU HERE?
HELLO, SIR.
OUR LOADER'S BROKEN.
COULD I BORROW YOUR TOOLS?

SHIRT: KOSHIEN

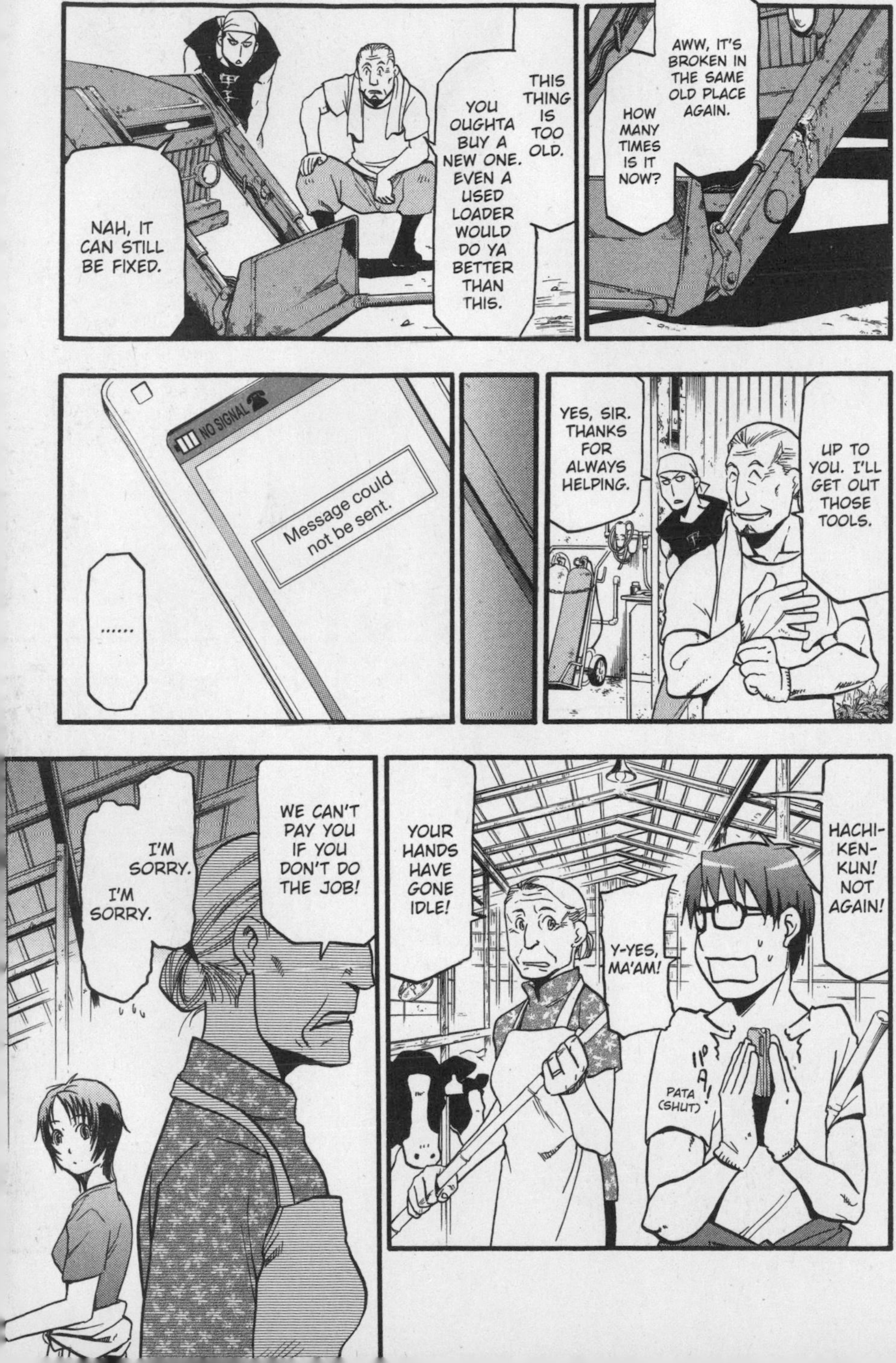
AWW, IT'S BROKEN IN THE SAME OLD PLACE AGAIN.
HOW MANY TIMES IS IT NOW?
THIS THING IS TOO OLD.
YOU OUGHTA BUY A NEW ONE. EVEN A USED LOADER WOULD DO YA BETTER THAN THIS.
NAH, IT CAN STILL BE FIXED.
UP TO YOU. I'LL GET OUT THOSE TOOLS.
YES, SIR. THANKS FOR ALWAYS HELPING.
NO SIGNAL
Message could not be sent.
......
HACHI-KEN-KUN! NOT AGAIN!
Y-YES, MA'AM!
PATA (SHUT)
YOUR HANDS HAVE GONE IDLE!
WE CAN'T PAY YOU IF YOU DON'T DO THE JOB!
I'M SORRY.
I'M SORRY.

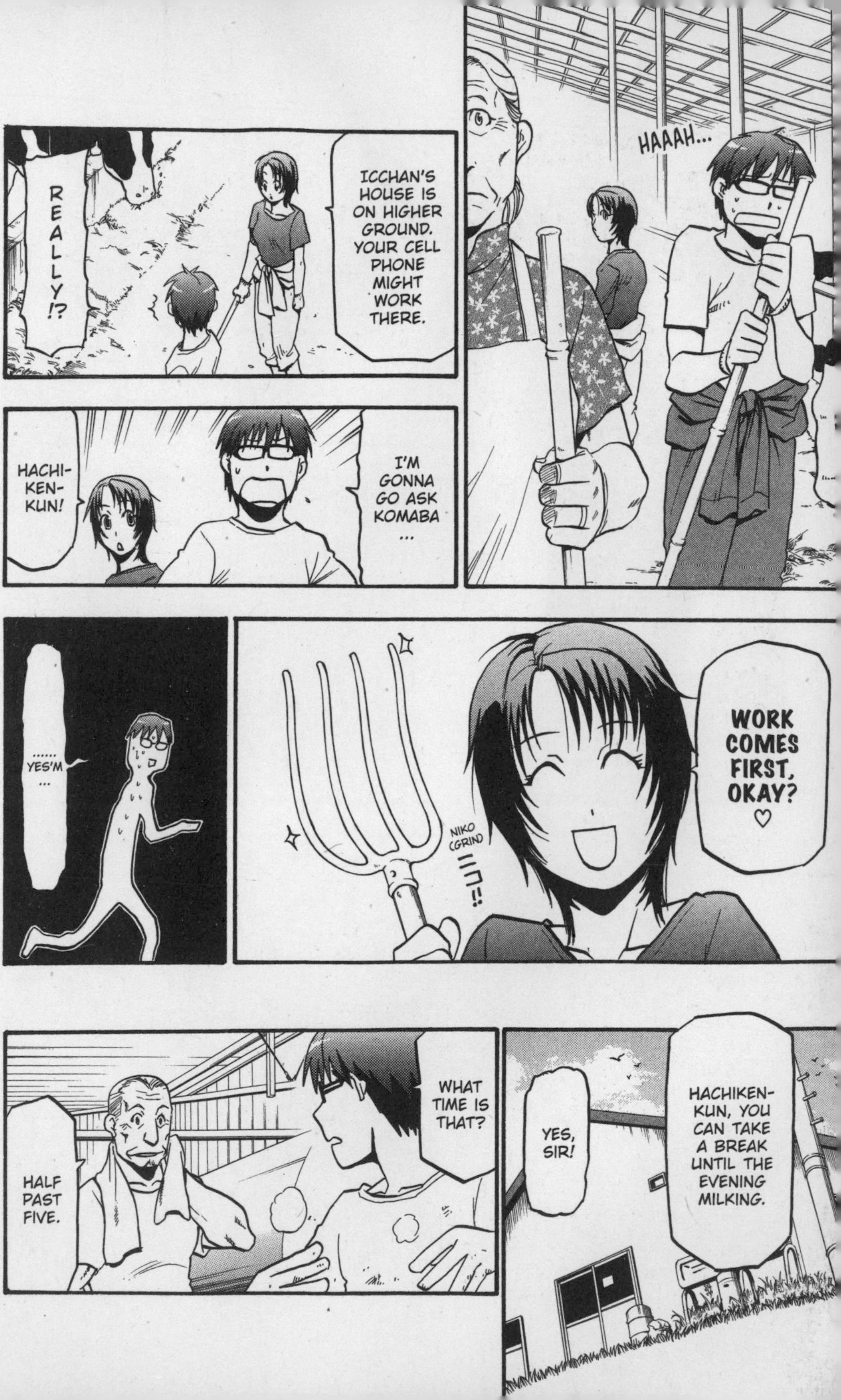
HAAAH...
ICCHAN'S HOUSE IS ON HIGHER GROUND. YOUR CELL PHONE MIGHT WORK THERE.
REALLY!?
I'M GONNA GO ASK KOMABA ...
HACHI-KEN-KUN!
WORK COMES FIRST, OKAY? ♡
NIKO (GRIN)
ニコ!!
...... YES'M ...
HACHIKEN-KUN, YOU CAN TAKE A BREAK UNTIL THE EVENING MILKING.
YES, SIR!
WHAT TIME IS THAT?
HALF PAST FIVE.

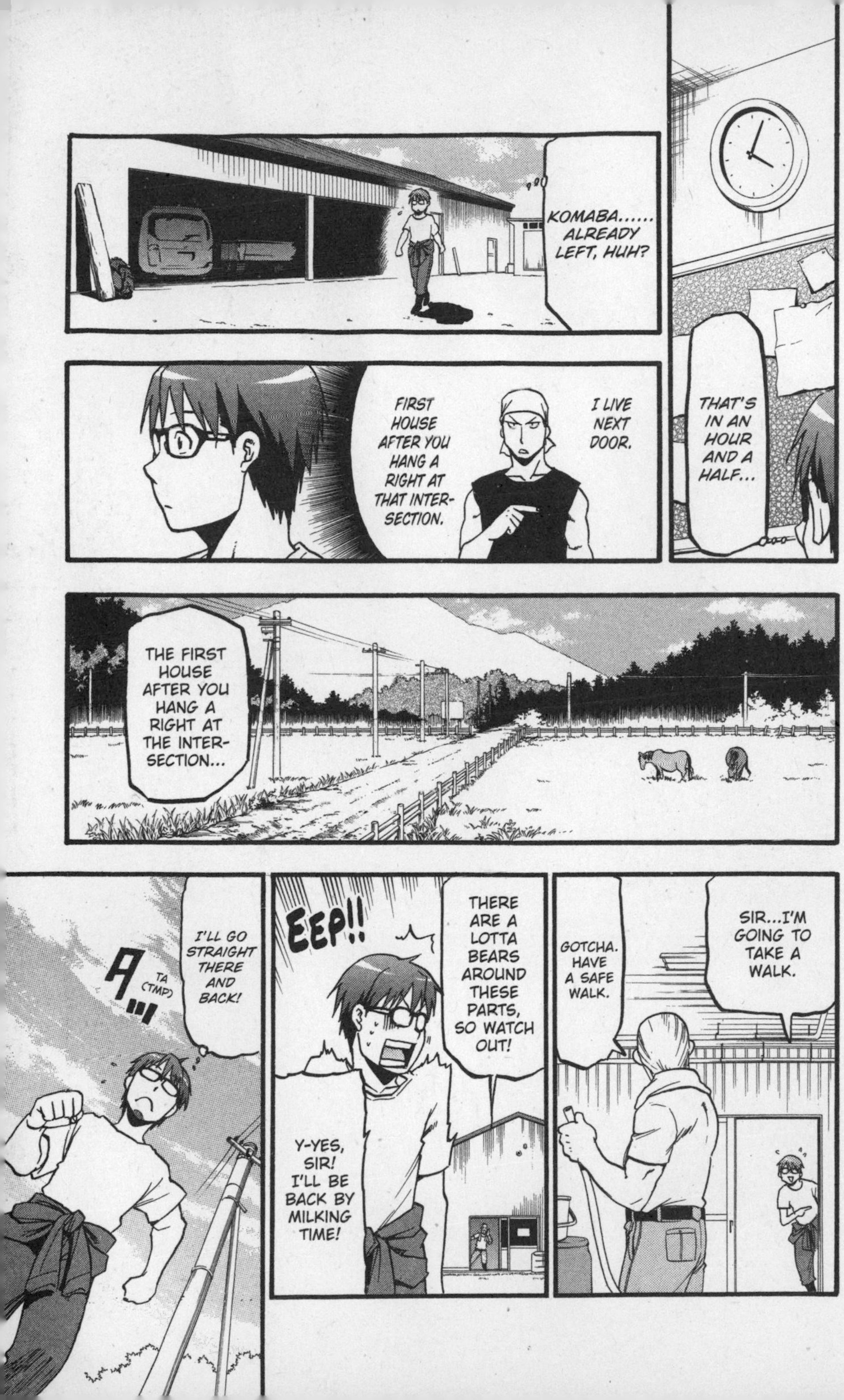
KOMABA...... ALREADY LEFT, HUH?
THAT'S IN AN HOUR AND A HALF...
I LIVE NEXT DOOR.
FIRST HOUSE AFTER YOU HANG A RIGHT AT THAT INTER-SECTION.
THE FIRST HOUSE AFTER YOU HANG A RIGHT AT THE INTER-SECTION...
SIR...I'M GOING TO TAKE A WALK.
GOTCHA. HAVE A SAFE WALK.
THERE ARE A LOTTA BEARS AROUND THESE PARTS, SO WATCH OUT!
EEP!!
Y-YES, SIR! I'LL BE BACK BY MILKING TIME!
I'LL GO STRAIGHT THERE AND BACK!
TA (TMP)

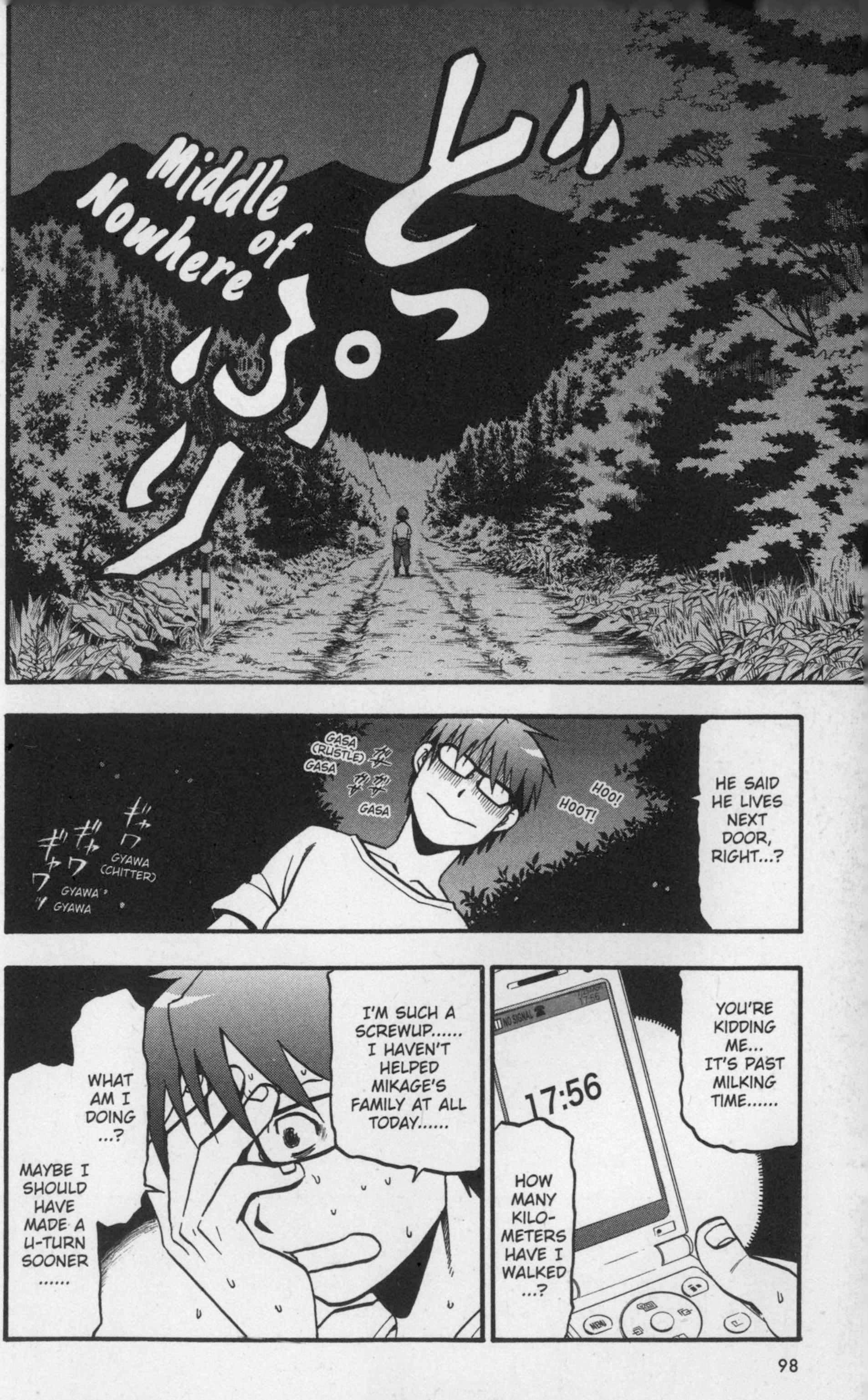
Middle of Nowhere
HE SAID HE LIVES NEXT DOOR, RIGHT...?
HOO! HOOT!
GASA (RUSTLE) GASA GASA
GYAWA (CHITTER) GYAWA GYAWA
YOU'RE KIDDING ME... IT'S PAST MILKING TIME......
NO SIGNAL
17:56
HOW MANY KILO-METERS HAVE I WALKED ...?
I'M SUCH A SCREWUP...... I HAVEN'T HELPED MIKAGE'S FAMILY AT ALL TODAY......
WHAT AM I DOING ...?
MAYBE I SHOULD HAVE MADE A U-TURN SOONER ......

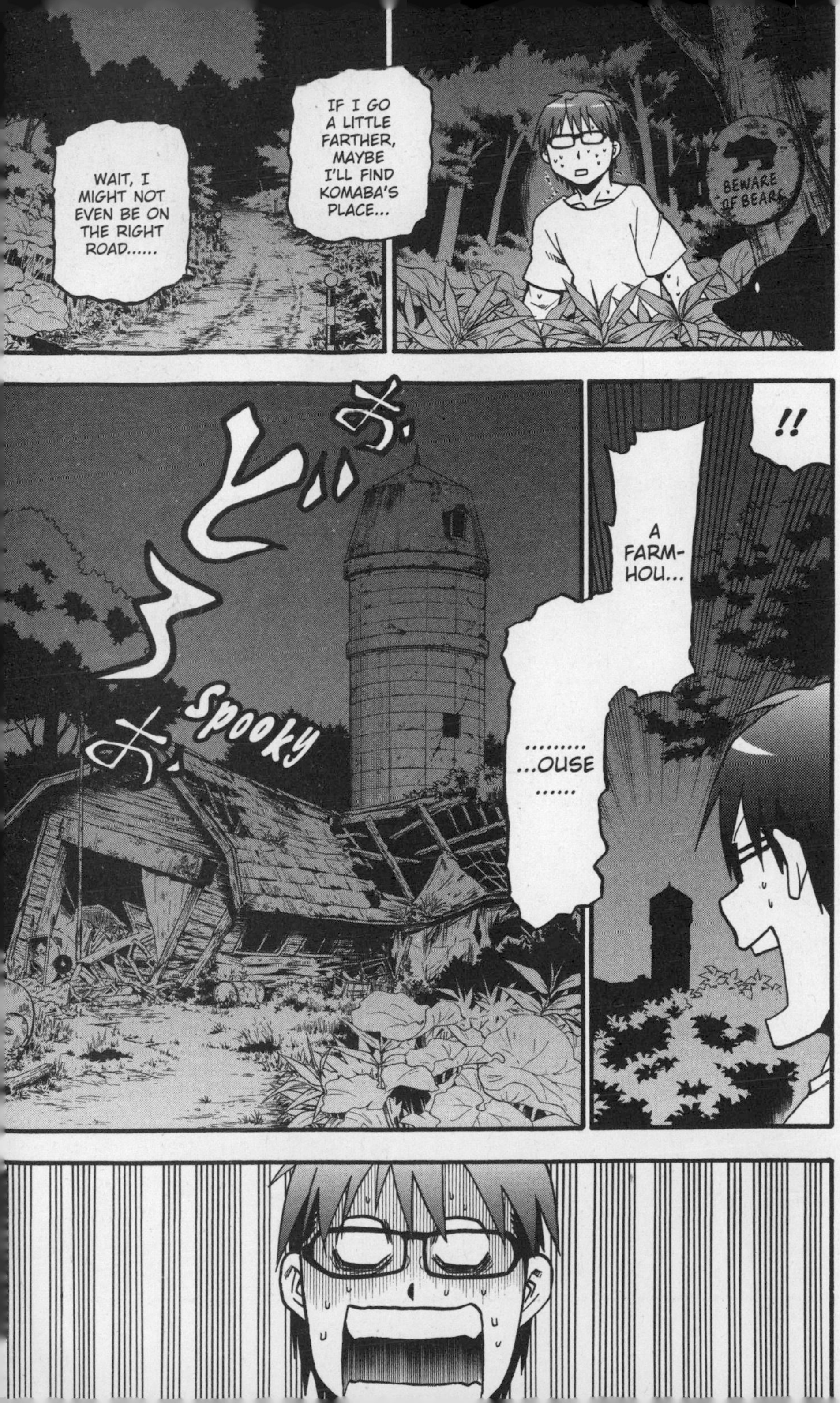
BEWARE OF BEARS
IF I GO A LITTLE FARTHER, MAYBE I'LL FIND KOMABA'S PLACE...
WAIT, I MIGHT NOT EVEN BE ON THE RIGHT ROAD......
!!
A FARM-HOU...
....
...OUSE
......
spooky

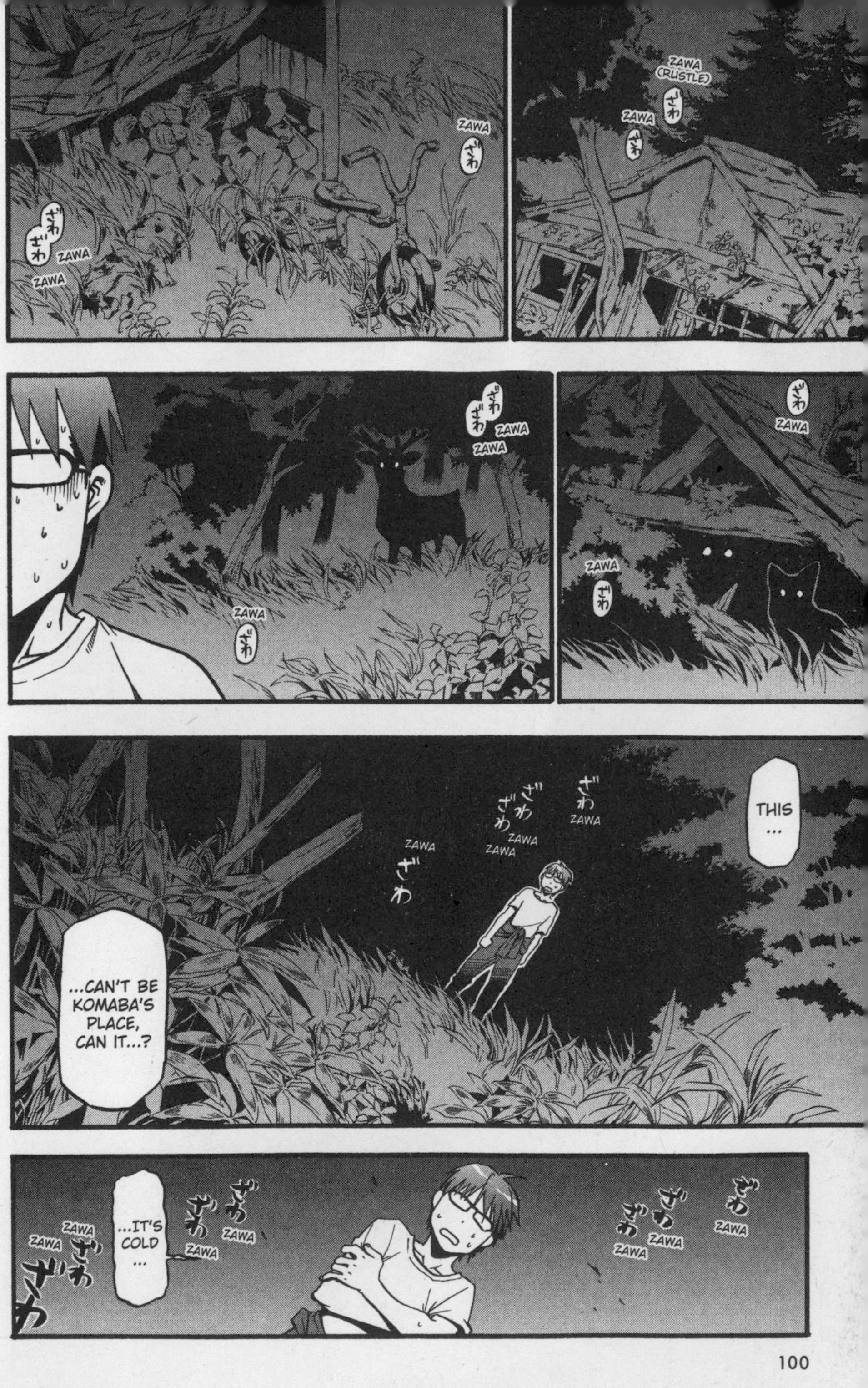
ざわ
ZAWA (RUSTLE)
ざわ
ZAWA
ざわ
ZAWA
ざわ ざわ
ZAWA ZAWA
ざわ
ZAWA
ざわ
ZAWA
ざわ ざわ
ZAWA ZAWA
ざわ
ZAWA
THIS ...
ざわ ざわ ざわ
ZAWA ZAWA ZAWA
ざわ
ZAWA
...CAN'T BE KOMABA'S PLACE, CAN IT...?
ざわ ざわ ざわ
ZAWA ZAWA ZAWA
...IT'S COLD ...
ざわ ざわ
ZAWA ZAWA
ざわ ざわ
ZAWA ZAWA

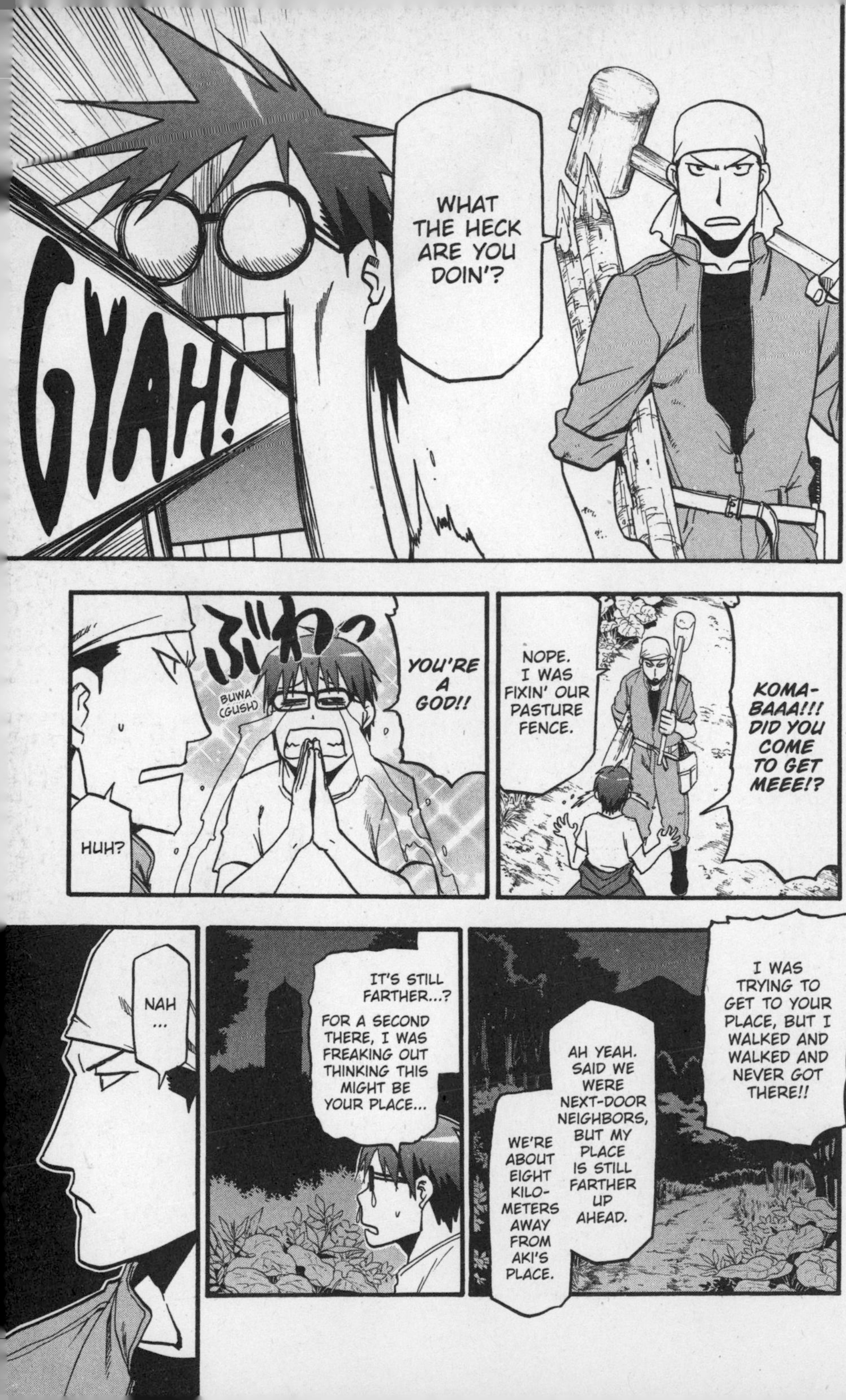
WHAT THE HECK ARE YOU DOIN'?
GYAH!
KOMA-BAAA!!! DID YOU COME TO GET MEEE!?
NOPE. I WAS FIXIN' OUR PASTURE FENCE.
YOU'RE A GOD!!
ぶわっ
BUWA (GUSH)
HUH?
I WAS TRYING TO GET TO YOUR PLACE, BUT I WALKED AND WALKED AND NEVER GOT THERE!!
AH YEAH. SAID WE WERE NEXT-DOOR NEIGHBORS, BUT MY PLACE IS STILL FARTHER UP AHEAD.
WE'RE ABOUT EIGHT KILO-METERS AWAY FROM AKI'S PLACE.
IT'S STILL FARTHER...?
FOR A SECOND THERE, I WAS FREAKING OUT THINKING THIS MIGHT BE YOUR PLACE...
NAH ...

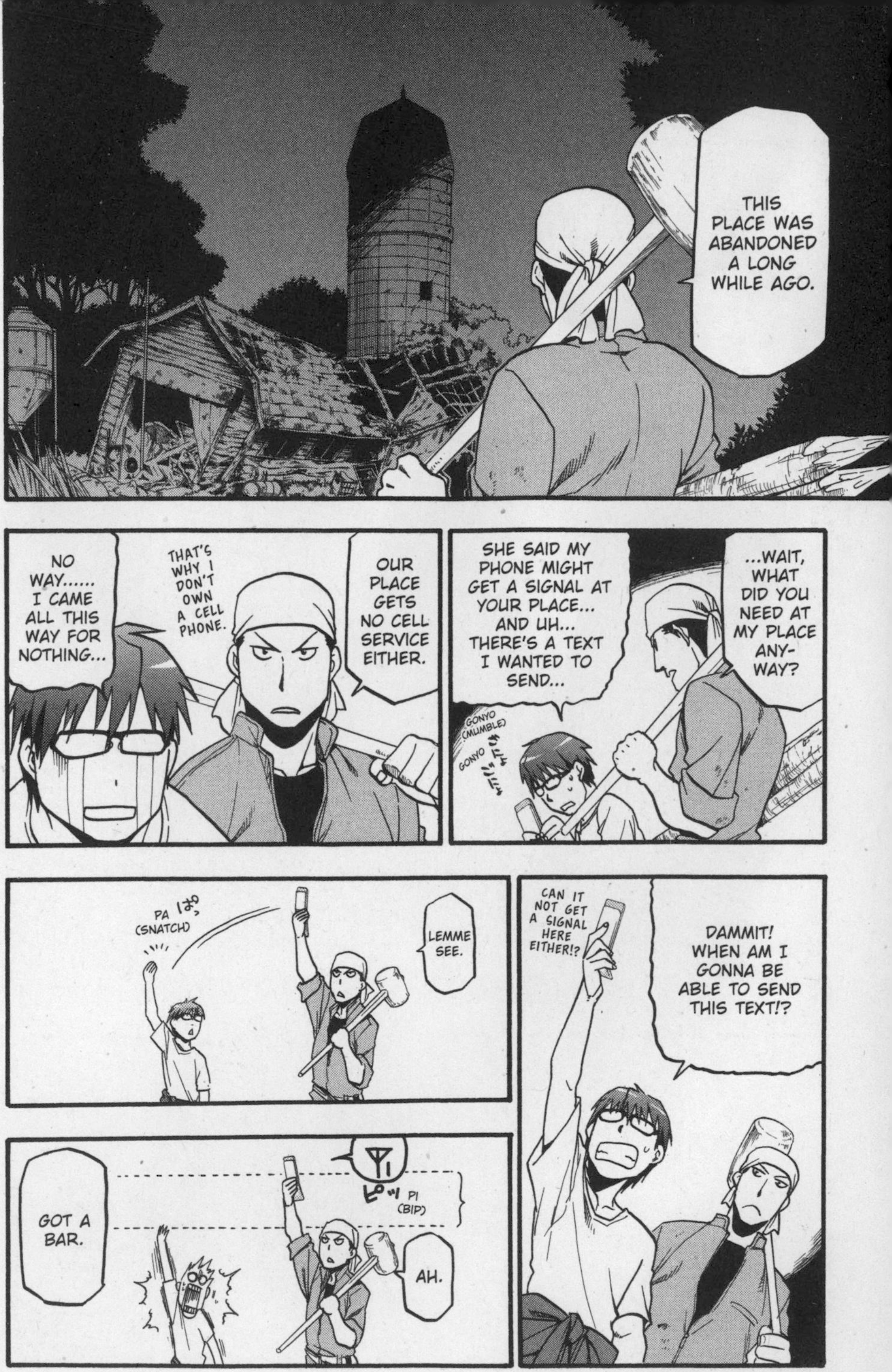
THIS PLACE WAS ABANDONED A LONG WHILE AGO.
...WAIT, WHAT DID YOU NEED AT MY PLACE ANY-WAY?
SHE SAID MY PHONE MIGHT GET A SIGNAL AT YOUR PLACE... AND UH... THERE'S A TEXT I WANTED TO SEND...
GONYO GONYO (MUMBLE)
OUR PLACE GETS NO CELL SERVICE EITHER.
THAT'S WHY I DON'T OWN A CELL PHONE.
NO WAY...... I CAME ALL THIS WAY FOR NOTHING...
DAMMIT! WHEN AM I GONNA BE ABLE TO SEND THIS TEXT!?
CAN IT NOT GET A SIGNAL HERE EITHER!?
LEMME SEE.
ぱっ PA (SNATCH)
AH.
ピッ PI (BIP)
GOT A BAR.

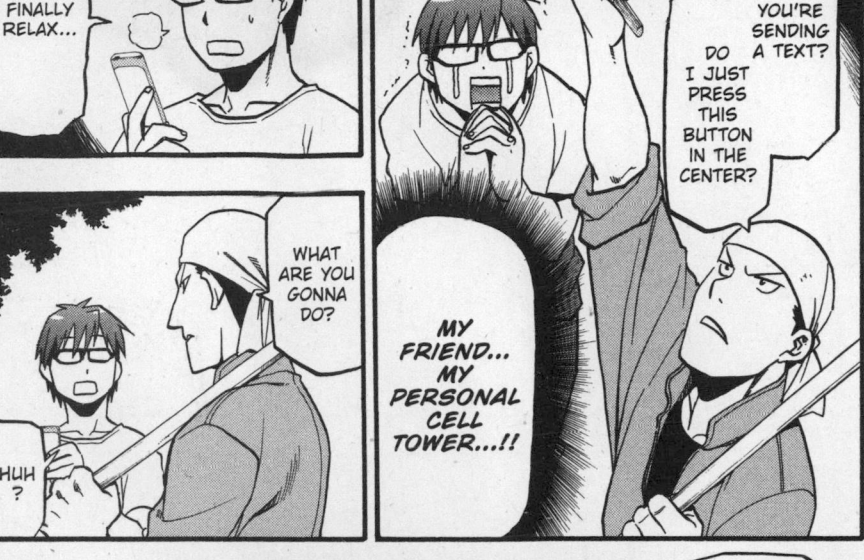

YOU'RE SENDING A TEXT?
DO I JUST PRESS THIS BUTTON IN THE CENTER?
ピッ
PI
OHHH...
MY FRIEND... MY PERSONAL CELL TOWER...!!
...NOW I CAN FINALLY RELAX...
AND BACK TO NO SIGNAL.
WHEW...
WHAT ARE YOU GONNA DO?
HUH?
EVEN IF YOU HEAD BACK, IT'S GONNA GET PITCH-DARK REAL SOON.
AH... CRAP...... I DIDN'T TELL THEM I WAS GOING TO YOUR PLACE!
EVEN IF I HEAD BACK NOW, I'M GONNA MISS THE REST OF THE DAY'S WORK...
CRAAAP... THEY'RE GONNA BE SO MAD...
YOU THINK THEY'RE GONNA BE MAD ABOUT THE WORK? DUMBASS!

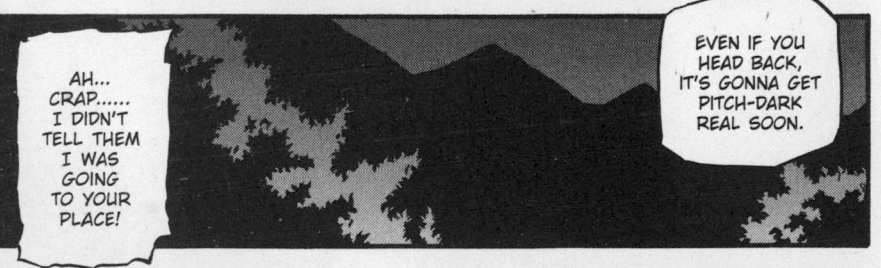

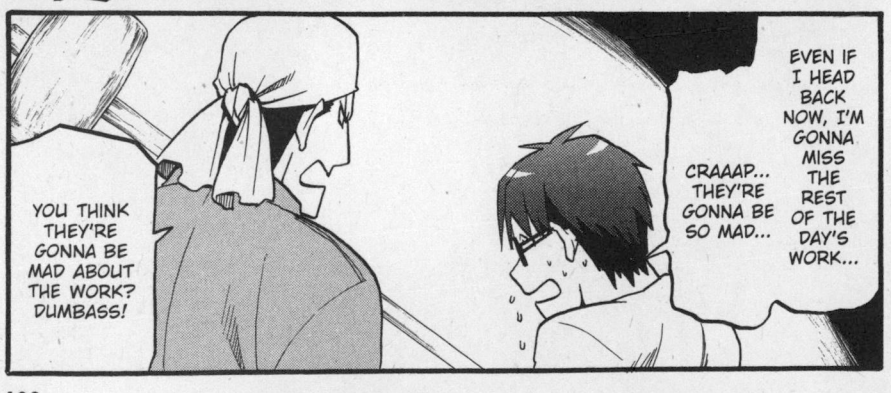

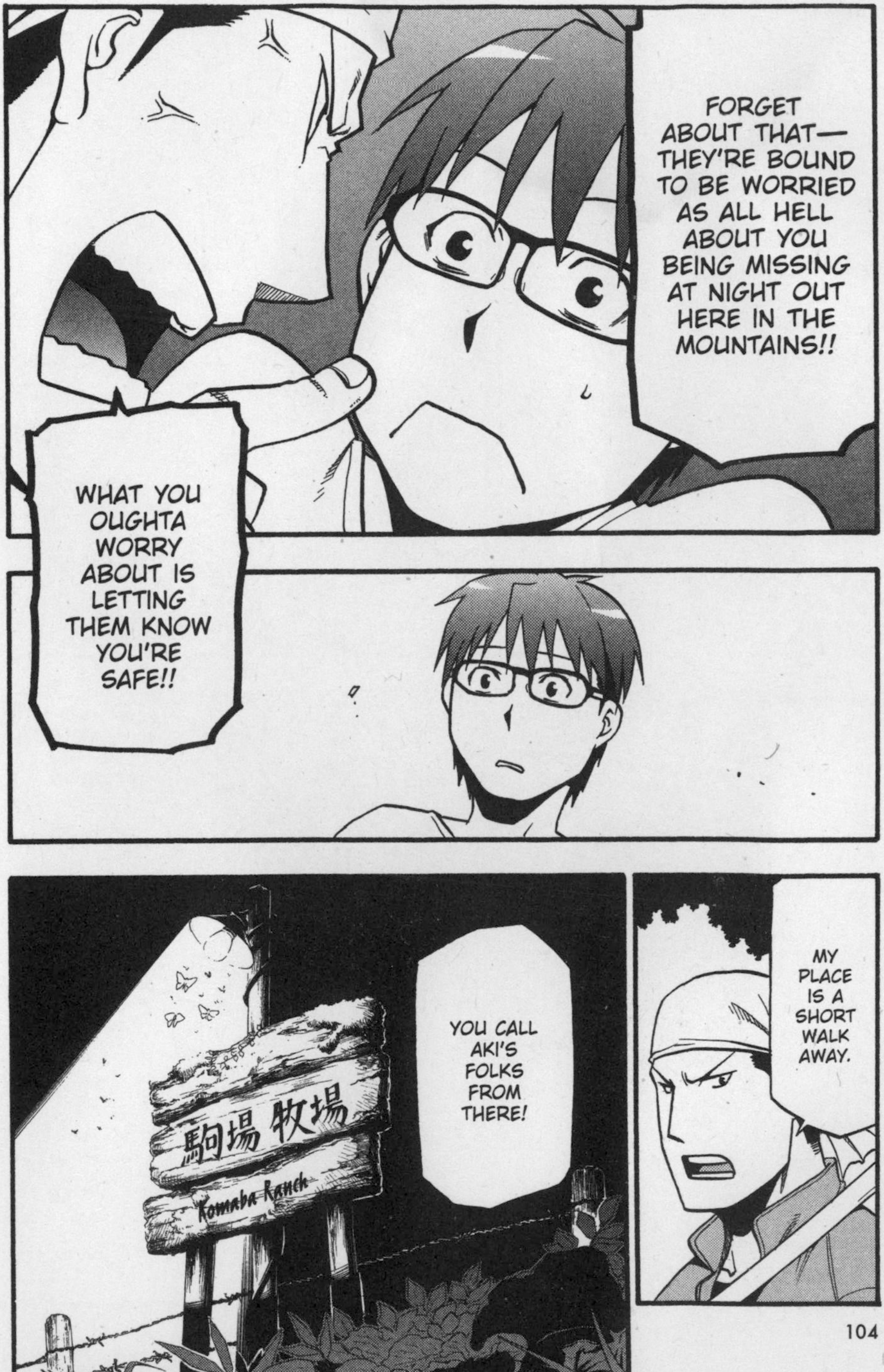
FORGET ABOUT THAT— THEY'RE BOUND TO BE WORRIED AS ALL HELL ABOUT YOU BEING MISSING AT NIGHT OUT HERE IN THE MOUNTAINS!!
WHAT YOU OUGHTA WORRY ABOUT IS LETTING THEM KNOW YOU'RE SAFE!!
MY PLACE IS A SHORT WALK AWAY.
YOU CALL AKI'S FOLKS FROM THERE!
駒場 牧場
Komaba Ranch

Silver Spoon

KAITO MEGURO

CAPE ERIMO
MIDDLE SCHOOL

RUGBY TEAM

CRAB IS
HIS SNACK OF
CHOICE.

Chapter 14:
Tale of Summer ④

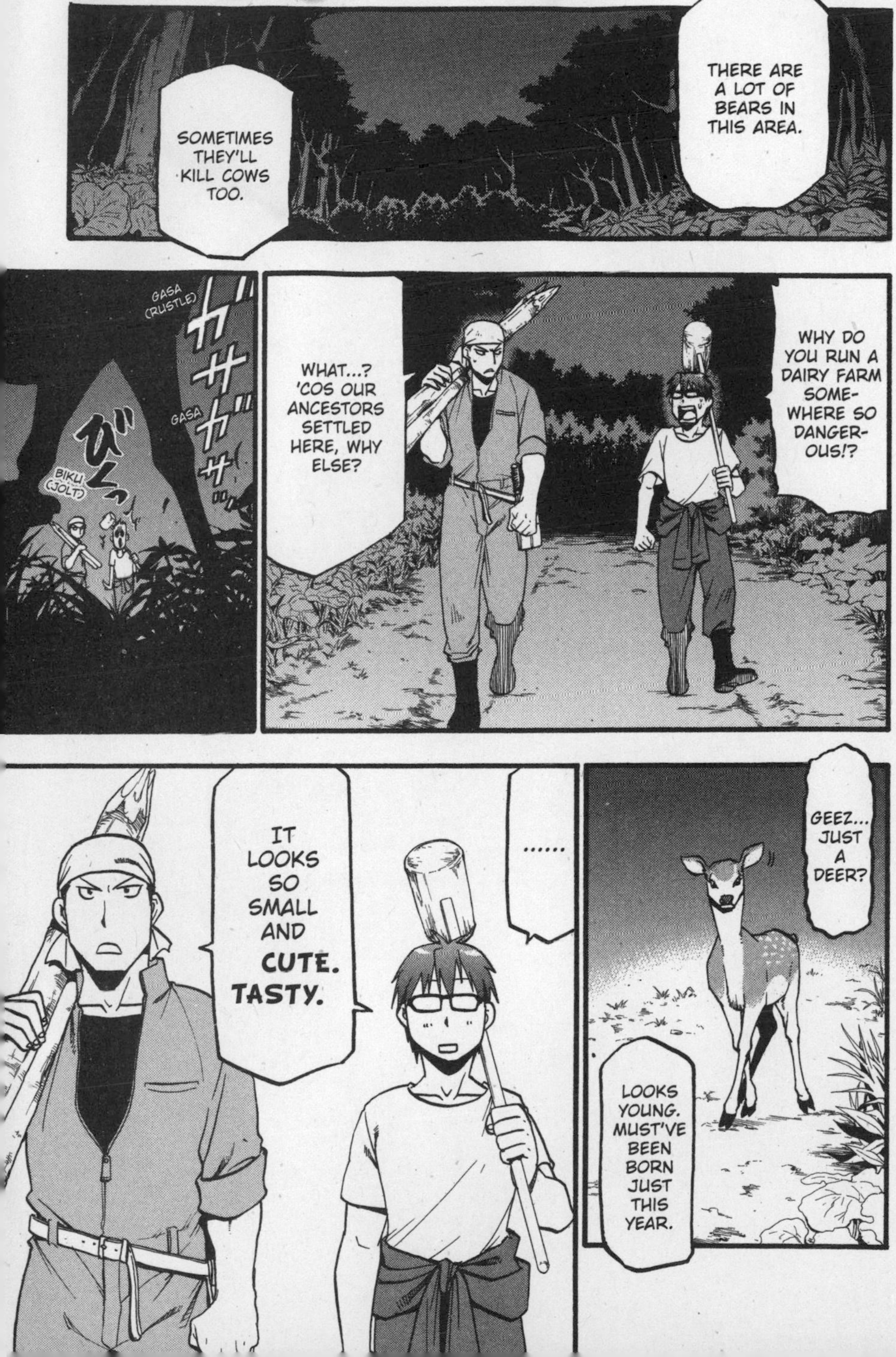
THERE ARE A LOT OF BEARS IN THIS AREA.
SOMETIMES THEY'LL KILL COWS TOO.
WHY DO YOU RUN A DAIRY FARM SOME-WHERE SO DANGER-OUS!?
WHAT...? 'COS OUR ANCESTORS SETTLED HERE, WHY ELSE?
GASA (RUSTLE)
GASA
BIKU (JOLT)
GEEZ... JUST A DEER?
LOOKS YOUNG. MUST'VE BEEN BORN JUST THIS YEAR.
......
IT LOOKS SO SMALL AND CUTE. TASTY.

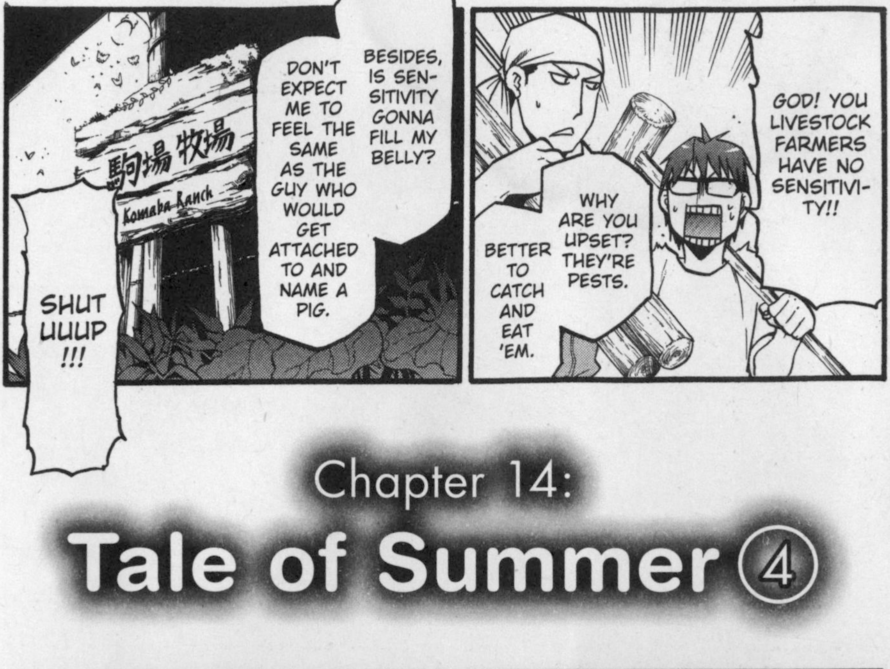
GOD! YOU LIVESTOCK FARMERS HAVE NO SENSITIVITY!!
WHY ARE YOU UPSET? THEY'RE PESTS.
BETTER TO CATCH AND EAT 'EM.
BESIDES, IS SENSITIVITY GONNA FILL MY BELLY?
DON'T EXPECT ME TO FEEL THE SAME AS THE GUY WHO WOULD GET ATTACHED TO AND NAME A PIG.
駒場牧場
Komaba Ranch
SHUT UUUP!!!

Chapter 14:
Tale of Summer ④

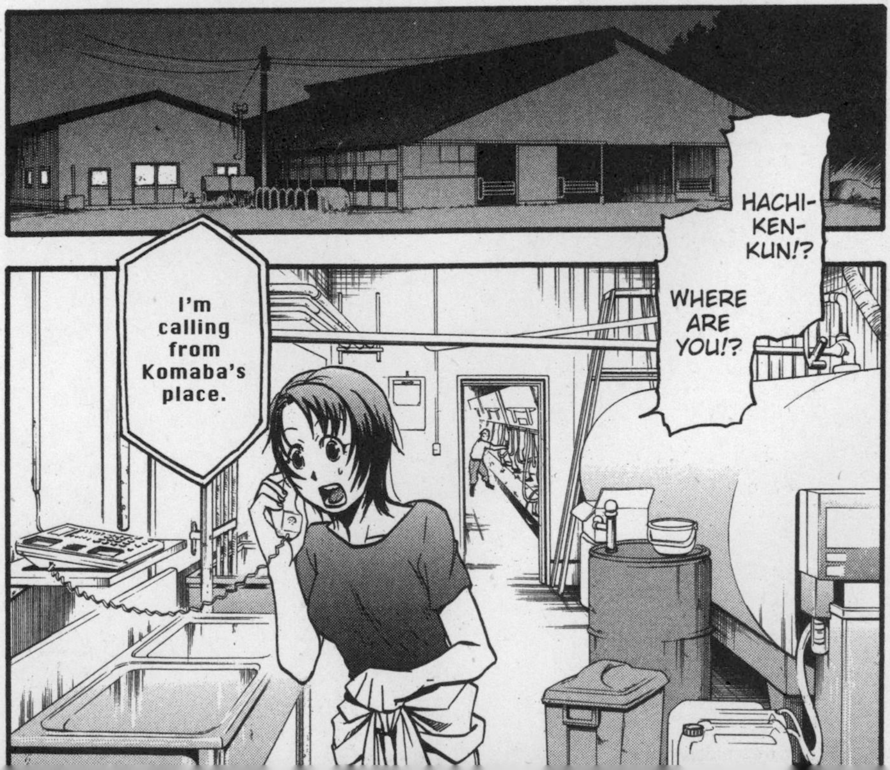
HACHI-KEN-KUN!?
WHERE ARE YOU!?
I'm calling from Komaba's place.

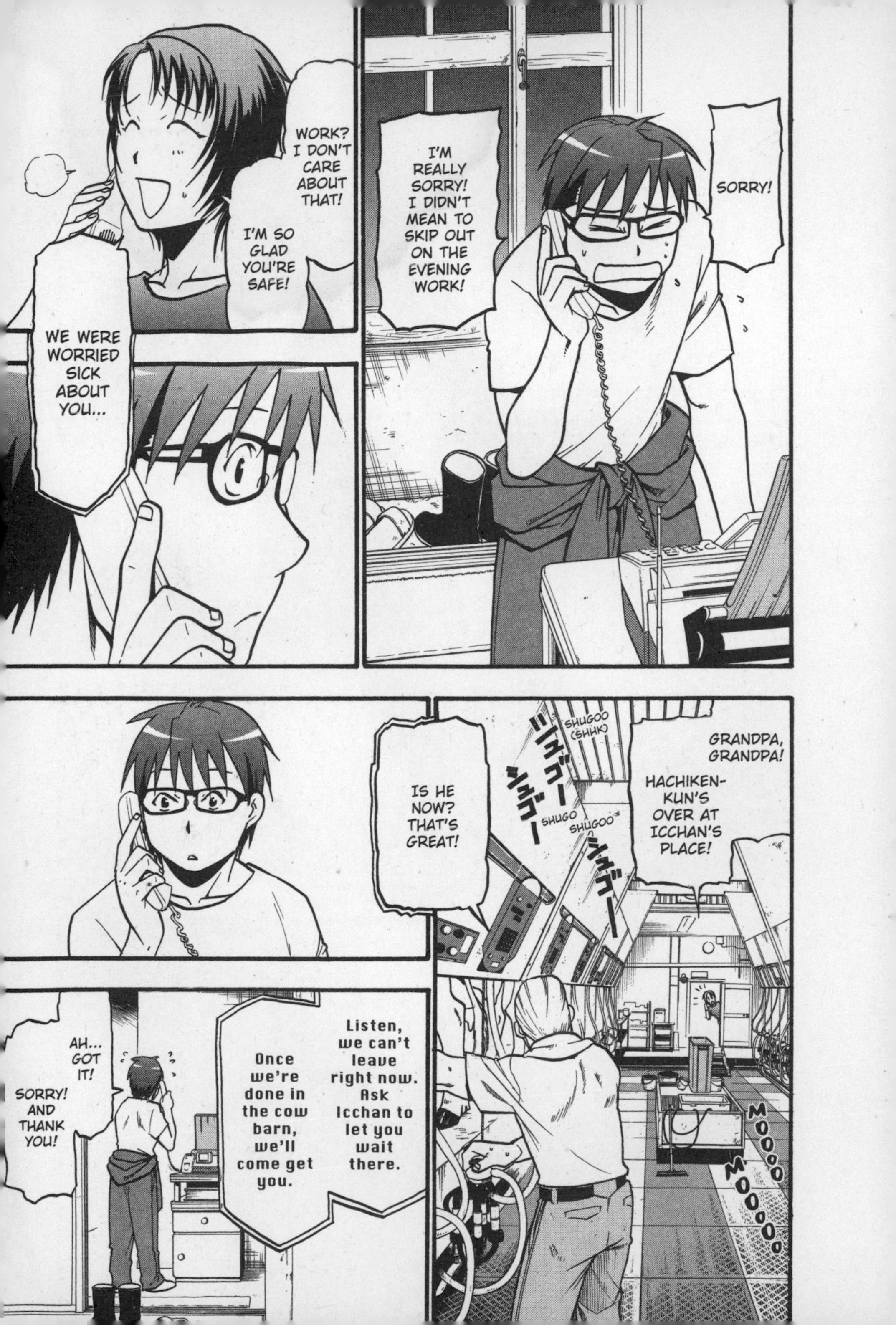
SORRY!
I'M REALLY SORRY! I DIDN'T MEAN TO SKIP OUT ON THE EVENING WORK!
WORK? I DON'T CARE ABOUT THAT!
I'M SO GLAD YOU'RE SAFE!
WE WERE WORRIED SICK ABOUT YOU...
GRANDPA, GRANDPA!
HACHIKEN-KUN'S OVER AT ICCHAN'S PLACE!
SHUGOO (SHHK)
SHUGO
SHUGOO
IS HE NOW? THAT'S GREAT!
MOOOO MOOOOO
Listen, we can't leave right now. Ask Icchan to let you wait there.
Once we're done in the cow barn, we'll come get you.
AH... GOT IT!
SORRY! AND THANK YOU!

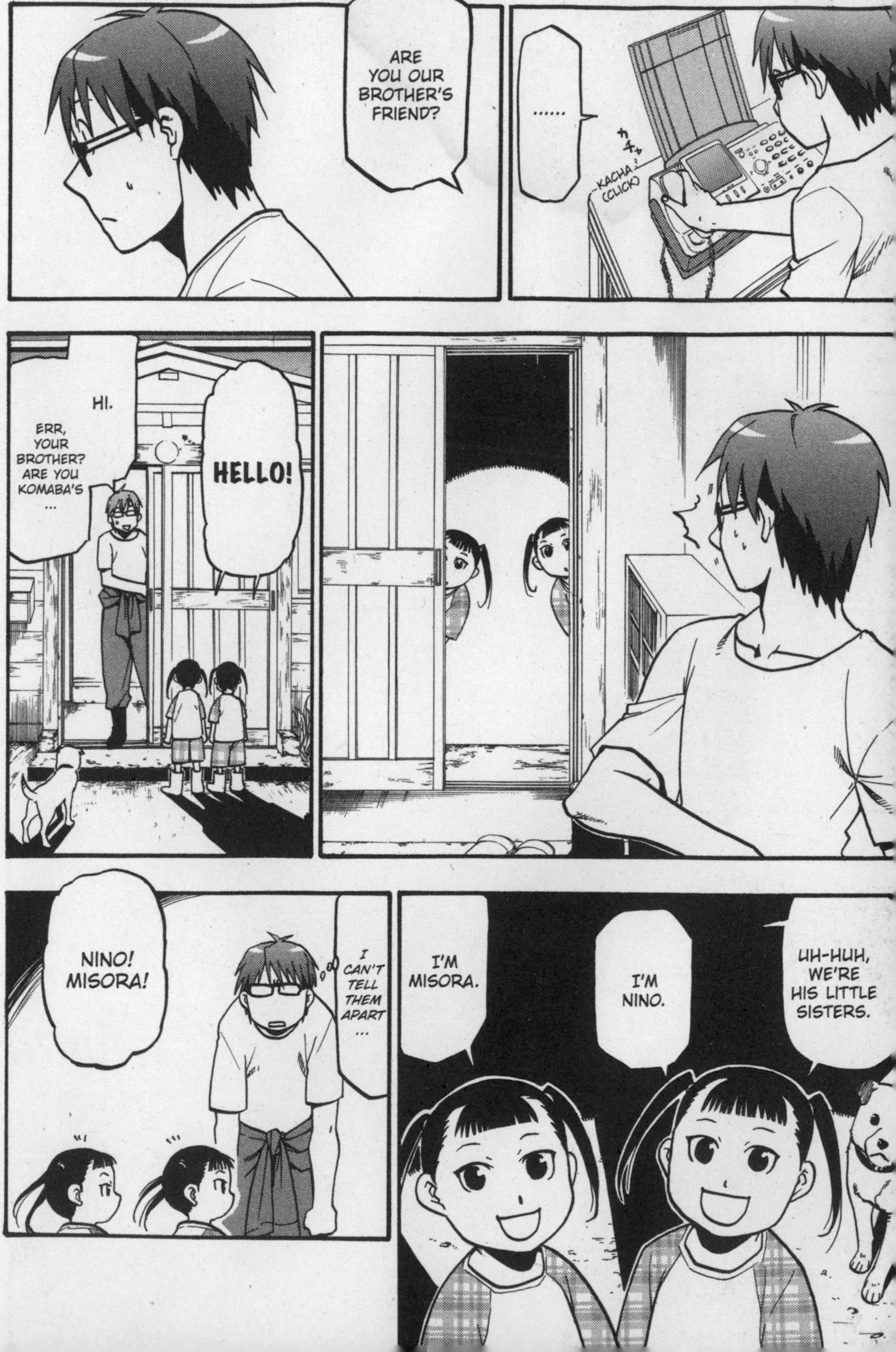

カチャ
KACHA (CLICK)
......
ARE YOU OUR BROTHER'S FRIEND?
HELLO!
HI.
ERR, YOUR BROTHER? ARE YOU KOMABA'S ...
UH-HUH, WE'RE HIS LITTLE SISTERS.
I'M NINO.
I'M MISORA.
I CAN'T TELL THEM APART ...
NINO! MISORA!

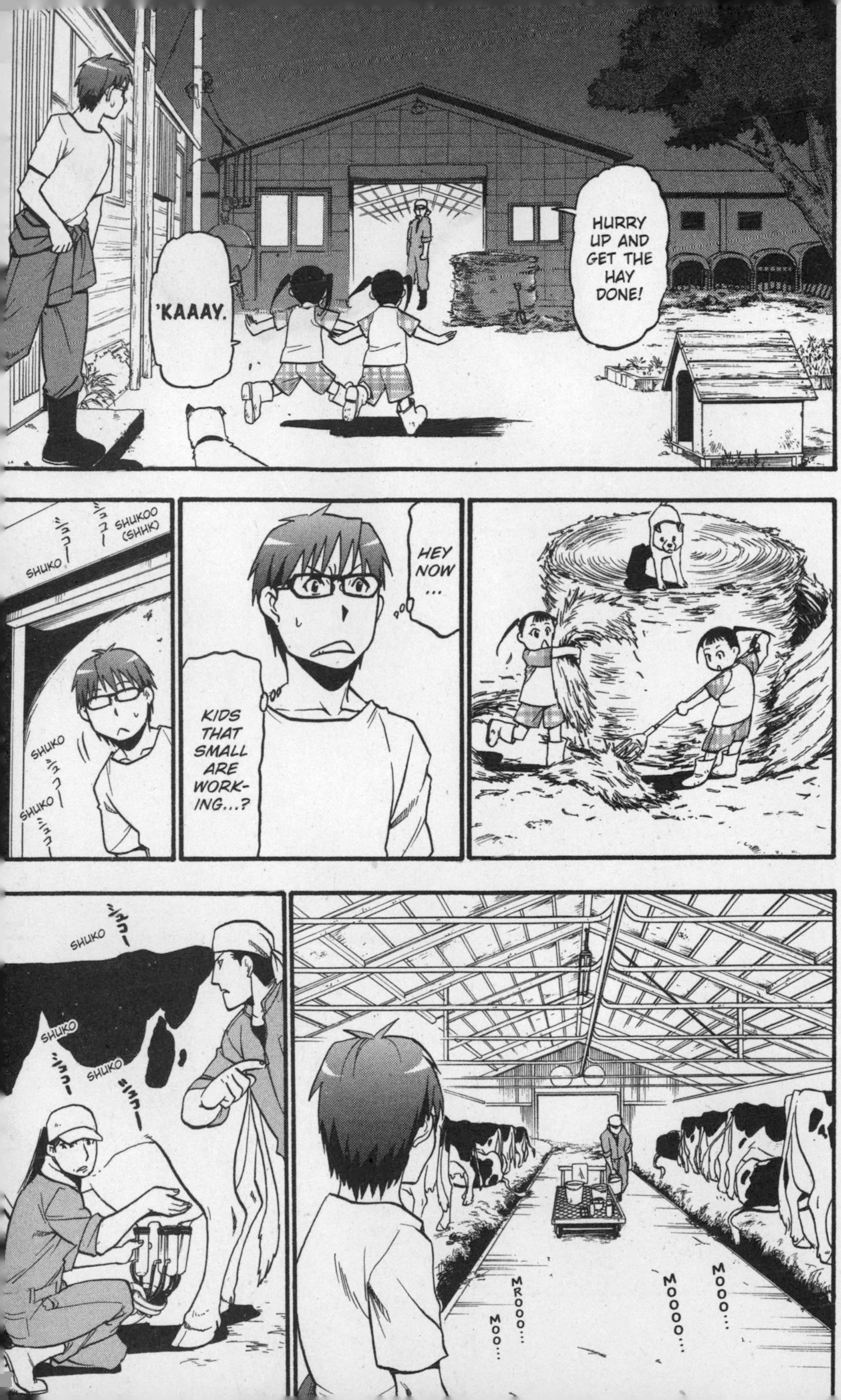
HURRY UP AND GET THE HAY DONE!
'KAAAY.
HEY NOW...
KIDS THAT SMALL ARE WORKING...?
SHUKOO (SHHK)
SHUKO
SHUKO
SHUKO
MOOO...
MOOOO...
MROOOO...
MOO...
SHUKO
SHUKO
SHUKO

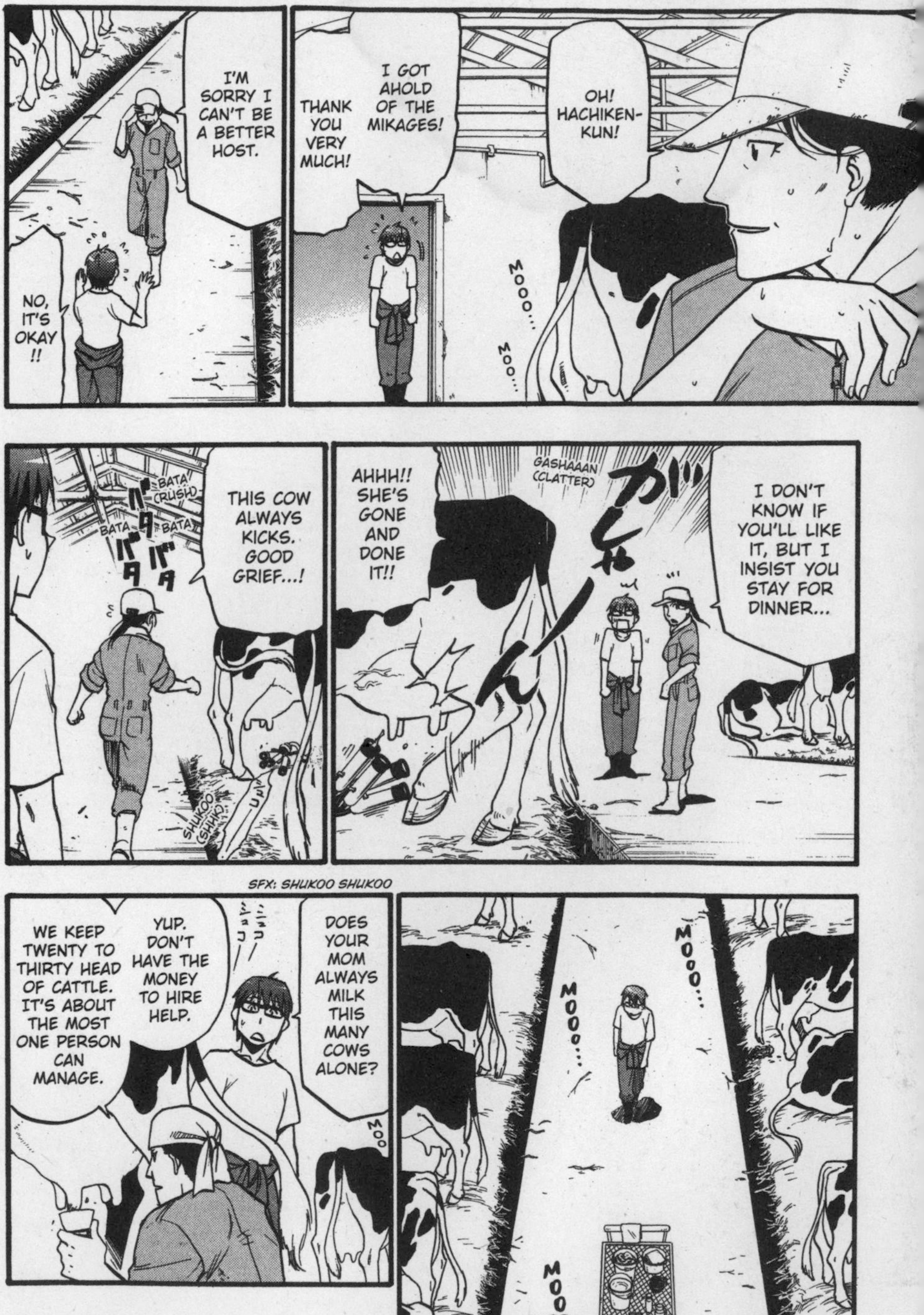
OH! HACHIKEN-KUN!
MOOO...
MOO...
I GOT AHOLD OF THE MIKAGES!
THANK YOU VERY MUCH!
I'M SORRY I CAN'T BE A BETTER HOST.
NO, IT'S OKAY!!
I DON'T KNOW IF YOU'LL LIKE IT, BUT I INSIST YOU STAY FOR DINNER...
GASHAAAN (CLATTER)
AHHH!! SHE'S GONE AND DONE IT!!
THIS COW ALWAYS KICKS. GOOD GRIEF...!
BATA (RUSH)
BATA
BATA
SHUKOO (SHHK)
SFX: SHUKOO SHUKOO
MOOO...
MOOO...
MOOOO...
DOES YOUR MOM ALWAYS MILK THIS MANY COWS ALONE?
YUP. DON'T HAVE THE MONEY TO HIRE HELP.
WE KEEP TWENTY TO THIRTY HEAD OF CATTLE. IT'S ABOUT THE MOST ONE PERSON CAN MANAGE.
MOO

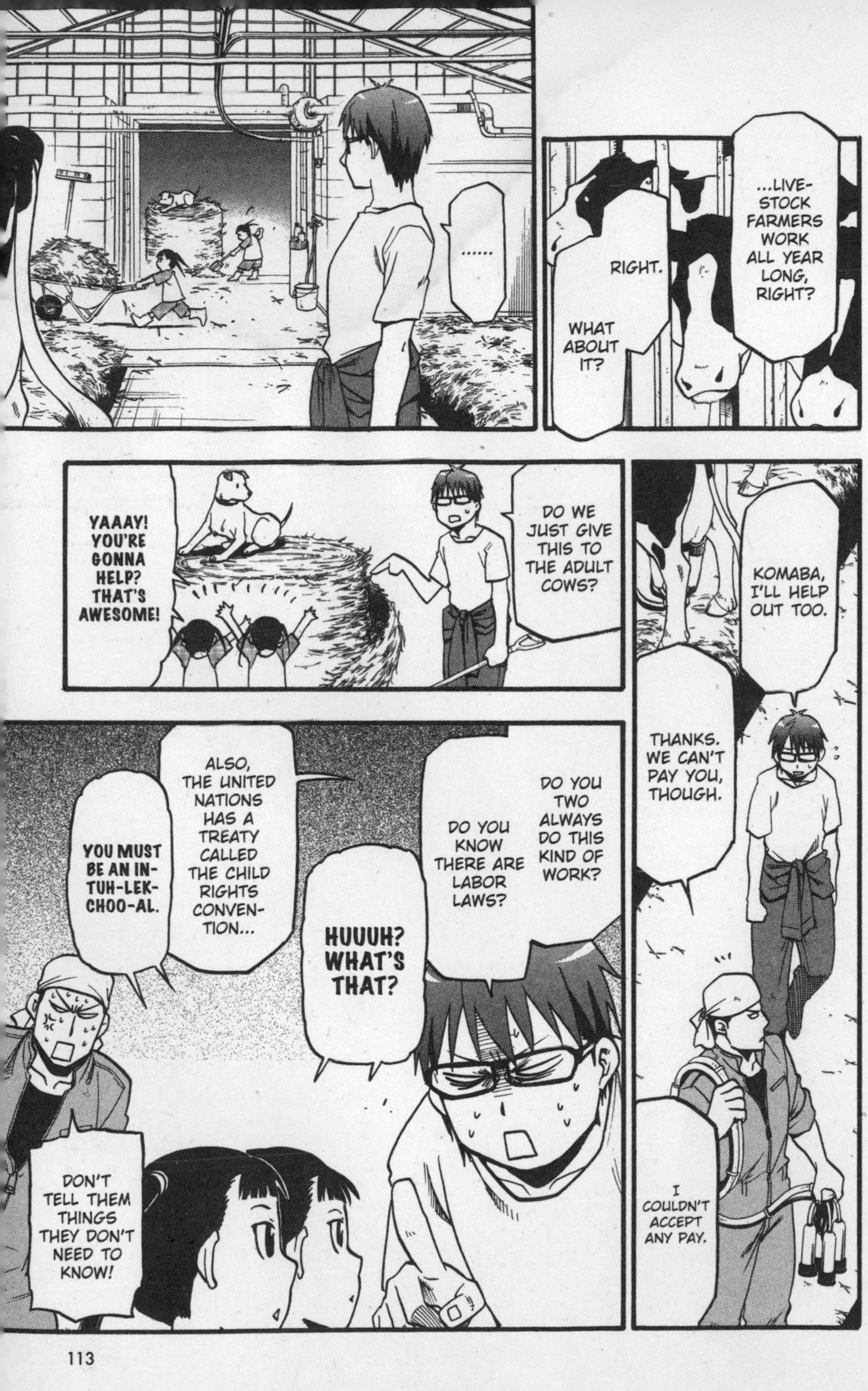

...LIVE-STOCK FARMERS WORK ALL YEAR LONG, RIGHT?
RIGHT.
WHAT ABOUT IT?
......
KOMABA, I'LL HELP OUT TOO.
THANKS. WE CAN'T PAY YOU, THOUGH.
I COULDN'T ACCEPT ANY PAY.
DO WE JUST GIVE THIS TO THE ADULT COWS?
YAAAY! YOU'RE GONNA HELP? THAT'S AWESOME!
DO YOU TWO ALWAYS DO THIS KIND OF WORK?
DO YOU KNOW THERE ARE LABOR LAWS?
HUUUH? WHAT'S THAT?
ALSO, THE UNITED NATIONS HAS A TREATY CALLED THE CHILD RIGHTS CONVEN-TION...
YOU MUST BE AN IN-TUH-LEK-CHOO-AL.
DON'T TELL THEM THINGS THEY DON'T NEED TO KNOW!

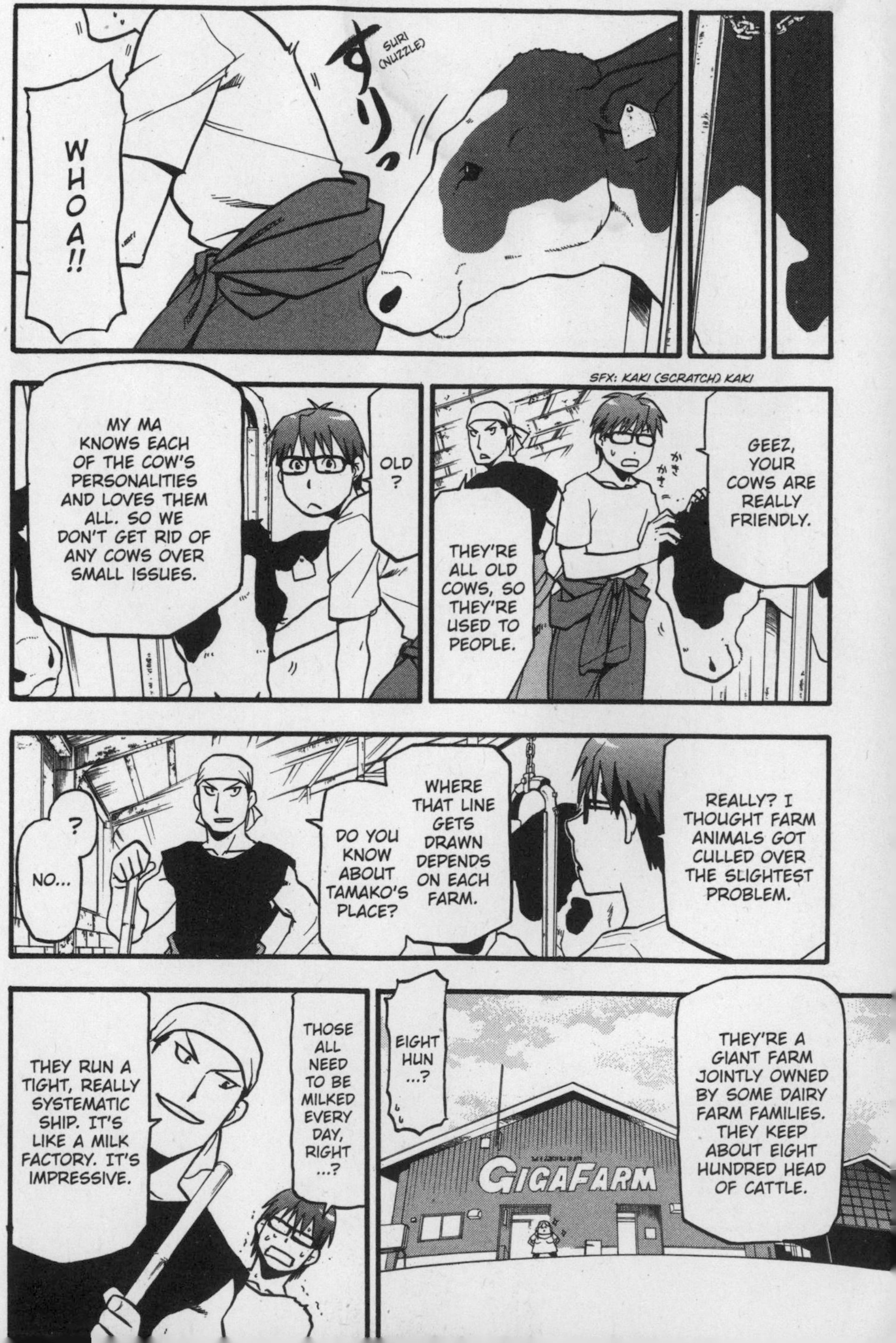
SURI (NUZZLE)
WHOA!!
GEEZ, YOUR COWS ARE REALLY FRIENDLY.
SFX: KAKI (SCRATCH) KAKI
THEY'RE ALL OLD COWS, SO THEY'RE USED TO PEOPLE.
OLD?
MY MA KNOWS EACH OF THE COW'S PERSONALITIES AND LOVES THEM ALL. SO WE DON'T GET RID OF ANY COWS OVER SMALL ISSUES.
REALLY? I THOUGHT FARM ANIMALS GOT CULLED OVER THE SLIGHTEST PROBLEM.
WHERE THAT LINE GETS DRAWN DEPENDS ON EACH FARM.
DO YOU KNOW ABOUT TAMAKO'S PLACE?
?
NO...
THEY'RE A GIANT FARM JOINTLY OWNED BY SOME DAIRY FARM FAMILIES. THEY KEEP ABOUT EIGHT HUNDRED HEAD OF CATTLE.
GIGAFARM
EIGHT HUN...?
THOSE ALL NEED TO BE MILKED EVERY DAY, RIGHT...?
THEY RUN A TIGHT, REALLY SYSTEMATIC SHIP. IT'S LIKE A MILK FACTORY. IT'S IMPRESSIVE.

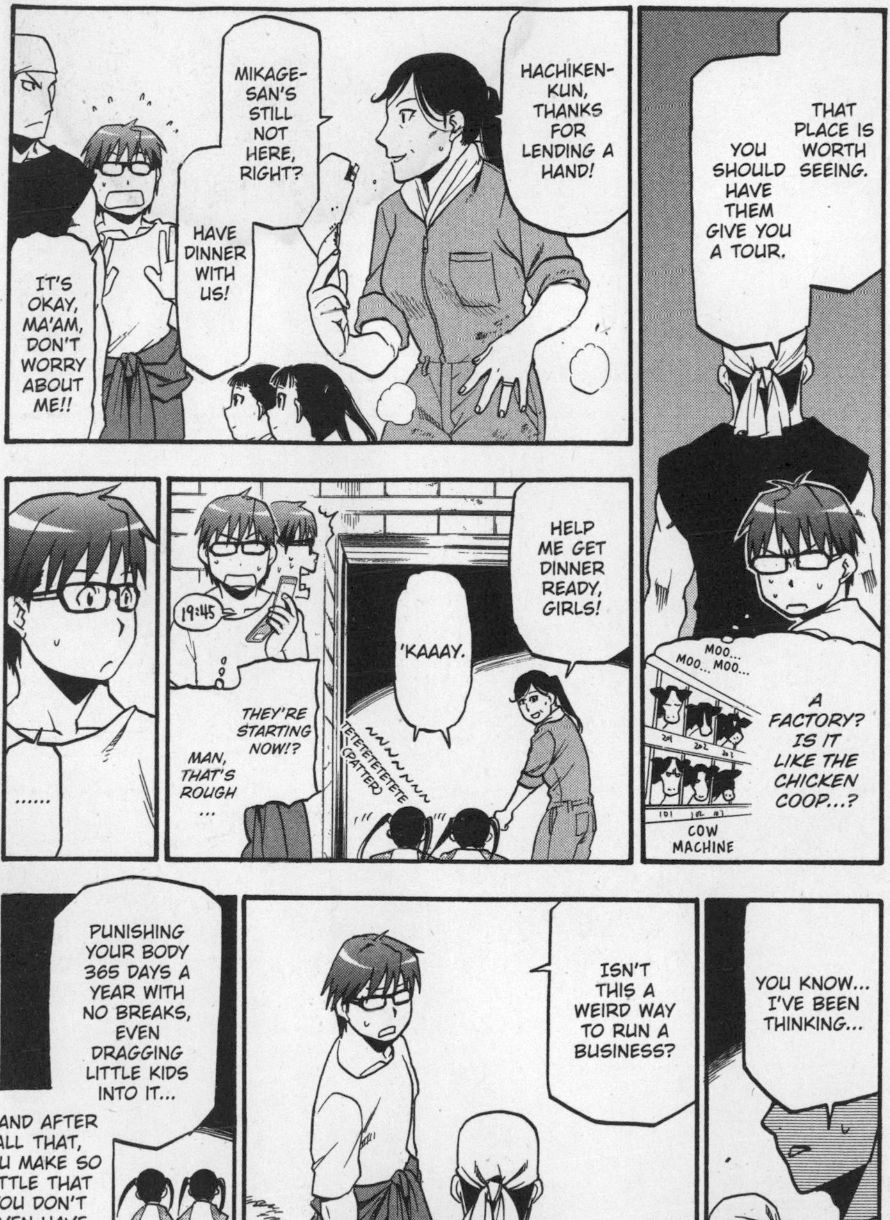
THAT PLACE IS WORTH SEEING.
YOU SHOULD HAVE THEM GIVE YOU A TOUR.
MOO... MOO... MOO...
A FACTORY? IS IT LIKE THE CHICKEN COOP...?
COW MACHINE
HACHIKEN-KUN, THANKS FOR LENDING A HAND!
MIKAGE-SAN'S STILL NOT HERE, RIGHT?
HAVE DINNER WITH US!
IT'S OKAY, MA'AM, DON'T WORRY ABOUT ME!!
HELP ME GET DINNER READY, GIRLS!
'KAAAY.
TETETETETETETE NNNNNNNN (PATTER)
19:45
THEY'RE STARTING NOW!?
MAN, THAT'S ROUGH...
......
YOU KNOW... I'VE BEEN THINKING...
ISN'T THIS A WEIRD WAY TO RUN A BUSINESS?
PUNISHING YOUR BODY 365 DAYS A YEAR WITH NO BREAKS, EVEN DRAGGING LITTLE KIDS INTO IT...
...AND AFTER ALL THAT, YOU MAKE SO LITTLE THAT YOU DON'T EVEN HAVE THE MONEY TO GO TO UNIVERSITY. IT'S NOT RATIONAL...

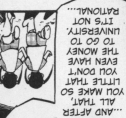

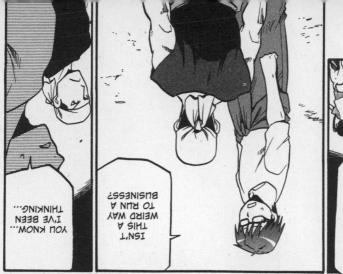

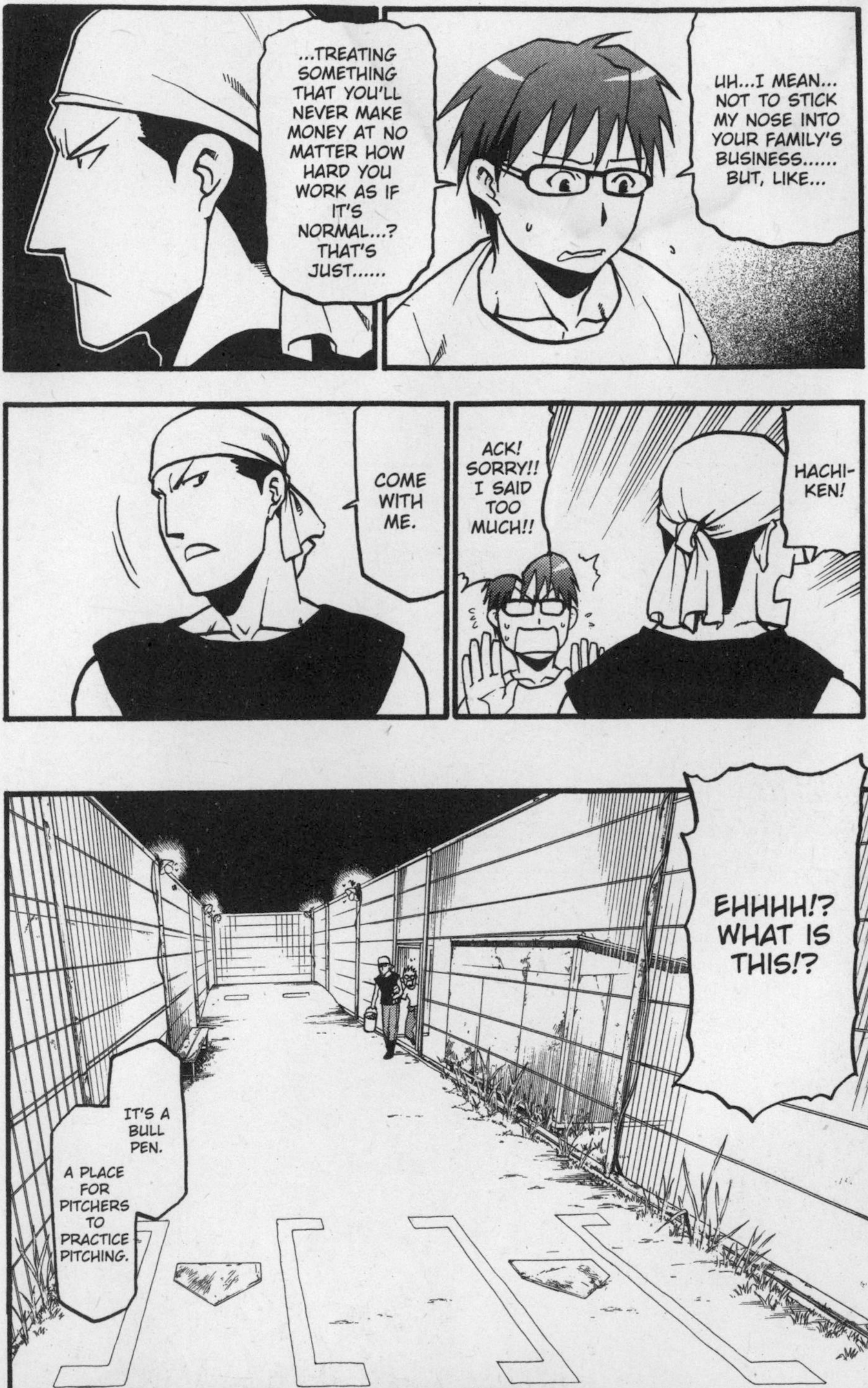
UH...I MEAN... NOT TO STICK MY NOSE INTO YOUR FAMILY'S BUSINESS...... BUT, LIKE...
...TREATING SOMETHING THAT YOU'LL NEVER MAKE MONEY AT NO MATTER HOW HARD YOU WORK AS IF IT'S NORMAL...? THAT'S JUST......
HACHI-KEN!
ACK! SORRY!! I SAID TOO MUCH!!
COME WITH ME.
EHHHH!? WHAT IS THIS!?
IT'S A BULL PEN.
A PLACE FOR PITCHERS TO PRACTICE PITCHING.

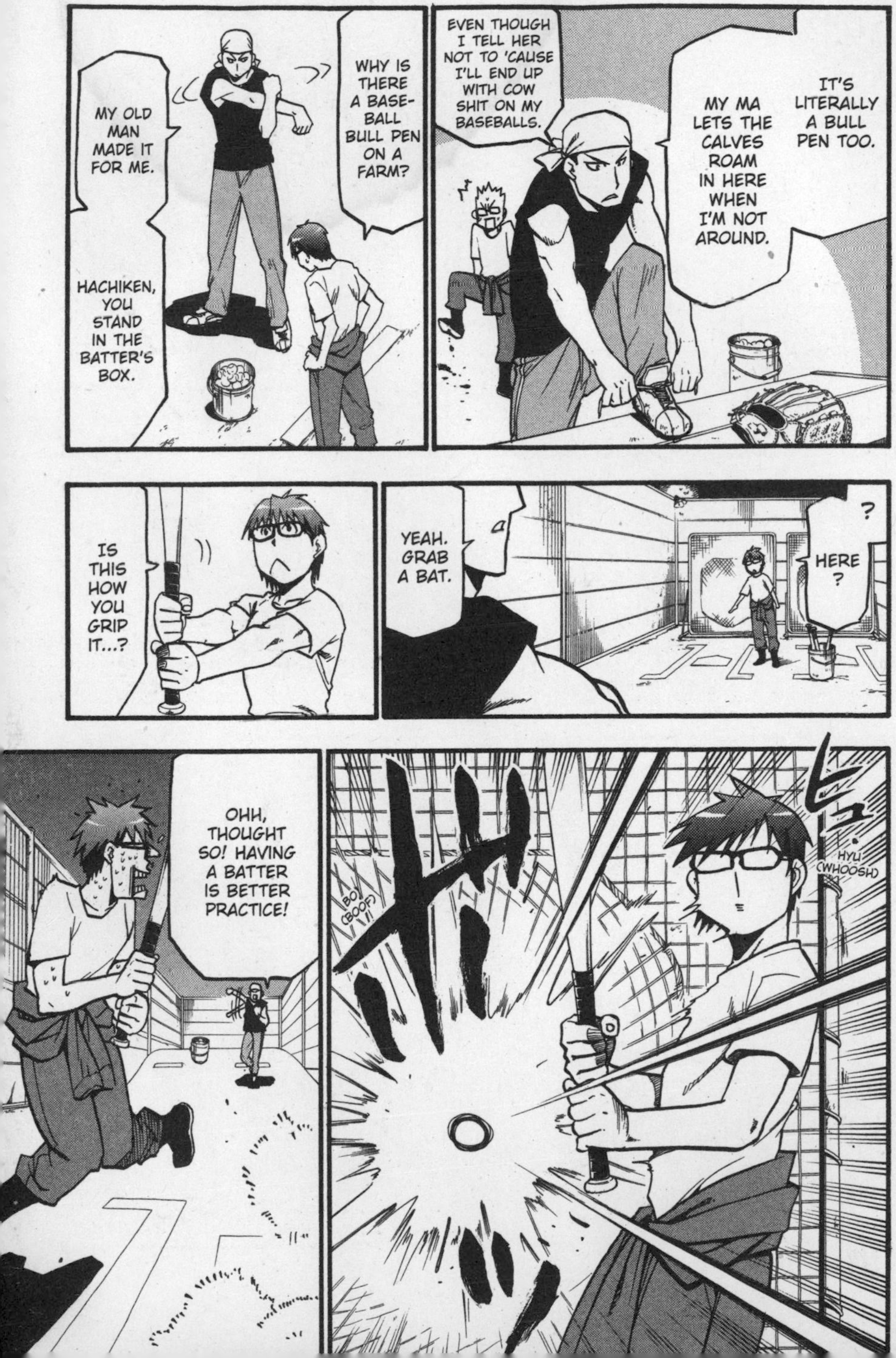
IT'S LITERALLY A BULL PEN TOO.
MY MA LETS THE CALVES ROAM IN HERE WHEN I'M NOT AROUND.
EVEN THOUGH I TELL HER NOT TO 'CAUSE I'LL END UP WITH COW SHIT ON MY BASEBALLS.
WHY IS THERE A BASE-BALL BULL PEN ON A FARM?
MY OLD MAN MADE IT FOR ME.
HACHIKEN, YOU STAND IN THE BATTER'S BOX.
HERE?
?
YEAH. GRAB A BAT.
IS THIS HOW YOU GRIP IT...?
HYU (WHOOSH)
BO (BOOF)
OHH, THOUGHT SO! HAVING A BATTER IS BETTER PRACTICE!

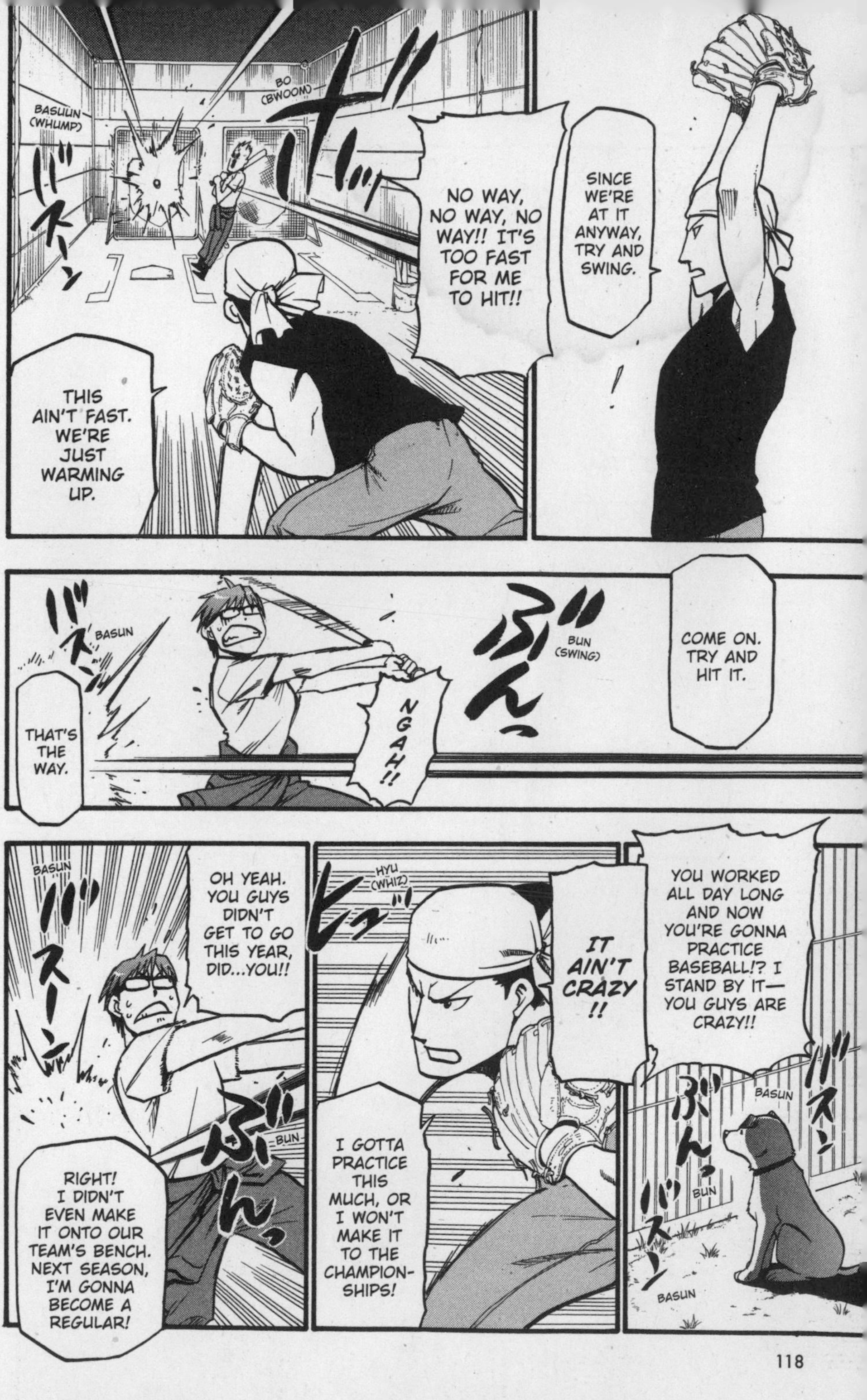
SINCE WE'RE AT IT ANYWAY, TRY AND SWING.
NO WAY, NO WAY, NO WAY!! IT'S TOO FAST FOR ME TO HIT!!
BO (BWOOM)
BASUUN (WHUMP)
THIS AIN'T FAST. WE'RE JUST WARMING UP.
COME ON. TRY AND HIT IT.
BUN (SWING)
NGAH!!
BASUN
THAT'S THE WAY.
YOU WORKED ALL DAY LONG AND NOW YOU'RE GONNA PRACTICE BASEBALL!? I STAND BY IT— YOU GUYS ARE CRAZY!!
BASUN
BUN
BASUN
IT AIN'T CRAZY!!
HYU (WHIZ)
I GOTTA PRACTICE THIS MUCH, OR I WON'T MAKE IT TO THE CHAMPION-SHIPS!
OH YEAH. YOU GUYS DIDN'T GET TO GO THIS YEAR, DID...YOU!!
BASUN
BUN
RIGHT! I DIDN'T EVEN MAKE IT ONTO OUR TEAM'S BENCH. NEXT SEASON, I'M GONNA BECOME A REGULAR!

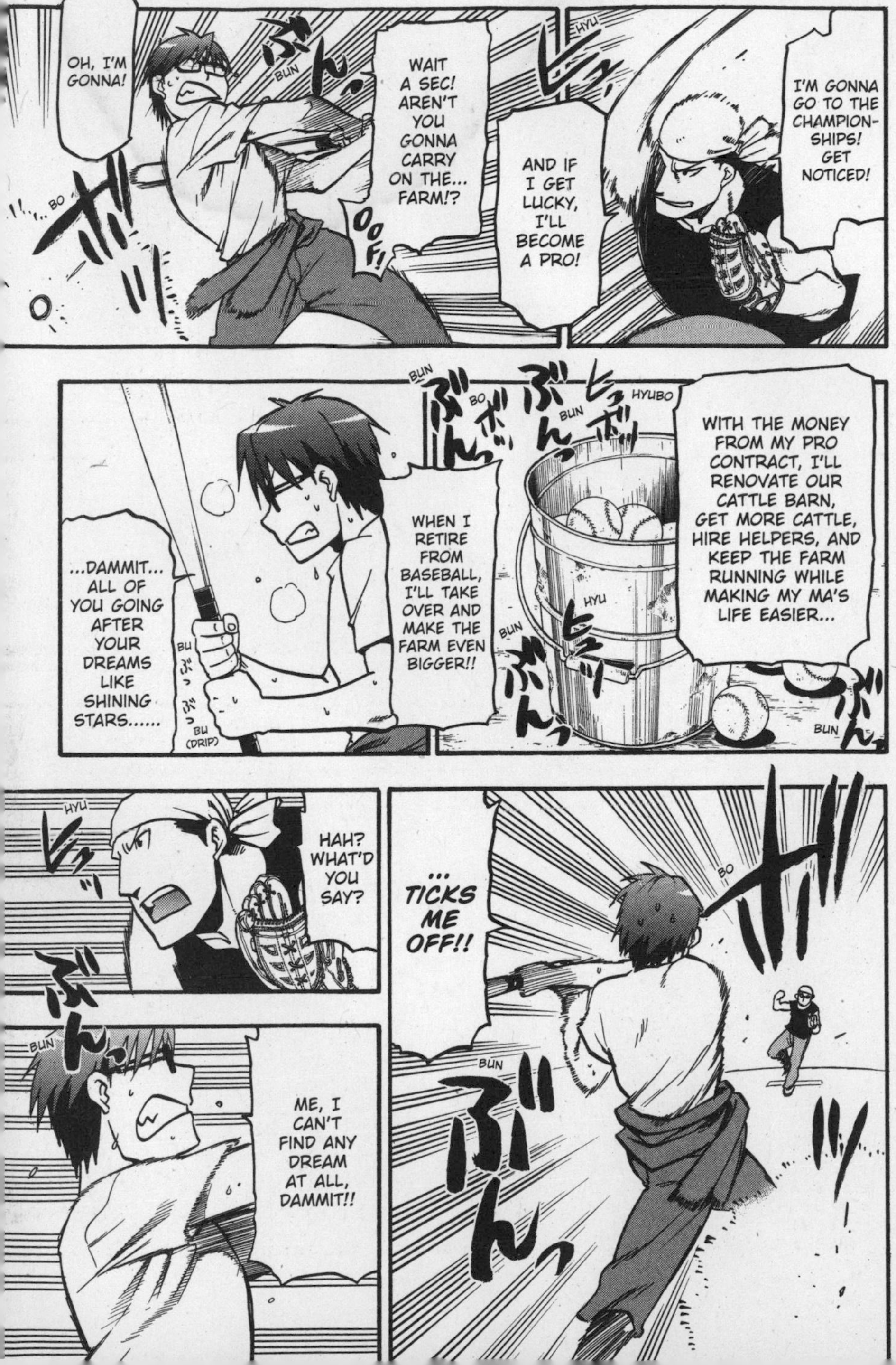
HYU
I'M GONNA GO TO THE CHAMPIONSHIPS! GET NOTICED!
AND IF I GET LUCKY, I'LL BECOME A PRO!
WAIT A SEC! AREN'T YOU GONNA CARRY ON THE... FARM!?
OOF!
BUN
OH, I'M GONNA!
BO
HYUBO
BUN
WITH THE MONEY FROM MY PRO CONTRACT, I'LL RENOVATE OUR CATTLE BARN, GET MORE CATTLE, HIRE HELPERS, AND KEEP THE FARM RUNNING WHILE MAKING MY MA'S LIFE EASIER...
HYU
BUN
BUN
BO
BUN
WHEN I RETIRE FROM BASEBALL, I'LL TAKE OVER AND MAKE THE FARM EVEN BIGGER!!
BU
BU
(DRIP)
...DAMMIT... ALL OF YOU GOING AFTER YOUR DREAMS LIKE SHINING STARS......
BO
... TICKS ME OFF!!
BUN
HYU
HAH? WHAT'D YOU SAY?
BUN
ME, I CAN'T FIND ANY DREAM AT ALL, DAMMIT!!

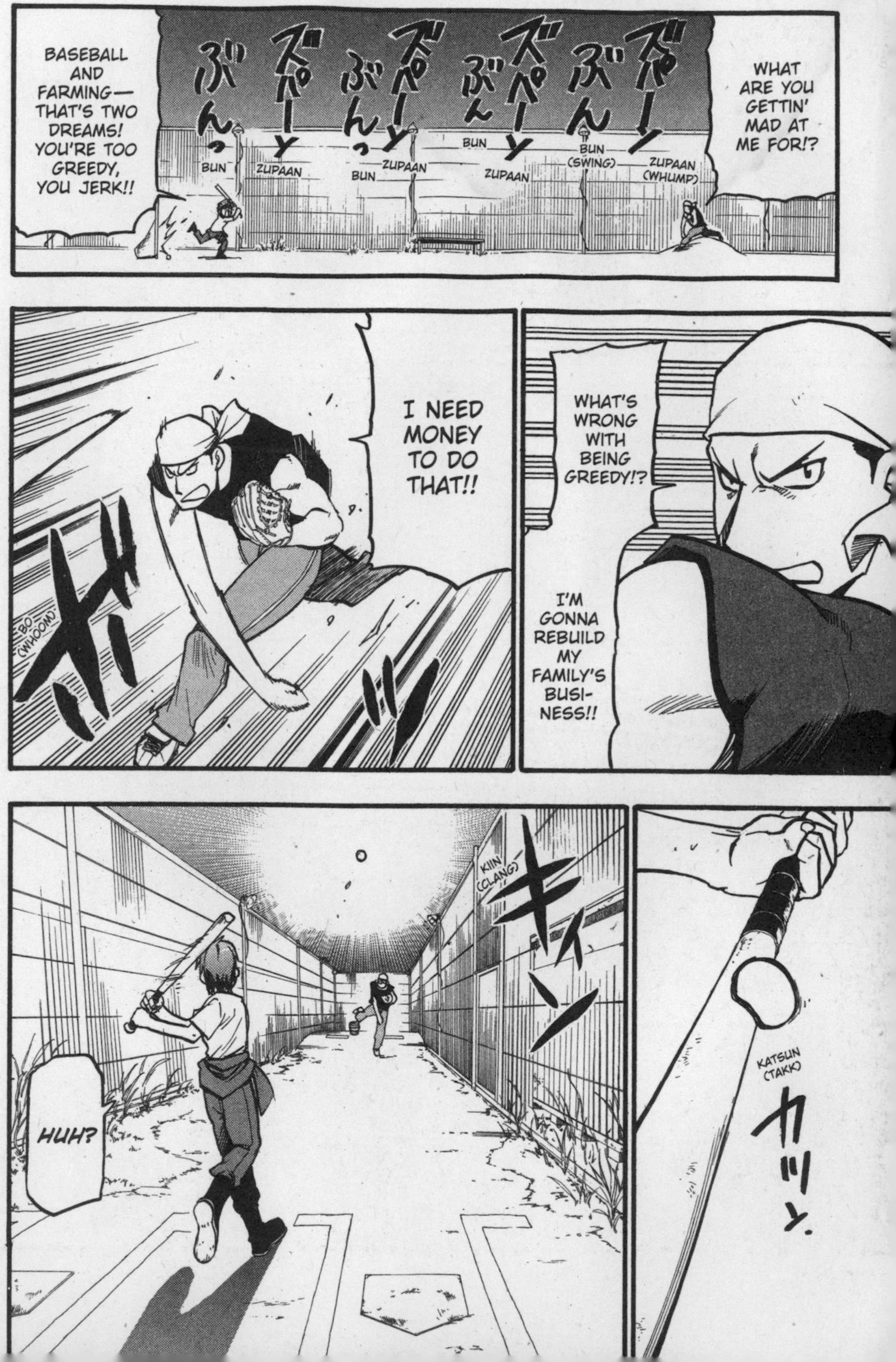
WHAT ARE YOU GETTIN' MAD AT ME FOR!?
ZUPAAN (WHUMP)
BUN (SWING)
ZUPAAN
BUN
ZUPAAN
BUN
ZUPAAN
BUN
BASEBALL AND FARMING—THAT'S TWO DREAMS! YOU'RE TOO GREEDY, YOU JERK!!
WHAT'S WRONG WITH BEING GREEDY!?
I'M GONNA REBUILD MY FAMILY'S BUSI-NESS!!
I NEED MONEY TO DO THAT!!
BO (WHOOM)
KATSUN (TAKK)
KIIN (CLANG)
HUH?

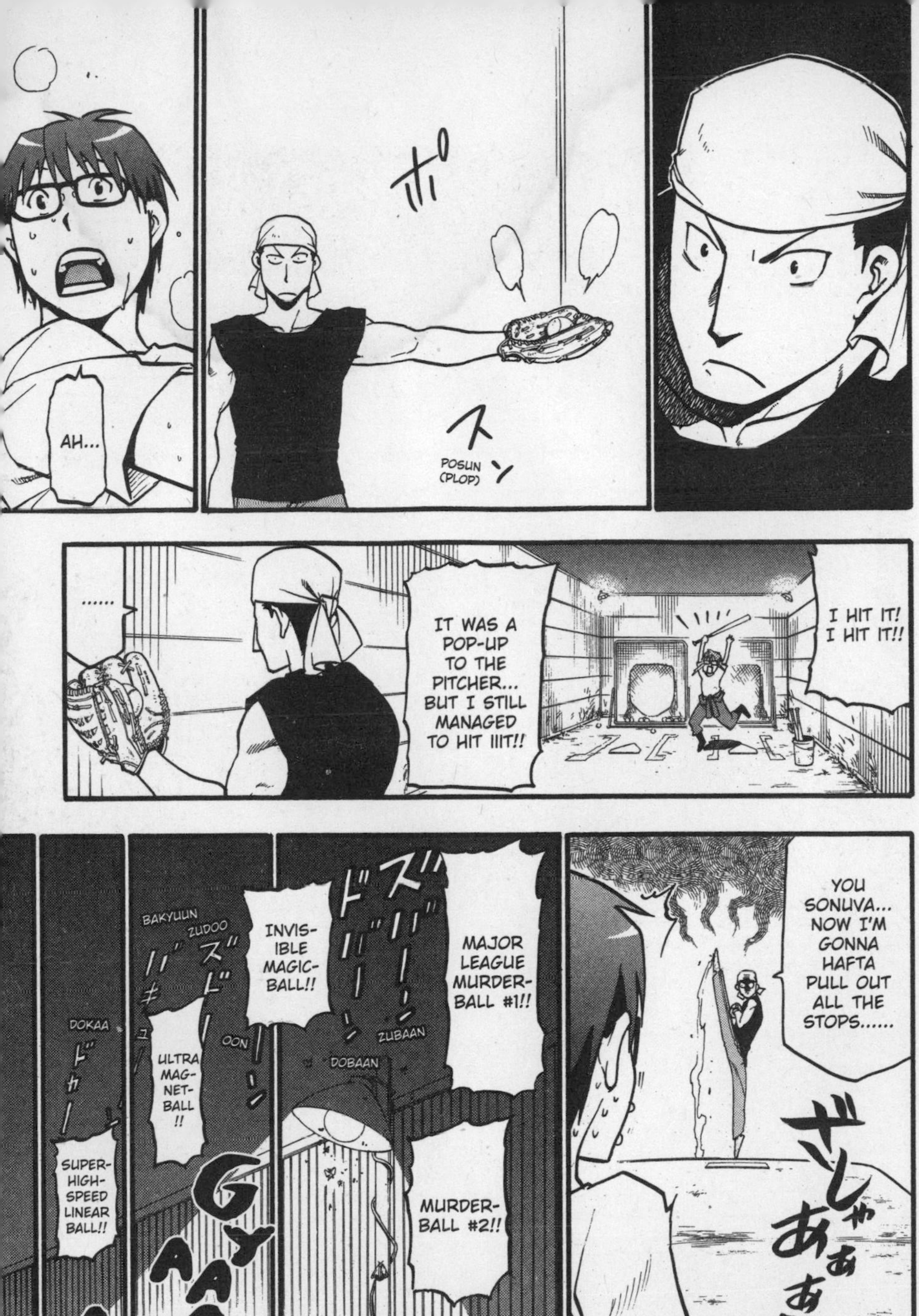
POSUN (PLOP)
AH...
I HIT IT! I HIT IT!!
IT WAS A POP-UP TO THE PITCHER... BUT I STILL MANAGED TO HIT IIIT!!
......
YOU SONUVA... NOW I'M GONNA HAFTA PULL OUT ALL THE STOPS......
ZASHAAAAAAA (CRACKLE)
MAJOR LEAGUE MURDER-BALL #1!!
ZUBAAN
MURDER-BALL #2!!
DOBAAN
INVISIBLE MAGIC-BALL!!
BAKYUUN
ZUDOO
ULTRA MAGNET-BALL!!
OON
DOKAA
SUPER-HIGH-SPEED LINEAR BALL!!
GYAAAAAAAAA

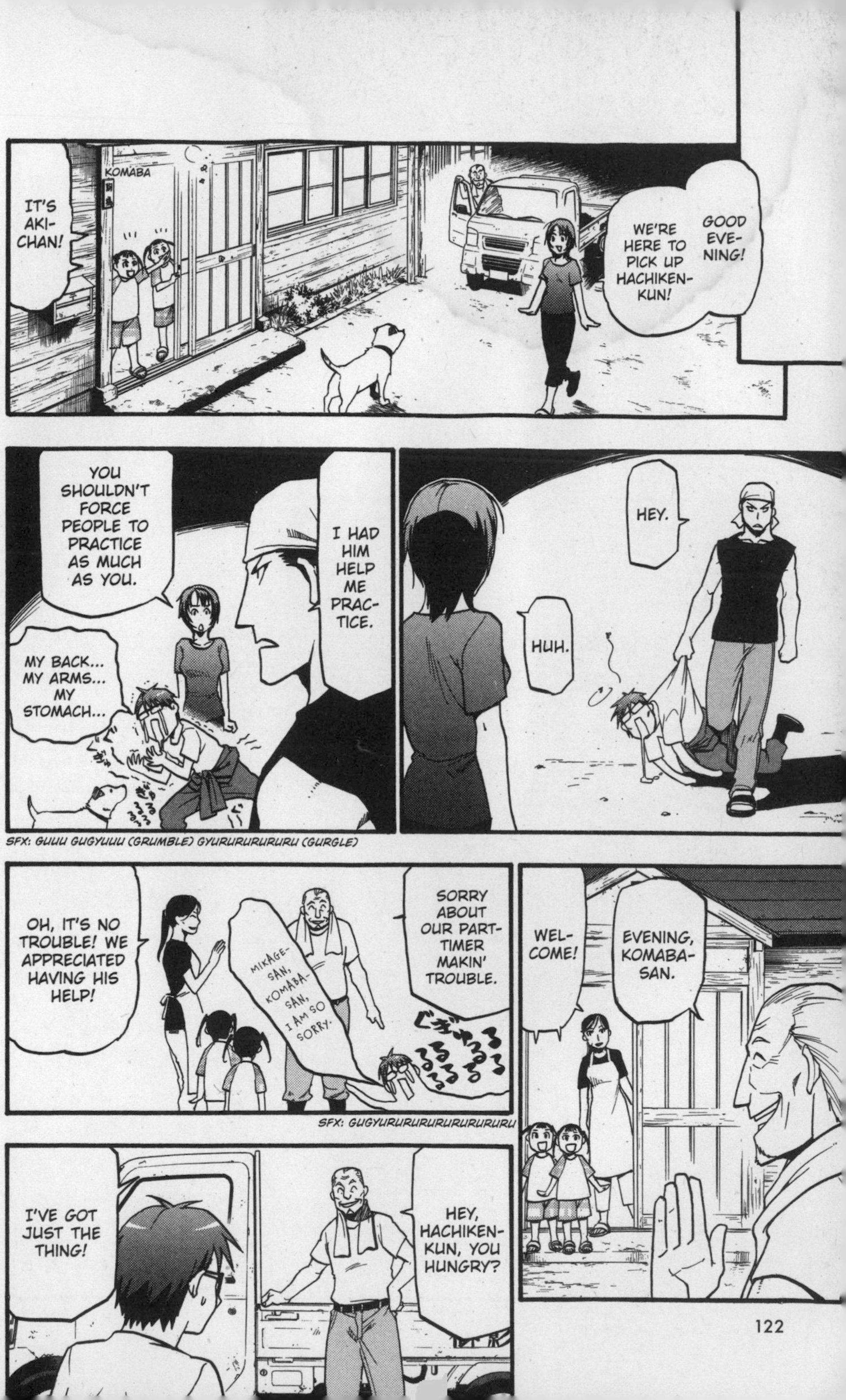
GOOD EVENING!
WE'RE HERE TO PICK UP HACHIKEN-KUN!
KOMABA
IT'S AKI-CHAN!
HEY.
HUH.
I HAD HIM HELP ME PRACTICE.
YOU SHOULDN'T FORCE PEOPLE TO PRACTICE AS MUCH AS YOU.
MY BACK... MY ARMS... MY STOMACH...
SFX: GUUU GUGYUUU (GRUMBLE) GYURURURURURU (GURGLE)
EVENING, KOMABA-SAN.
WEL-COME!
SORRY ABOUT OUR PART-TIMER MAKIN' TROUBLE.
MIKAGE-SAN, KOMABA-SAN, I AM SO SORRY.
OH, IT'S NO TROUBLE! WE APPRECIATED HAVING HIS HELP!
SFX: GUGYURURURURURURURURU
HEY, HACHIKEN-KUN, YOU HUNGRY?
I'VE GOT JUST THE THING!

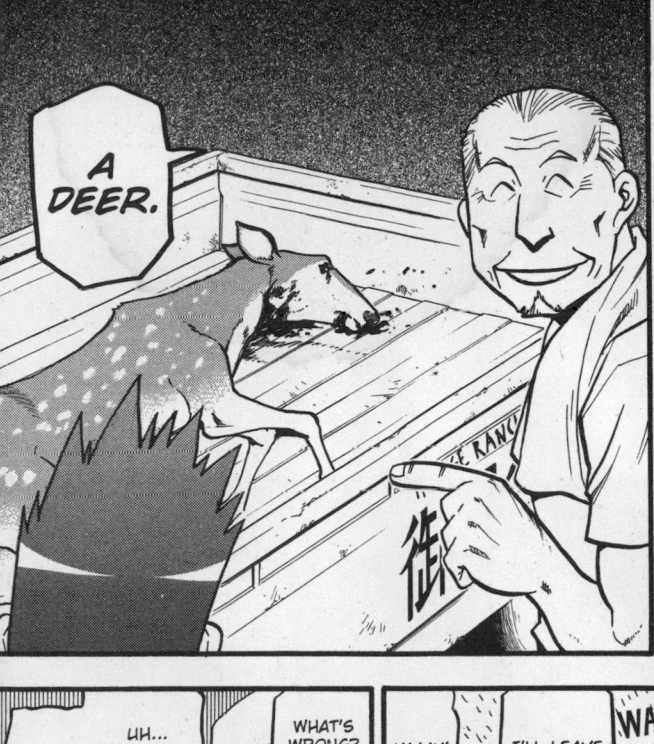

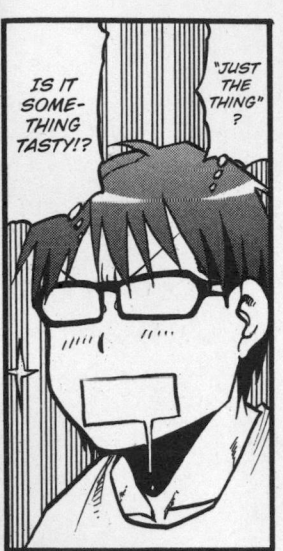

"JUST THE THING"?
IS IT SOMETHING TASTY!?
A DEER.
RAN INTO IT ON THE WAY HERE!
I DRAINED THE BLOOD RIGHT THERE ON THE SIDE OF THE ROAD. IT'LL BE TASTY!
WAHAHAHAHA
I'LL LEAVE HALF OF IT WITH YOU FOLKS.
YAAAY! VENISON!
WHAT'S WRONG? YOU'RE HUNGRY, AREN'T YOU? YOU DON'T LIKE VENISON?
UH... IT'S NOT ABOUT THE FOOD I LIKE...
IT'S LIKE...YOU KNOW... SENSITIVITY...
IF YOU TAKE VENISON THAT'S BEEN AGED IN A REFRIGERATOR FOR SEVERAL DAYS, TOSS IT IN A POT WITH LOTS OF GINGER, SOY SAUCE, AND SAKE, AND LET IT SIMMER IN THERE ALL DAY, THE SINEW WILL BE SOFT ENOUGH TO MELT IN YOUR MOUTH, THE RED MEAT'LL BE SO JUICY, AND YOU WON'T TASTE EVEN A HINT OF GAMINESS IN THE FAT—
CUT IT OUT, ICCHAN. DON'T TALK ABOUT HOW WHEN YOU PUT GOOD-QUALITY VENISON—WHICH CREATES BARELY ANY SOUP SCUM AND IS OVERFLOWING WITH RUSTIC FLAVOR, YET IS STILL DELICATE—ON TOP OF PIPING-HOT, FRESHLY COOKED RICE, AND THE SOY SAUCE THAT'S ABSORBED THE VENISON'S SAVORY TASTE SOAKS DOWN INTO THE WHITE RICE, IT'S INDESCRIBABLY DELICIOUS!
STOOOP!! YOU DEEEMONS!!!
THE APPETITE WINS OVER ANY SENSE OF "SEN-SEE-TEE-VEE-TEE."
RIGHT?
どばば
DOBABA (DROOL)
SFX: GUGYURURURURURU GUU GUGUU

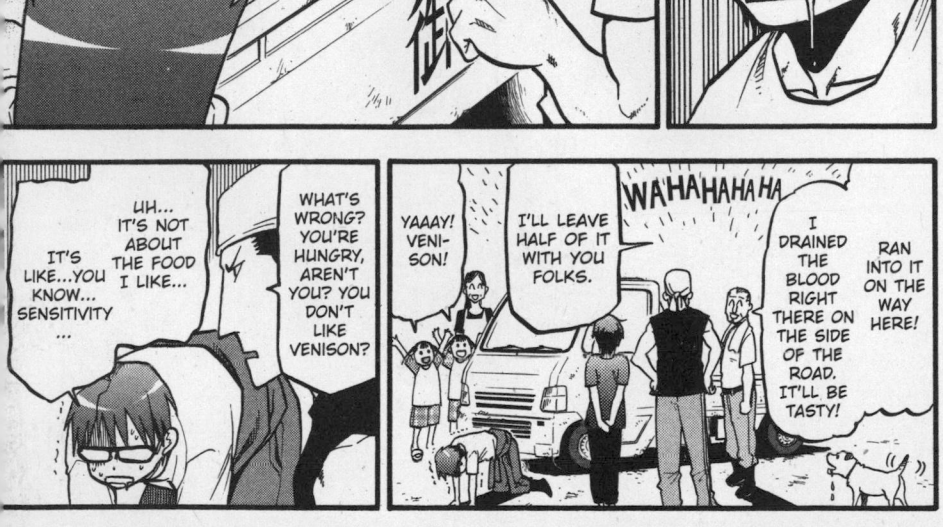

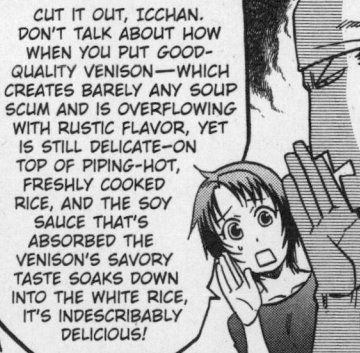

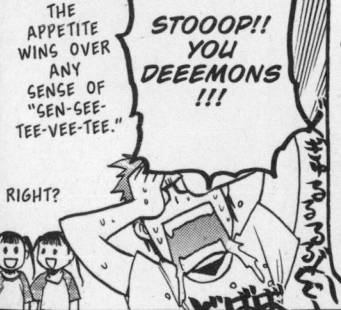

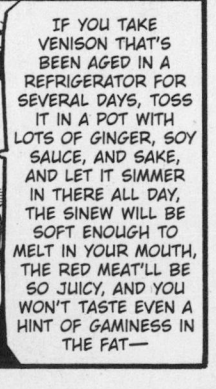

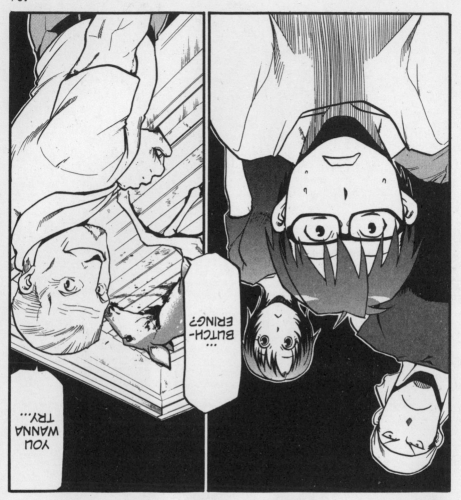

...
BUTCH-
ERING?

YOU
WANNA
TRY...

WELP,
LET'S GET IT
TAKEN CARE
OF LICKETY-
SPLIT.

HACHI-
KEN-
KUN.

Silver Spoon

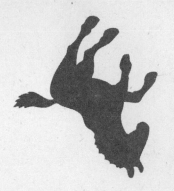

EISAKU TOWARI

SHIBETSU IWAONAI
MIDDLE SCHOOL

HIS FAMILY RAISES
SHEEP AND BEEF
CATTLE.

PREFERS ADDING
SAUCE TO HIS
JINGISUKAN AFTER
IT'S COOKED.

RUGBY
TEAM

Chapter 15: Tale of Summer ⑤

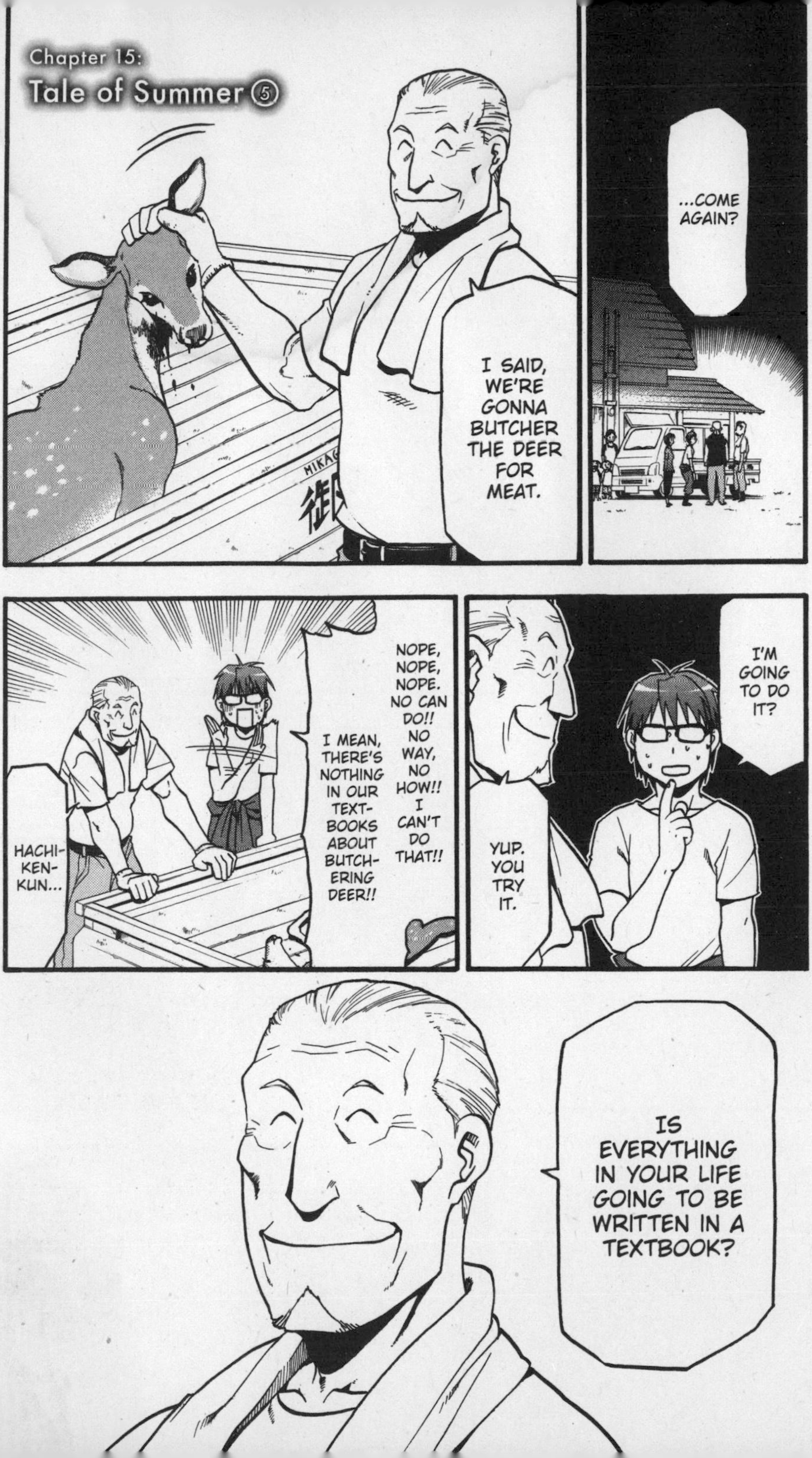

...COME AGAIN?
I SAID, WE'RE GONNA BUTCHER THE DEER FOR MEAT.
I'M GOING TO DO IT?
YUP. YOU TRY IT.
NOPE, NOPE, NOPE. NO CAN DO!! NO WAY, NO HOW!! I CAN'T DO THAT!!
I MEAN, THERE'S NOTHING IN OUR TEXT-BOOKS ABOUT BUTCH-ERING DEER!!
HACHI-KEN-KUN...
IS EVERYTHING IN YOUR LIFE GOING TO BE WRITTEN IN A TEXTBOOK?

Chapter 15: Tale of Summer ⑤

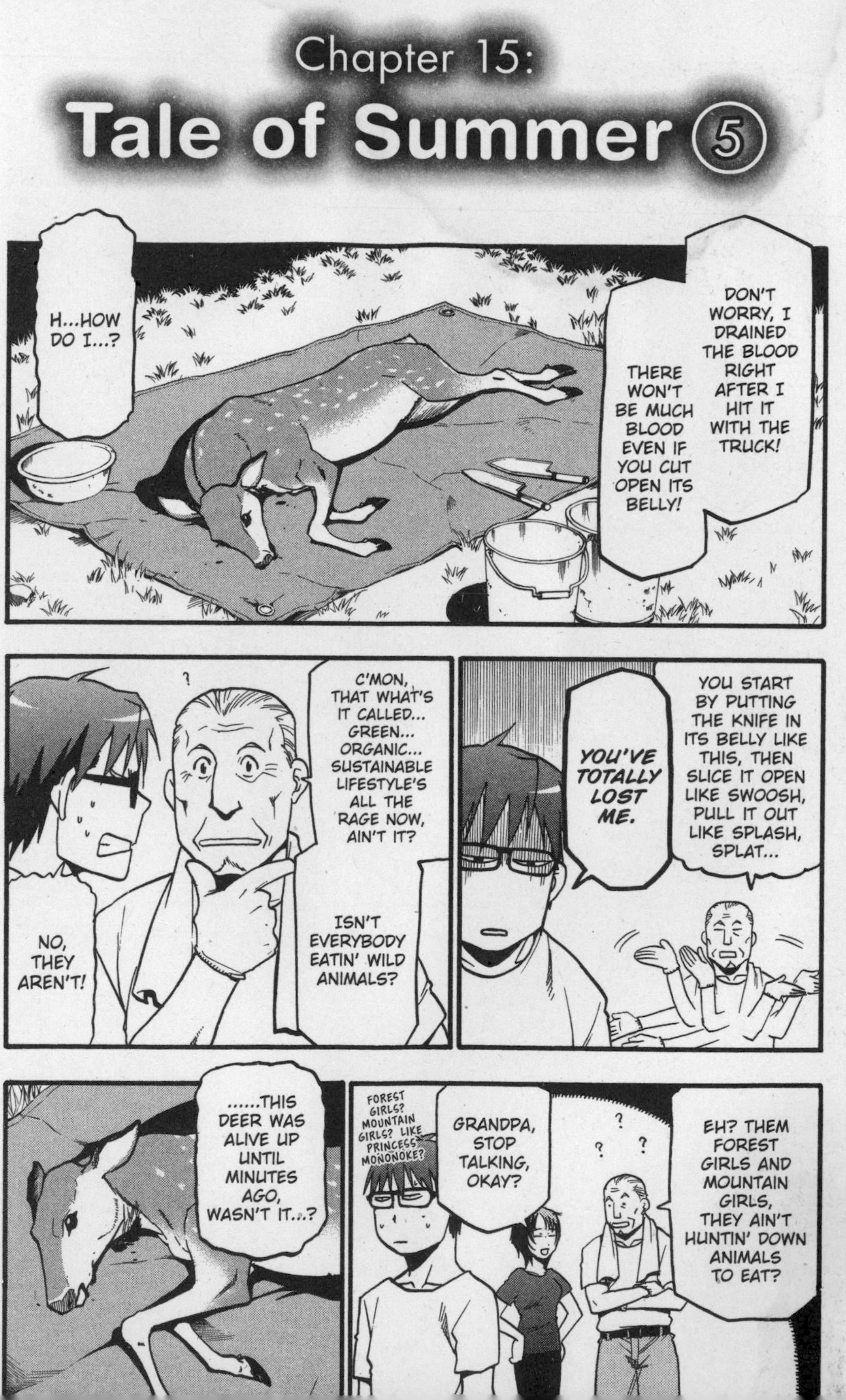

DON'T WORRY, I DRAINED THE BLOOD RIGHT AFTER I HIT IT WITH THE TRUCK!
THERE WON'T BE MUCH BLOOD EVEN IF YOU CUT OPEN ITS BELLY!
H...HOW DO I...?
YOU START BY PUTTING THE KNIFE IN ITS BELLY LIKE THIS, THEN SLICE IT OPEN LIKE SWOOSH, PULL IT OUT LIKE SPLASH, SPLAT...
YOU'VE TOTALLY LOST ME.
?
C'MON, THAT WHAT'S IT CALLED... GREEN... ORGANIC... SUSTAINABLE LIFESTYLE'S ALL THE RAGE NOW, AIN'T IT?
ISN'T EVERYBODY EATIN' WILD ANIMALS?
NO, THEY AREN'T!
EH? THEM FOREST GIRLS AND MOUNTAIN GIRLS, THEY AIN'T HUNTIN' DOWN ANIMALS TO EAT?
? ? ?
GRANDPA, STOP TALKING, OKAY?
FOREST GIRLS? MOUNTAIN GIRLS? LIKE PRINCESS MONONOKE?
......THIS DEER WAS ALIVE UP UNTIL MINUTES AGO, WASN'T IT...?

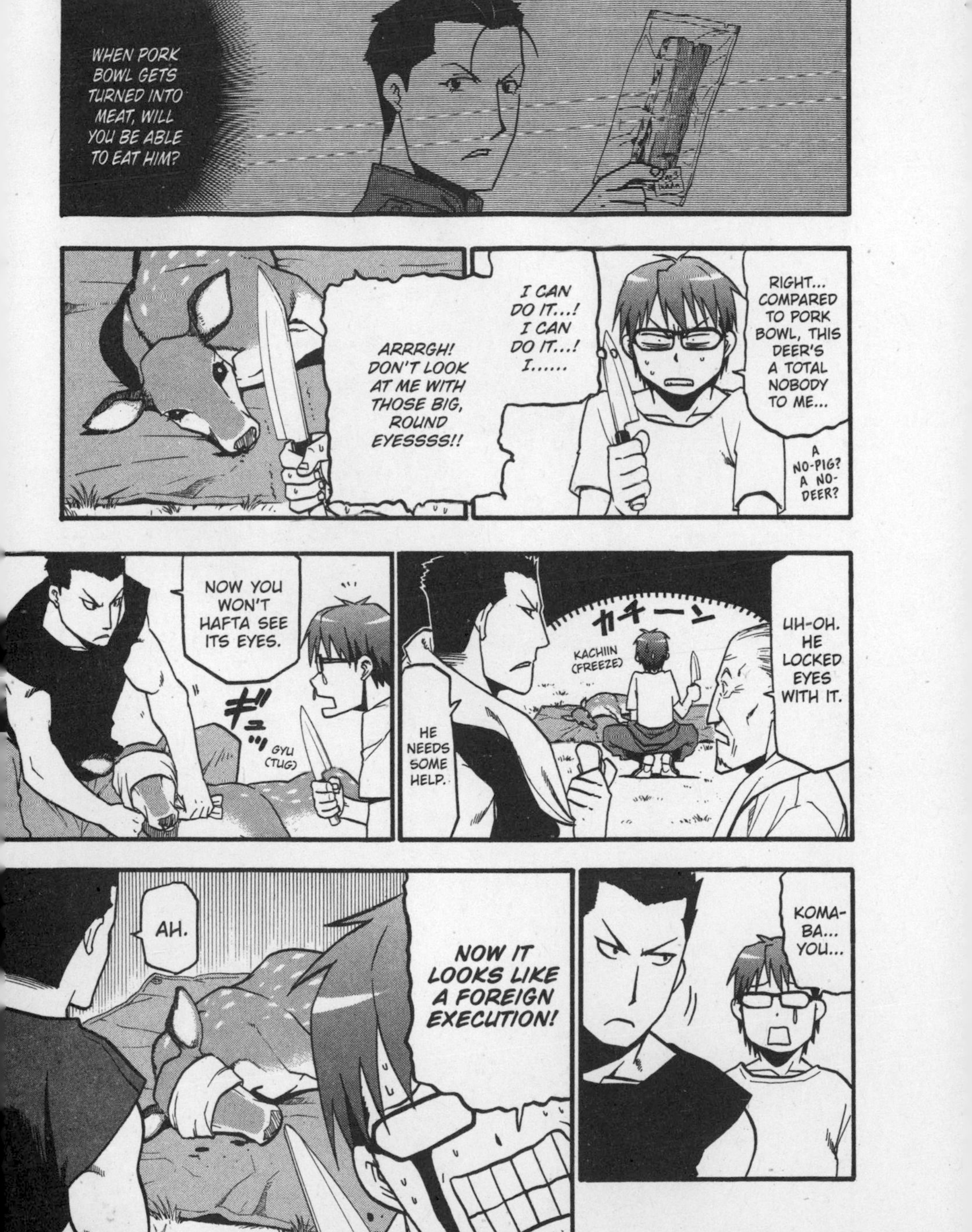
WHEN PORK BOWL GETS TURNED INTO MEAT, WILL YOU BE ABLE TO EAT HIM?
RIGHT... COMPARED TO PORK BOWL, THIS DEER'S A TOTAL NOBODY TO ME...
A NO-PIG? A NO-DEER?
I CAN DO IT...! I CAN DO IT...! I......
ARRRGH! DON'T LOOK AT ME WITH THOSE BIG, ROUND EYESSSS!!
UH-OH. HE LOCKED EYES WITH IT.
カチーン
KACHIIN (FREEZE)
HE NEEDS SOME HELP.
NOW YOU WON'T HAFTA SEE ITS EYES.
ギュ
GYU (TUG)
KOMA-BA... YOU...
NOW IT LOOKS LIKE A FOREIGN EXECUTION!
AH.

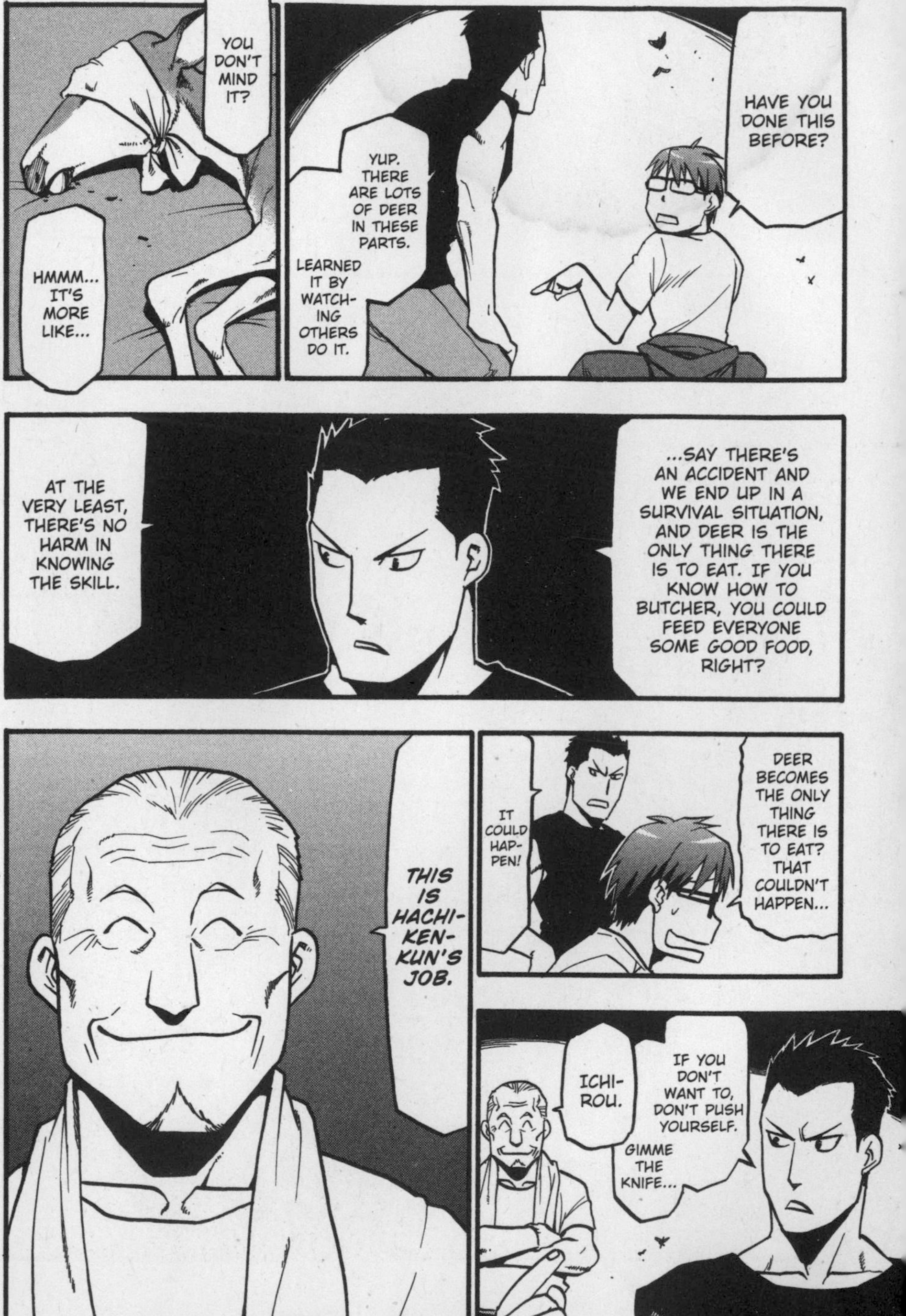
HAVE YOU DONE THIS BEFORE?
YUP. THERE ARE LOTS OF DEER IN THESE PARTS.
LEARNED IT BY WATCHING OTHERS DO IT.
YOU DON'T MIND IT?
HMMM... IT'S MORE LIKE...
...SAY THERE'S AN ACCIDENT AND WE END UP IN A SURVIVAL SITUATION, AND DEER IS THE ONLY THING THERE IS TO EAT. IF YOU KNOW HOW TO BUTCHER, YOU COULD FEED EVERYONE SOME GOOD FOOD, RIGHT?
AT THE VERY LEAST, THERE'S NO HARM IN KNOWING THE SKILL.
DEER BECOMES THE ONLY THING THERE IS TO EAT? THAT COULDN'T HAPPEN...
IT COULD HAPPEN!
IF YOU DON'T WANT TO, DON'T PUSH YOURSELF.
GIMME THE KNIFE...
ICHIROU.
THIS IS HACHIKEN-KUN'S JOB.

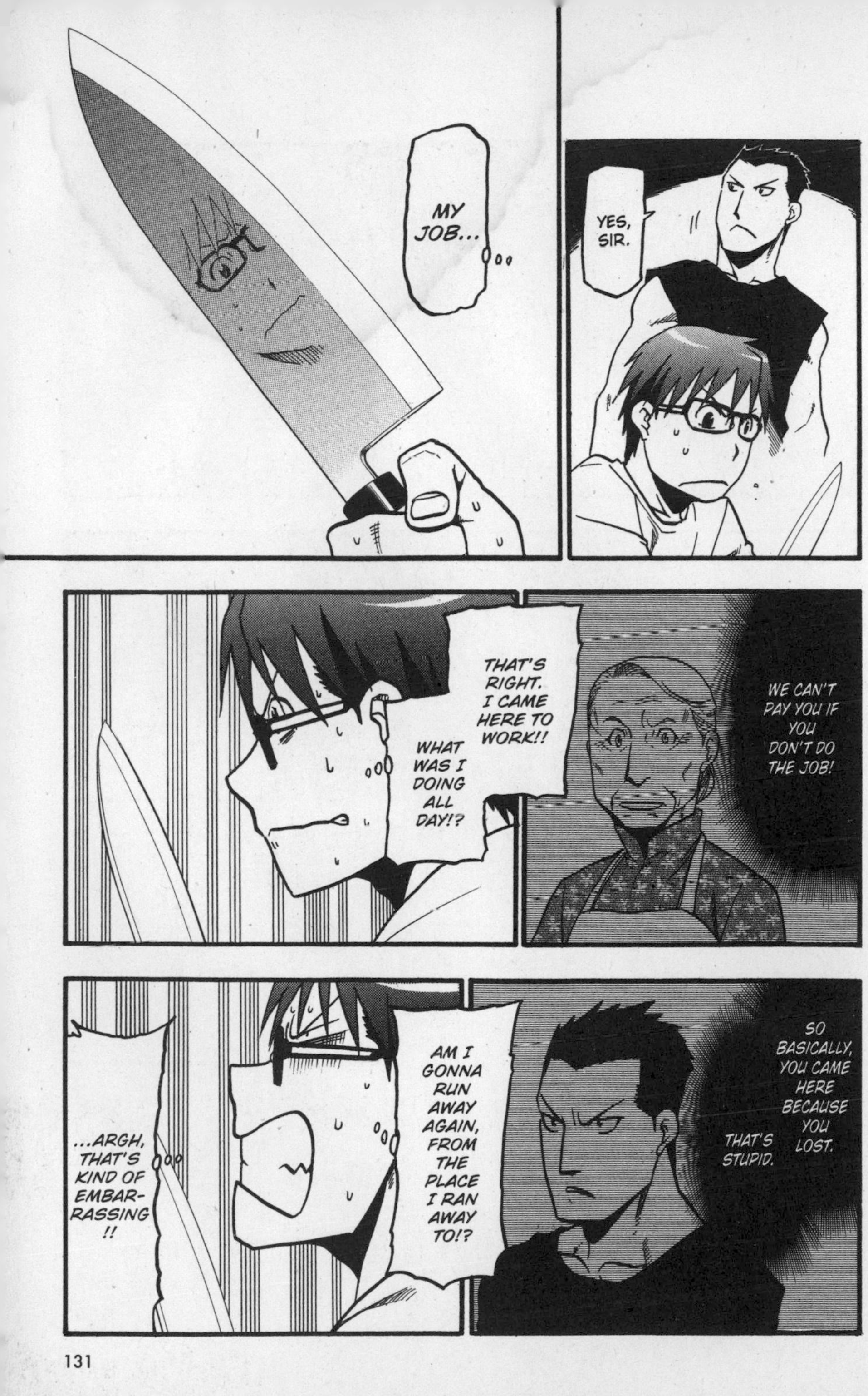
YES, SIR.
MY JOB...
WE CAN'T PAY YOU IF YOU DON'T DO THE JOB!
THAT'S RIGHT. I CAME HERE TO WORK!!
WHAT WAS I DOING ALL DAY!?
SO BASICALLY, YOU CAME HERE BECAUSE YOU LOST.
THAT'S STUPID.
AM I GONNA RUN AWAY AGAIN, FROM THE PLACE I RAN AWAY TO!?
...ARGH, THAT'S KIND OF EMBAR-RASSING!!

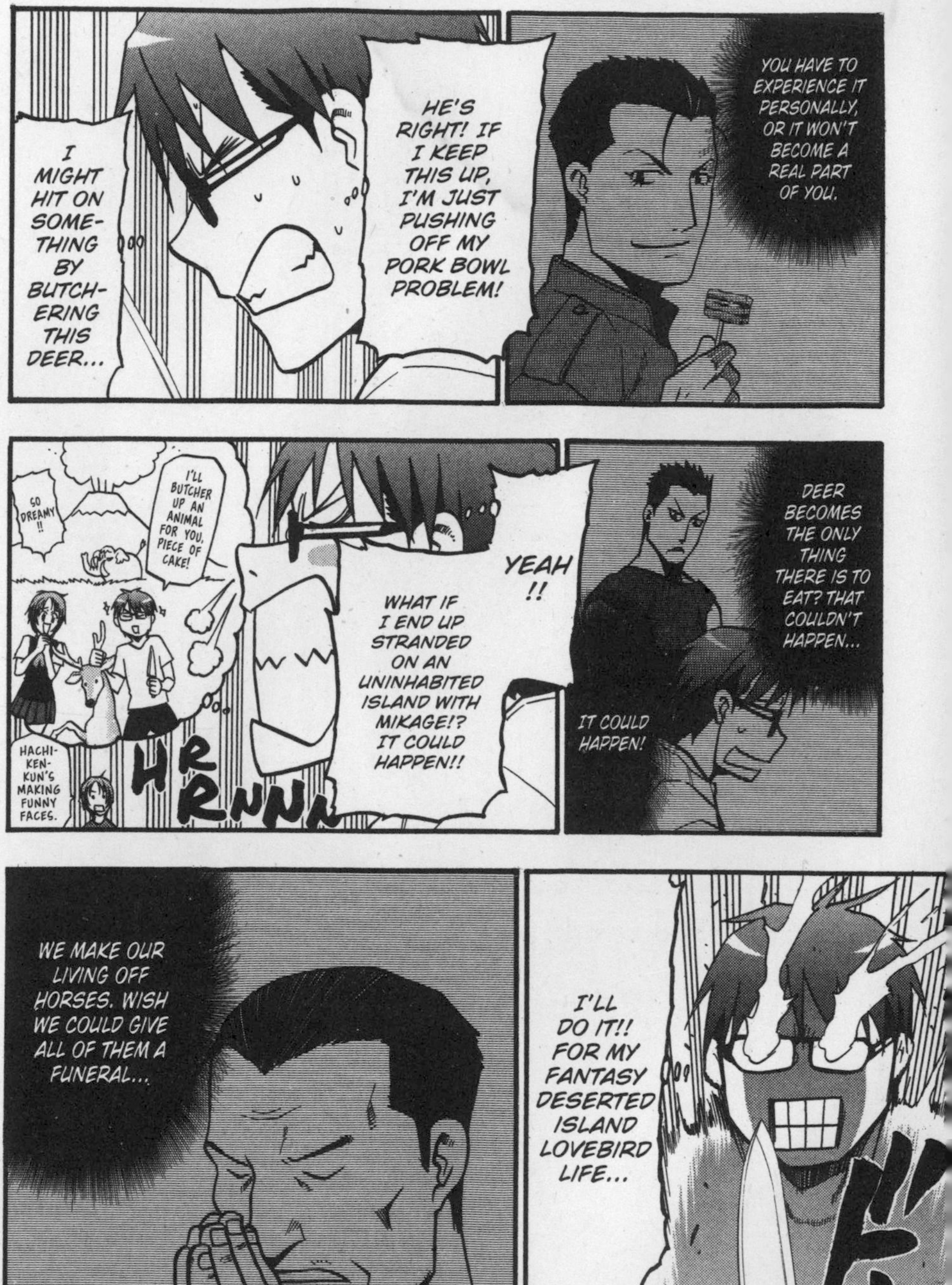
YOU HAVE TO EXPERIENCE IT PERSONALLY, OR IT WON'T BECOME A REAL PART OF YOU.
HE'S RIGHT! IF I KEEP THIS UP, I'M JUST PUSHING OFF MY PORK BOWL PROBLEM!
I MIGHT HIT ON SOME-THING BY BUTCH-ERING THIS DEER...
DEER BECOMES THE ONLY THING THERE IS TO EAT? THAT COULDN'T HAPPEN...
IT COULD HAPPEN!
YEAH !!
WHAT IF I END UP STRANDED ON AN UNINHABITED ISLAND WITH MIKAGE!? IT COULD HAPPEN!!
HRRNNN
I'LL BUTCHER UP AN ANIMAL FOR YOU, PIECE OF CAKE!
SO DREAMY !!
HACHI-KEN-KUN'S MAKING FUNNY FACES.
I'LL DO IT!! FOR MY FANTASY DESERTED ISLAND LOVEBIRD LIFE...
DO (BOOM)
WE MAKE OUR LIVING OFF HORSES. WISH WE COULD GIVE ALL OF THEM A FUNERAL...

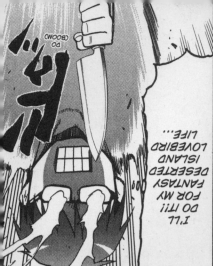

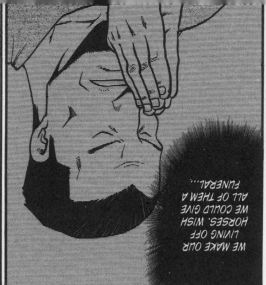

PAN (CLAP)

PAN

PATA (TAP)

NO GOOD AFTER ALL....?

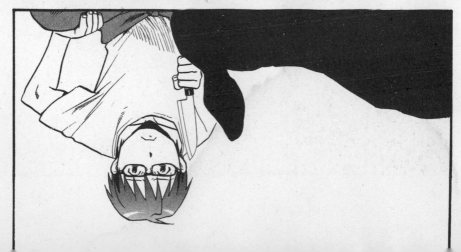

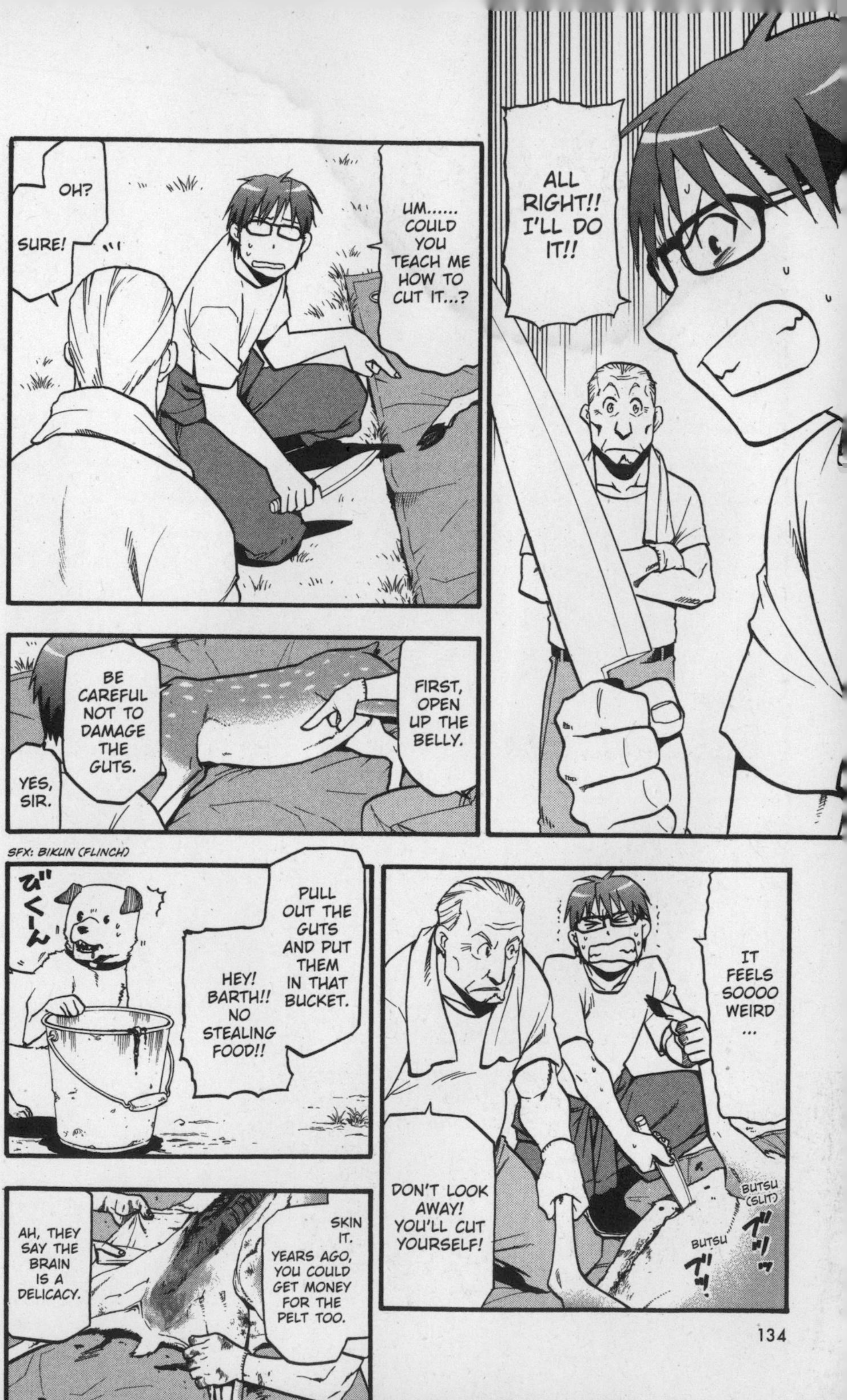
ALL RIGHT!! I'LL DO IT!!
UM...... COULD YOU TEACH ME HOW TO CUT IT...?
OH?
SURE!
FIRST, OPEN UP THE BELLY.
BE CAREFUL NOT TO DAMAGE THE GUTS.
YES, SIR.
SFX: BIKUN (FLINCH)
IT FEELS SOOOO WEIRD ...
BUTSU (SLIT)
BUTSU
DON'T LOOK AWAY! YOU'LL CUT YOURSELF!
PULL OUT THE GUTS AND PUT THEM IN THAT BUCKET.
HEY! BARTH!! NO STEALING FOOD!!
びくーん
SKIN IT. YEARS AGO, YOU COULD GET MONEY FOR THE PELT TOO.
AH, THEY SAY THE BRAIN IS A DELICACY.

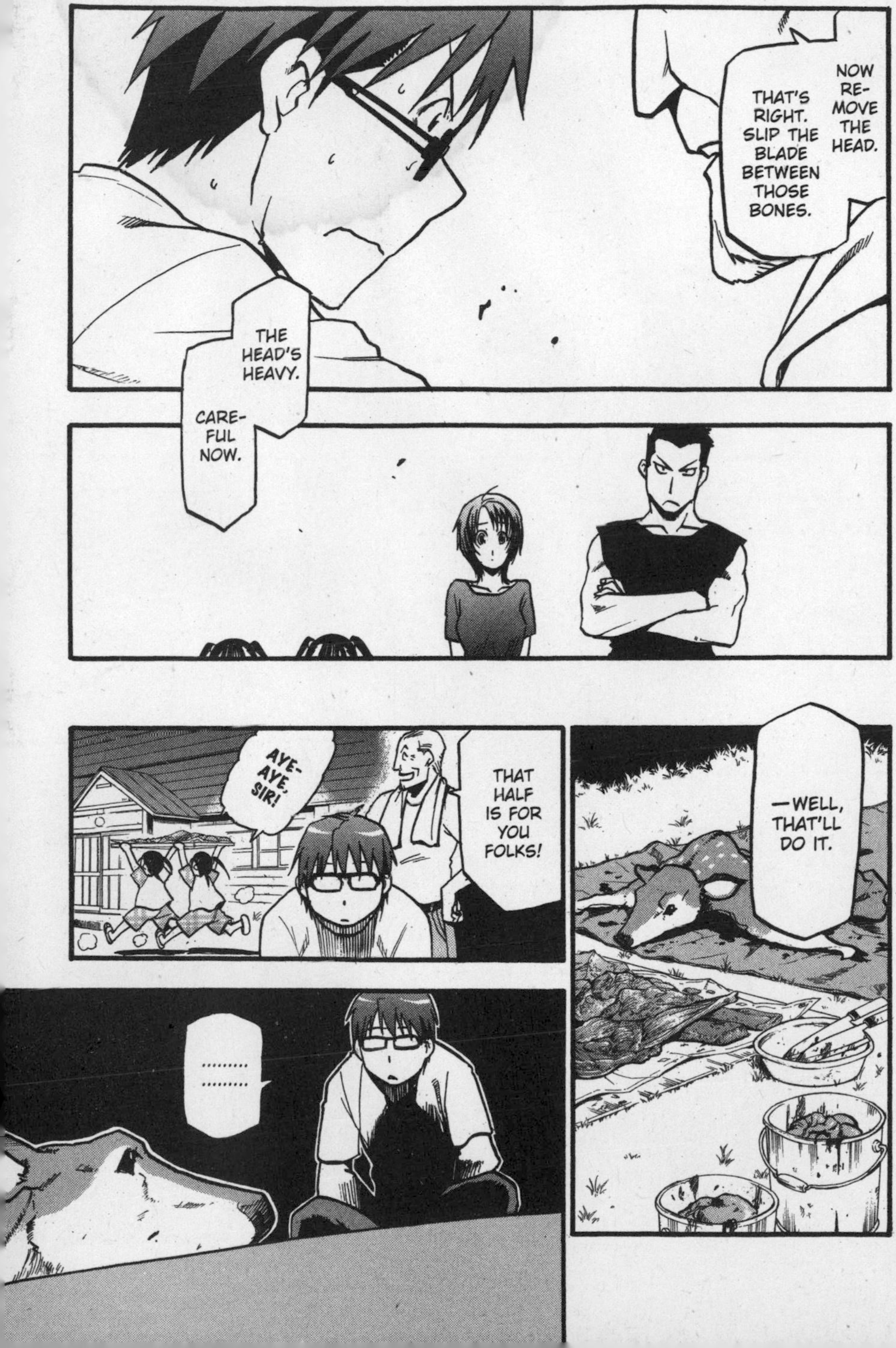
NOW RE-MOVE THE HEAD.
THAT'S RIGHT. SLIP THE BLADE BETWEEN THOSE BONES.
THE HEAD'S HEAVY.
CARE-FUL NOW.
—WELL, THAT'LL DO IT.
THAT HALF IS FOR YOU FOLKS!
AYE-AYE, SIR!
………
………

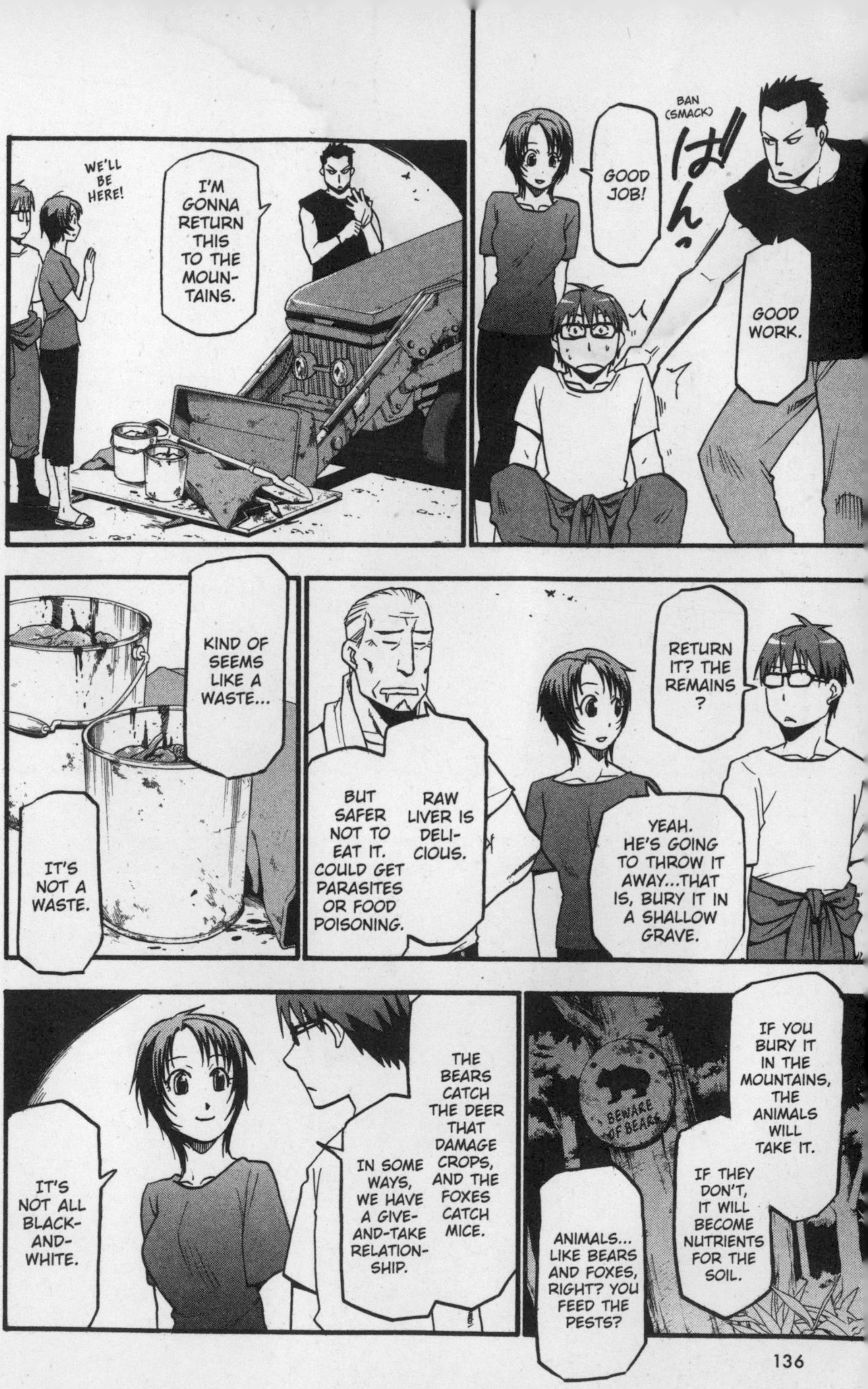
BAN (SMACK)
GOOD JOB!
GOOD WORK.
I'M GONNA RETURN THIS TO THE MOUN-TAINS.
WE'LL BE HERE!
RETURN IT? THE REMAINS?
YEAH. HE'S GOING TO THROW IT AWAY...THAT IS, BURY IT IN A SHALLOW GRAVE.
RAW LIVER IS DELI-CIOUS.
BUT SAFER NOT TO EAT IT. COULD GET PARASITES OR FOOD POISONING.
KIND OF SEEMS LIKE A WASTE...
IT'S NOT A WASTE.
IF YOU BURY IT IN THE MOUNTAINS, THE ANIMALS WILL TAKE IT.
IF THEY DON'T, IT WILL BECOME NUTRIENTS FOR THE SOIL.
BEWARE OF BEARS
ANIMALS... LIKE BEARS AND FOXES, RIGHT? YOU FEED THE PESTS?
THE BEARS CATCH THE DEER THAT DAMAGE CROPS, AND THE FOXES CATCH MICE.
IN SOME WAYS, WE HAVE A GIVE-AND-TAKE RELATION-SHIP.
IT'S NOT ALL BLACK-AND-WHITE.

SFX: DODODODODO (PUTTER)
BUT BEARS ARE SCARY, SO YOU NEED TO GO PRETTY DEEP INTO THE MOUNTAINS WHEN YOU BURY REMAINS.
C'MON, BARTH!
ドドドドド
HACHI-KEN-KUN, WHY DON'T YOU GO WASH YOUR HANDS?
EH?
AH! WHOA, LOOK AT THAT BLOOD!!!
JAAA (FSSH)
じゃ
BABABA (SPLASH)
ばばば
JAAA
じゃー
......

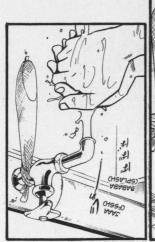

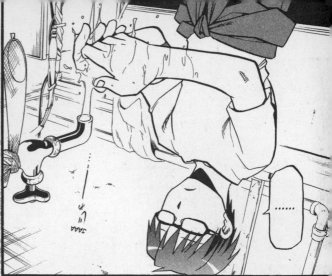

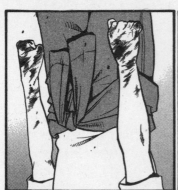

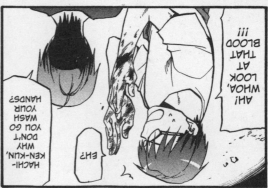

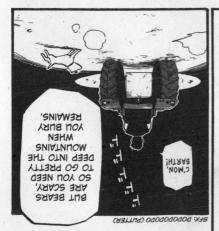

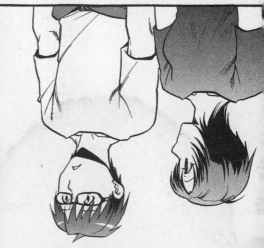

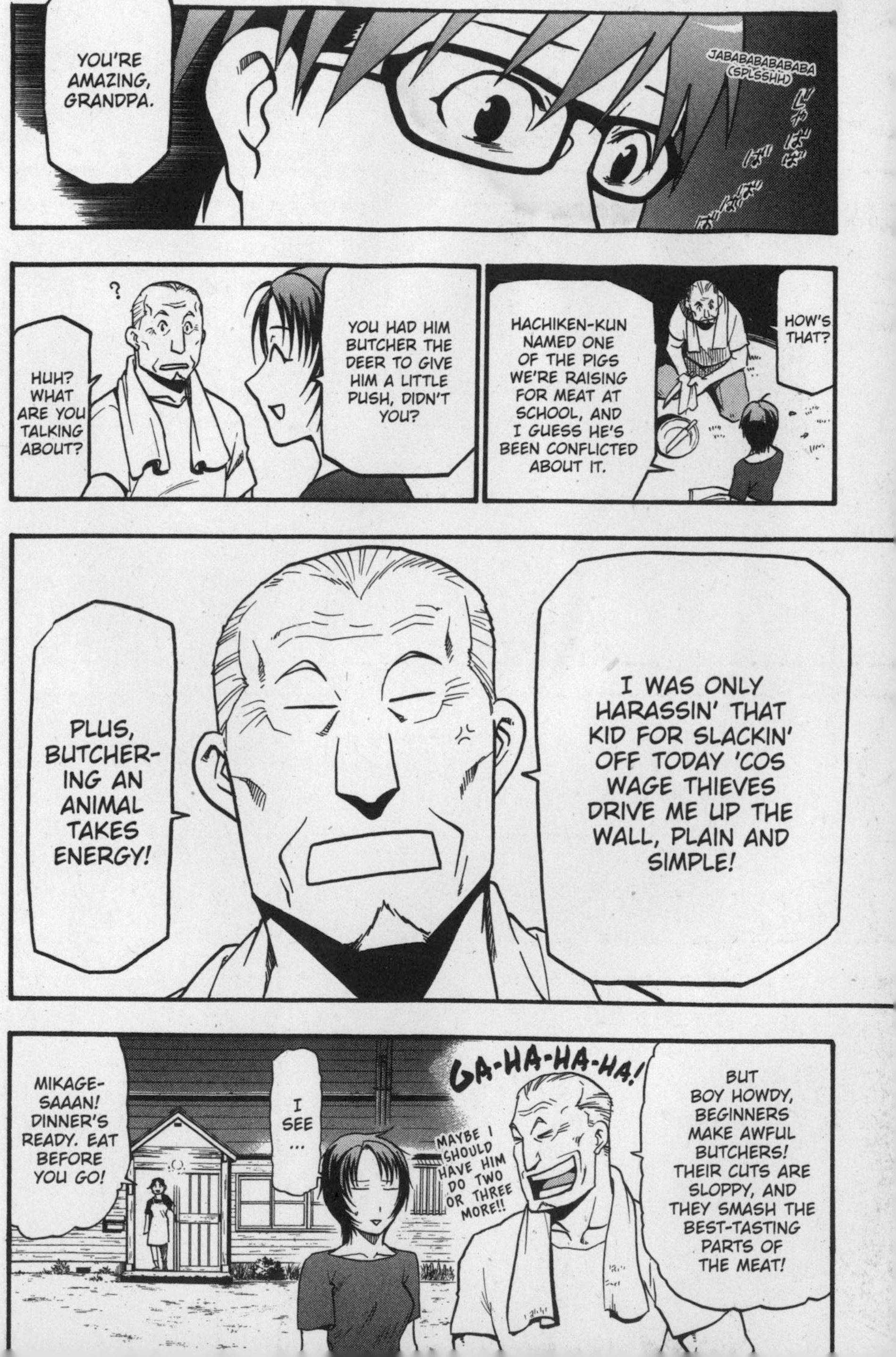
JABABABABABA (SPLSSHH)
YOU'RE AMAZING, GRANDPA.
HOW'S THAT?
HACHIKEN-KUN NAMED ONE OF THE PIGS WE'RE RAISING FOR MEAT AT SCHOOL, AND I GUESS HE'S BEEN CONFLICTED ABOUT IT.
YOU HAD HIM BUTCHER THE DEER TO GIVE HIM A LITTLE PUSH, DIDN'T YOU?
HUH? WHAT ARE YOU TALKING ABOUT?
I WAS ONLY HARASSIN' THAT KID FOR SLACKIN' OFF TODAY 'COS WAGE THIEVES DRIVE ME UP THE WALL, PLAIN AND SIMPLE!
PLUS, BUTCHER-ING AN ANIMAL TAKES ENERGY!
BUT BOY HOWDY, BEGINNERS MAKE AWFUL BUTCHERS! THEIR CUTS ARE SLOPPY, AND THEY SMASH THE BEST-TASTING PARTS OF THE MEAT!
GA-HA-HA-HA!
MAYBE I SHOULD HAVE HIM DO TWO OR THREE MORE!!
I SEE ...
MIKAGE-SAAAN! DINNER'S READY. EAT BEFORE YOU GO!

MEAT!!
EAT UP BEFORE IT GETS COLD!
LOOKS GOOD. I'M STARVING.
LET'S EAT!
GARI (GNAW)
GARI
GARI GARI
THIS MEAT ......
...WAS A LIVING THING AN HOUR AGO...
......
MOSO (NIBBLE)
THANK YOU FOR THE FOOD ...

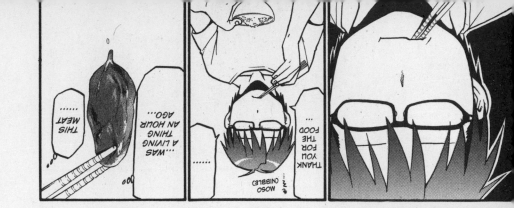

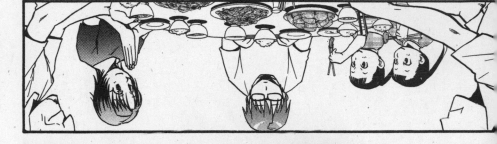

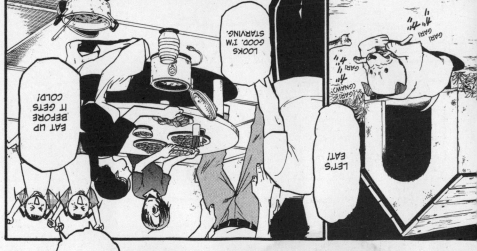

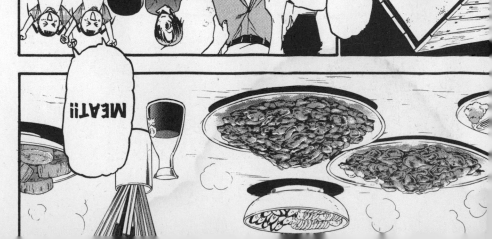

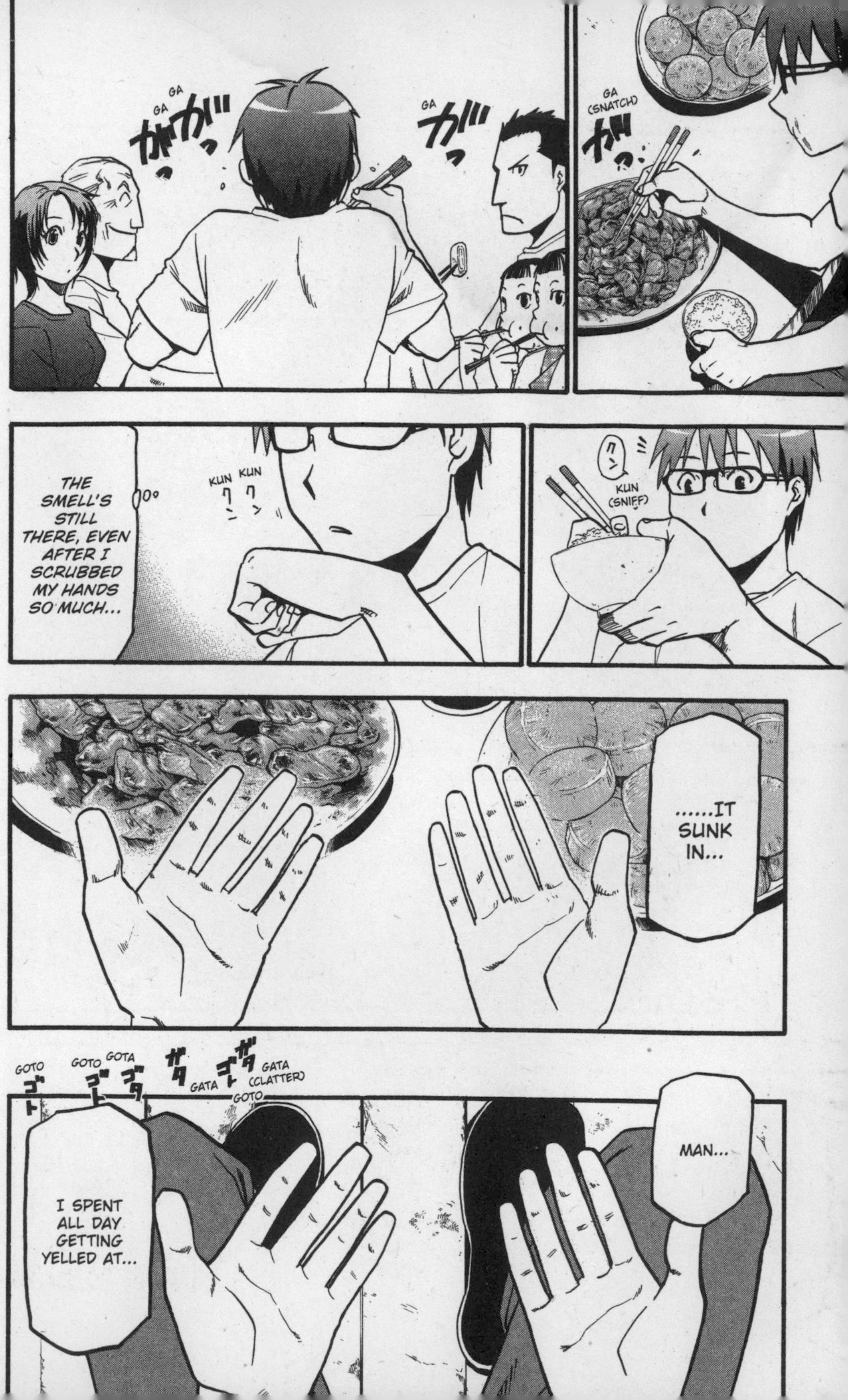
GA (SNATCH)
GA
GA GA
KUN (SNIFF)
KUN KUN
THE SMELL'S STILL THERE, EVEN AFTER I SCRUBBED MY HANDS SO MUCH...
......IT SUNK IN...
GOTO GOTO GOTA GATA GOTO GATA (CLATTER)
MAN...
I SPENT ALL DAY GETTING YELLED AT...

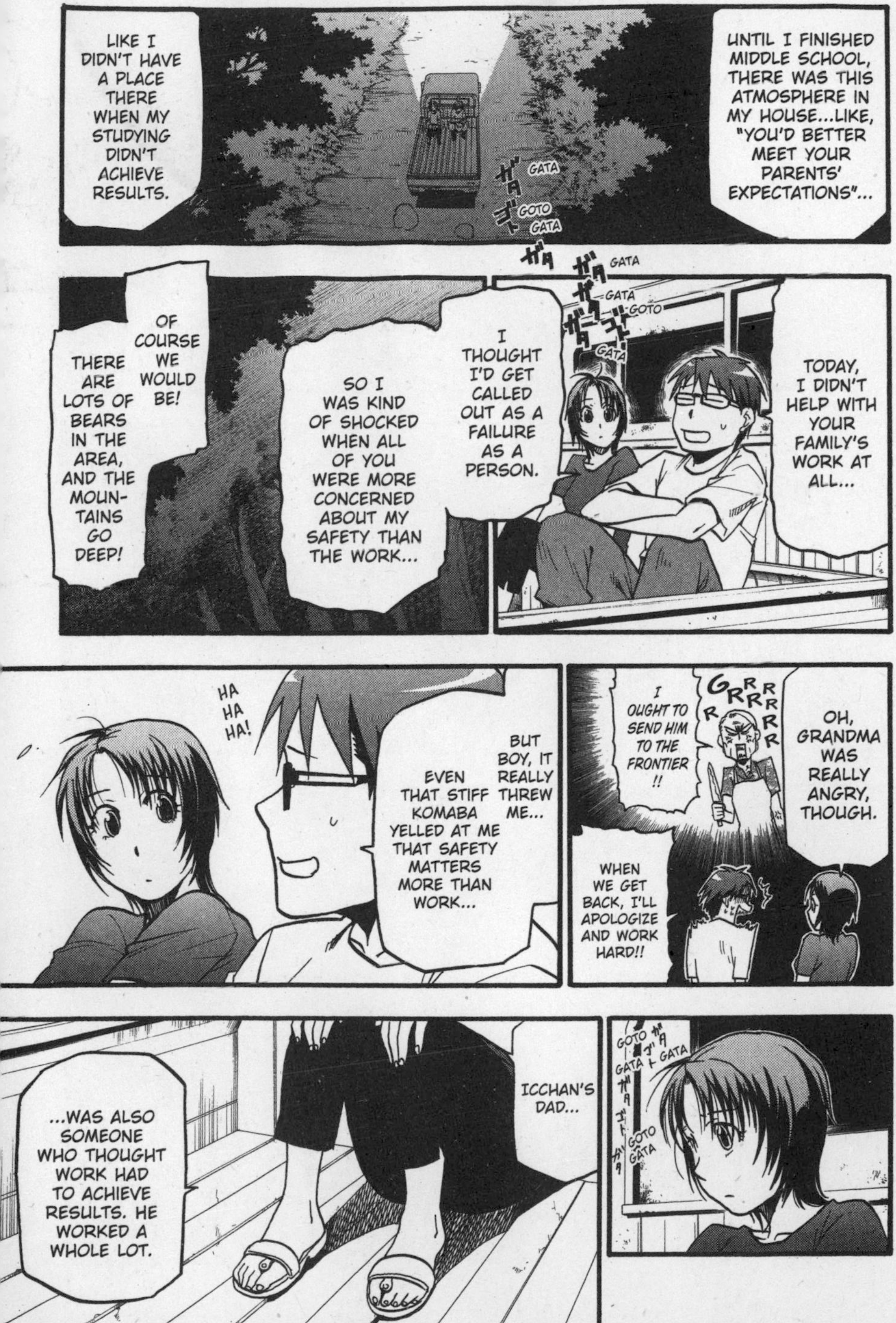
UNTIL I FINISHED MIDDLE SCHOOL, THERE WAS THIS ATMOSPHERE IN MY HOUSE...LIKE, "YOU'D BETTER MEET YOUR PARENTS' EXPECTATIONS"...
GATA
GOTO GATA
LIKE I DIDN'T HAVE A PLACE THERE WHEN MY STUDYING DIDN'T ACHIEVE RESULTS.
GATA
GATA GOTO GATA
TODAY, I DIDN'T HELP WITH YOUR FAMILY'S WORK AT ALL...
I THOUGHT I'D GET CALLED OUT AS A FAILURE AS A PERSON.
SO I WAS KIND OF SHOCKED WHEN ALL OF YOU WERE MORE CONCERNED ABOUT MY SAFETY THAN THE WORK...
OF COURSE WE WOULD BE!
THERE ARE LOTS OF BEARS IN THE AREA, AND THE MOUN-TAINS GO DEEP!
OH, GRANDMA WAS REALLY ANGRY, THOUGH.
GRRRRRRRR
I OUGHT TO SEND HIM TO THE FRONTIER !!
WHEN WE GET BACK, I'LL APOLOGIZE AND WORK HARD!!
HA HA HA!
BUT BOY, IT REALLY THREW ME...
EVEN THAT STIFF KOMABA YELLED AT ME THAT SAFETY MATTERS MORE THAN WORK...
GOTO GATA
GATA
GOTO GATA
ICCHAN'S DAD...
...WAS ALSO SOMEONE WHO THOUGHT WORK HAD TO ACHIEVE RESULTS. HE WORKED A WHOLE LOT.

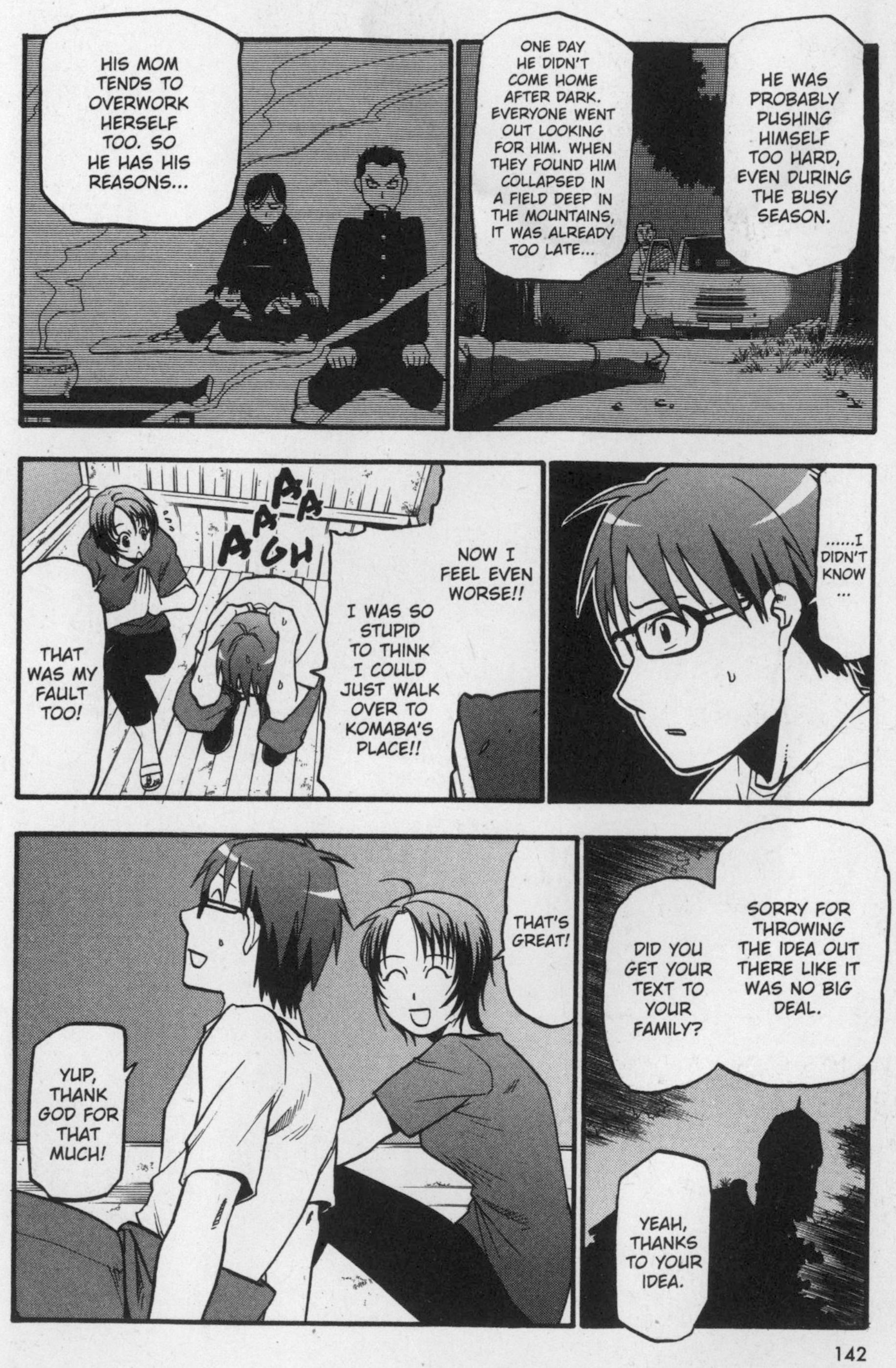
HE WAS PROBABLY PUSHING HIMSELF TOO HARD, EVEN DURING THE BUSY SEASON.
ONE DAY HE DIDN'T COME HOME AFTER DARK. EVERYONE WENT OUT LOOKING FOR HIM. WHEN THEY FOUND HIM COLLAPSED IN A FIELD DEEP IN THE MOUNTAINS, IT WAS ALREADY TOO LATE...
HIS MOM TENDS TO OVERWORK HERSELF TOO. SO HE HAS HIS REASONS...
......I DIDN'T KNOW ...
NOW I FEEL EVEN WORSE!!
AAAAGH
I WAS SO STUPID TO THINK I COULD JUST WALK OVER TO KOMABA'S PLACE!!
THAT WAS MY FAULT TOO!
SORRY FOR THROWING THE IDEA OUT THERE LIKE IT WAS NO BIG DEAL.
DID YOU GET YOUR TEXT TO YOUR FAMILY?
YEAH, THANKS TO YOUR IDEA.
THAT'S GREAT!
YUP, THANK GOD FOR THAT MUCH!

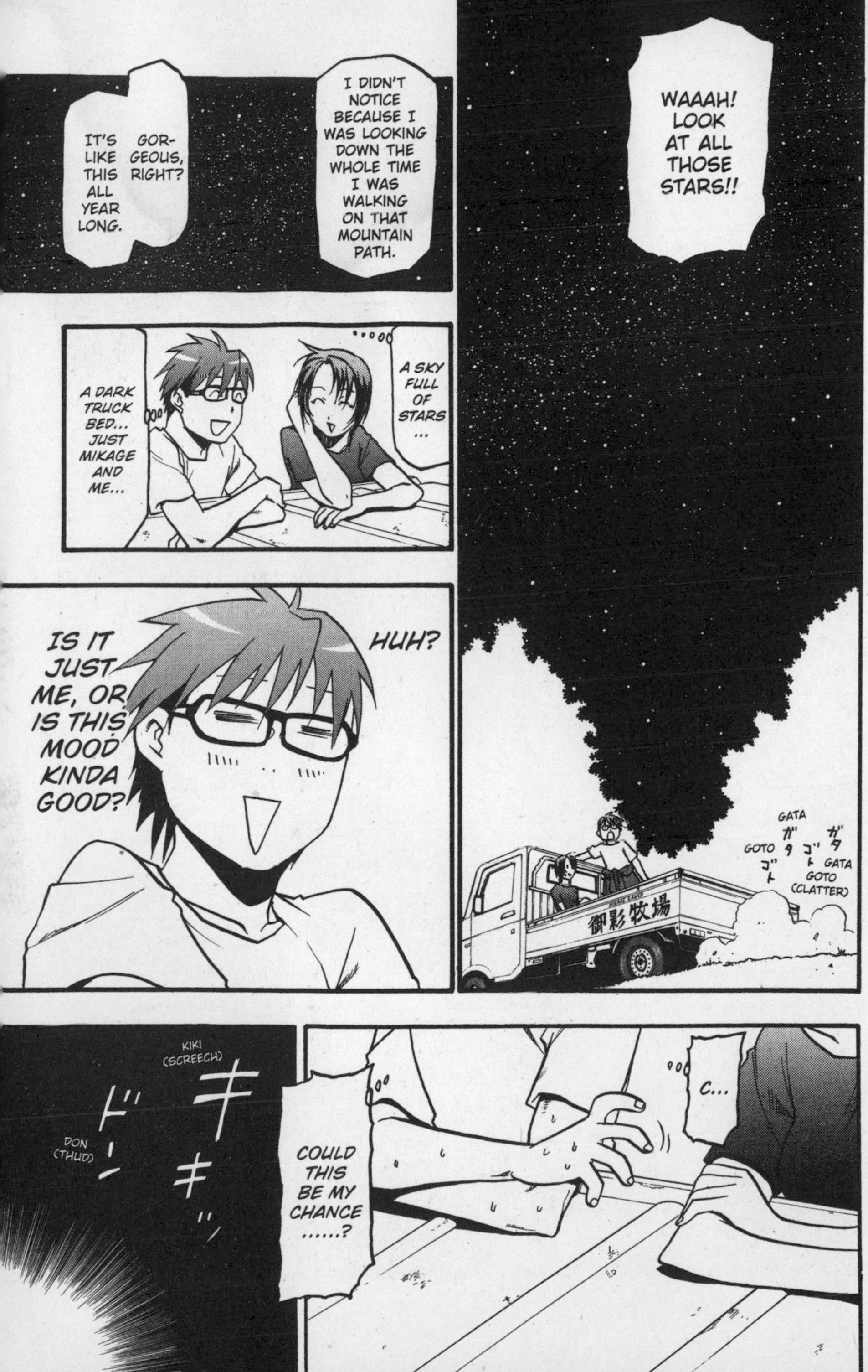
WAAAH! LOOK AT ALL THOSE STARS!!
GATA GOTO GATA GOTO (CLATTER)
御影牧場
I DIDN'T NOTICE BECAUSE I WAS LOOKING DOWN THE WHOLE TIME I WAS WALKING ON THAT MOUNTAIN PATH.
GORGEOUS, RIGHT?
IT'S LIKE THIS ALL YEAR LONG.
A SKY FULL OF STARS...
A DARK TRUCK BED... JUST MIKAGE AND ME...
HUH?
IS IT JUST ME, OR IS THIS MOOD KINDA GOOD?
C...
COULD THIS BE MY CHANCE......?
KIKI (SCREECH)
DON (THUD)

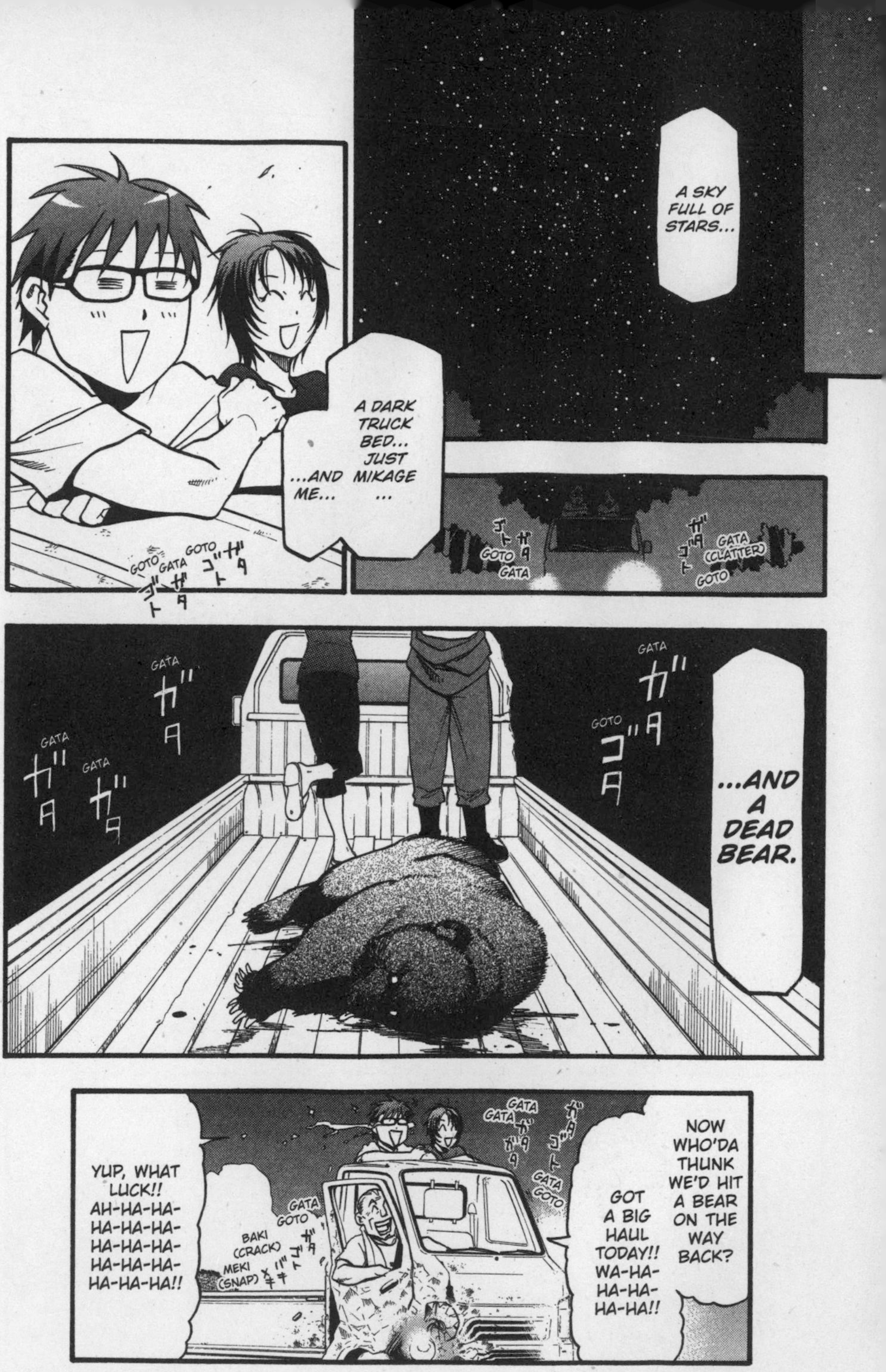
A SKY FULL OF STARS...
GATA (CLATTER) GOTO
GOTO GATA
A DARK TRUCK BED... JUST MIKAGE ...
...AND ME...
GOTO GATA GOTO GATA
...AND A DEAD BEAR.
GOTO GATA
GATA
GATA GATA
NOW WHO'DA THUNK WE'D HIT A BEAR ON THE WAY BACK?
GOT A BIG HAUL TODAY!! WA-HA-HA-HA-HA-HA!!
GATA GATA GATA GOTO
GATA GOTO
BAKI (CRACK) MEKI (SNAP)
YUP, WHAT LUCK!! AH-HA-HA-HA-HA-HA-HA-HA-HA-HA-HA-HA-HA-HA-HA!!

Silver Spoon

YUTAKA
KONDOU

NISEKO VILLAGE
MIDDLE SCHOOL
BASKETBALL TEAM

I'M SO SORRY FOR THE TROUBLE...
IT'S GOOD THAT YOU'RE SAFE, BUT YOU REALLY GAVE US A FRIGHT!
I'M VERY SORRY! I'LL HAVE MY ACT TOGETHER TOMORROW!
PEKO PEKO
PEKO (BOW)
Chapter 16:
Tale of Summer ⑥
SO, YOU BUTCHERED A DEER?
AH, YES, MA'AM!
GASA (RUSTLE)
WE LEFT HALF WITH THE KOMABAS, AND THIS HALF IS FOR YOU...
GASA GASA

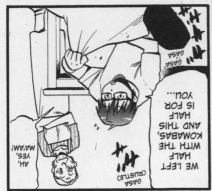

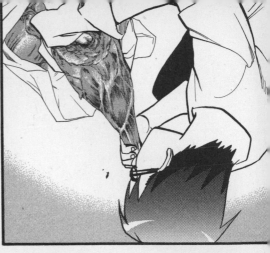

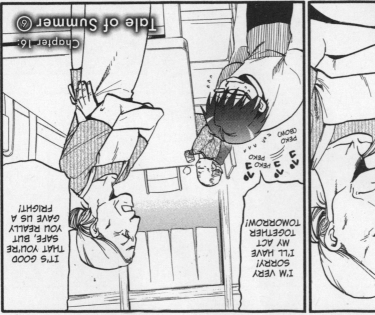

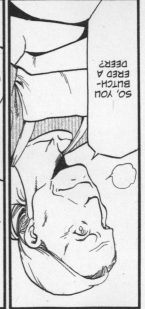

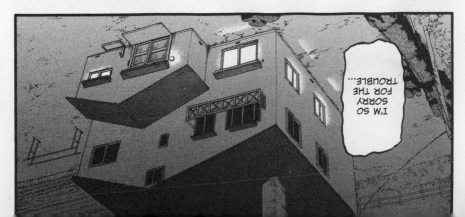

HEAVY ......
HOO BOY, WHAT A DAY!
HIT A BEAR ON THE WAY HOME. THE TRUCK'S ALL DENTED UP!
BEAR ...
BOSO (MUMBLE) ぼそ…
SHE SPOKE !!
BOSO ぼそ
BOSO ぼそ BOSO ぼそ
THE YEAR WE SETTLED HERE, JIROU-SAN'S WIFE AND DAUGHTER WERE EATEN BY A BEAR...
THE AINU HUNTERS AND THE MENFOLK ALL GOT TOGETHER AND WENT ON A MOUNTAIN HUNT, BUT THEY COULDN'T KILL IT.
TWO DAYS LATER, IT GOT GENICHI-SAN'S WHOLE FAMILY.
IT WAS A GIANT BEAR.
ぼそ BOSO ぼそ BOSO
ぼそ BOSO
ぼそ BOSO ぼそ BOSO ぼそ BOSO
MOGO (CHEW) もご MOGO もご
HEAVYYYY......

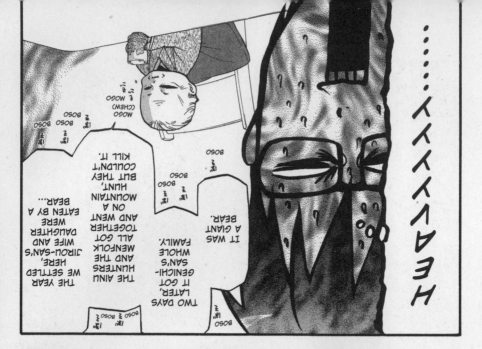

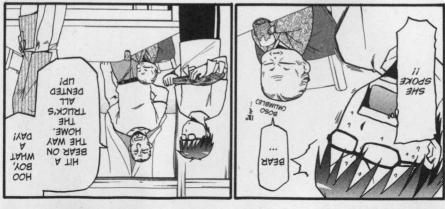

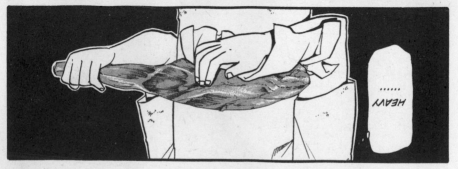

Chapter 16: Tale of Summer ⑥

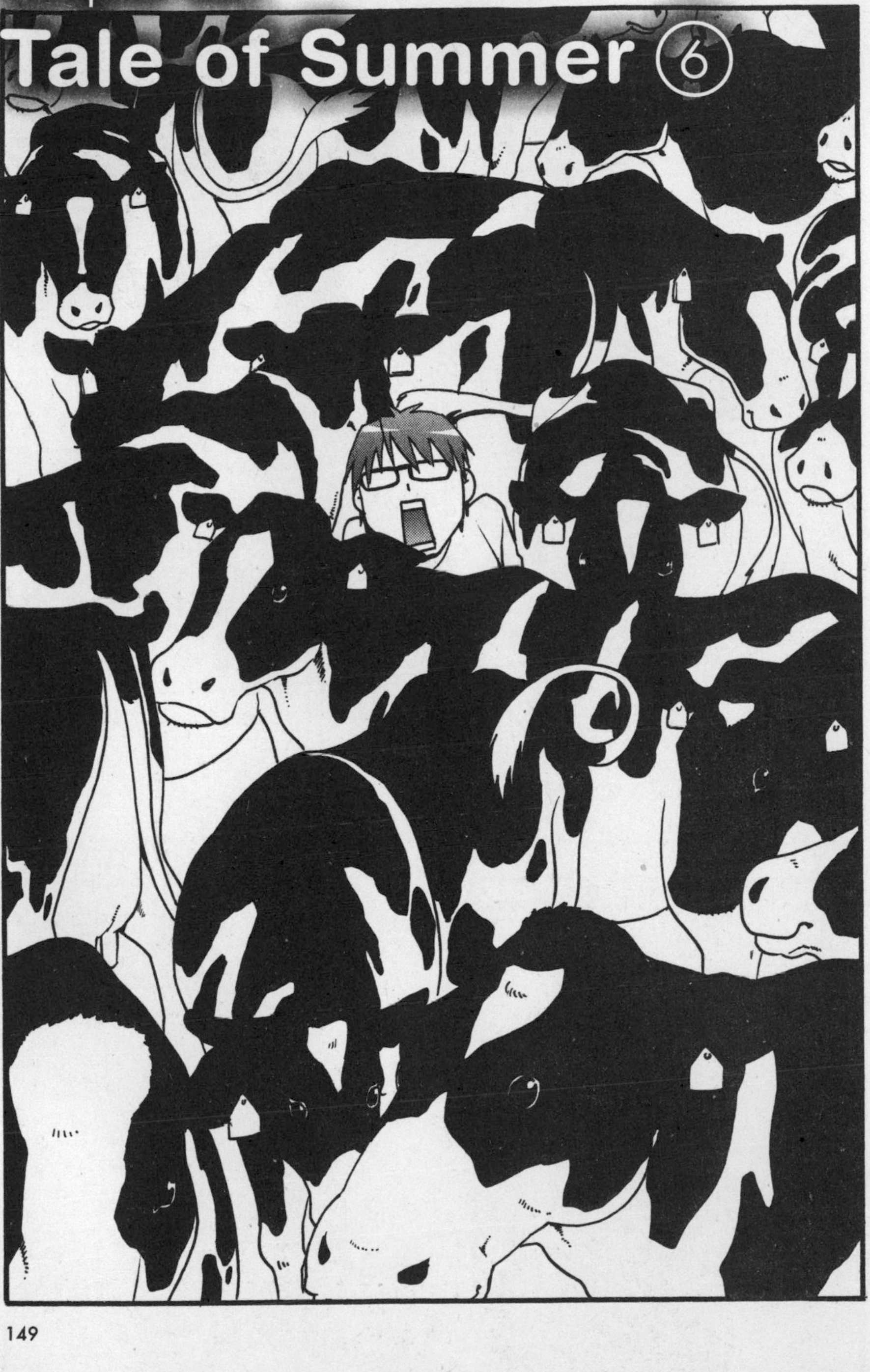

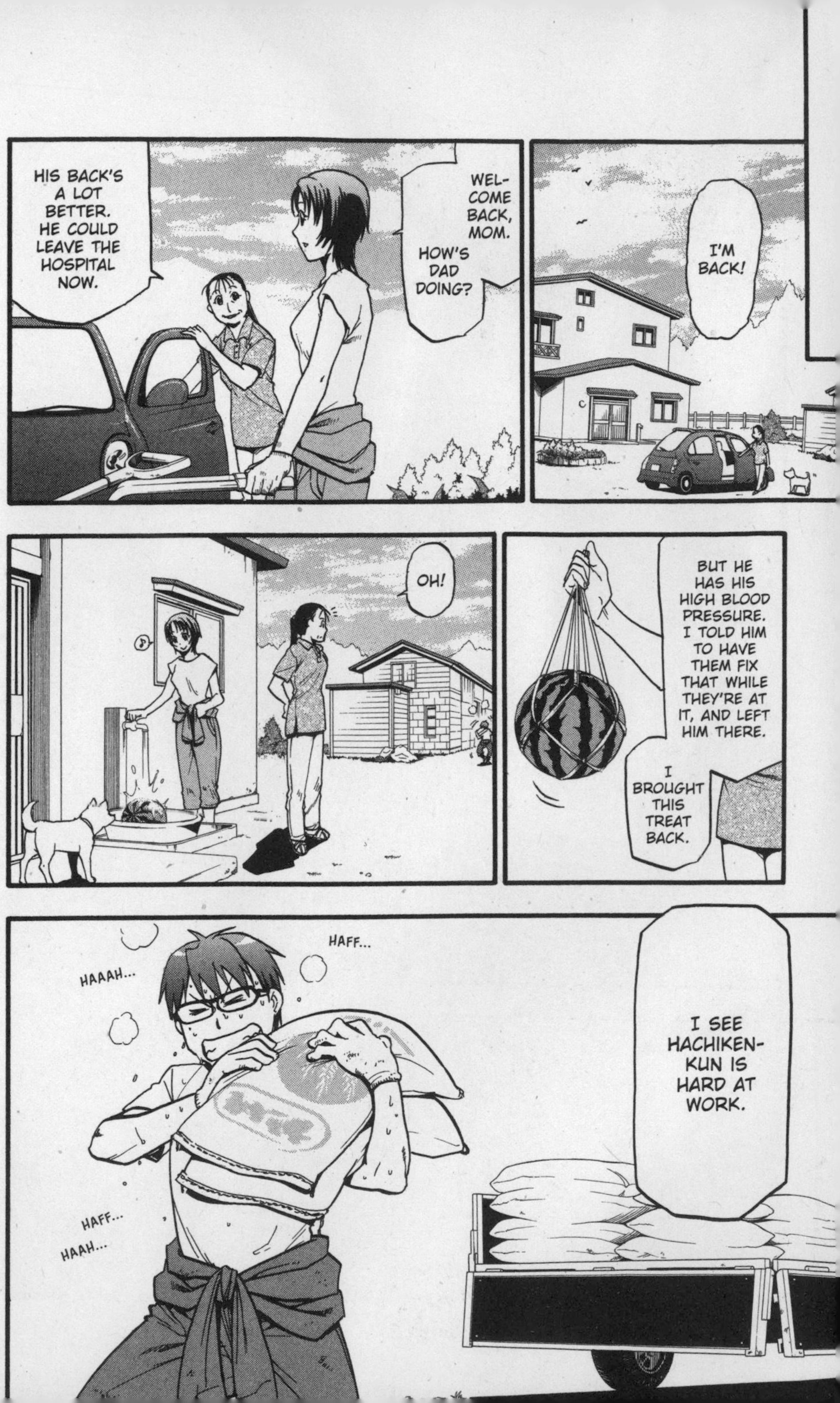
I'M BACK!
WEL-COME BACK, MOM.
HOW'S DAD DOING?
HIS BACK'S A LOT BETTER. HE COULD LEAVE THE HOSPITAL NOW.
BUT HE HAS HIS HIGH BLOOD PRESSURE. I TOLD HIM TO HAVE THEM FIX THAT WHILE THEY'RE AT IT, AND LEFT HIM THERE.
I BROUGHT THIS TREAT BACK.
OH!
I SEE HACHIKEN-KUN IS HARD AT WORK.
HAFF...
HAAAH...
HAFF...
HAAH...

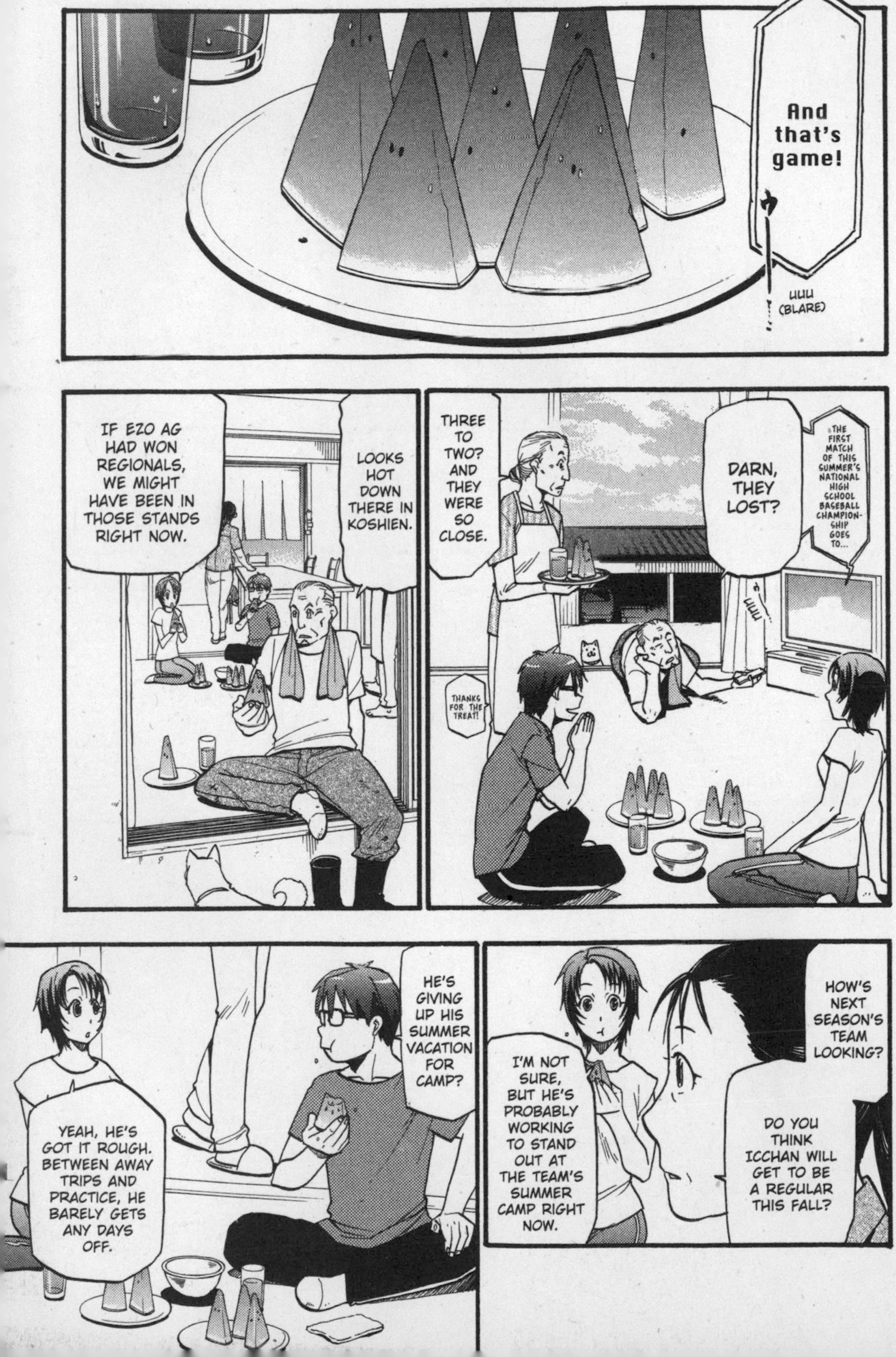
And that's game!
UUU (BLARE)
THE FIRST MATCH OF THIS SUMMER'S NATIONAL HIGH SCHOOL BASEBALL CHAMPIONSHIP GOES TO...
DARN, THEY LOST?
UUU
THREE TO TWO? AND THEY WERE SO CLOSE.
THANKS FOR THE TREAT!
LOOKS HOT DOWN THERE IN KOSHIEN.
IF EZO AG HAD WON REGIONALS, WE MIGHT HAVE BEEN IN THOSE STANDS RIGHT NOW.
HOW'S NEXT SEASON'S TEAM LOOKING?
DO YOU THINK ICCHAN WILL GET TO BE A REGULAR THIS FALL?
I'M NOT SURE, BUT HE'S PROBABLY WORKING TO STAND OUT AT THE TEAM'S SUMMER CAMP RIGHT NOW.
HE'S GIVING UP HIS SUMMER VACATION FOR CAMP?
YEAH, HE'S GOT IT ROUGH. BETWEEN AWAY TRIPS AND PRACTICE, HE BARELY GETS ANY DAYS OFF.

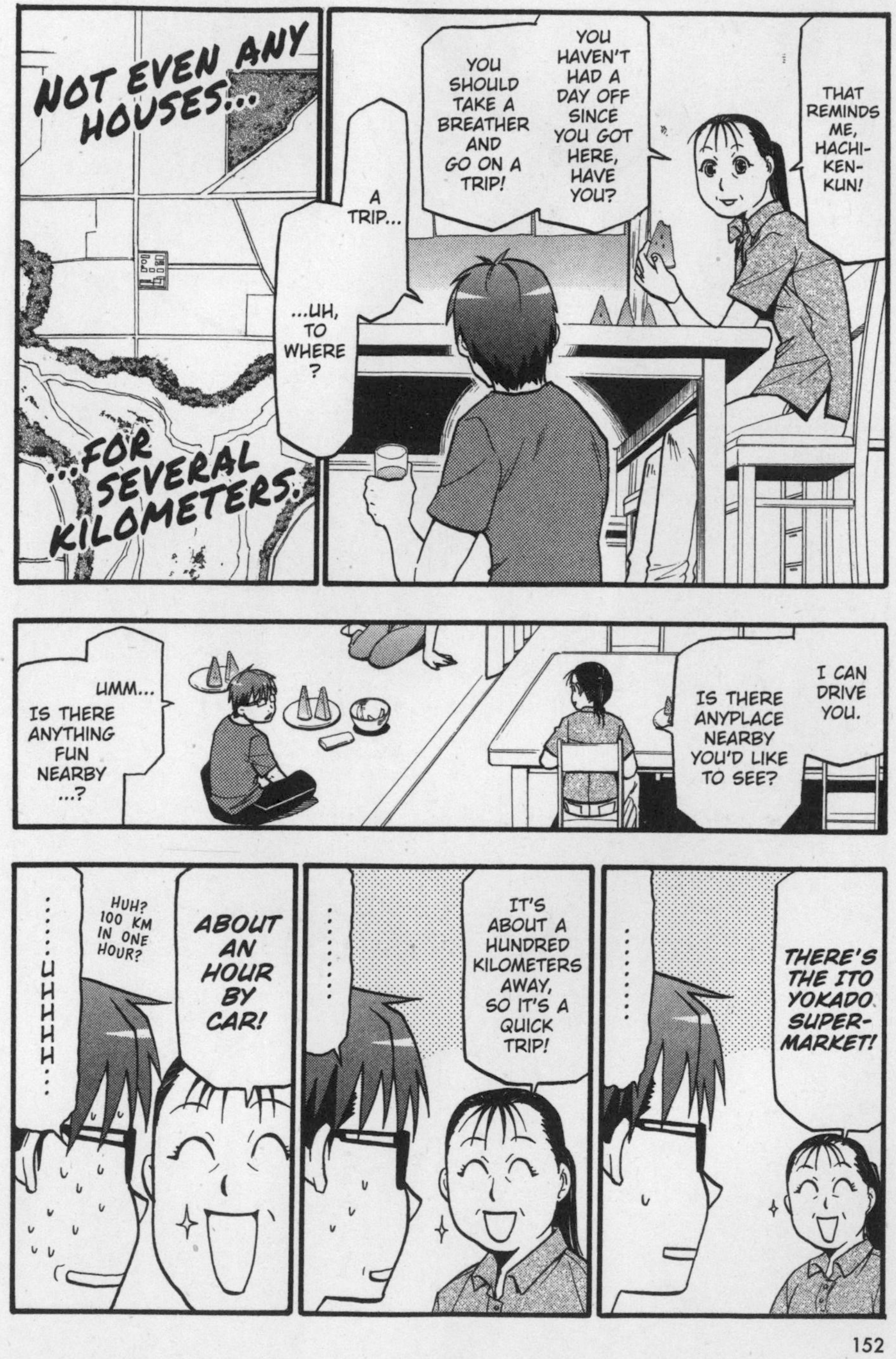
THAT REMINDS ME, HACHI-KEN-KUN!
YOU HAVEN'T HAD A DAY OFF SINCE YOU GOT HERE, HAVE YOU?
YOU SHOULD TAKE A BREATHER AND GO ON A TRIP!
A TRIP...
...UH, TO WHERE ?
NOT EVEN ANY HOUSES...
...FOR SEVERAL KILOMETERS.
I CAN DRIVE YOU.
IS THERE ANYPLACE NEARBY YOU'D LIKE TO SEE?
UMM... IS THERE ANYTHING FUN NEARBY ...?
THERE'S THE ITO YOKADO SUPER-MARKET!
....
IT'S ABOUT A HUNDRED KILOMETERS AWAY, SO IT'S A QUICK TRIP!
....
ABOUT AN HOUR BY CAR!
HUH? 100 KM IN ONE HOUR?
......UHHHH...

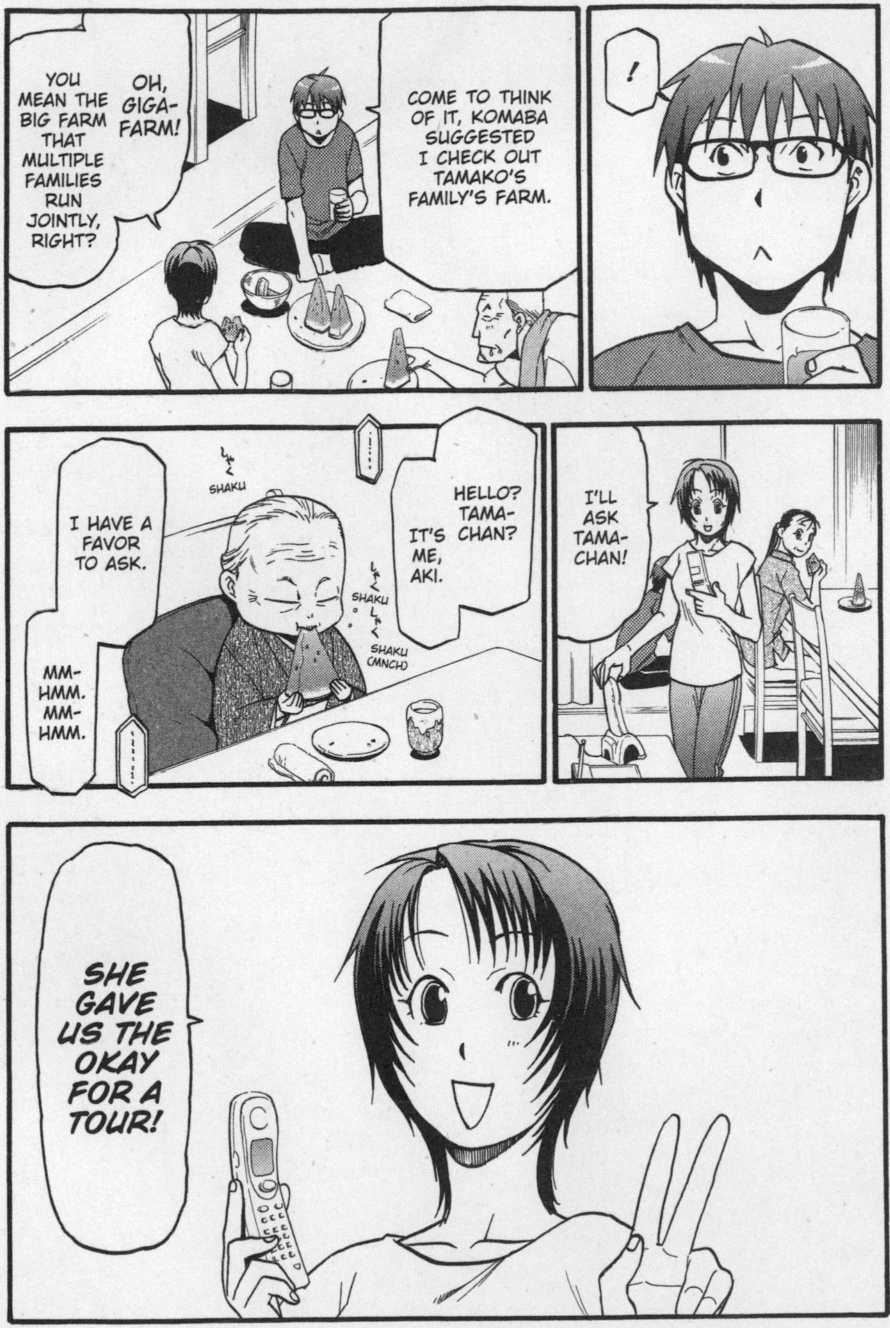
!
COME TO THINK OF IT, KOMABA SUGGESTED I CHECK OUT TAMAKO'S FAMILY'S FARM.
OH, GIGA-FARM!
YOU MEAN THE BIG FARM THAT MULTIPLE FAMILIES RUN JOINTLY, RIGHT?
I'LL ASK TAMA-CHAN!
HELLO? TAMA-CHAN?
IT'S ME, AKI.
SHAKU
SHAKU
SHAKU (MNCH)
I HAVE A FAVOR TO ASK.
MM-HMM. MM-HMM.
SHE GAVE US THE OKAY FOR A TOUR!

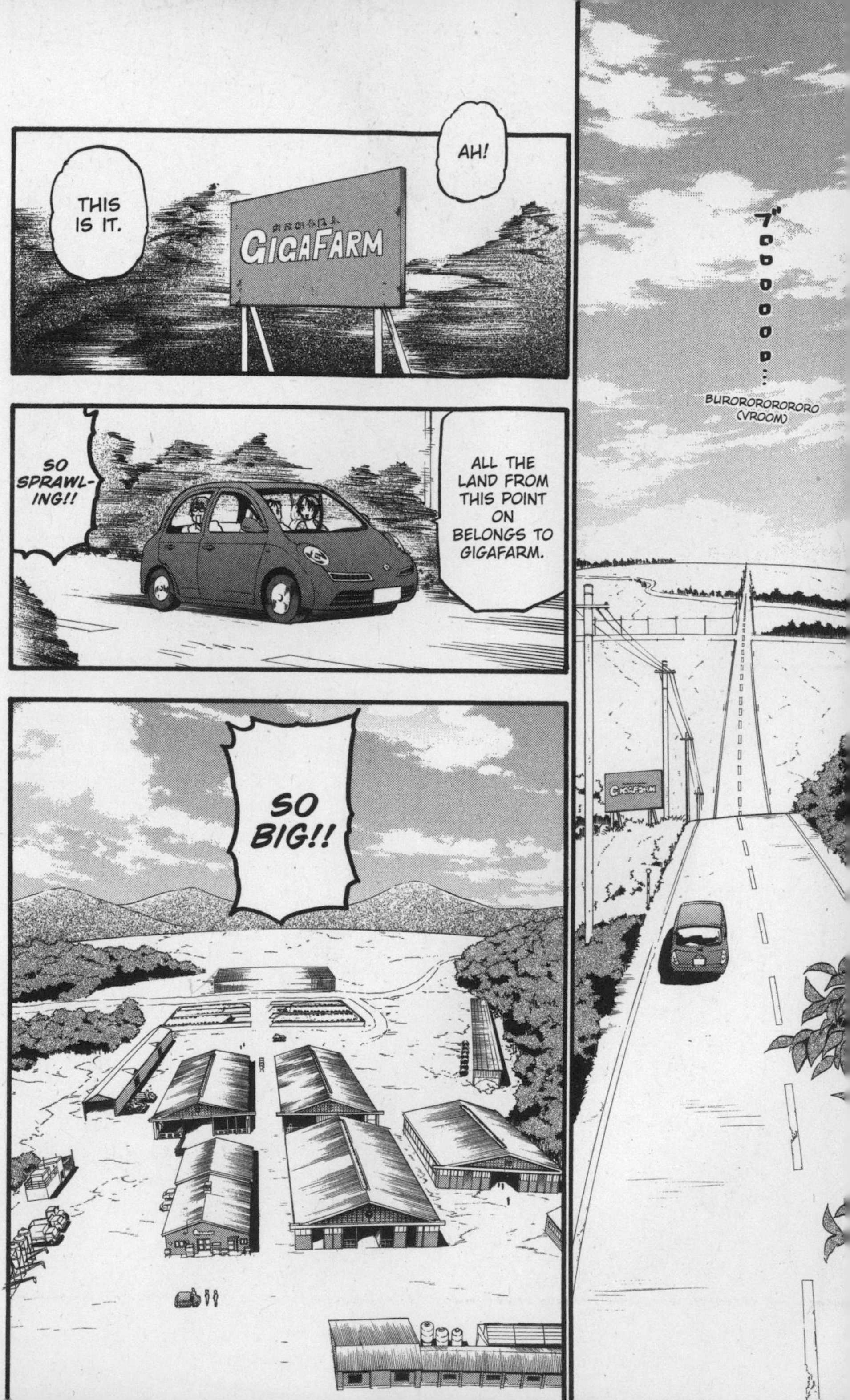
BURORORORORORO
(VROOM)
GIGAFARM
AH!
THIS IS IT.
GIGAFARM
ALL THE LAND FROM THIS POINT ON BELONGS TO GIGAFARM.
SO SPRAWLING!!
SO BIG!!

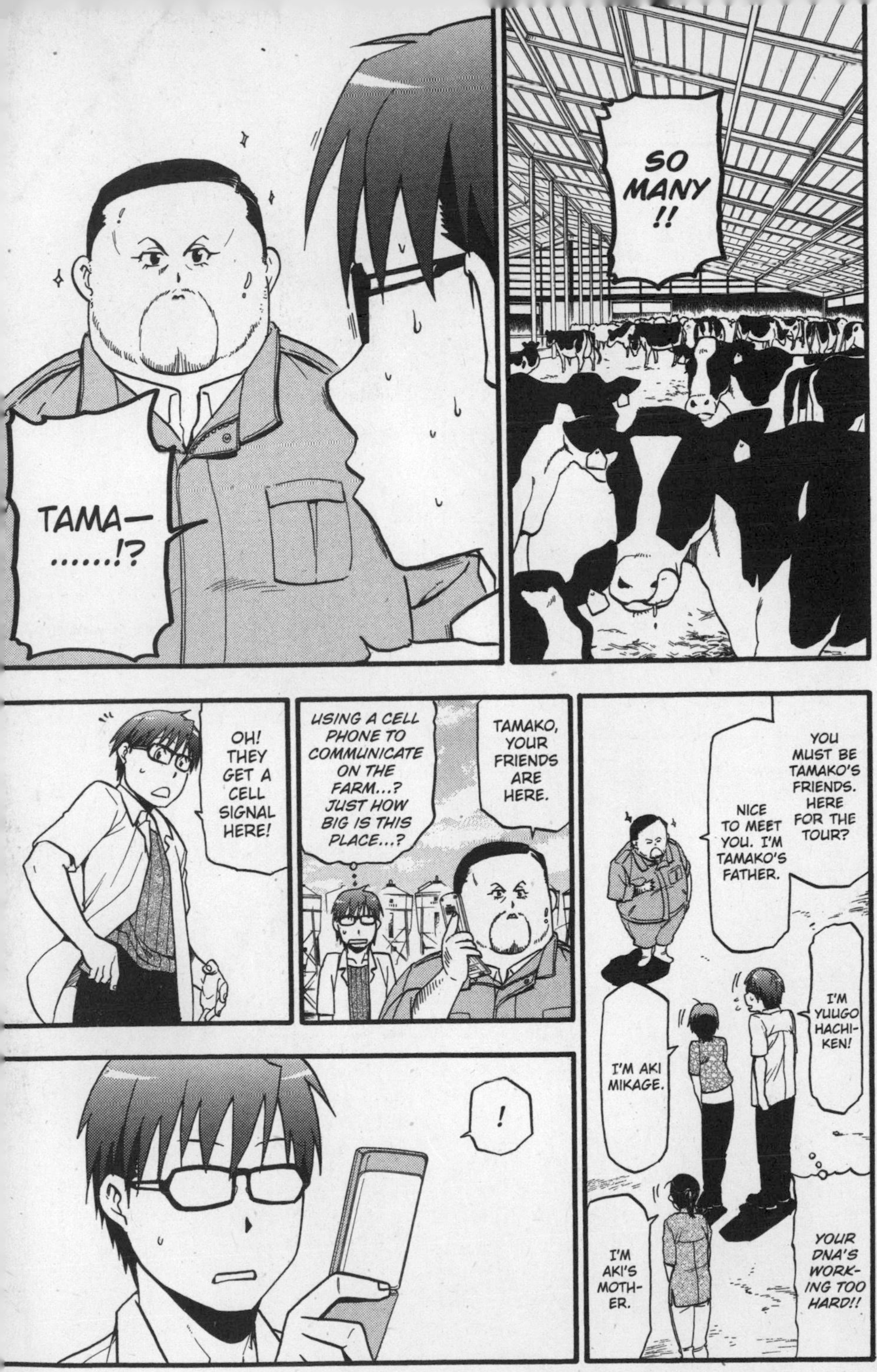
SO MANY !!
TAMA— ......!?
YOU MUST BE TAMAKO'S FRIENDS. HERE FOR THE TOUR?
NICE TO MEET YOU. I'M TAMAKO'S FATHER.
I'M YUUGO HACHIKEN!
I'M AKI MIKAGE.
YOUR DNA'S WORKING TOO HARD!!
I'M AKI'S MOTHER.
TAMAKO, YOUR FRIENDS ARE HERE.
USING A CELL PHONE TO COMMUNICATE ON THE FARM...? JUST HOW BIG IS THIS PLACE...?
OH! THEY GET A CELL SIGNAL HERE!
!

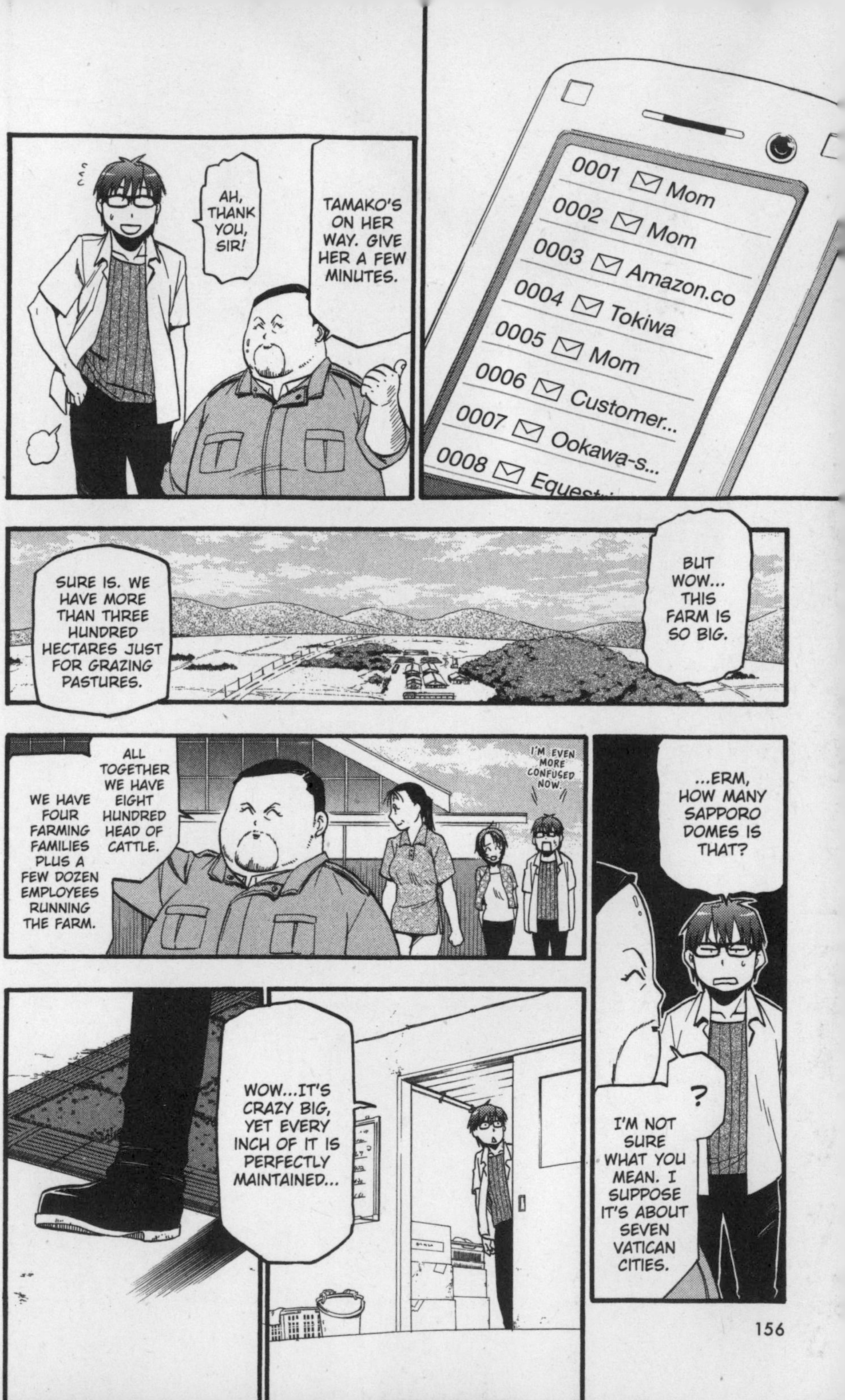
0001 Mom
0002 Mom
0003 Amazon.co
0004 Tokiwa
0005 Mom
0006 Customer...
0007 Ookawa-s...
TAMAKO'S ON HER WAY. GIVE HER A FEW MINUTES.
AH, THANK YOU, SIR!
BUT WOW... THIS FARM IS SO BIG.
SURE IS. WE HAVE MORE THAN THREE HUNDRED HECTARES JUST FOR GRAZING PASTURES.
...ERM, HOW MANY SAPPORO DOMES IS THAT?
I'M EVEN MORE CONFUSED NOW.
ALL TOGETHER WE HAVE EIGHT HUNDRED HEAD OF CATTLE.
WE HAVE FOUR FARMING FAMILIES PLUS A FEW DOZEN EMPLOYEES RUNNING THE FARM.
?
I'M NOT SURE WHAT YOU MEAN. I SUPPOSE IT'S ABOUT SEVEN VATICAN CITIES.
WOW...IT'S CRAZY BIG, YET EVERY INCH OF IT IS PERFECTLY MAINTAINED...

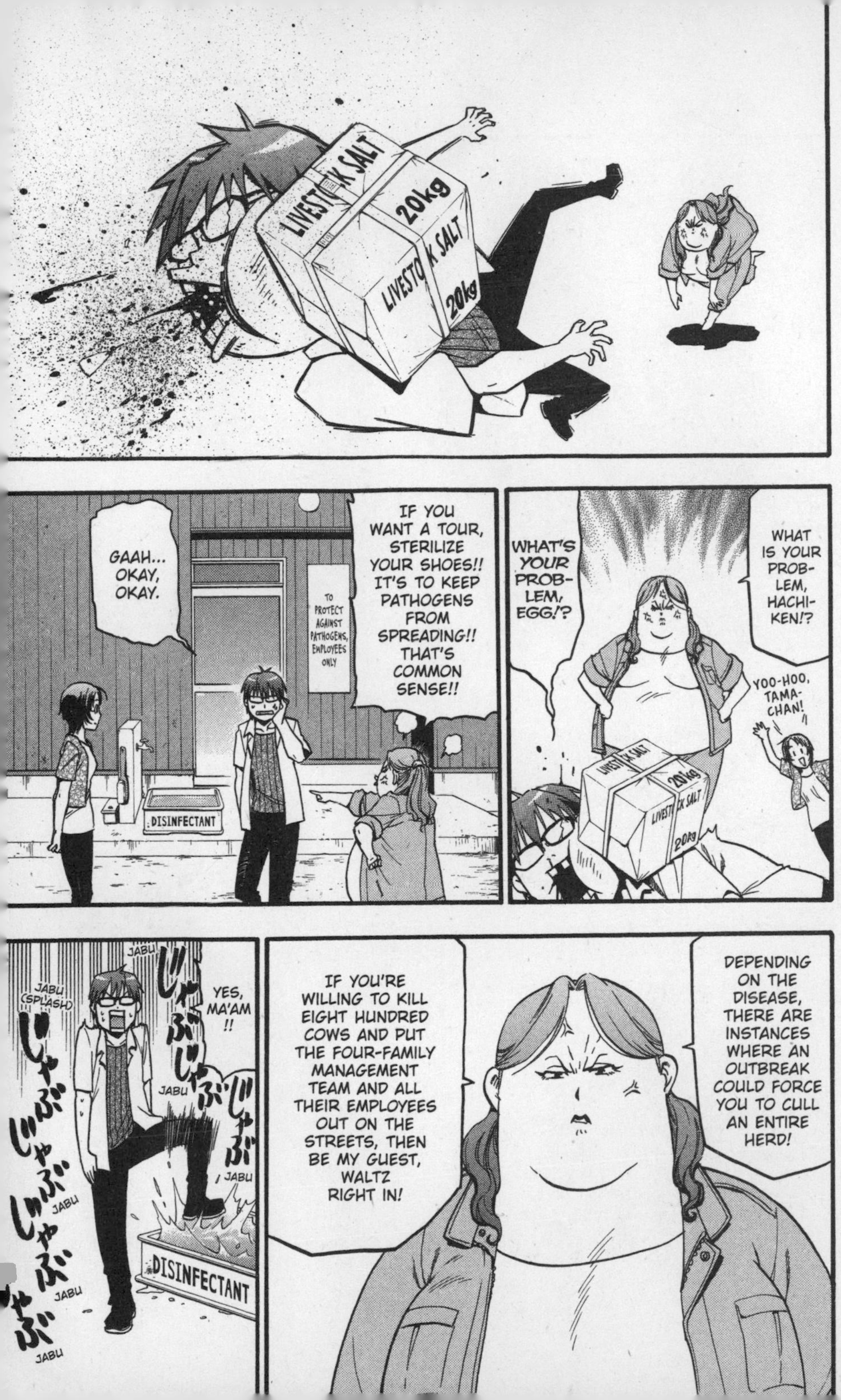
LIVESTOCK SALT
20kg
LIVESTOCK SALT
20kg
WHAT IS YOUR PROB-LEM, HACHI-KEN!?
WHAT'S YOUR PROB-LEM, EGG!?
YOO-HOO, TAMA-CHAN!
LIVESTOCK SALT
20kg
IF YOU WANT A TOUR, STERILIZE YOUR SHOES!! IT'S TO KEEP PATHOGENS FROM SPREADING!! THAT'S COMMON SENSE!!
GAAH... OKAY, OKAY.
TO PROTECT AGAINST PATHOGENS, EMPLOYEES ONLY
DISINFECTANT
DEPENDING ON THE DISEASE, THERE ARE INSTANCES WHERE AN OUTBREAK COULD FORCE YOU TO CULL AN ENTIRE HERD!
IF YOU'RE WILLING TO KILL EIGHT HUNDRED COWS AND PUT THE FOUR-FAMILY MANAGEMENT TEAM AND ALL THEIR EMPLOYEES OUT ON THE STREETS, THEN BE MY GUEST, WALTZ RIGHT IN!
YES, MA'AM!!
JABU
JABU (SPLASH)
JABU
JABU
JABU
JABU
JABU
DISINFECTANT

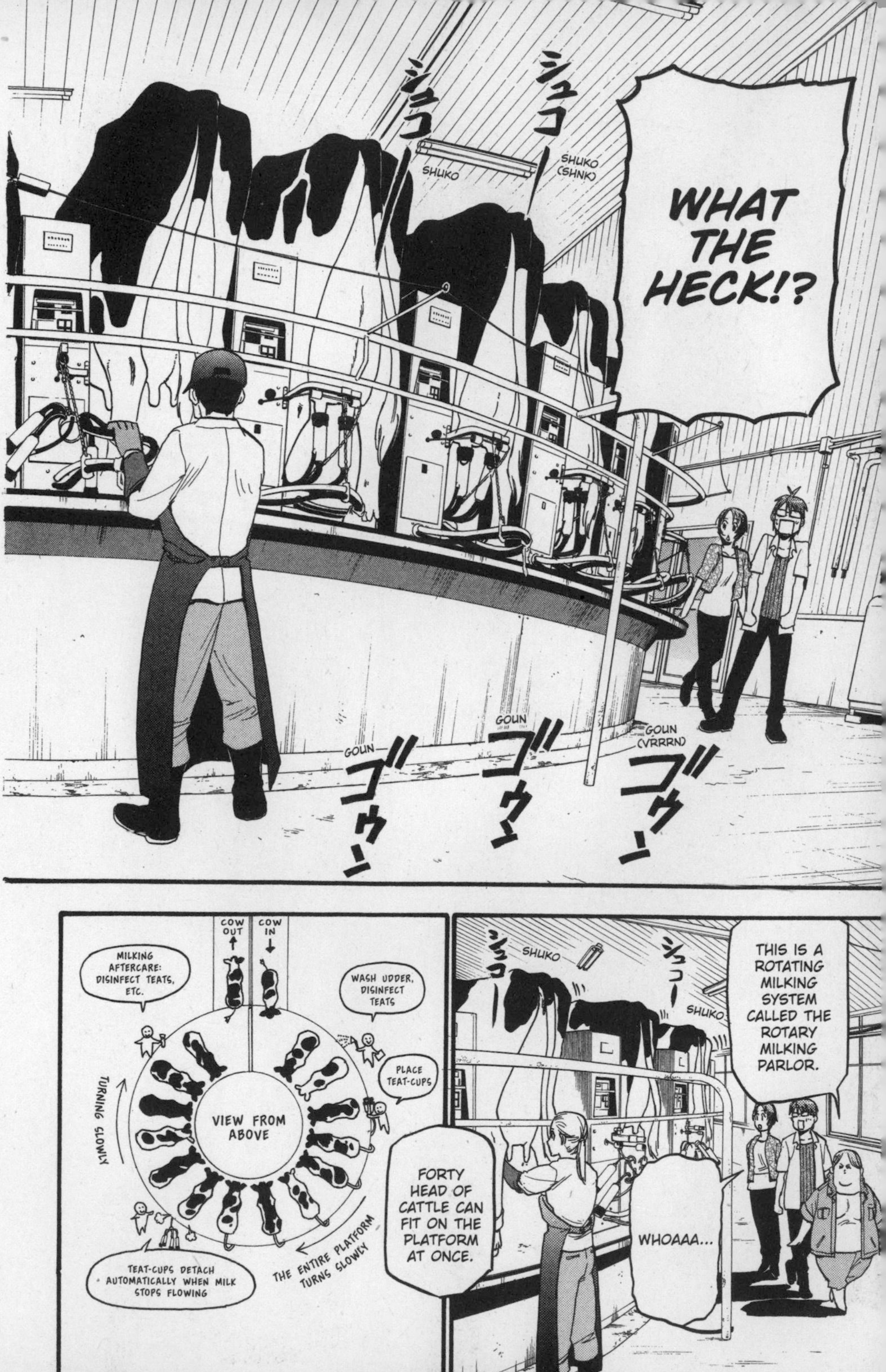
WHAT THE HECK!?
シュコ
SHUKO (SHNK)
シュコ
SHUKO
ゴウン
GOUN (VRRRN)
ゴウン
GOUN
ゴウン
GOUN
THIS IS A ROTATING MILKING SYSTEM CALLED THE ROTARY MILKING PARLOR.
シュコー
SHUKO
シュコー
SHUKO
WHOAAA...
FORTY HEAD OF CATTLE CAN FIT ON THE PLATFORM AT ONCE.
COW OUT
COW IN
MILKING AFTERCARE: DISINFECT TEATS, ETC.
WASH UDDER, DISINFECT TEATS
PLACE TEAT-CUPS
VIEW FROM ABOVE
TURNING SLOWLY
THE ENTIRE PLATFORM TURNS SLOWLY
TEAT-CUPS DETACH AUTOMATICALLY WHEN MILK STOPS FLOWING

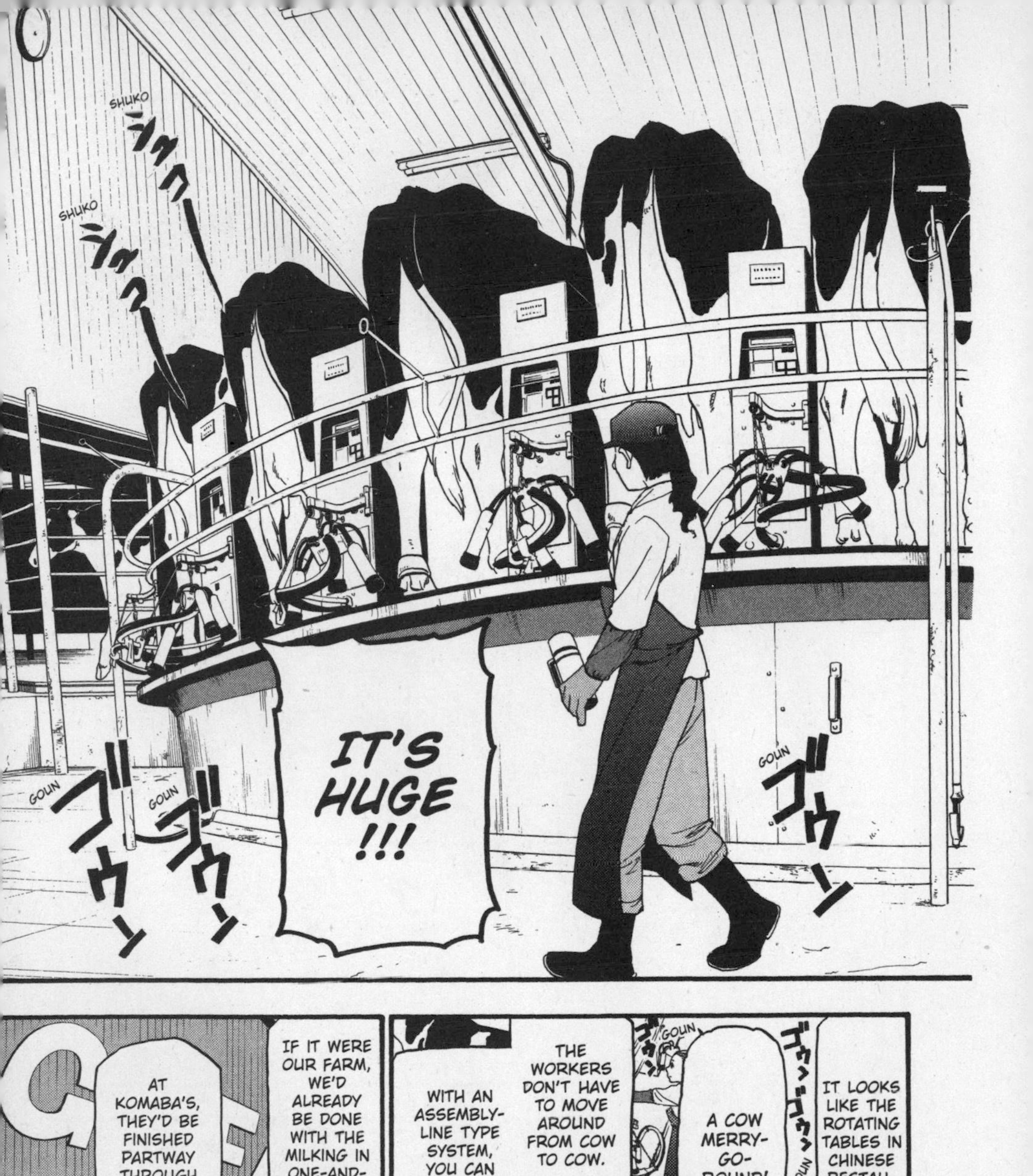
GOUN
IT'S HUGE!!!
GOUN
GOUN
SHUKO
SHUKO
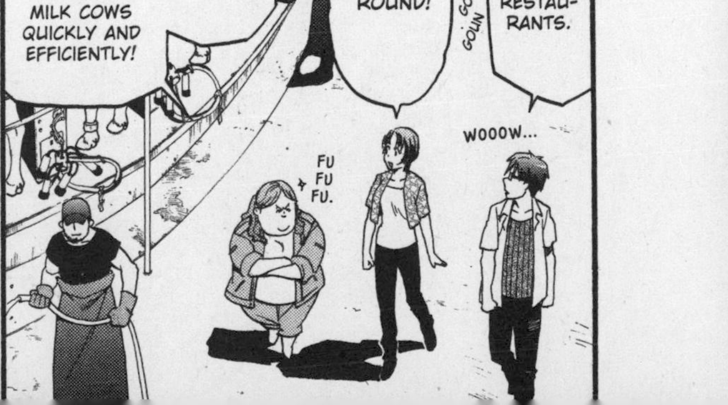
IT LOOKS LIKE THE ROTATING TABLES IN CHINESE RESTAURANTS.
WOOOW...
GOUN GOUN
A COW MERRY-GO-ROUND!
GOUN
THE WORKERS DON'T HAVE TO MOVE AROUND FROM COW TO COW.
WITH AN ASSEMBLY-LINE TYPE SYSTEM, YOU CAN MILK COWS QUICKLY AND EFFICIENTLY!
FU FU FU.
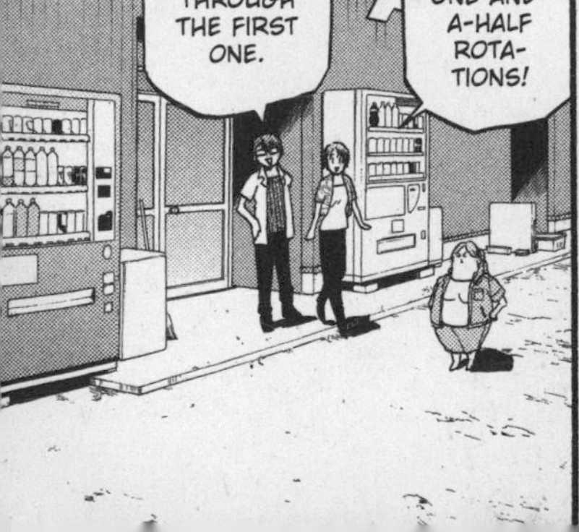
IF IT WERE OUR FARM, WE'D ALREADY BE DONE WITH THE MILKING IN ONE-AND-A-HALF ROTATIONS!
AT KOMABA'S, THEY'D BE FINISHED PARTWAY THROUGH THE FIRST ONE.

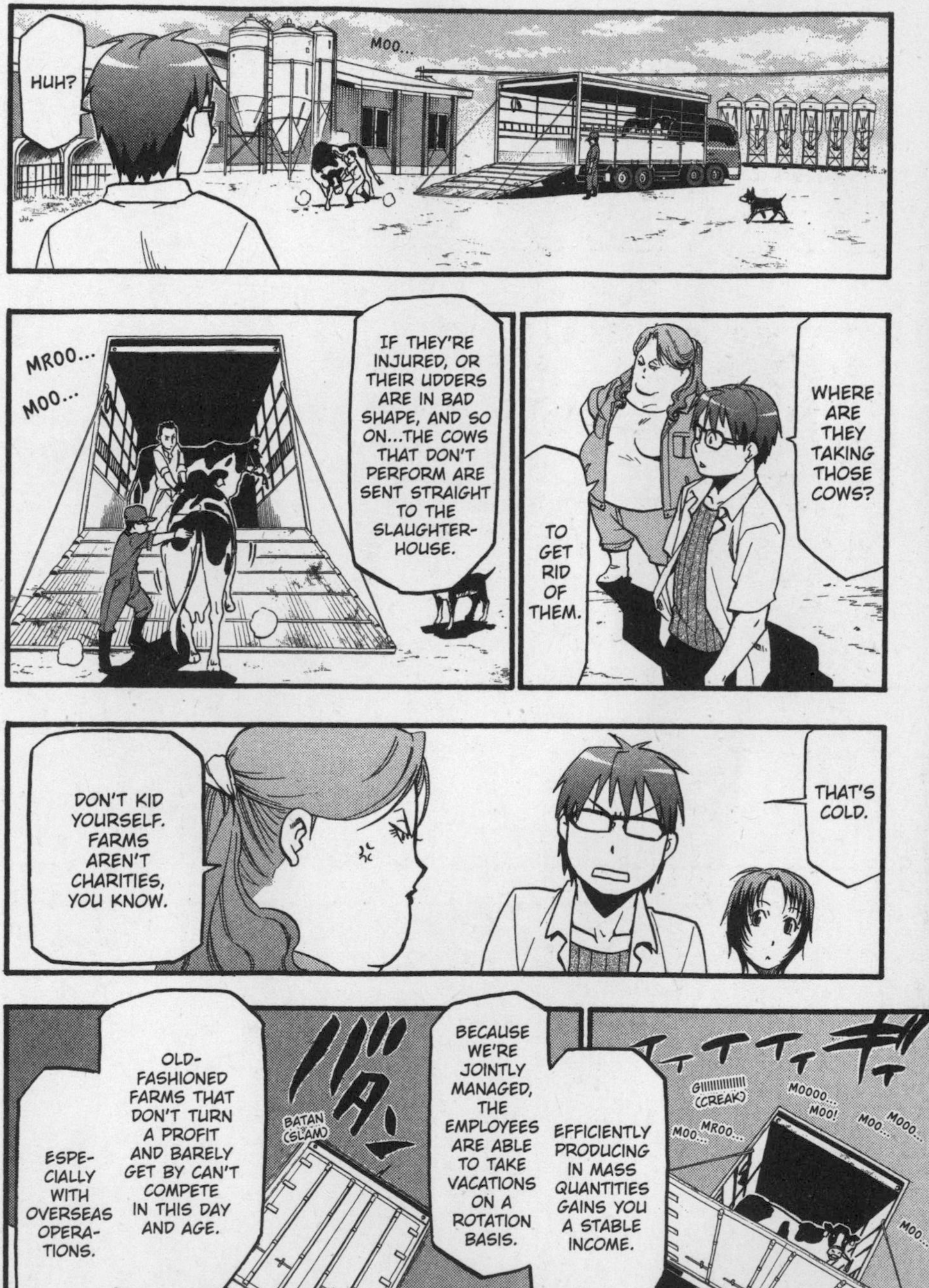
HUH?
MOO...
WHERE ARE THEY TAKING THOSE COWS?
TO GET RID OF THEM.
IF THEY'RE INJURED, OR THEIR UDDERS ARE IN BAD SHAPE, AND SO ON...THE COWS THAT DON'T PERFORM ARE SENT STRAIGHT TO THE SLAUGHTER-HOUSE.
MROO...
MOO...
THAT'S COLD.
DON'T KID YOURSELF. FARMS AREN'T CHARITIES, YOU KNOW.
GIIIIIIIIIII (CREAK)
MOOOO...
MOO!
MOOO...
MROO...
MOO...
MOO...
BECAUSE WE'RE JOINTLY MANAGED, THE EMPLOYEES ARE ABLE TO TAKE VACATIONS ON A ROTATION BASIS.
EFFICIENTLY PRODUCING IN MASS QUANTITIES GAINS YOU A STABLE INCOME.
BATAN (SLAM)
OLD-FASHIONED FARMS THAT DON'T TURN A PROFIT AND BARELY GET BY CAN'T COMPETE IN THIS DAY AND AGE.
ESPE-CIALLY WITH OVERSEAS OPERA-TIONS.

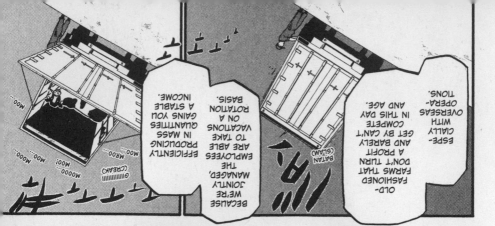

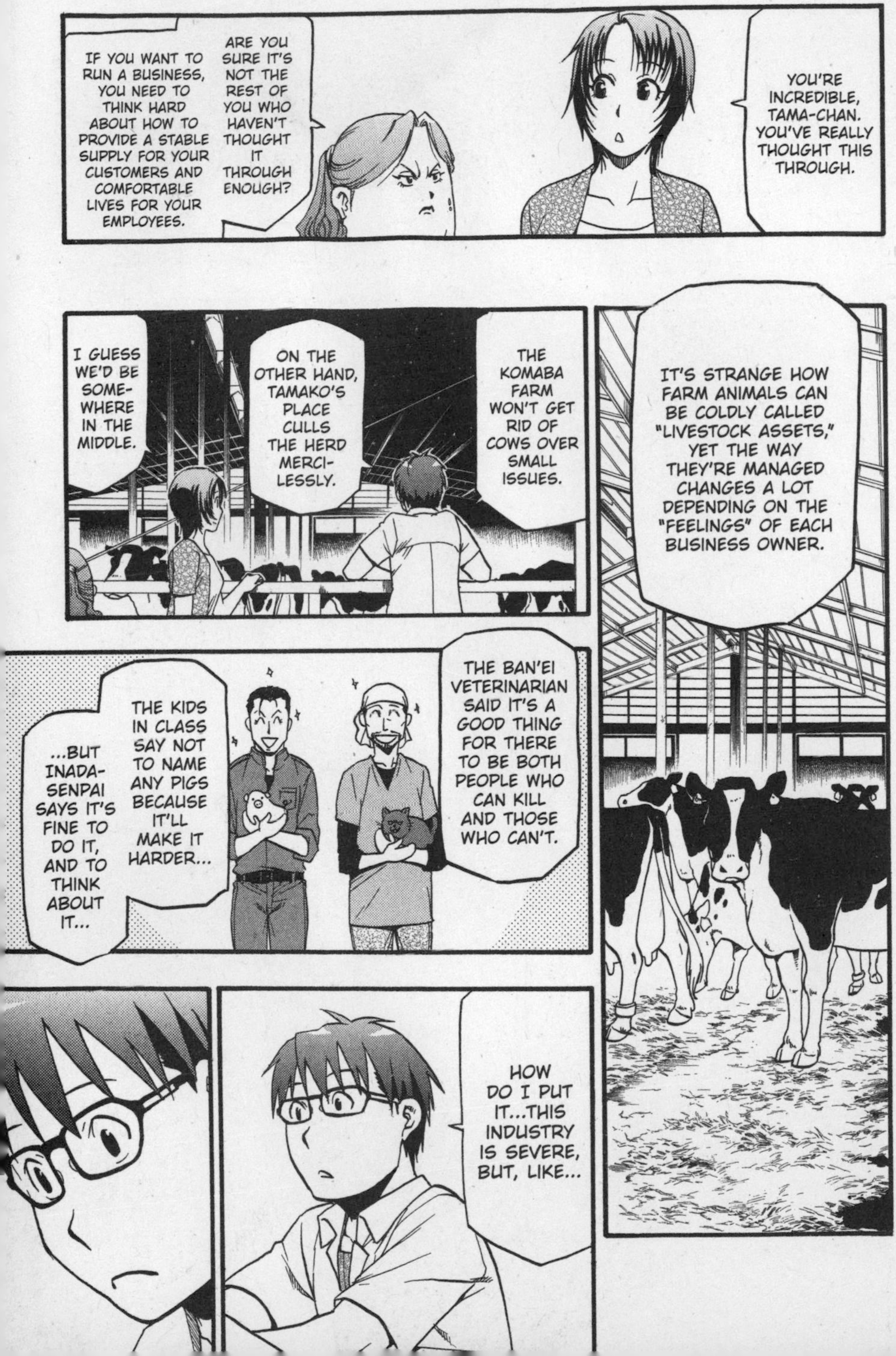
YOU'RE INCREDIBLE, TAMA-CHAN. YOU'VE REALLY THOUGHT THIS THROUGH.
ARE YOU SURE IT'S NOT THE REST OF YOU WHO HAVEN'T THOUGHT IT THROUGH ENOUGH?
IF YOU WANT TO RUN A BUSINESS, YOU NEED TO THINK HARD ABOUT HOW TO PROVIDE A STABLE SUPPLY FOR YOUR CUSTOMERS AND COMFORTABLE LIVES FOR YOUR EMPLOYEES.
IT'S STRANGE HOW FARM ANIMALS CAN BE COLDLY CALLED "LIVESTOCK ASSETS," YET THE WAY THEY'RE MANAGED CHANGES A LOT DEPENDING ON THE "FEELINGS" OF EACH BUSINESS OWNER.
THE KOMABA FARM WON'T GET RID OF COWS OVER SMALL ISSUES.
ON THE OTHER HAND, TAMAKO'S PLACE CULLS THE HERD MERCILESSLY.
I GUESS WE'D BE SOMEWHERE IN THE MIDDLE.
THE BAN'EI VETERINARIAN SAID IT'S A GOOD THING FOR THERE TO BE BOTH PEOPLE WHO CAN KILL AND THOSE WHO CAN'T.
THE KIDS IN CLASS SAY NOT TO NAME ANY PIGS BECAUSE IT'LL MAKE IT HARDER...
...BUT INADA-SENPAI SAYS IT'S FINE TO DO IT, AND TO THINK ABOUT IT...
HOW DO I PUT IT...THIS INDUSTRY IS SEVERE, BUT, LIKE...

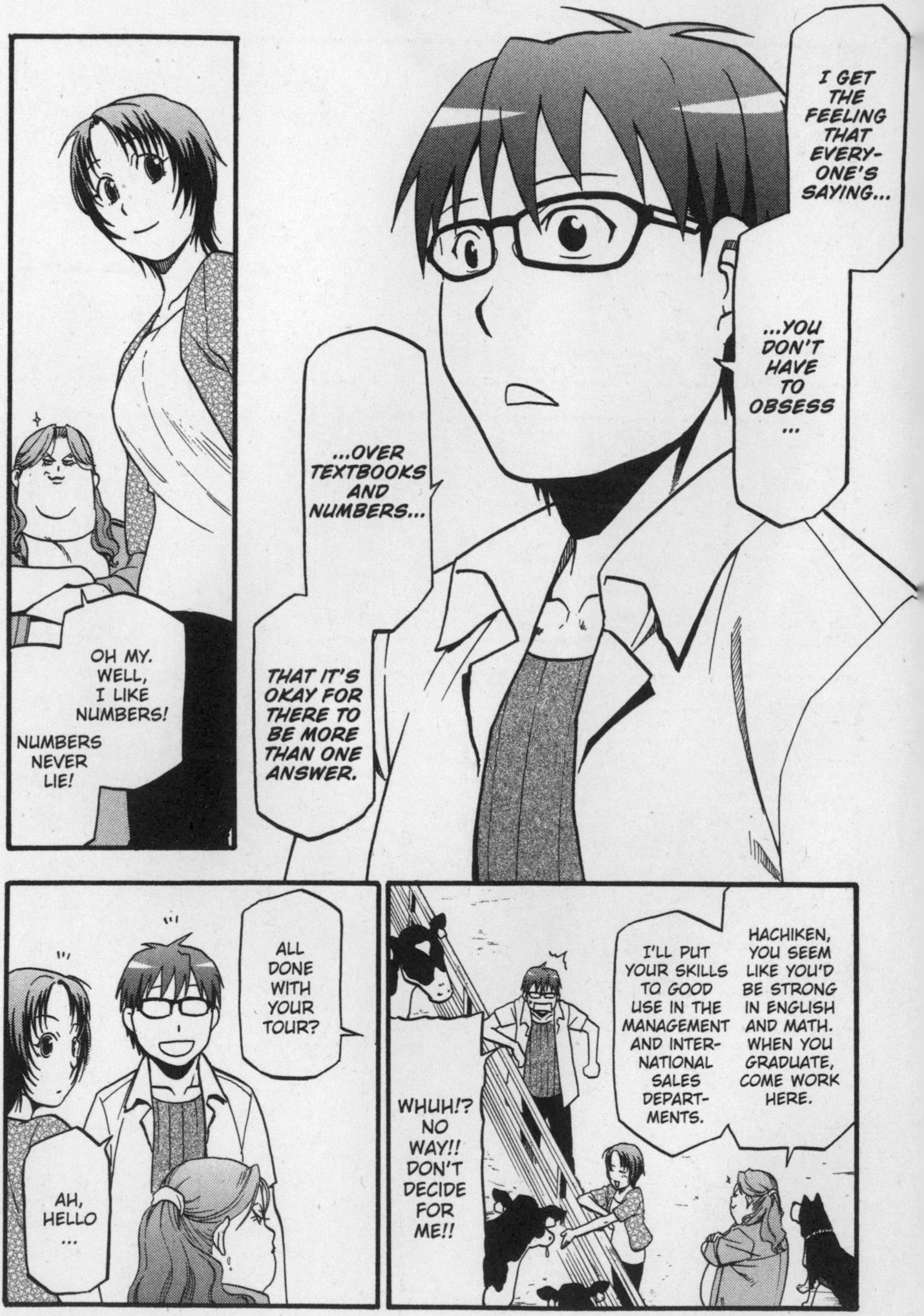
I GET THE FEELING THAT EVERY-ONE'S SAYING...
...YOU DON'T HAVE TO OBSESS ...
...OVER TEXTBOOKS AND NUMBERS...
THAT IT'S OKAY FOR THERE TO BE MORE THAN ONE ANSWER.
OH MY. WELL, I LIKE NUMBERS!
NUMBERS NEVER LIE!
HACHIKEN, YOU SEEM LIKE YOU'D BE STRONG IN ENGLISH AND MATH. WHEN YOU GRADUATE, COME WORK HERE.
I'LL PUT YOUR SKILLS TO GOOD USE IN THE MANAGEMENT AND INTER-NATIONAL SALES DEPART-MENTS.
WHUH!? NO WAY!! DON'T DECIDE FOR ME!!
ALL DONE WITH YOUR TOUR?
AH, HELLO ...

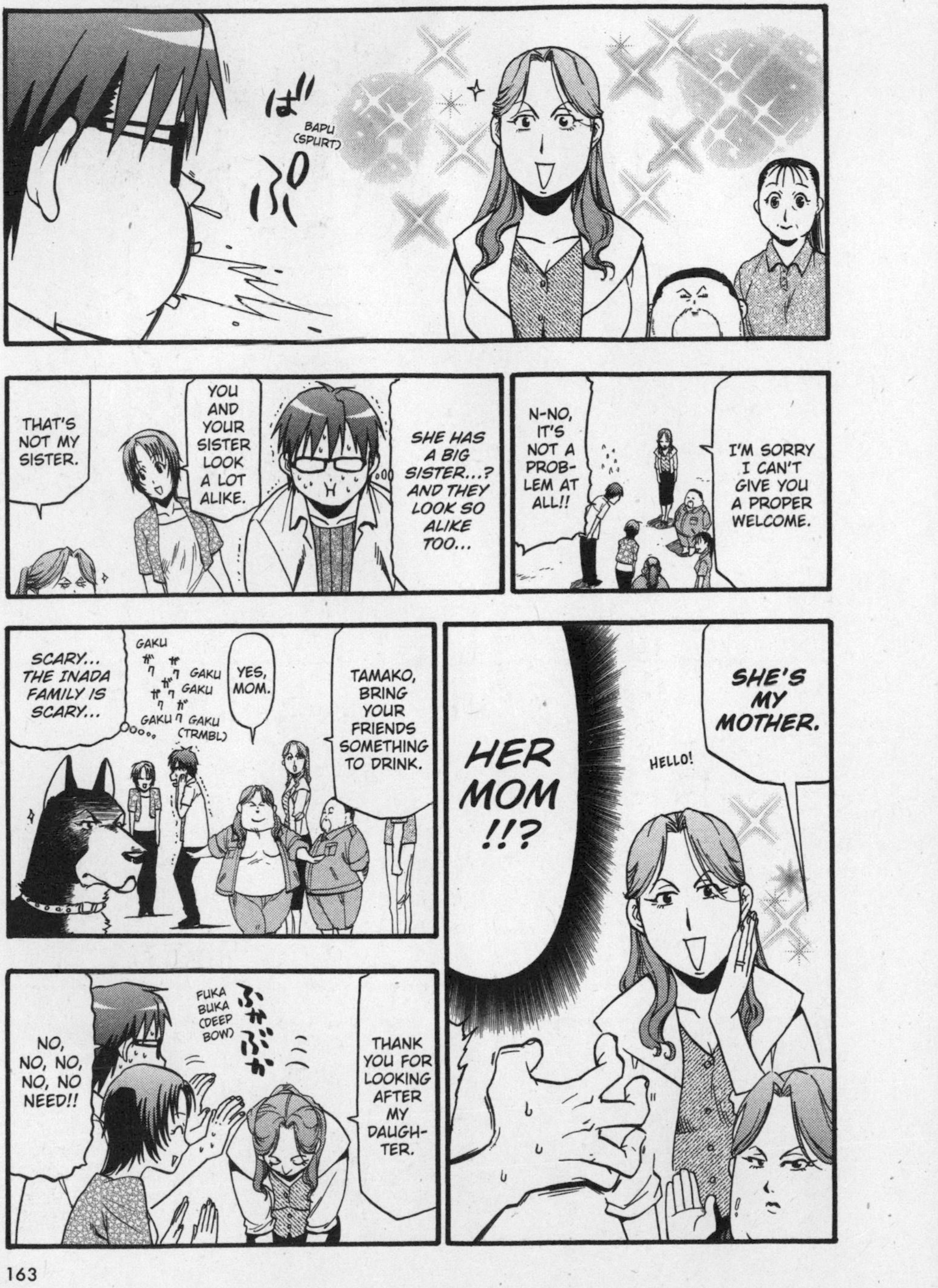
ばぷ
BAPU (SPURT)
I'M SORRY I CAN'T GIVE YOU A PROPER WELCOME.
N-NO, IT'S NOT A PROB-LEM AT ALL!!
SHE HAS A BIG SISTER...? AND THEY LOOK SO ALIKE TOO...
YOU AND YOUR SISTER LOOK A LOT ALIKE.
THAT'S NOT MY SISTER.
SHE'S MY MOTHER.
HELLO!
HER MOM !!?
TAMAKO, BRING YOUR FRIENDS SOMETHING TO DRINK.
YES, MOM.
GAKU GAKU GAKU GAKU GAKU (TRMBL)
SCARY... THE INADA FAMILY IS SCARY...
THANK YOU FOR LOOKING AFTER MY DAUGH-TER.
ふかぶか
FUKA BUKA (DEEP BOW)
NO, NO, NO, NO, NO NEED!!

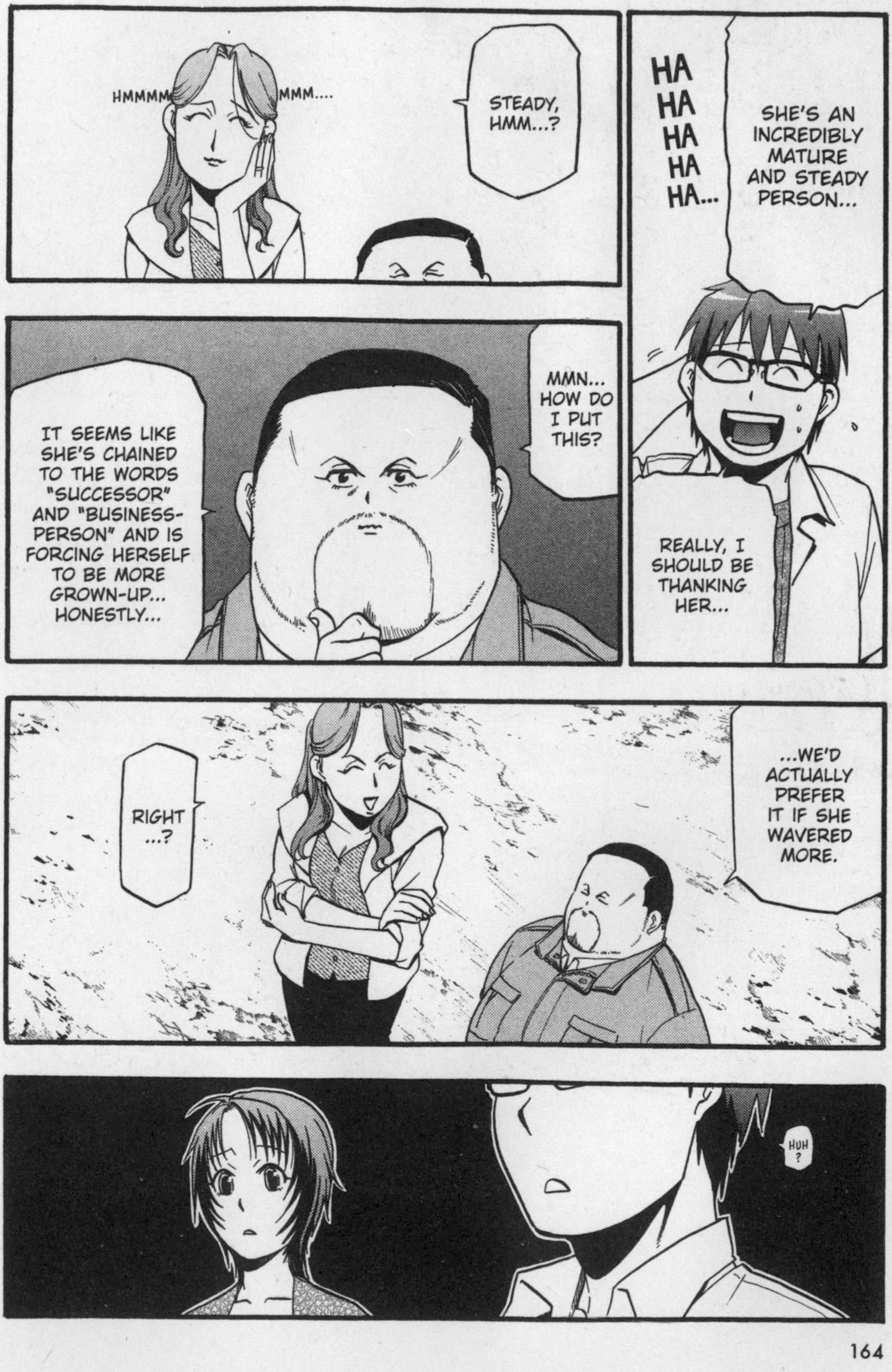
SHE'S AN INCREDIBLY MATURE AND STEADY PERSON...
HA HA HA HA HA...
REALLY, I SHOULD BE THANKING HER...
STEADY, HMM...?
HMMMMMMM....
MMN... HOW DO I PUT THIS?
IT SEEMS LIKE SHE'S CHAINED TO THE WORDS "SUCCESSOR" AND "BUSINESS-PERSON" AND IS FORCING HERSELF TO BE MORE GROWN-UP... HONESTLY...
...WE'D ACTUALLY PREFER IT IF SHE WAVERED MORE.
RIGHT ...?
HUH ?

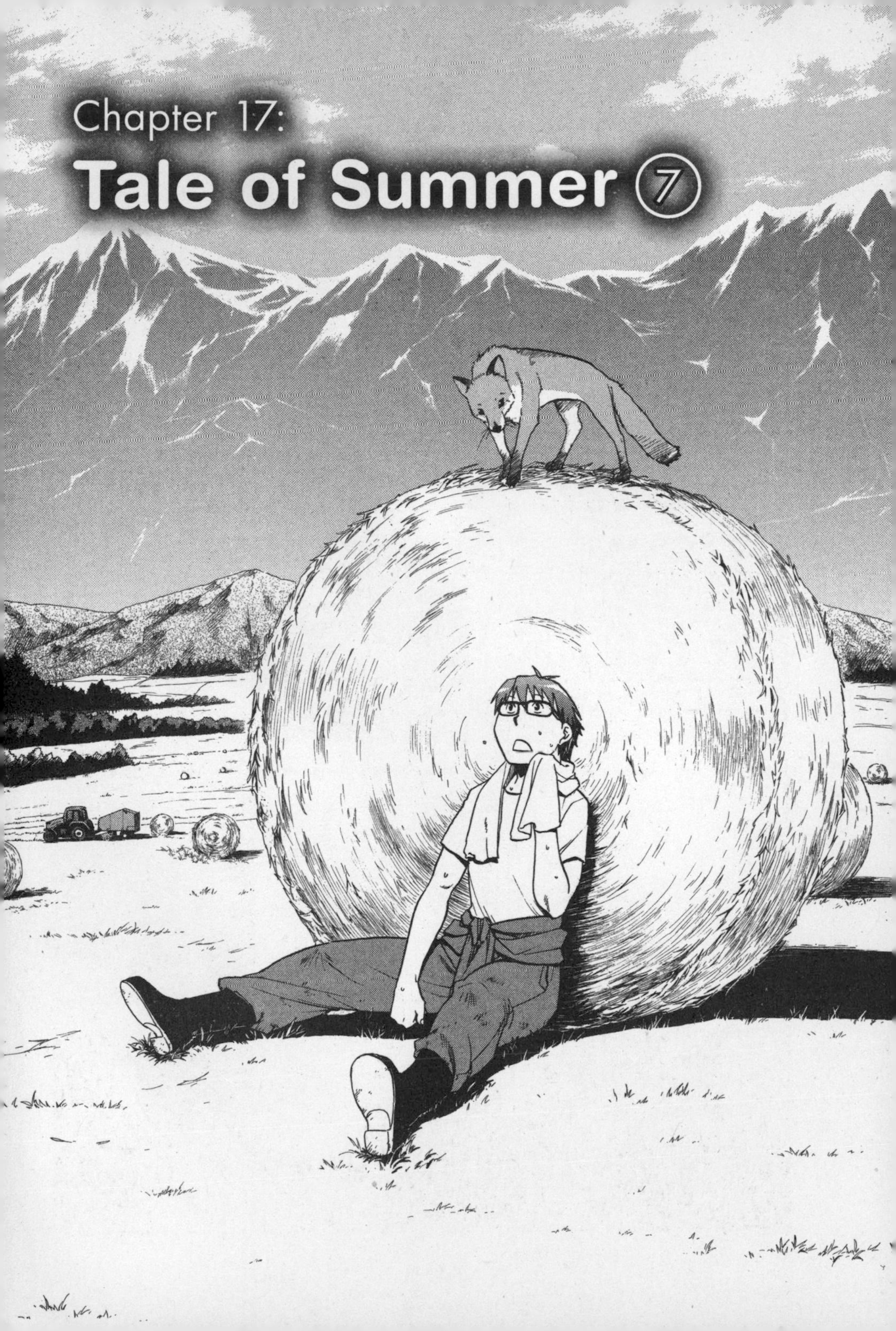
Chapter 17:
Tale of Summer ⑦

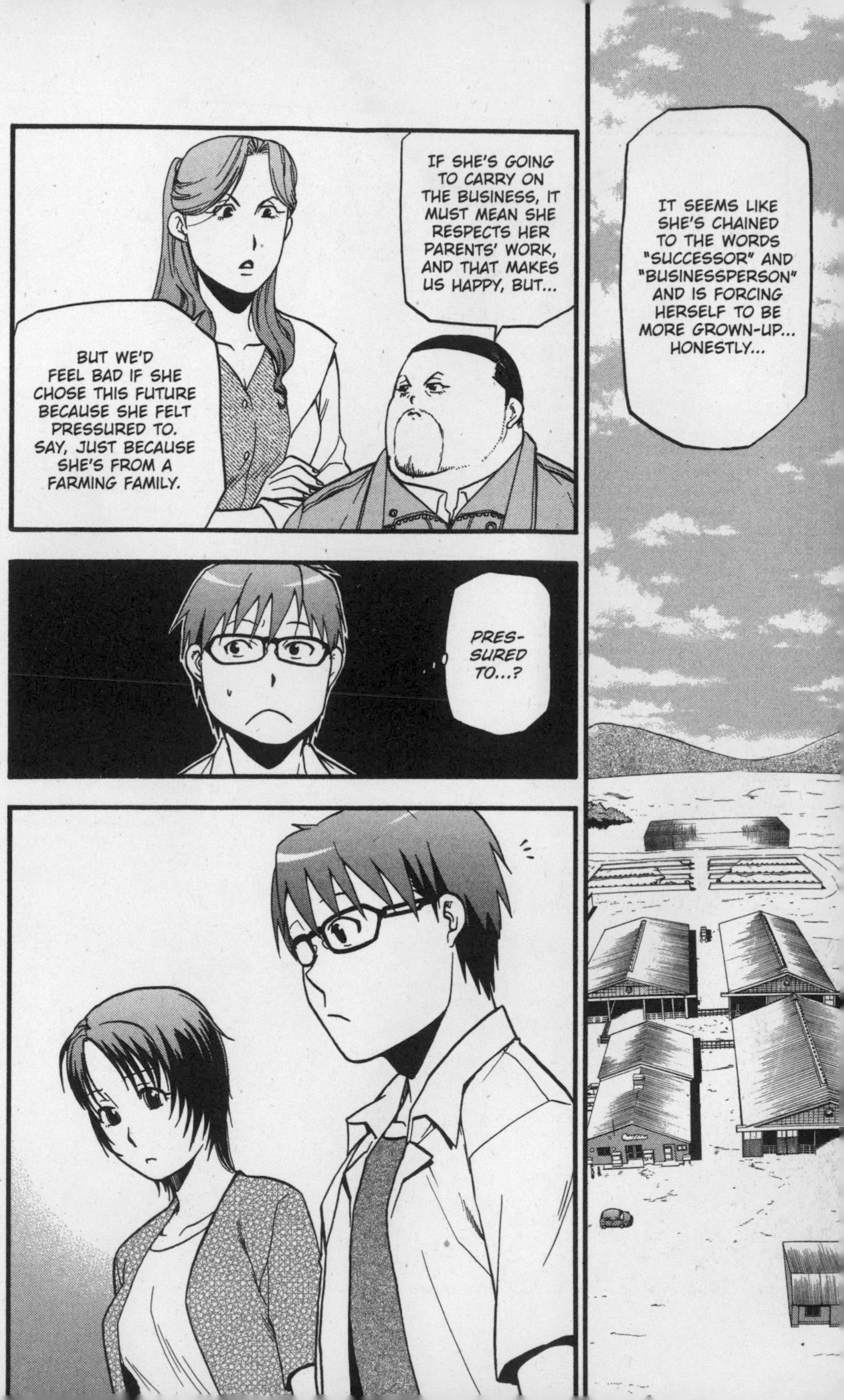
IT SEEMS LIKE SHE'S CHAINED TO THE WORDS "SUCCESSOR" AND "BUSINESSPERSON" AND IS FORCING HERSELF TO BE MORE GROWN-UP... HONESTLY...
IF SHE'S GOING TO CARRY ON THE BUSINESS, IT MUST MEAN SHE RESPECTS HER PARENTS' WORK, AND THAT MAKES US HAPPY, BUT...
BUT WE'D FEEL BAD IF SHE CHOSE THIS FUTURE BECAUSE SHE FELT PRESSURED TO. SAY, JUST BECAUSE SHE'S FROM A FARMING FAMILY.
PRES-SURED TO...?

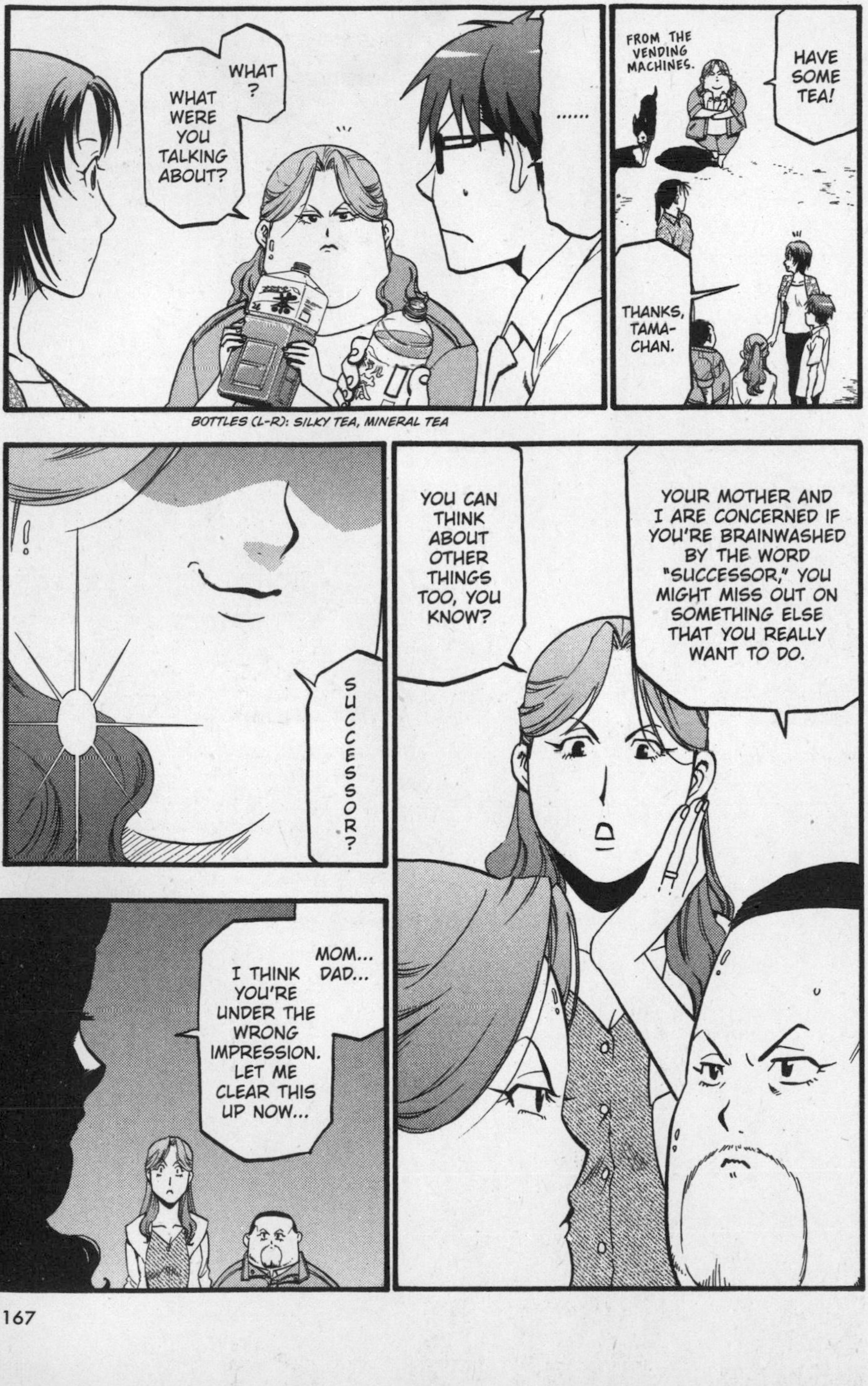
HAVE SOME TEA!
FROM THE VENDING MACHINES.
THANKS, TAMA-CHAN.
......
WHAT?
WHAT WERE YOU TALKING ABOUT?
BOTTLES (L-R): SILKY TEA, MINERAL TEA
YOUR MOTHER AND I ARE CONCERNED IF YOU'RE BRAINWASHED BY THE WORD "SUCCESSOR," YOU MIGHT MISS OUT ON SOMETHING ELSE THAT YOU REALLY WANT TO DO.
YOU CAN THINK ABOUT OTHER THINGS TOO, YOU KNOW?
SUCCESSOR?
MOM... DAD...
I THINK YOU'RE UNDER THE WRONG IMPRESSION. LET ME CLEAR THIS UP NOW...

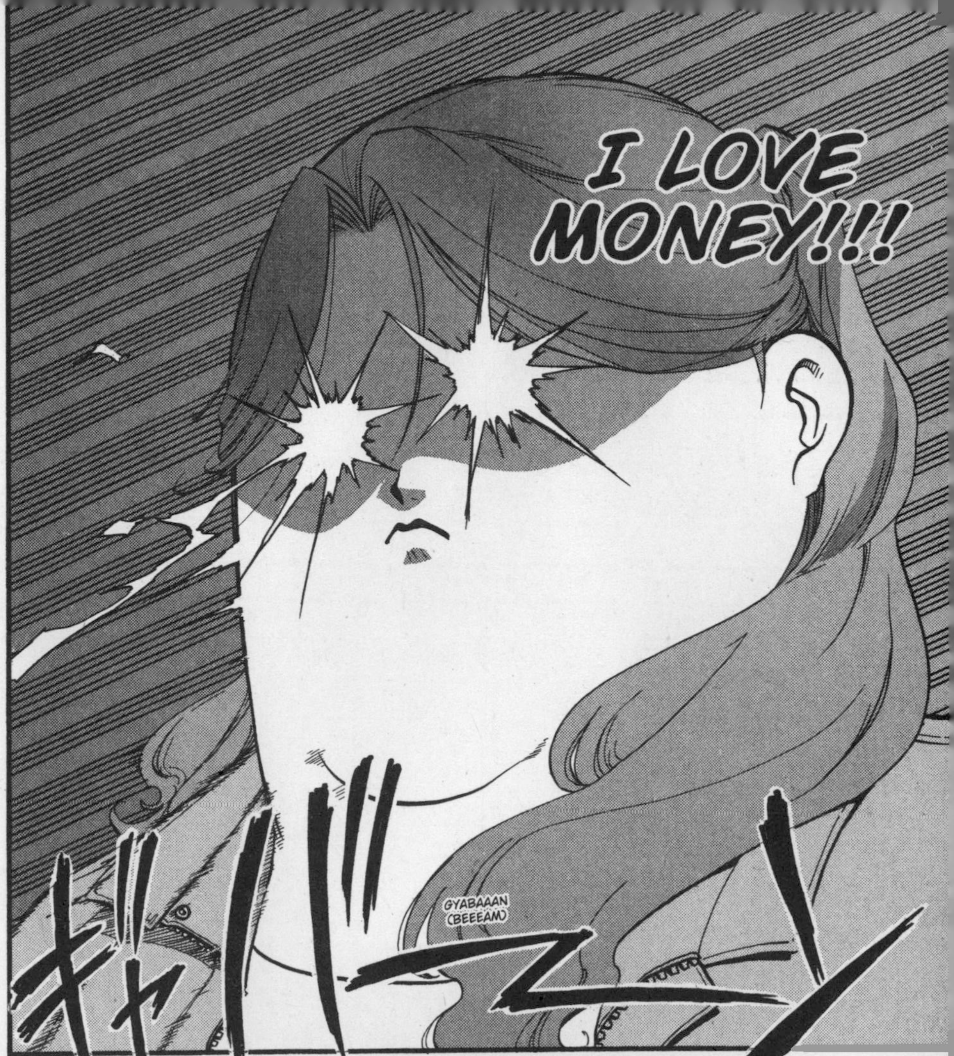
I LOVE MONEY!!!
GYABAAAN (BEEEAM)
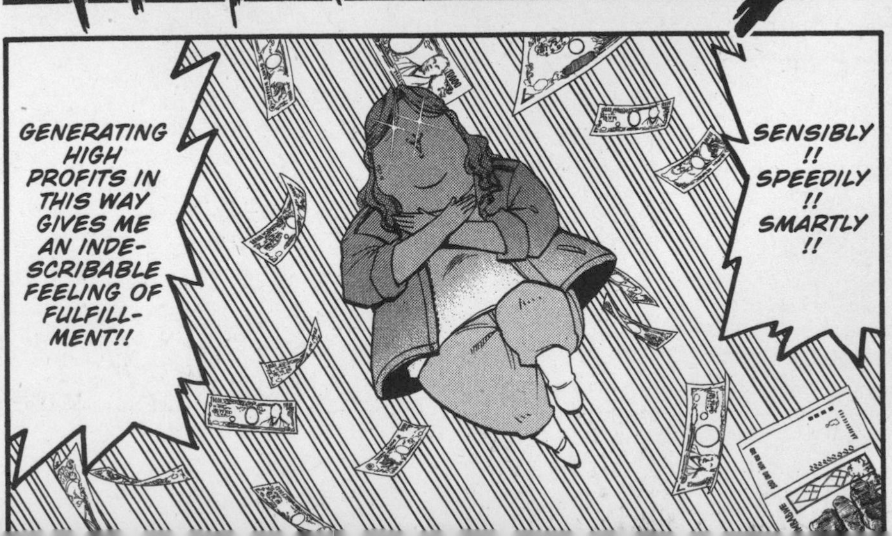
SENSIBLY !! SPEEDILY !! SMARTLY !!
GENERATING HIGH PROFITS IN THIS WAY GIVES ME AN INDE-SCRIBABLE FEELING OF FULFILL-MENT!!

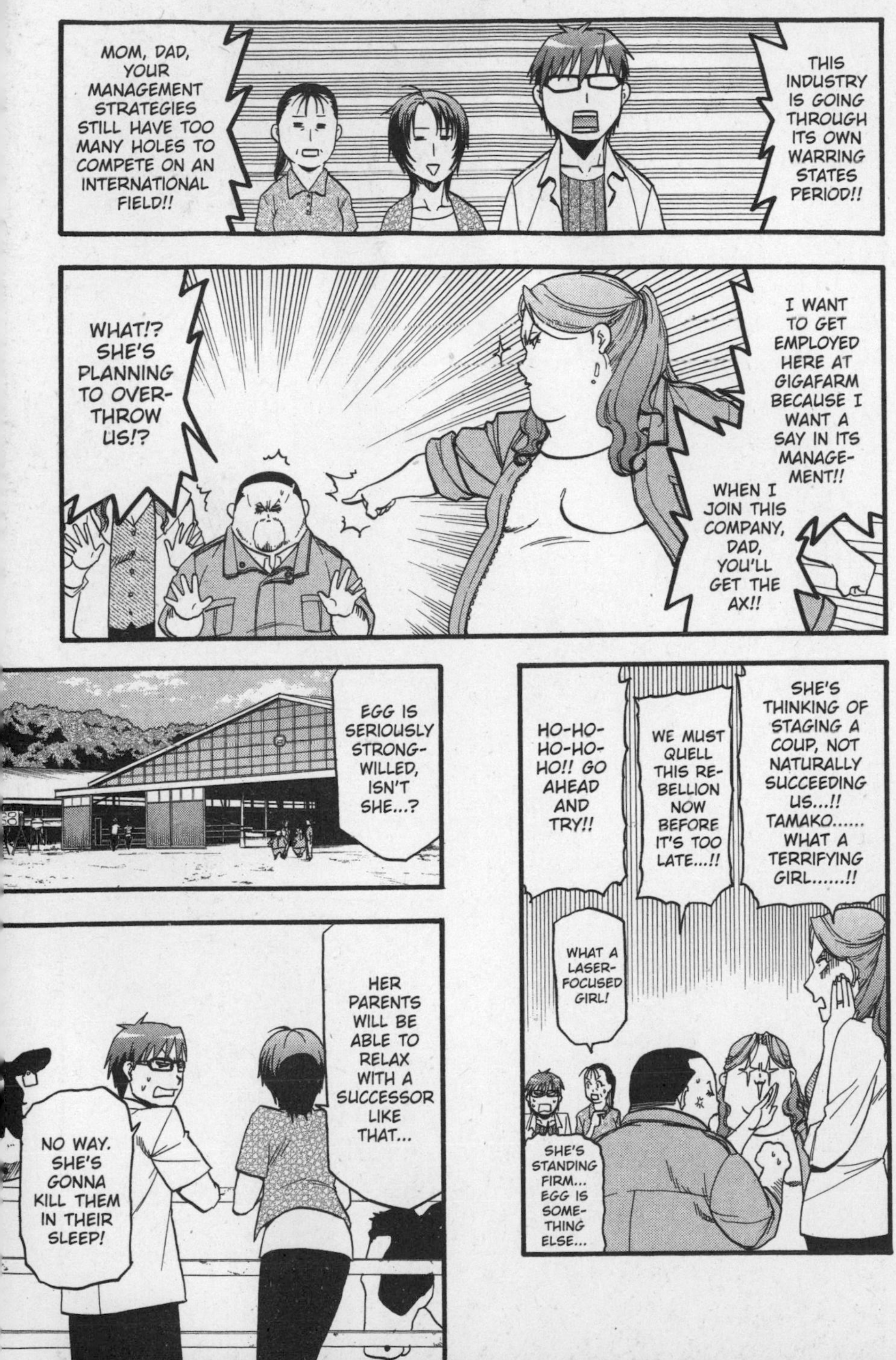
THIS INDUSTRY IS GOING THROUGH ITS OWN WARRING STATES PERIOD!!
MOM, DAD, YOUR MANAGEMENT STRATEGIES STILL HAVE TOO MANY HOLES TO COMPETE ON AN INTERNATIONAL FIELD!!
I WANT TO GET EMPLOYED HERE AT GIGAFARM BECAUSE I WANT A SAY IN ITS MANAGEMENT!!
WHEN I JOIN THIS COMPANY, DAD, YOU'LL GET THE AX!!
WHAT!? SHE'S PLANNING TO OVERTHROW US!?
SHE'S THINKING OF STAGING A COUP, NOT NATURALLY SUCCEEDING US...!! TAMAKO...... WHAT A TERRIFYING GIRL......!!
WE MUST QUELL THIS REBELLION NOW BEFORE IT'S TOO LATE...!!
HO-HO-HO-HO-HO!! GO AHEAD AND TRY!!
WHAT A LASER-FOCUSED GIRL!
SHE'S STANDING FIRM... EGG IS SOMETHING ELSE...
EGG IS SERIOUSLY STRONG-WILLED, ISN'T SHE...?
HER PARENTS WILL BE ABLE TO RELAX WITH A SUCCESSOR LIKE THAT...
NO WAY. SHE'S GONNA KILL THEM IN THEIR SLEEP!

HEY, UH...
MIKAGE ......
...ARE YOU NOT SURE ABOUT CARRYING ON YOUR FAMILY'S BUSINESS?
UH, IF I'M READING YOU WRONG, I'M SORRY.
IT'S JUST LIKE... ERR...
I KNOW! I CAN HELP YOU FIGURE IT OUT IF YOU WANT?

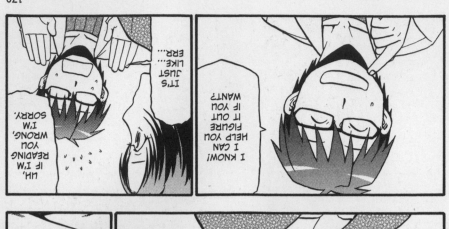

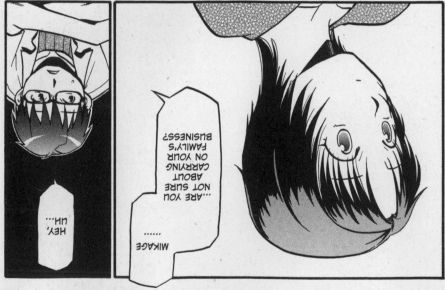

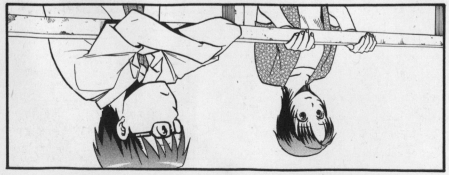

WAIT A...
AH.
AM I A TOTAL IDIOT !!?
A GUY WHO RAN AWAY FROM THE COLLEGE PREP PROGRAM AND IS NOW WANDERING AROUND WITH NO FOCUS, UNABLE TO SEE EVEN HIS OWN FUTURE, OFFERING TO GIVE CAREER ADVICE TO SOMEONE ELSE...?
WHO AM I KIDDING!!?
I AM SO LAME RIGHT NOW...
AH AH AH AH
AH AH AH AH AH
AH AH AH AH AH AH
LIKE A DUMB-ASS...
SO EMBAR-RASSED ...

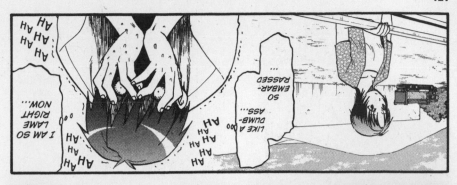

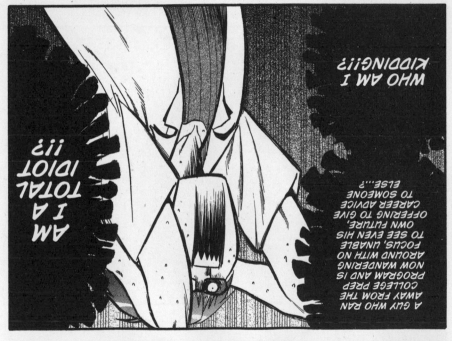

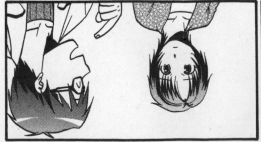

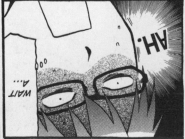

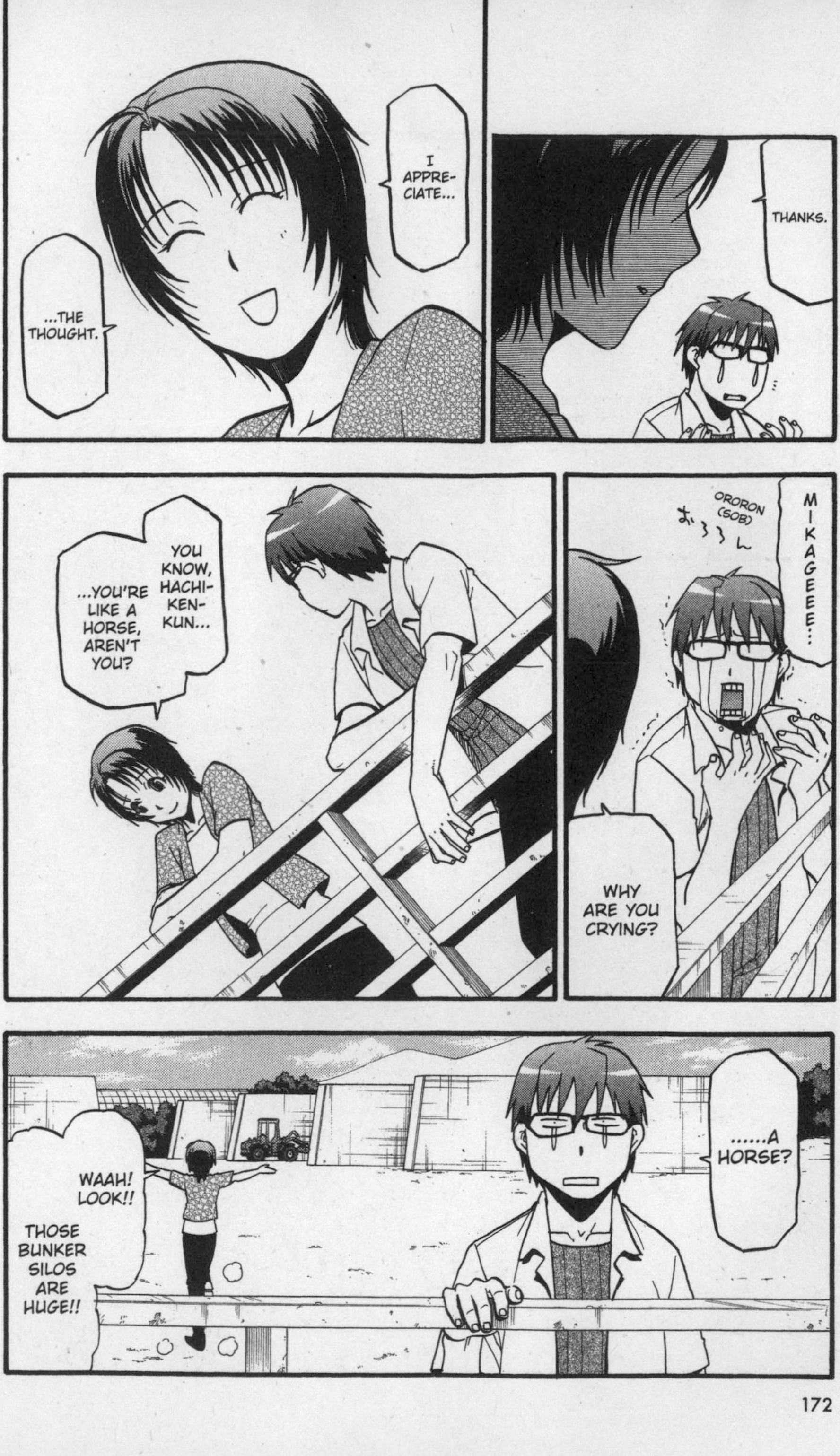
THANKS.
I APPRE-CIATE...
...THE THOUGHT.
MIKAGEEE...
ORORON (SOB) おろろん
WHY ARE YOU CRYING?
YOU KNOW, HACHI-KEN-KUN...
...YOU'RE LIKE A HORSE, AREN'T YOU?
......A HORSE?
WAAH! LOOK!!
THOSE BUNKER SILOS ARE HUGE!!

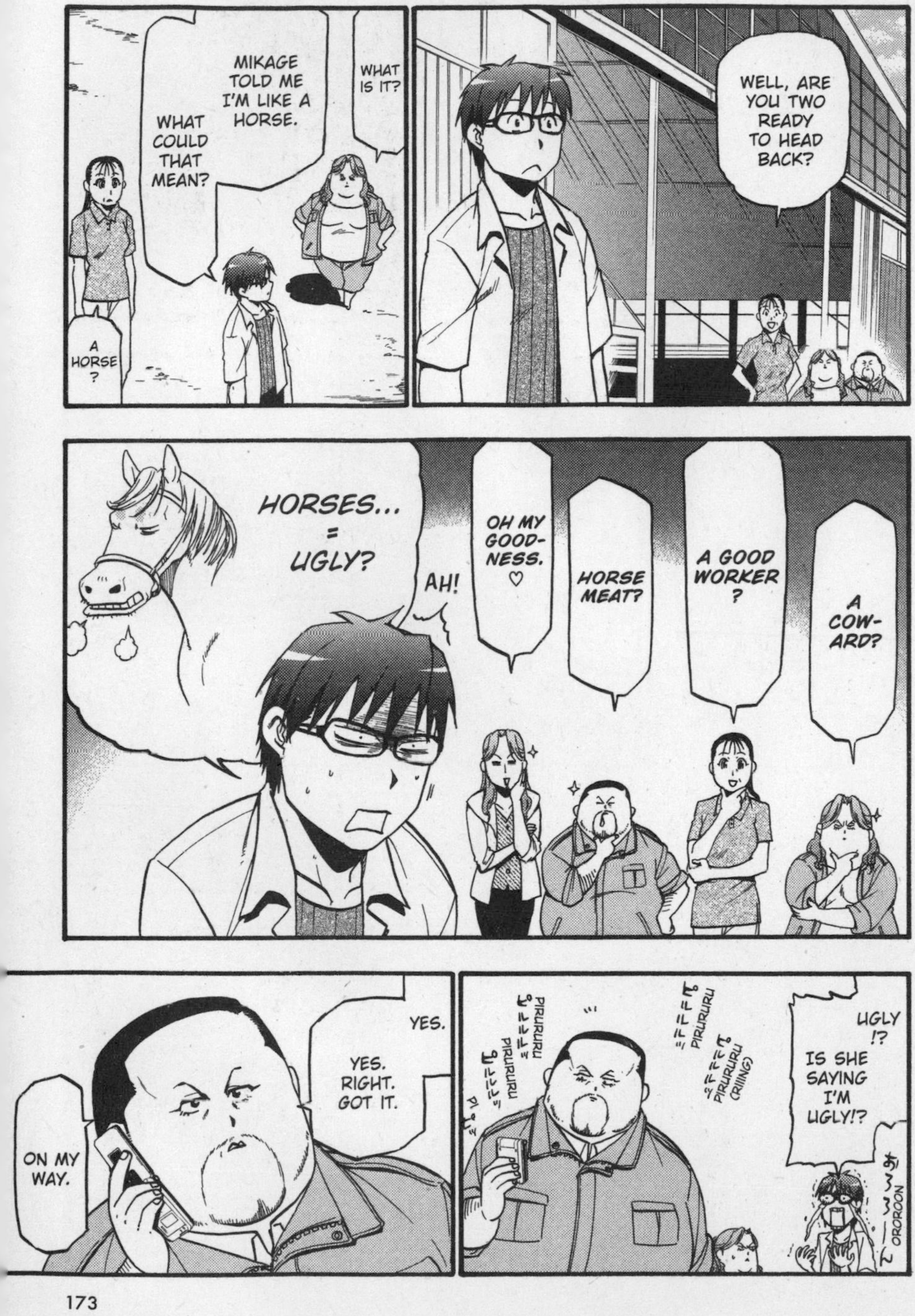
WELL, ARE YOU TWO READY TO HEAD BACK?
WHAT IS IT?
MIKAGE TOLD ME I'M LIKE A HORSE.
WHAT COULD THAT MEAN?
A HORSE?
A COW-ARD?
A GOOD WORKER?
HORSE MEAT?
OH MY GOOD-NESS. ♡
AH!
HORSES... = UGLY?
UGLY!? IS SHE SAYING I'M UGLY!?
OROROON
PIRURURU (RIIING)
PIRURURU
PIRURURU
PIRURURU
PI
YES.
YES. RIGHT. GOT IT.
ON MY WAY.

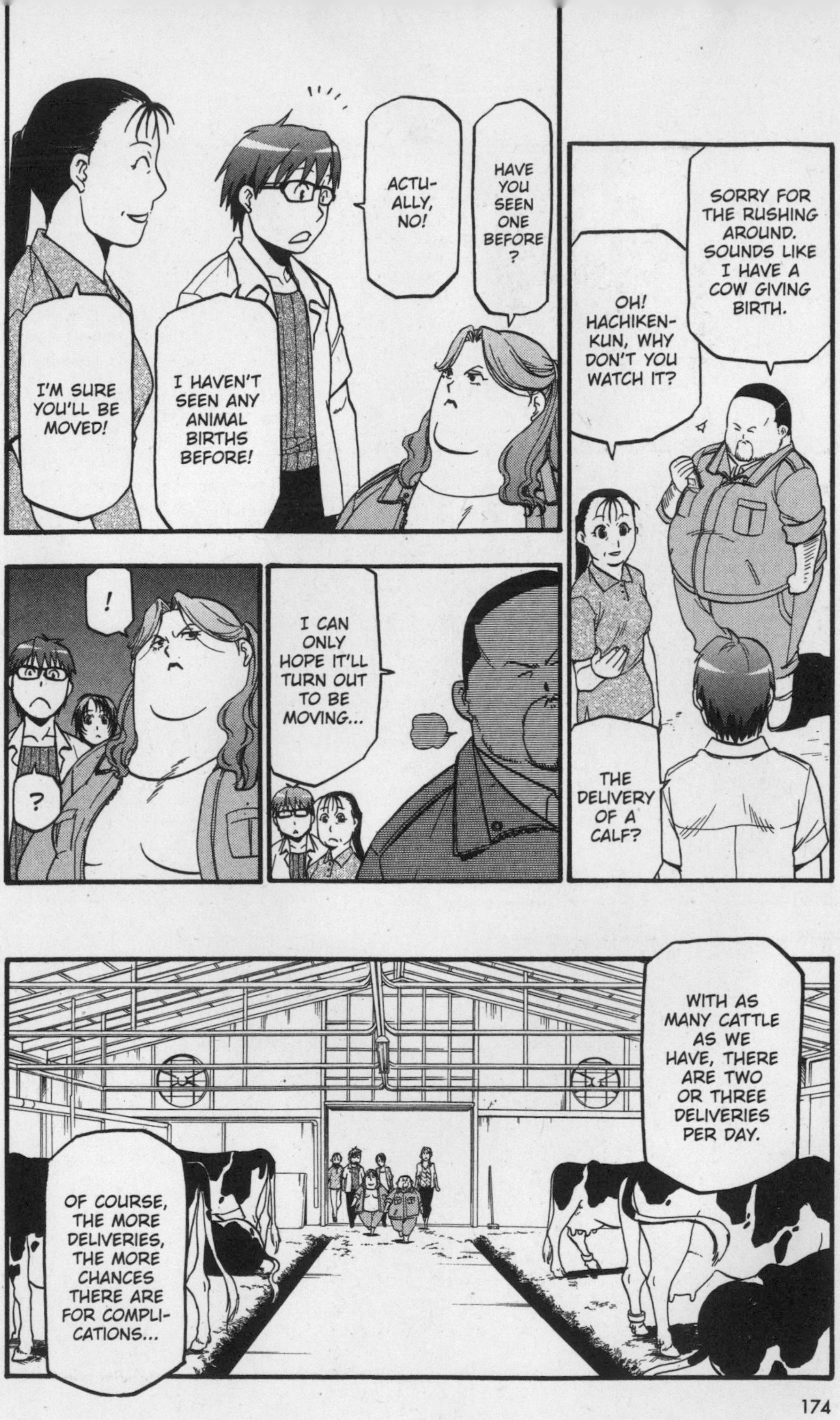
SORRY FOR THE RUSHING AROUND. SOUNDS LIKE I HAVE A COW GIVING BIRTH.
OH! HACHIKEN-KUN, WHY DON'T YOU WATCH IT?
THE DELIVERY OF A CALF?
HAVE YOU SEEN ONE BEFORE ?
ACTU-ALLY, NO!
I HAVEN'T SEEN ANY ANIMAL BIRTHS BEFORE!
I'M SURE YOU'LL BE MOVED!
I CAN ONLY HOPE IT'LL TURN OUT TO BE MOVING...
!
?
WITH AS MANY CATTLE AS WE HAVE, THERE ARE TWO OR THREE DELIVERIES PER DAY.
OF COURSE, THE MORE DELIVERIES, THE MORE CHANCES THERE ARE FOR COMPLI-CATIONS...

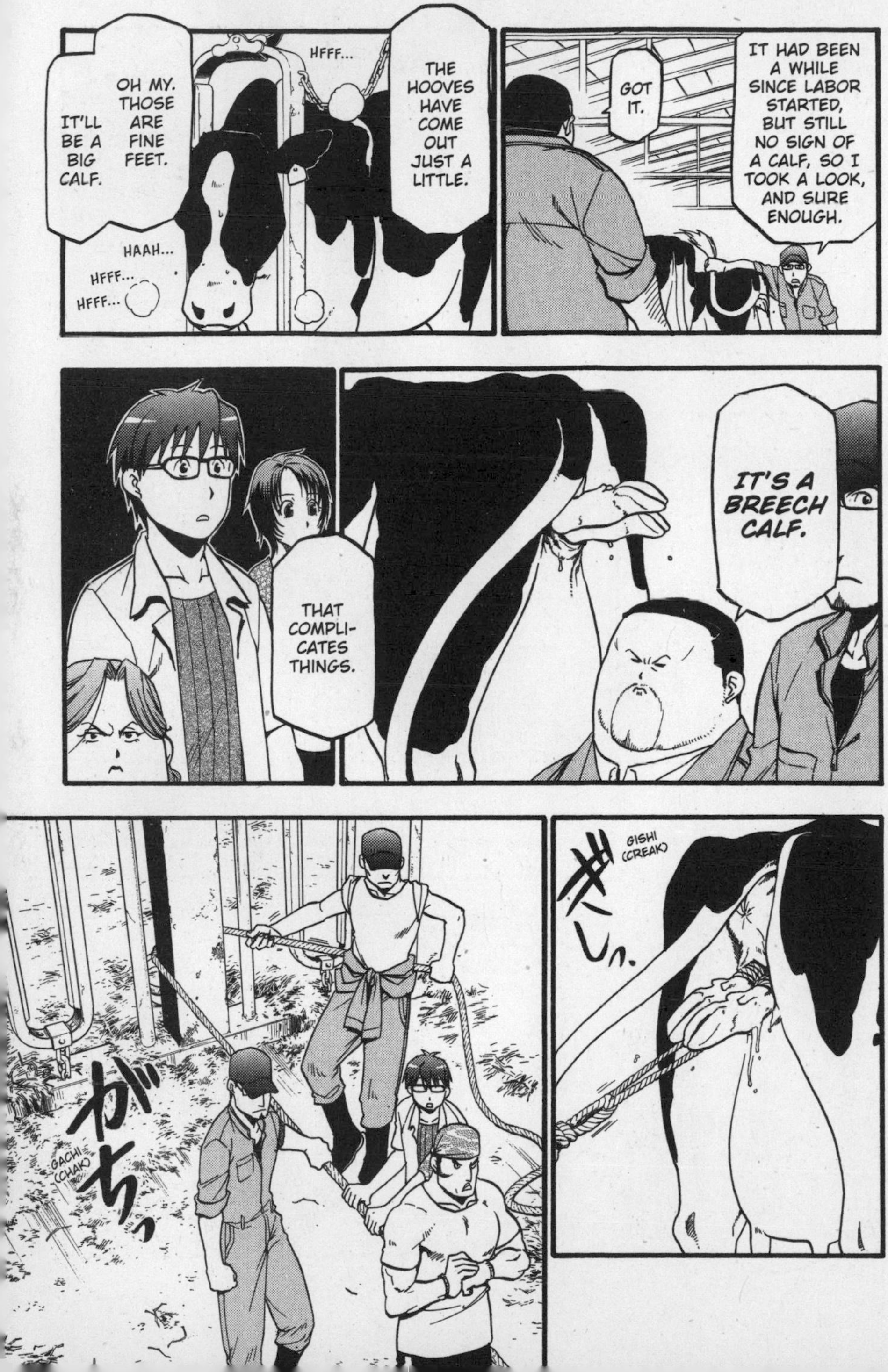
IT HAD BEEN A WHILE SINCE LABOR STARTED, BUT STILL NO SIGN OF A CALF, SO I TOOK A LOOK, AND SURE ENOUGH.
GOT IT.
THE HOOVES HAVE COME OUT JUST A LITTLE.
HFFF...
OH MY. THOSE ARE FINE FEET.
IT'LL BE A BIG CALF.
HAAH...
HFFF...
HFFF...
IT'S A BREECH CALF.
THAT COMPLI-CATES THINGS.
GISHI (CREAK)
GACHI (CHAK)

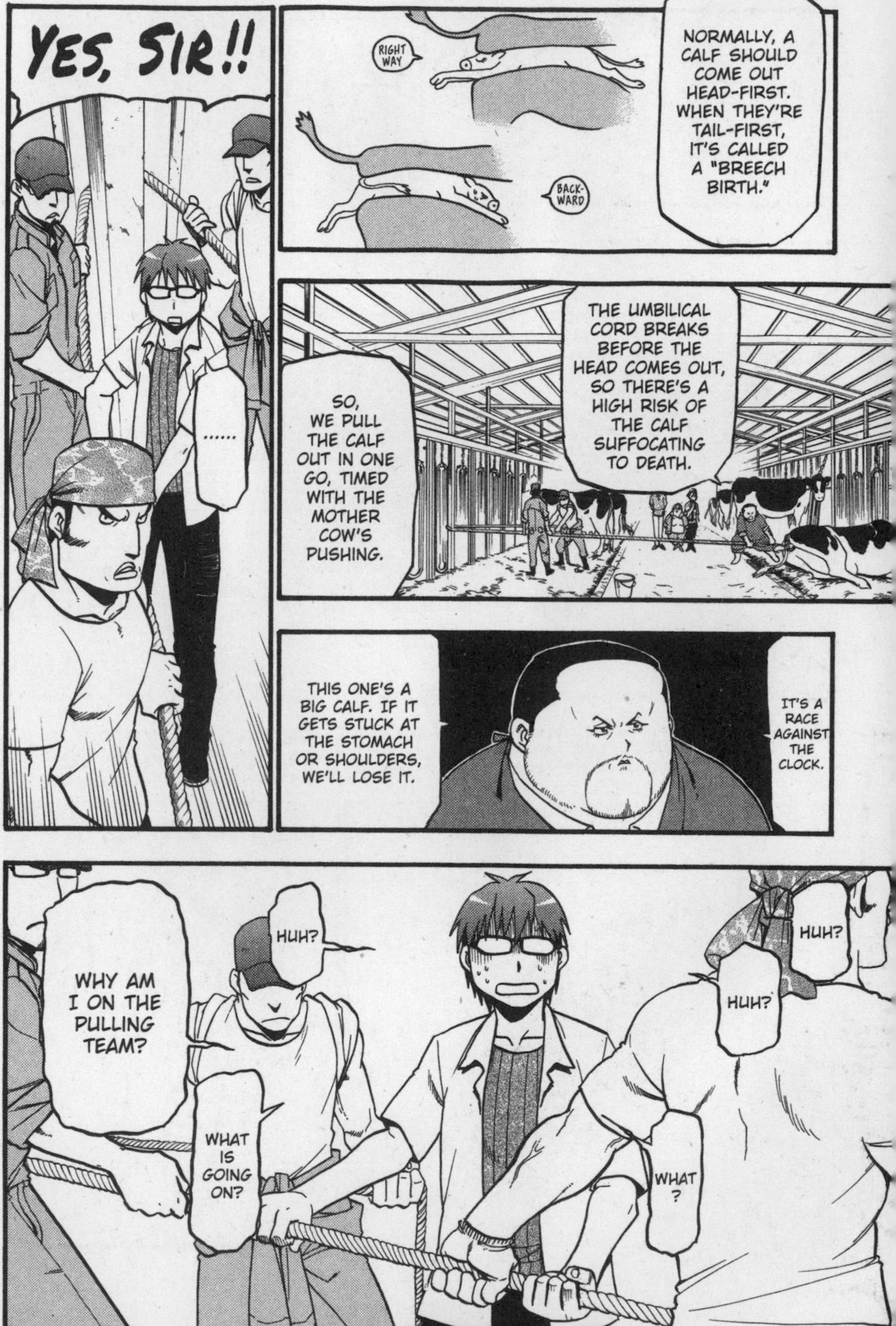
NORMALLY, A CALF SHOULD COME OUT HEAD-FIRST. WHEN THEY'RE TAIL-FIRST, IT'S CALLED A "BREECH BIRTH."
RIGHT WAY
BACK-WARD
THE UMBILICAL CORD BREAKS BEFORE THE HEAD COMES OUT, SO THERE'S A HIGH RISK OF THE CALF SUFFOCATING TO DEATH.
SO, WE PULL THE CALF OUT IN ONE GO, TIMED WITH THE MOTHER COW'S PUSHING.
IT'S A RACE AGAINST THE CLOCK.
THIS ONE'S A BIG CALF. IF IT GETS STUCK AT THE STOMACH OR SHOULDERS, WE'LL LOSE IT.
YES, SIR!!
......
HUH?
HUH?
WHAT ?
HUH?
WHAT IS GOING ON?
WHY AM I ON THE PULLING TEAM?

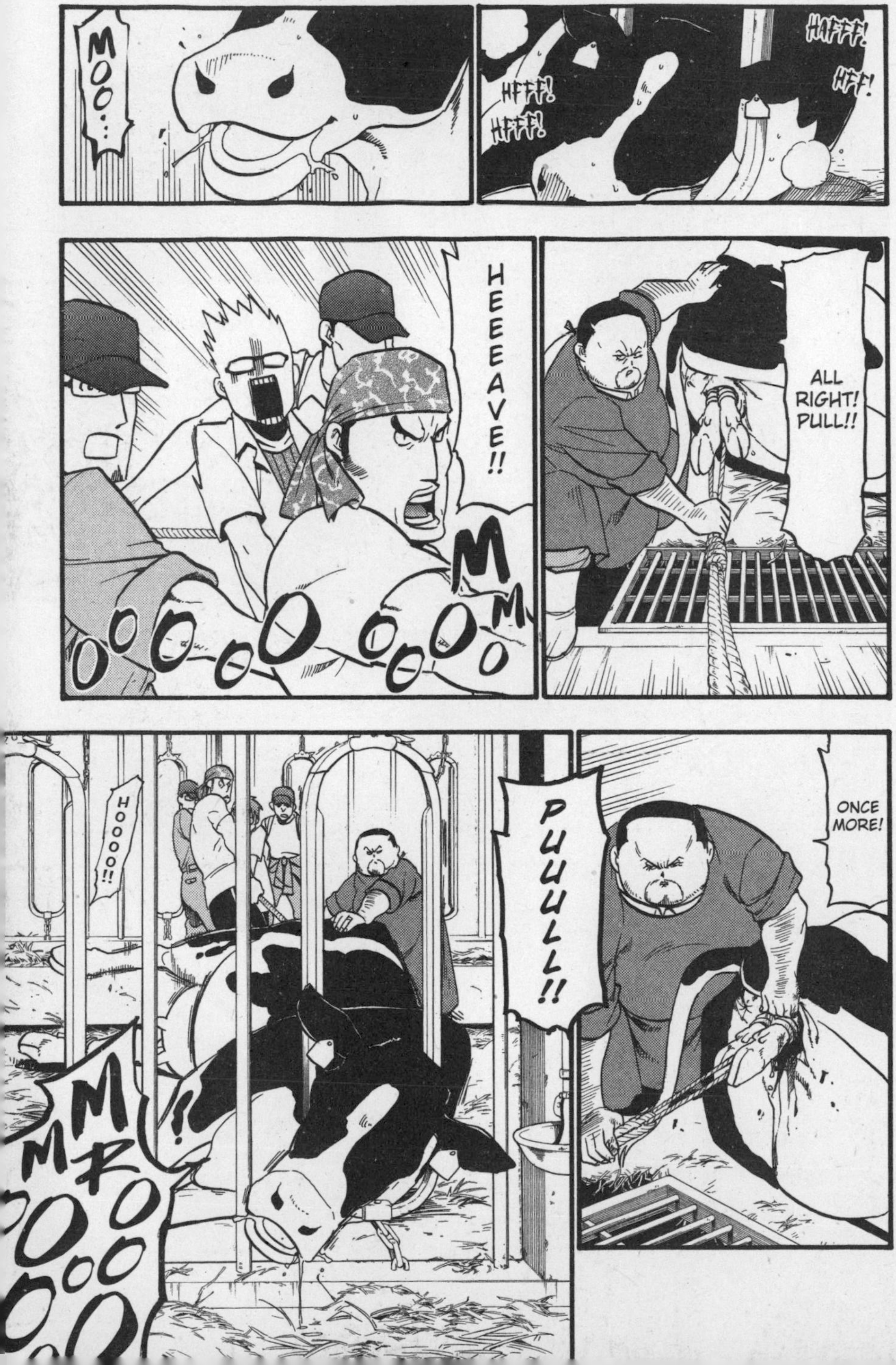
HAFFF!
HFF!
HFFF!
HFFF!
MOO...!
ALL RIGHT! PULL!!
HEEEAVE!!
MMOOOOOOOOOO
ONCE MORE!
PUUULLL!!
HOOOOO!!
MMROOOOOOO

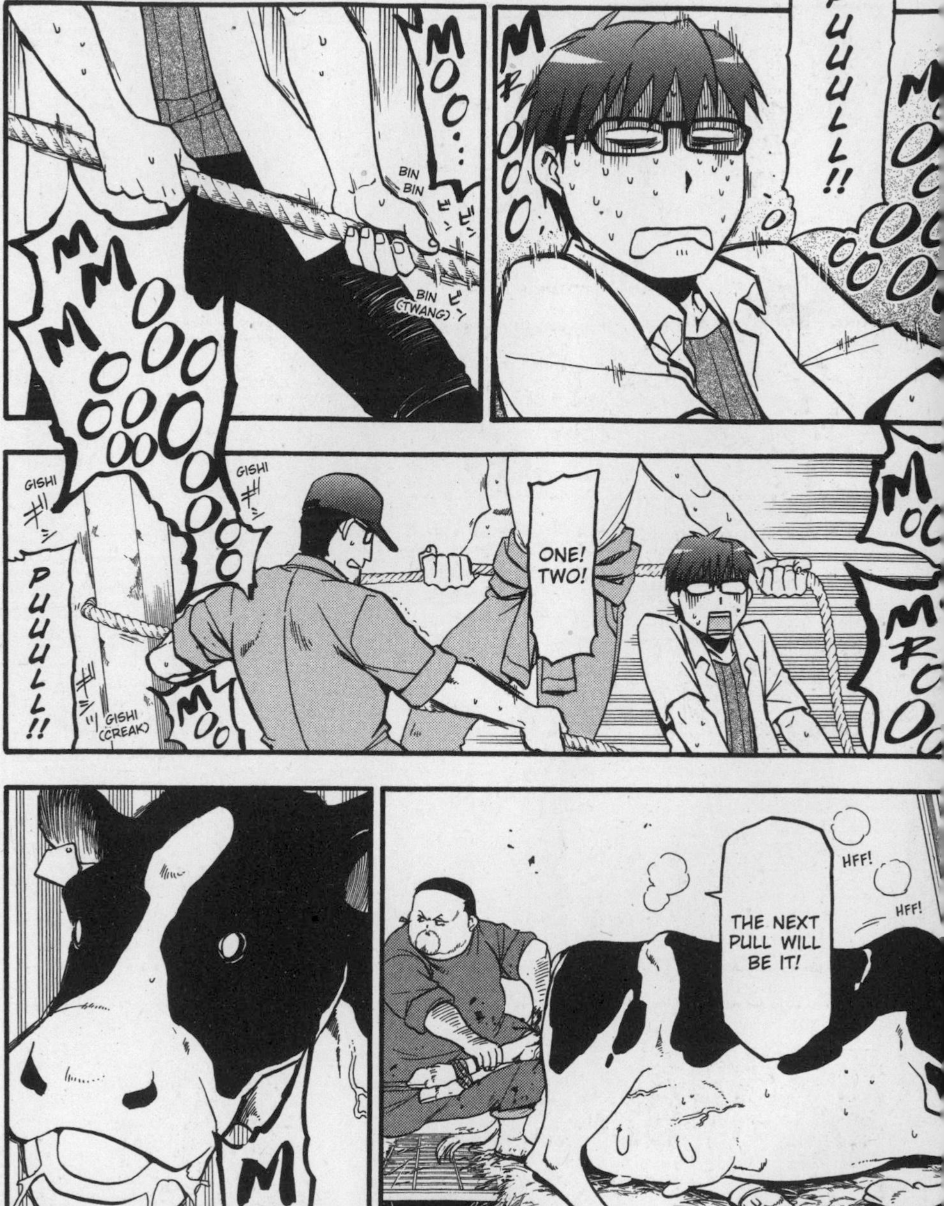
MOOOOOO
PUUULLL!!
MROOOO
MOO...
BIN BIN
BIN (TWANG)
MMMOOOOOOOOOOOOOO
MOO
MROOO
ONE! TWO!
GISHI
PUUULLL!!
GISHI (CREAK)
MOO
HFF!
HFF!
THE NEXT PULL WILL BE IT!
MOO...

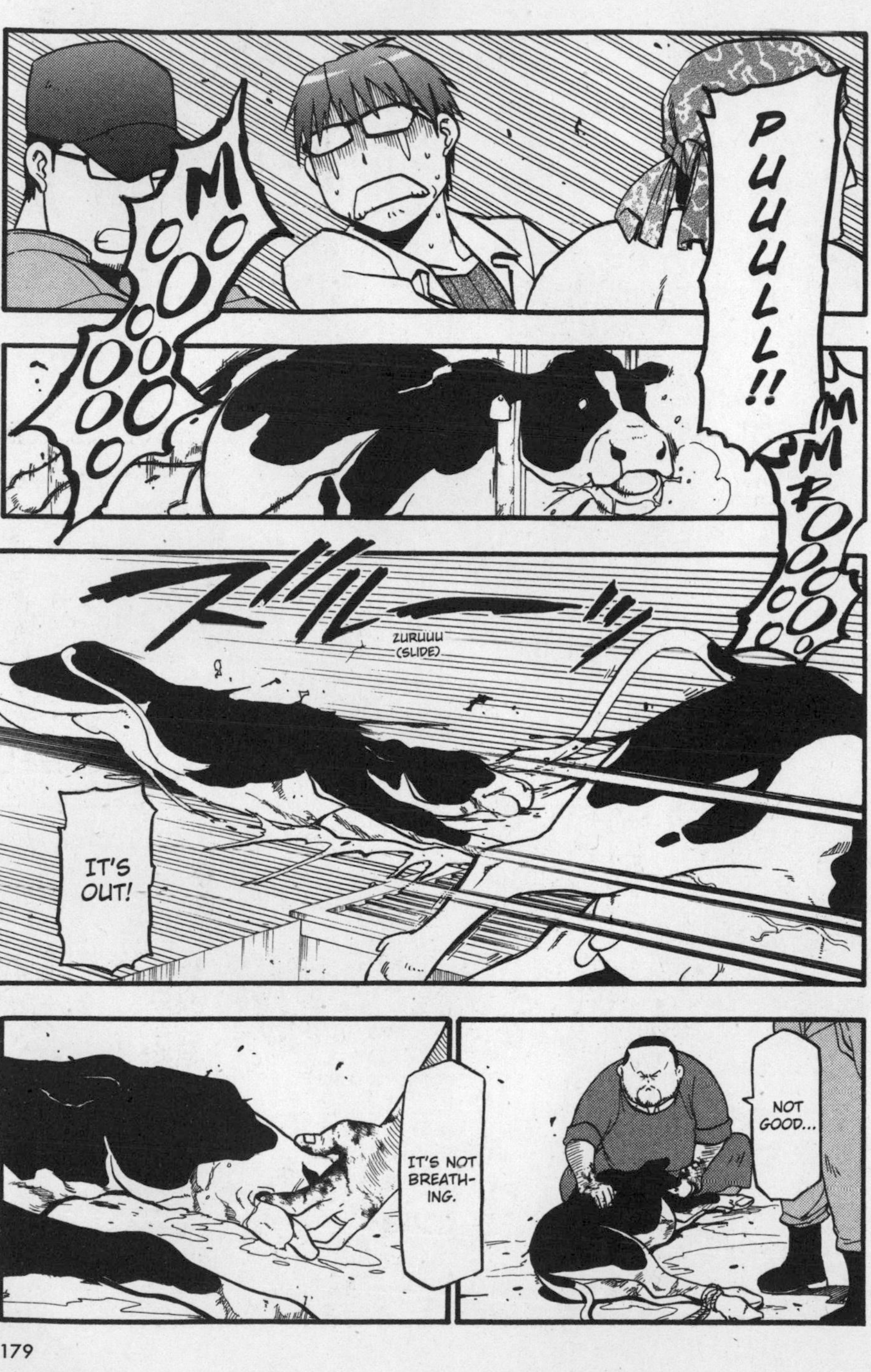
PUUULLL!!
MOOOOOOOOOOOOO
MMROOOOOOOO
ZURUUU (SLIDE)
IT'S OUT!
NOT GOOD...
IT'S NOT BREATH-ING.

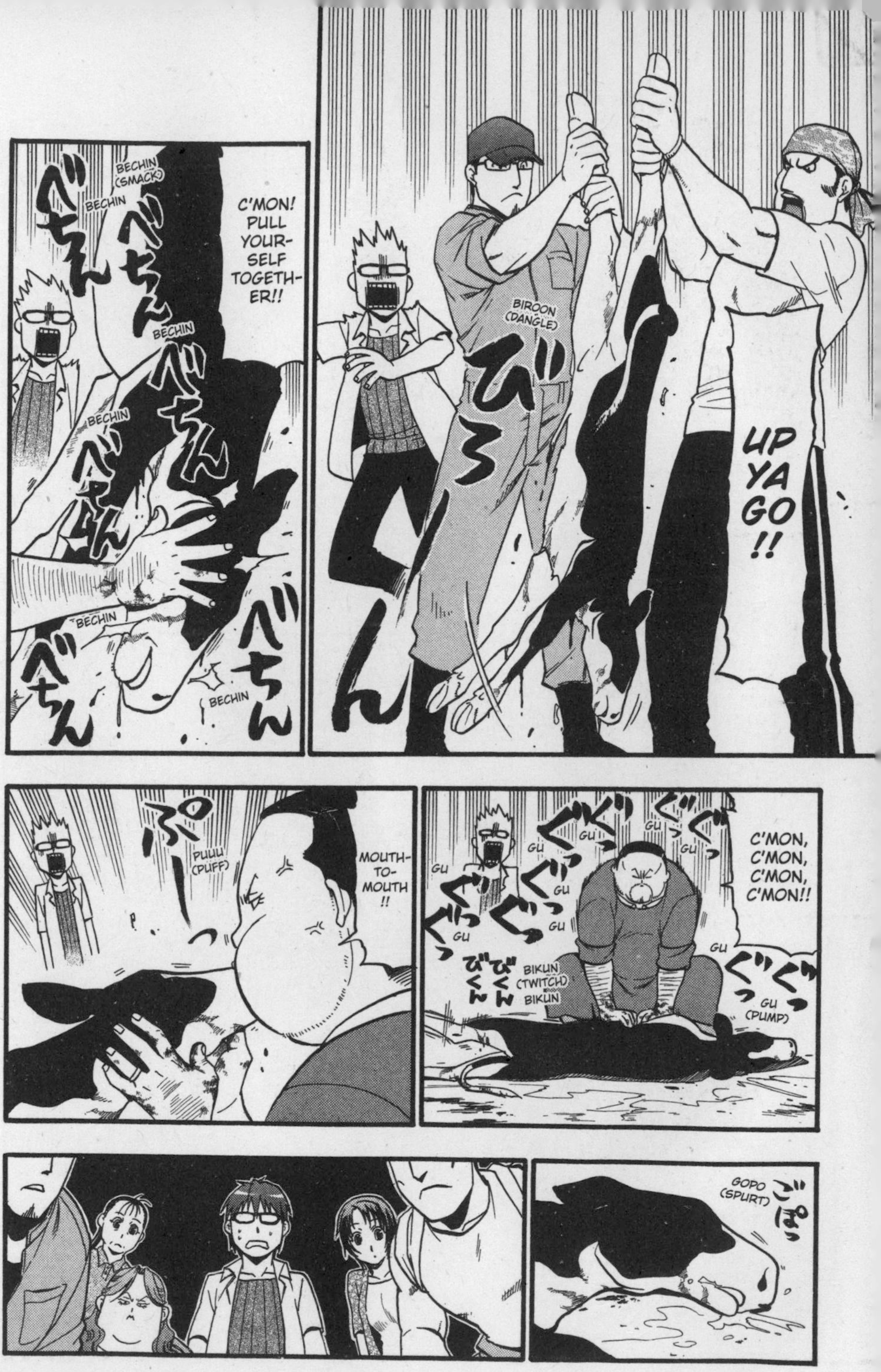
UP YA GO!!
BIROON (DANGLE)
びろ〜ん
C'MON! PULL YOURSELF TOGETHER!!
BECHIN (SMACK)
BECHIN
BECHIN
BECHIN
BECHIN
BECHIN
C'MON, C'MON, C'MON, C'MON!!
GU (PUMP)
GU
GU
GU
GU
GU
GU
GU
BIKUN (TWITCH) BIKUN
MOUTH-TO-MOUTH!!
PUUU (PUFF)
GOPO (SPURT)

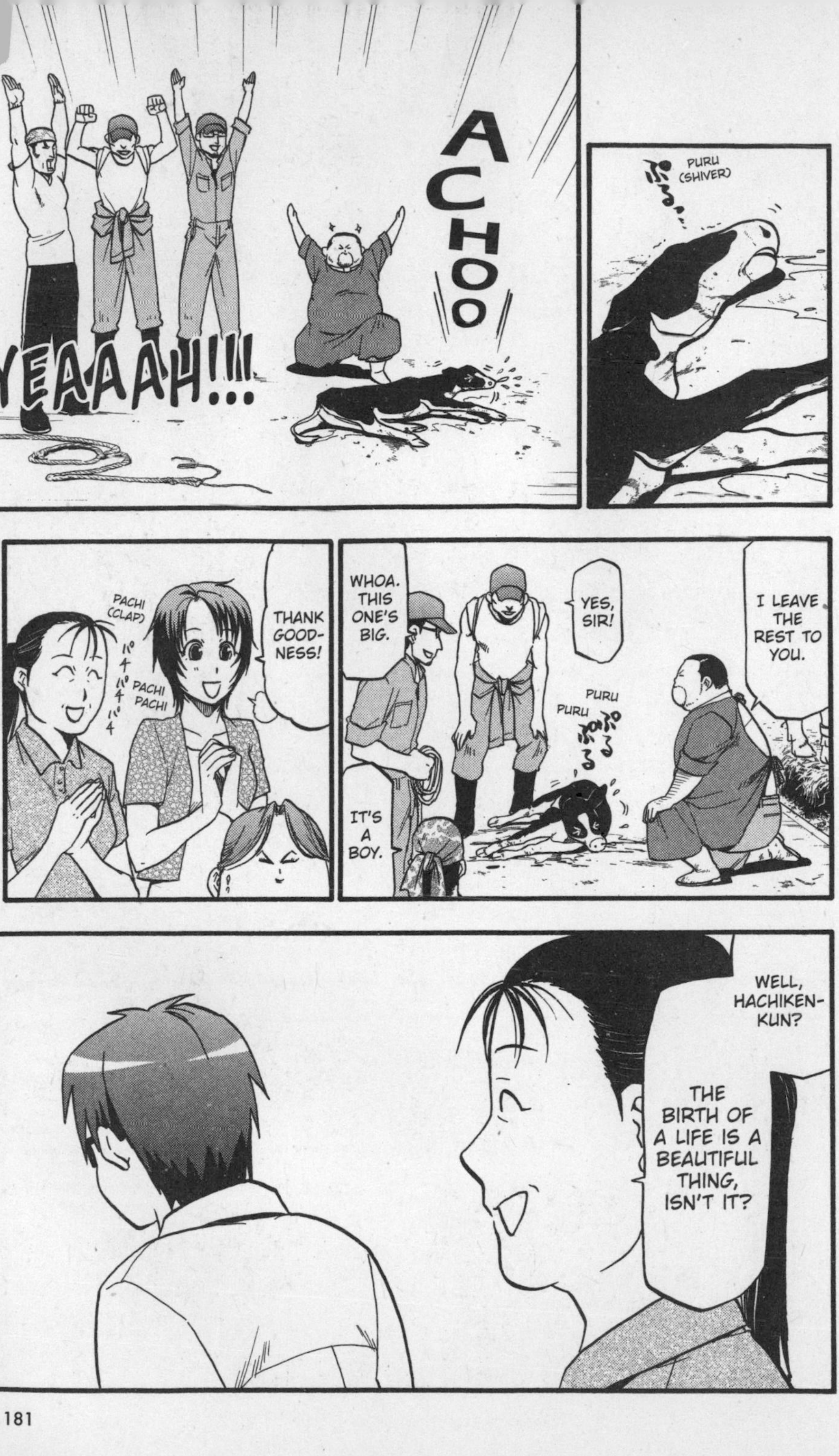
PURU (SHIVER)
ACHOO
YEAAAH!!!
I LEAVE THE REST TO YOU.
PURU PURU
YES, SIR!
WHOA. THIS ONE'S BIG.
IT'S A BOY.
THANK GOOD-NESS!
PACHI (CLAP)
PACHI PACHI
WELL, HACHIKEN-KUN?
THE BIRTH OF A LIFE IS A BEAUTIFUL THING, ISN'T IT?

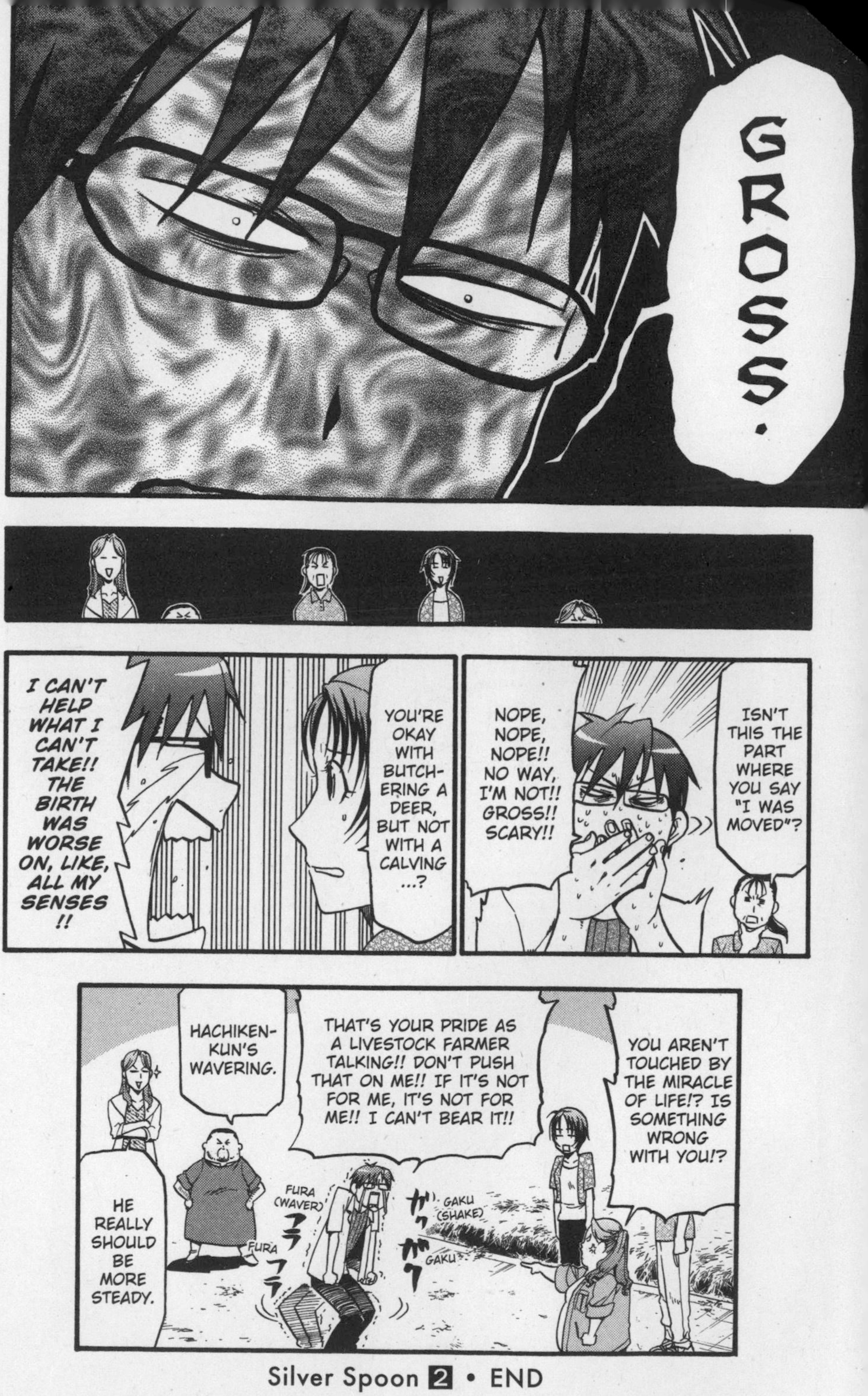
GROSS.
ISN'T THIS THE PART WHERE YOU SAY "I WAS MOVED"?
NOPE, NOPE, NOPE!! NO WAY, I'M NOT!! GROSS!! SCARY!!
YOU'RE OKAY WITH BUTCHERING A DEER, BUT NOT WITH A CALVING ...?
I CAN'T HELP WHAT I CAN'T TAKE!! THE BIRTH WAS WORSE ON, LIKE, ALL MY SENSES !!
YOU AREN'T TOUCHED BY THE MIRACLE OF LIFE!? IS SOMETHING WRONG WITH YOU!?
THAT'S YOUR PRIDE AS A LIVESTOCK FARMER TALKING!! DON'T PUSH THAT ON ME!! IF IT'S NOT FOR ME, IT'S NOT FOR ME!! I CAN'T BEAR IT!!
HACHIKEN-KUN'S WAVERING.
GAKU (SHAKE)
GAKU
FURA (WAVER)
FURA
HE REALLY SHOULD BE MORE STEADY.

Silver Spoon 2 • END

Silver
Spoon

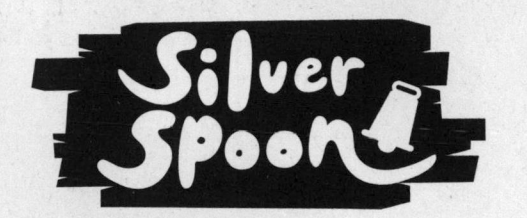

Hachiken-kun

*HACHI = EIGHT

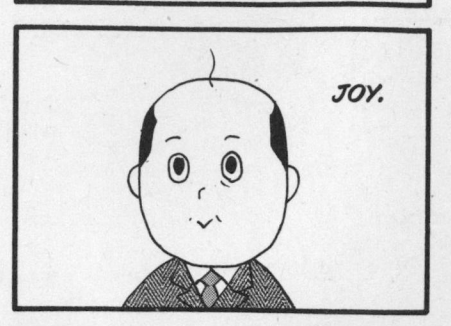

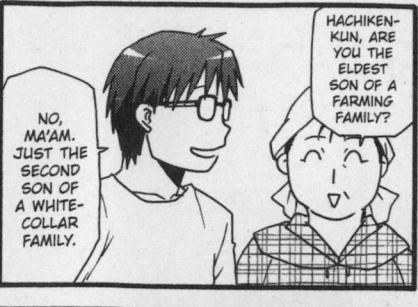

HACHIKEN-KUN, ARE YOU THE ELDEST SON OF A FARMING FAMILY?
NO, MA'AM. JUST THE SECOND SON OF A WHITE-COLLAR FAMILY.
OH WOW... I DIDN'T KNOW HACHIKEN HAS AN OLDER BROTH-ER.
I WONDER WHAT HIS NAME IS...?
"SHICHI-KEN"?
HOW DID YOU ARRIVE AT THAT?

*SHICHI = SEVEN

The Principal

JOY.
ANGER.
PATHOS.
HUMOR.

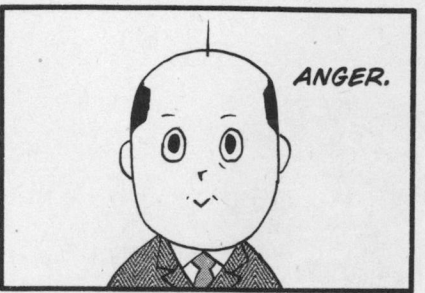

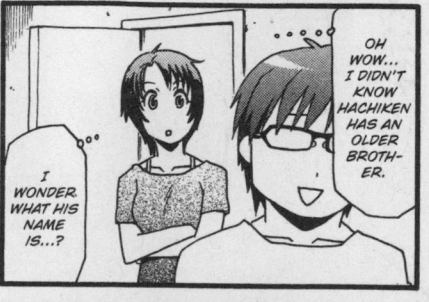

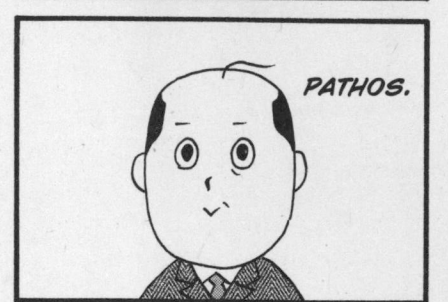

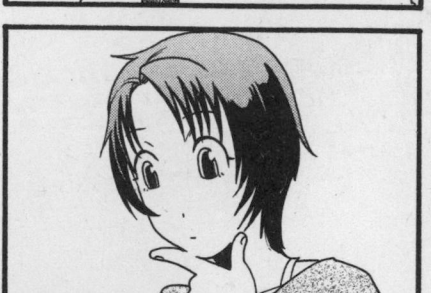

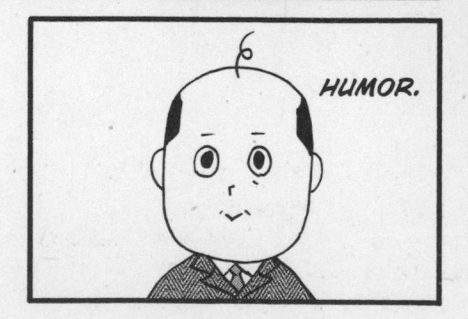

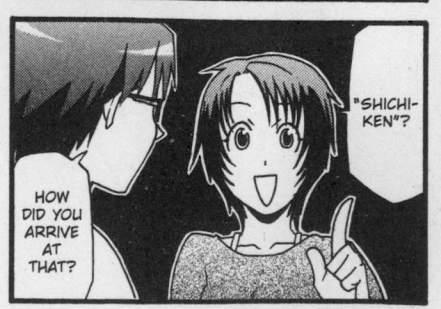

Cow Shed Diaries: Cow, Cow, Cow Chapter

THREE COWS.

ONE COW.

TWO COWS.

FOUR COWS.

KAKI (SKRITCH)

KAKI

THERE ARE A LOT OF COWS IN THIS MANGA.

I FOUND OUT IT DOESN'T HAVE TO BE SHEEP YOU'RE COUNTING FOR YOU TO FALL ASLEEP.

I DOZED OFF!

AH!!

FRESH DAIKON RADISHES

THIRTEEN C......

....

KAKI

FRESH DAIKON RADISHES

TEN COWS.

EIGHT COWS.

SEVEN COWS.

FIVE COWS.

NINE COWS.

SIX COWS.

ELEVEN COWS.

KAKI

KAKI

KAKI

FRESH DAIKON RADISHES

Silver Spoon 2!
Thanks so much for reading the second volume. I'd be thrilled if you joined us for the next volume too.

Hiromu Arakawa

~ Special Thanks ~
All of my assistants,
Everyone who helped with collecting material and interviews,
My editor, Takashi Tsubouchi,
AND YOU!!

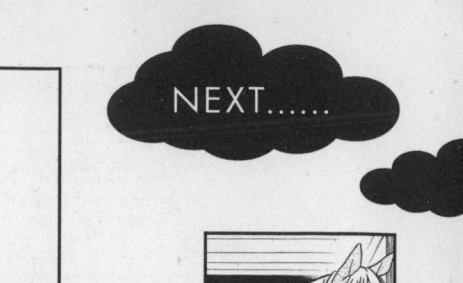

NEXT......

SURI (NUZZLE)
HFF... HAAH... HAGK...
LOOK AT HIM GO.
...ARE YOU ALL RIGHT?
AH...
SHUGOO (SHWRR)
SHUGOO
SHUGOO

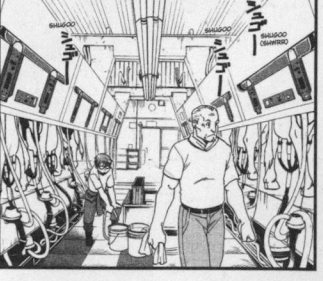

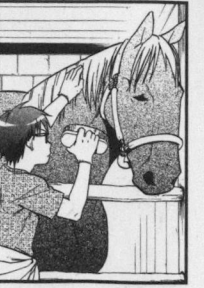

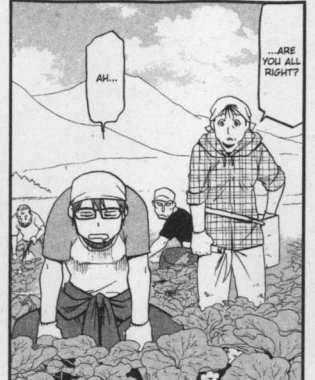

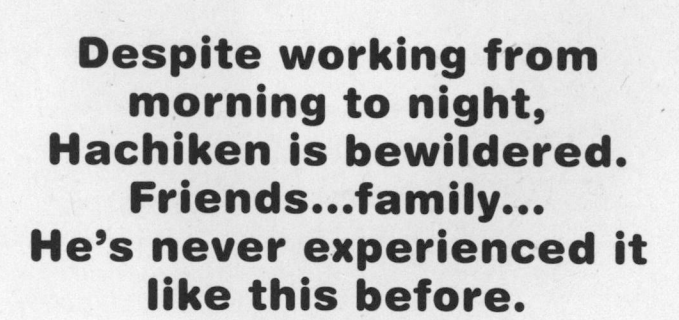

Despite working from morning to night, Hachiken is bewildered. Friends...family... He's never experienced it like this before.

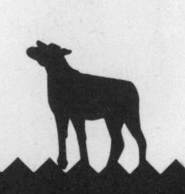

MOOOO...
MOO...
MOOO...
AAAAAA AAAAAA AAAAAA AAAAAA AAAAH!
BOBOBO (PUTTER)
MOO
ZAZAZA (SKREECH)
AFTER SUMMER VACATION, PORK BOWL'S GONNA BE TURNED INTO BACON...

Hachiken's summer of firsts isn't over yet...

Silver Spoon **Volume 3 coming June 2018!!**

to be continued......

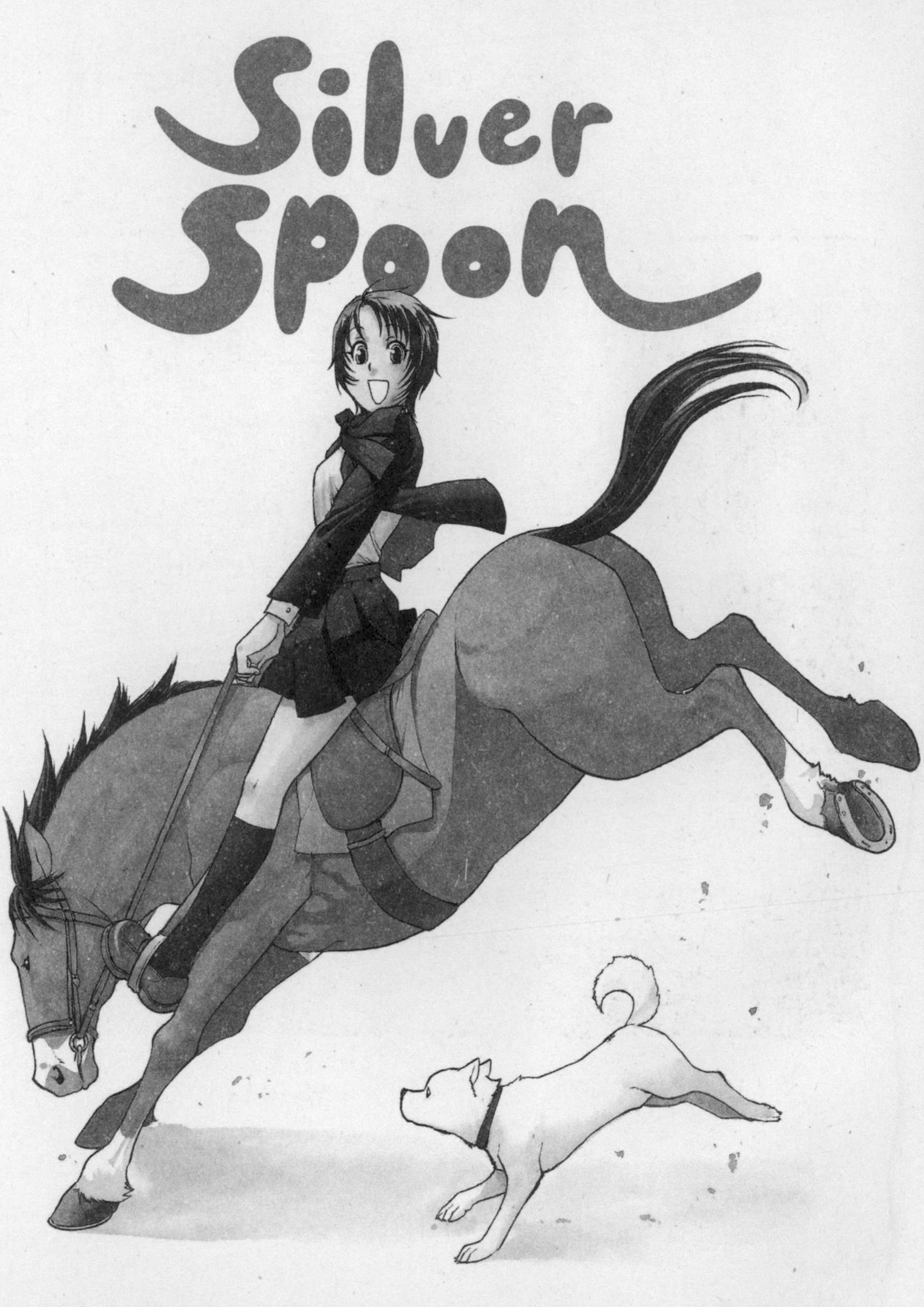
Silver Spoon

Beware of Horses

HORSES NUZZLE ME AN AWFUL LOT.
※
※ CHAPTER 1
SURI SURI (NUZZLE)
GOSHI (RUB) GOSHI
AM I THE KIND OF PERSON HORSES LIKE?
TEE HEE HEE! ♥
AH... ABOUT THAT...
WHEN THEY RUB AGAINST YOU EXCES-SIVELY...
...THEY'RE TREATING YOU THE SAME AS A PILLAR OR A FENCE THEY'D USE TO SCRATCH AN ITCH.
GOSHI
GOSHI

Translation Notes

Common Honorifics

no honorific: Indicates familiarity or closeness; if used without permission or reason, addressing someone in this manner would constitute an insult.

-san: The Japanese equivalent of Mr./Mrs./Miss. If a situation calls for politeness, this is the fail-safe honorific.

-sama: Conveys great respect; may also indicate the social status of the speaker is lower than that of the addressee.

-kun: Used most often when referring to boys, this honorific indicates affection or familiarity. Occasionally used by older men among their peers, but it may also be used by anyone referring to a person of lower standing.

-chan: An affectionate honorific indicating familiarity used mostly in reference to girls; also used in reference to cute persons or animals of either gender.

-sensei: A respectful term for teachers, artists, or high-level professionals.

-niisan, nii-san, aniki, etc.: A term of endearment meaning "big brother" that may be more widely used to address any young man who is like a brother, regardless of whether he is related or not.

-neesan, nee-san, aneki, etc.: The female counterpart of the above, nee-san means "big sister."

Currency Conversion

While conversion rates fluctuate, an easy estimate for Japanese Yen conversion is ¥100 to 1 USD.

Page 9

Cheese is less abundant and more expensive in Japan than in, say, the United States. This is why Hachiken lists mozzarella cheese as one of the things he might have trouble learning about or obtaining; it's not commonplace for him.

Page 44

One Hundred Poems by One Hundred Poets is a classic Japanese anthology of waka poems commonly taught in school. It's also used for the card game karuta. In this game, cards for each poem are laid out between contestants; a reader begins to recite a poem, and the contestants compete to see who has faster reflexes and a better memory for pouncing on the correct card. Typically, each poem is read from the beginning, but in the Hokkaido variation of the game, the poems are read from the second half instead.

Page 45

In Japanese, Hachiken's nickname for Chestnut, "Dot-brows," is "maromayu." In the Heian Period (AD 794–1185), aristocratic women would remove their eyebrows and paint on new ones, sometimes as small dots similar to the "eyebrow" dots Chestnut has. Maro was a first-person pronoun often used by nobility at the time, and mayu means "eyebrows"—thus maromayu. "Chestnut" is "maron" in Japanese, so the nickname sounds more similar to his real name in the Japanese.

Page 54

Jingisukan is a Hokkaido grilled mutton dish.

Page 55

Mock cavalry battles are a common event on sports day in Japanese schools. Three students (as the horse) carry one student (the rider). Two teams clash against each other, and the team whose riders fall first loses. So normally, the riders have the important role, which is why Hachiken is moved by what he thinks is the power of friendship.

Page 60

Dosukoi is a shout associated with sumo wrestlers.

Page 78

The Meiji Period lasted from 1868 to 1912, during which time Japan went through an industrial revolution and modernization. Aki's great-grandma also would have lived through the Taishō Period (1912–1926) and the Showa Period (1926–1989). Silver Spoon takes place in the Heisei Period (1989–present, as of 2017), so she's been a witness to four distinct periods of Japanese history.

Page 94
Japan's National High School Baseball Championship takes place at the Hanshin Koshien Stadium in Koshien. It's a two-week tournament with forty-nine teams competing during summer vacation.

Page 110
One naming convention (albeit one that is becoming rarer) for children in Japan is to use numbers, particularly for sons. Japanese readers can safely assume that Ichirou is the eldest son of his parents because *ichi* means "one." As for the twins, the *"ni"* in Nino is "two" and the *"mi"* in Misora is "three," so we know that Nino was born before her sister.

Page 128
"Forest girl" and "mountain girl" are actually names of different fashion styles. Forest girl (*mori girl*) fashion favors vintage-inspired designs, shawls, natural colors, layers, etc., for a soft, fairy tale–like look. Mountain girl (*yama girl*) fashion employs clothes that would be suitable for hiking or other outdoor activities while still maintaining a feminine aesthetic.

Princess Mononoke is a Studio Ghibli film in which the titular Princess Mononoke is a wild girl of the forest who was raised by wolves. Hachiken doesn't seem to be familiar with forest/mountain girl fashions either, so this is what the terms bring to mind for him.

Page 148
The Ainu were the native hunter-gatherer inhabitants of Hokkaido. Like many indigenous peoples, they became marginalized in their own land when it was colonized, in this case by Japan.

Page 151
Koshien is located on Honshu island (Japan's main island) in the Kansai region (the south-central area of the island). Hachiken and the Mikages are watching the match from up in Hokkaido, Japan's northernmost and coldest region.

Page 152
Ito Yokado is one of Japan's largest supermarket chains, so for a city kid like Hachiken, it would be weird for the Mikages to consider a trip to Ito Yokado to be a special outing.

Page 157
In Japanese, "egg" is *"tamago,"* so the nickname is not only a comment on Tamako's shape but also a play on her name.

Page 169
The Warring States Period (also known as the Sengoku Period, 1467–1603) was an age of military conflict as different factions fought for power.

Page 184
Hachiken's name includes the word for "eight" ("*hachi*") in it, so going back to the name-by-numbers convention (see note for page 110), Aki concludes his older brother might be named Shichiken (where "*shichi*" is "seven"). But it doesn't quite add up; if that were the naming convention his parents used, it would make Hachiken their eighth son, not the second...

Silver Spoon 2

HIROMU ARAKAWA

Translation: **Amanda Haley** / Lettering: **Abigail Blackman**

This book is a work of fiction. Names, characters, places, and incidents are the product of the author's imagination or are used fictitiously. Any resemblance to actual events, locales, or persons, living or dead, is coincidental.

GIN NO SAJI SILVER SPOON Vol. 2
by Hiromu ARAKAWA
© 2011 Hiromu ARAKAWA
Original Japanese edition published by SHOGAKUKAN.
English translation rights in the United States of America, Canada, the United Kingdom, Ireland, Australia and New Zealand arranged with SHOGAKUKAN through Tuttle-Mori Agency, Inc.

English translation © 2018 by Yen Press, LLC

Yen Press
1290 Avenue of the Americas
New York, NY 10104

Visit us at yenpress.com
facebook.com/yenpress
twitter.com/yenpress
yenpress.tumblr.com
instagram.com/yenpress

First Yen Press Edition: April 2018

Yen Press is an imprint of Yen Press, LLC.
The Yen Press name and logo are trademarks of Yen Press, LLC.

The publisher is not responsible for websites (or their content) that are not owned by the publisher.

Library of Congress Control Number: 2017959207

ISBN: 978-1-9753-2619-7

10 9 8 7 6 5 4 3 2 1

WOR

Printed in the United States of America